THE COLLEGIATE BAPTIST HISTORY WORKBOOK

*A Work Text History of the Baptized Believers
From the Time of Christ to the Twentieth Century*

*With Short Biographies
And Articles of Interest by
The Classic Baptist Historians*

Compiled, Edited and Written by James R. Beller

The **Collegiate** *Baptist History Workbook*
James R. Beller

ISBN 0-9668766-0-1
Copyright © 2002 Prairie Fire Press
Second Edition Copyright © 2005
Third printing 2006
On the worldwide web at
http://www.21tnt.com/pfp/

Notes on the Second Edition, third printing

The first edition of the *Baptist History Workbook* was published in 2002 and saw use across America and foreign countries.

The new edition includes several useful changes. Although the layout is essentially the same, the size of the publication has been changed to enhance viewing and study.

A timeline has been added and an appendix. The appendix includes the author's ten affirmations, and a helpful map. The map will help the student identify Baptist groups from each era. Included in the appendix is the article *Which Church was the First Baptist Church in America?* This controversy is briefly discussed in chapter twelve. The first edition has been corrected by better evidence.

Every student of church history must be versed in the false theology of Augustine. Every student of the Baptist Christian view of history must understand *Augustinianism*. A brief discussion of the difference between Pauline and Augustinian theology is found in chapter four. Please note that this third printing gives slightly more detail on this matter on page 56. Also note "identifying marks" on page 59.

For this edition, we have included information on the origin of the camp-meetings and the great Baptist evangelists. We have also documented the controversial Mosheim and Hosius quotes on pages 72, 121, and 130.

Our main historians:

- **Heny D'Anvers**
- **Thieleman J. Van Braght**
- **Thomas Crosby**
- **G. H. Orchard**
- **Isaac Backus**
- **David Benedict**
- **William Cathcart**
- **Thomas Armitage**
- **J. M. Carroll**
- **John Taylor Christian**

For this edition we have added some information on the long forgotten but immensely important **Henry D'Anvers**, one of the first English Baptist historians. D'Anver's *Treatise on Baptism* has finally been reprinted for the glory of God and the benefit of this present generation.

Timelines are from Robinson's *Compilation of History*, with edits by the author.

An instructor's guide with quizzes, tests and answer key is available from Prairie Fire Press at www.21tnt.com/pfp.

—James R. Beller

The Collegiate Baptist History Workbook

Chapter One— Introduction
p. 1   *Section One*: Origins of the Baptist Churches
         Section Two: Baptist Distinctives and Earmarks of the N. T. Church
Chapter Two— The Churches of the Second Century
p. 17 *Section One*: The Transmission of the Text and the Beginning of the Corruption of the Ordinances.
         Section Two: Apostolic Successors and early Leaders
Chapter Three—The Churches of the Third Century
p. 33 *Section One*: The Novatianists. The Apostle's Creed
         Section Two: The Birth of the Sacraments
Chapter Four— The Churches of the Fourth Century
p. 47 *Section One*: The Century of Corruption. The Donatists
         Section Two: The Apostle's Creed vs. The Nicene Creed
Chapter Five— The Churches of the Fifth and Sixth Centuries
p. 61 *Section One*: The Dark Ages in Full Fright
         Section Two: Soul Winning Stations of the Fifth and Sixth Centuries
Chapter Six— The Churches of the Seventh, Eighth, and Ninth Centuries
p. 75 *Section One*: The Rise of the Waldenses, Albigenses and Paulicians
         Section Two: The Kingdom of Charlemagne. Mohammed & Islam
Chapter Seven—The Churches of Tenth, Eleven and Twelfth Centuries
p. 89 *Section One*: The Freefall of the Papacy
         Section Two: The Crusades, The Henricians, The Petrobrussians
Chapter Eight—The Churches of Thirteenth and Fourteenth Centuries
p. 101 *Section One*: The Lateran Councils. The War on the Albigenses.
         Section Two: John Wycliff.
Chapter Nine— The Churches of the Fifteenth Century
p. 115 *Section One*: Sawtree, Huss, and Savonarola.
         Section Two: Evidences of Baptist people in Europe and England.
Chapter Ten— The Churches of the Sixteenth Century
p. 127 *Section One*: The Reformation in Europe. The Anabaptists.
         Section Two: The Reformation Debate on Baptism.
Chapter Eleven- The Churches of Sixteenth Century Part II
p. 141 *Section One*: The Reformation in England.
         Section Two: The Baptists come out of Concealment.

Chapter Twelve-The Churches of the Seventeenth Century
p. 153
    Section One: Independents, Puritans, Dissenters and Pilgrims.
    Section Two: Roger Williams and John Clarke. Clarke's confession.

Ch. Thirteen—   **The Churches of the Seventeenth Century Part II**
p. 167
    Section One: Struggle in England. London Confession.
    Section Two: Struggle in America. Obadiah Holmes, Boston.

Ch. Fourteen—   **The Churches of the Eighteenth Century**
p. 183
    Section One: The Decline of Religion in England and America
    Section Two: The Philadelphia Baptist Association. The Philadelphia Confession of Faith.

Ch. Fifteen—   **The Churches of the Eighteenth Century Part II**
p. 195
    Section One: The Great Awakening in America and England. George Whitefield, Jonathan Edwards.
    Section Two: The "New Lights." Separates and Isaac Backus.

Ch. Sixteen—   **The Churches of the Eighteenth Century Part III**
p. 209
    Section One: Shubal Stearns and the Separate Baptist Revival.
    Section Two: Baptists in the Revolution. John Gano. John Leland. The Forging of the American System of Government from Baptist principles.

Ch. Seventeen—The Churches of the Nineteenth Century
p. 229
    Section One: The Rise of English Baptist Missions.
    Section Two: The 100-Year War for Souls in America. American Baptist Missions. Satan's Plan for America.

Ch. Eighteen—   **The Churches of the Twentieth Century.**
p. 247
    Section One: Ev. Alliance gives way to Ecumenicalism.
    Section Two: Fundamentalism and the fight for Baptist Principles (First Principles)

Map, Appendix A, B —
p. 257

Bibliography—
p. 263

Index—
p. 265

Collegiate Baptist History Workbook

33. **Descent of the Holy Ghost** on the Day of Pentecost
62. Martyrdom of James the Less
63. **Pudence and Claudia take the Gospel to Wales**
64. Persecution by Nero begins
68. Martyrdom of Peter and Paul
70. Destruction of Jerusalem by Titus
95. Persecution by Domitian
100. Death of John
116. Martyrdom of Ignatius
120. **First evidences of the Vaudois**
166. Martyrdom of Justin and Polycarp
168. **Montanus publishes writings**
190. Tertullian flourishes
248. Cyprian, bishop of Carthage
249. Persecution by Decius
251. Council at Carthage, Novatian excommunicated. Novatianists arise
254. Death of Origen
258. Martyrdom of Cyprian
260. Conversion of the Goths begins
298. Diocletian requires idolatry from soldiers
305. Council of Elvira or Grenada
311. **Separation of the Donatists from the apostate church**
313. End of persecution by pagan Rome
314. Council of Arles about the Donatists
319. Arius begins to publish his heresy
324. Emperor Constantine defeats Licinius, declares himself Christian
325. The First General Council held at Nicaea Arius condemned
335. Athanasius banished to Treves
337. Death of Constantine
343. Persecution in Persia
347. **Banishment of the Donatists**
348. Ulfilas, bishop of the Goths
360. Council of Laodicea
361. Julian emperor, Paganism restored
363. Death of Julian
370. Basil, bishop of Caesarea, 373. Death of Athanasius
374. Ambrose, bishop of Milan born
378. Gregory of Nazianzum goes to Constantinople
379. Theodosius, emperor
381. Second General Council held at Constantinople **Chiliasm condemned**
385. Execution of Priscillian
387. Baptism of Augustine
390. Massacre at Thessalonica
395. Augustine made bishop of Hippo
397. Chrysostom, at Constantinople

398. **Council of Carthage, A. D.**
400. Pelagius teaches at Rome
405. Patrick begins his ministry in Ireland (Hibernia)
407. Death of Chrysostom
409. Romans withdraw from Britain
410. Rome taken by Alaric
410. Pelagius and Celestius in Africa
411. Conference with Augustine and the Donatists at Carthage
412. Ninian bishop of Whithorn
416. Infant Baptism becomes compulsory. Lyonists or Vaudois, (Waldensians) seek refuge in the Piedmont.
429. Pelagianism put down in Britain by German & Lupus
430. Death of Augustine of Hippo
431. Third General Council held at Ephesus Condemnation of Nestorius
449. Landing of the Saxons in England
451. Fourth General Council held at Chalcedon
451. Attila the Hun in France,
465. **Death of Patrick**
484-519. Schism between Rome and Constantinople
529. Benedict institutes Monks
553. Fifth General Council held at Constantinople
565. Columba settles at Iona
565. Death of Justinian
589. Third Council of Toledo
589. **Columbanus goes into France**
590. Gregory the Great of Rome
596. Augustine II to England
597. "Conversion" of Ethelbert
589-615. **Missionary labours of Columbanus**
604. Deaths of Gregory, Augustine II
612. Mohammed publishes sentiments
627. Jerusalem taken by the Muslims
632. Death of Mohammed
635. **Settlement of Scottish missionaries in the Holy Land**
660. **Beginning of the Paulicians**
690. **Constantine of the Paulicians stoned. 100,000 Paulicians put to death by Theodora.**
700. **Albigensians (Cathari) arise in France from the Paulicians**
720. **Bogomils arise in the Balkins from the Paulicians**

724. Controversy of images
724. Victory of Martel over the Muslims
734. Death of the Venerable Bede
787. Second Council of Nicea
794. Council of Frankfort
800. Charles the Great crowned as emperor. Forgery of Donation of Constantine
860-870. "Conversion" of Bulgarians, Moravians, Bohemians
912. Foundation of the Order of Clugny
999. Sylvester II, pope
994-1030. "Conversion" of Norwegians.
1000. Paterines, descendents of the Novatianists emerge in Italy
1048. Pope Leo IX., Beginning of Hildebrand's influence over the papacy
1073. Hildebrand elected pope (Gregory VII)
1099. Jerusalem taken back in first crusade
1113. St John (Hospitallers) founded
1116. Templar Knights founded
1116. Henry of Clugny begins his ministry. Henricians begin
1126. **Peter de Bruys burned at the stake in St. Gilles. Petrobrussians begin their ministry.**
1147-1149. The Second Crusade
1153. Death of St. Bernard
1155. Arnold of Brescia burned at the stake. Arnoldists begin their ministry.
1154. Nicolas Breakspeare, an Englishman, Pope Adrian IV
1170. Murder of Archbishop Becket
1189. The Third Crusade
1198. Innocent III elected pope
1203. Constantinople taken Crusaders
1208-1238. **War on the Albigenses**
1215. Fourth Council of the Lateran. Innocent sanctions the Dominican and Franciscan Orders of Friars

Time Line

1229. The Council of Toulouse. Reading of the Bible forbidden. Oath of allegiance instigated.
1240. First Crusade of St. Louis
1270. Second Crusade and death of St. Louis
1274. Second Council of Lyons
1300. **Picards** arise in Bohemia from Waldensians, Walter Lollard converted.
1310. The popes settle at Avignon
1312. Council of Vienne; Templars dissolved
1330. Walter Lollard burnt, Lollards begin their ministry.
1377. Gregory XI moves the papacy from Avignon to Rome
1378. Beginning of the Great Schism of the West
1384. Death of John Wycliff (Lollard)
1400. Sawtre (Lollard) burnt
1414-1418. Council of Constance
1415. Pope John XXIII deposed
1415. John Huss burnt
1418. Religious war in Bohemia breaks out
1453. The Turks, under Sultan Mohammed II, became masters of Constantinople.
1455. Invention of Printing
1498. Death of Savonarola
1481. Hubmaier born in Bavaria
1483. Luther born
1484. Ulrich Zwingli born
1503. Death of Pope Alexander VI
1517. October 31, Martin Luther, 95 theses tacked to the door at Wittenberg
1515. Ministry of Zwingli begins in Switzerland
1520. Emergence of the Anabaptists in Switzerland
1528. **Hubmaier** and his wife martyred in Austria
1530. Augsburg Confession (Lutheran) presented to the imperial diet
1530. Waldensians absorbed into the Reformed movement
1536. Menno Simons joins the Anabaptists in Germany
1538. Henry the VIII's decree
1551. **Joan of Kent** burned at the stake in England
1559 Royal edict was published, any person holding to the Reformed faith or to *Anabaptism*) punishable by death. Extermination of the Huguenots begun.
1559. "Puritanism" begins in England

1559. John Calvin published his *Institutes of the Christian faith*
1530. Jesuits founded
1531. Henry VIII recognized as head of the English Church
1539. Henry's decree of death to those denying infant baptism
1551. Joan Boucher burned at Smithfield
1553. "B*loody*" Mary begins her reign of death in England
1572. St. Bartholomew's Day Massacre, Huguenots murdered
1579. Brownist (Congregationalist) movement started in England
1603. King James VI of Scotland becomes King James I of all England
1609. Jamestown Settlement in Virginia
1610. Anglican worship enforced in England
1611. Authorized Version
1612. Edward Wightman burned
1620. *Humble Supplication* presented to Parliament
1620. Pilgrims arrive
1625. Charles I becomes King
1628. Charles I dissolves parliament, pressures Puritans to desist
1629. Massachusetts Bay colony begins
1633. Laud becomes Archbishop
1637. First Baptist Church in America, under **Dr. John Clarke**, worships in New Hampshire
1644. London Confession (Particular Baptist) published
1644. Richard Baxter publishes his "Plain Scripture Proof" tirade against believer's baptism
1644. Roger Williams publishes *The Bloudy Tenet of Persecution*
1649. Civil War in England, the Presbyterians appointed Oliver Cromwell, Lord Protector
1649. Long parliament, death penalty for denying infant baptism is reinstated.
1651. The Beating of **Obadiah Holmes** in Boston
1655. The Massacre of the Waldensians
1660. Charles II restored to the throne.
1661. Address of toleration presented to Charles II by Thomas Grantham
1662. Act of Uniformity was passed

1663. Conventicle act; Bunyan jailed
1665. Plague 100,000 die in London
1666. Drought and the London fire
1689. Act of Toleration under William of Orange
1700. The Adoption of the Half-way covenant by the Congregational Church
1702. Publishing Mather's *Magnalia*
1703. Birth of Jonathan Edwards
1704. Birth of John Comer
1706. Birth of Daniel Marshall
1706. Birth of Shubal Stearns
1707. The Philadelphia Baptist Association formed
1708. Frst Baptist church in Conn. formed by Valentine Wightman
1714. Birth of George Whitefield
1724. Birth of Isaac Backus
1727. Birth of John Gano
1732. Birth of George Washington
1754. Birth of John Leland
1755-75. Separate Baptist Revival in the American South
1776. Declaration of Independence
1781. Surrender at Yorktown
1786. Virginia Statute for Religious Liberty
1792. London Baptist Missionary Society founded
1793. William Carey sails to India
1800. Second Great Awakening
1812. Judson sails to Burma
1814. Triennial Convention
1817. Isaac McCoy begins his mission to the Indians of America
1845. Southern Baptist Convention
1850. Spurgeon begins his ministry
1850. Bible revision controversy
1880. Whitsitt publishes 1641 theory
1905. Landmark Baptists begin association
1910. Fundamentalism arises
1920. Independent Baptist movement begins

V1I

WHY STUDY BAPTIST HISTORY?

1. Fulfillment in Gods Promises
2. Appreciate the sufferings of the past
3. Establish our own doctrinal foundation
4. Because it Helps us to recognize Godly heros

The Collegiate Baptist History Workbook

Chapter One

The Distinctives of a New Testament Church
An Introduction

      Section One: Origin of the Baptist Churches
      Section Two: Baptist Distinctives and Earmarks of the New Testament Church

SECTION ONE
Introduction to Baptist Church History

Welcome: **Our** prayer is that this overview of history will stir you to serve the living God. Our Baptist heritage has rarely been examined, and most of the true interest to inquisitive minds has been omitted.

Jesus went about "doing good." During His ministry, He established a genuine New Testament church. It was a *church*, or by definition, a *called-out assembly.* It was organized to hold up the truth for the world to see. It was to be the "pillar and ground of the truth" (I Timothy 3:15).

This workbook tells the story of truth, heroism, loyalty and betrayal. It tells the story of what the Christian life is all about and what living the will of God accomplishes. You will read about preachers, martyrs and missionaries. You will read about persecutions, revivals and awakenings. You will read about the *baptized believers* who paid a price for standing for scriptural baptism. They experienced revival through their courageous testimony and soul winning efforts.

Each chapter will contain two sections of material with checkpoints along the way. We will ask you to consider ***What is surely Believed***, learn some ***Definitions***, study the ***Scripture to Memorize***, get acquainted with the ***Pivotal Points to Ponder,*** and bring to mind the ***People to Remember***. At certain times we will ask, ***"Where is the Word of God?"*** in relation to key junctures in Christian history. May God bless you as you study, (II Timothy 2:15) and may He set your heart on fire to serve Him!

Scripture to Memorize

There is a key to understanding church history. It is Matthew 23:34:

Chapter 1—Distinctives of a New Testament Church

Wherefore, behold, I send unto you prophets, and wise men, and scribes: and some of them ye shall kill and crucify; and some of them shall ye scourge in your synagogues, and persecute them from city to city.

This verse will guide us in our study of the *baptized believers*. We shall look for **prophets**: those who fearlessly preached the word of God. We shall look for **wise men**: those men who took the word of God, won souls, and established churches. We shall look for **scribes**: those that preserved the word of God for us. Once again:

Matthew 23:34: *Wherefore, behold, I send unto you **prophets**, and **wise men**, and **scribes**: and some of them ye shall kill and crucify; and some of them shall ye scourge in your synagogues, and persecute them from city to city:*

In this passage Jesus promised three things:
1. To send prophets.
2. To send wise men.
3. To send scribes.

Definitions

1. **Prophet: A forth teller.** In the Old Testament the prophet was a *fore-teller*; he foretold the future. He was required to be accurate without exception. Notice Deuteronomy 18:22:

> *When a prophet speaketh in the name of the LORD, if the thing follow not, nor come to pass, that is the thing which the LORD hath not spoken, but the prophet hath spoken it presumptuously: thou shalt not be afraid of him.*

Prophets predicted the future because God told them what was going to happen. Then they recorded the words of God. That is how God gave us our Bible. Jesus promised to send prophets. These men, in the beginning, were to be fore-tellers **and** forth-tellers. After the scriptures were fully revealed, the fore-tellers then became exclusively forth-tellers. The group of prophets Jesus sent included Paul and the other apostles. Their mission was to complete the New Testament revelation. This was completed about the year A.D. 90.

2. **Wise men: Those who apply the word of God to life**. This would especially mean those that win souls. Proverbs 11:30 says, "He that winneth souls is wise." We may conclude that the wise men Jesus said He would send were **the church builders**. They

---

Pivotal Points to Ponder

Old Testament Commission to a New Testament Commission

The promise to God's people who "goeth forth and weepeth, bearing precious seed" was at first **an Old Testament commission** (Psalm 126:6) that the children of Israel were commanded to keep. In Daniel 12:2 we are told: "they that be wise shall shine as the brightness of the firmament, and they that turn many to righteousness as the stars forever." Indeed the commission from God to His people to "turn many to righteousness" was first an Old Testament commission for the nation of Israel to fulfill. **It became a New Testament commission** for the New Testament churches to fulfill.

When did this commission change hands? The following verses shed light on this:

Matt. 15:22-28 And, behold, a woman of Canaan came out of the same coasts, and cried unto him, saying, Have mercy on me, O Lord, thou Son of David; my daughter is grievously vexed with a devil. But he answered her not a word. And his disciples came and besought him, saying, Send her away; for she crieth after us. But he answered and said, I am not sent but unto the lost sheep of the house of Israel. Then came she and worshipped him, saying, Lord, help me. But he answered and said, It is not meet to take the children's bread, and to cast it to dogs. And she said, Truth, Lord: yet the dogs eat of the crumbs which fall from their masters' table. Then Jesus answered and said unto her, O woman, great is thy faith: be it unto thee even as thou wilt.

Matt. 21:43 Therefore say I unto you, The Kingdom of God **shall be taken from you**, and given to a nation bringing forth the fruits thereof.

Acts 28:28 Be it known therefore unto you, that the salvation of God is sent unto the Gentiles, and that **they will hear it**.

won souls and birthed churches as Jesus commanded in Matthew 28:19 and 20. This passage is sometimes called **The Great Commission**.

Wise men will always fulfill this commission.

3. **Scribe: Someone who copied the word of God for future generations**. Just as the scribes fulfilled a vital role in the life of the nation of Israel, so scribes fulfilled a role for the New Testament churches. We should be grateful to these people, but we should also be cautious about receiving everything they do as being correct and right. Many scribes did not like authority. (See Matthew 7:2.) Remember scribes helped put Jesus to death. (See Matthew 16:21.) Many scribes were put in the same category as the Pharisees. (See Matthew 23.) So in Mark 12:38 we are told to "beware of the scribes." The disciples ran into the *scribe problem* in Acts 4, 6 and 23. Nevertheless, **Jesus** promised to send these people. Satan, knowing Jesus would send the scribes, began immediately to counter-act the plan of God. If we are to understand the history of the true churches of Jesus Christ, we need an understanding of the scribe problem, and properly identify *the right scribes*.

> *Pivotal Points to Ponder*
>
> Therefore, it is important to realize that Jesus Himself promised to send forth prophets to finish the word of God, others to use it to start the right kind of churches and others to preserve or copy the word of God through the ages. Our study of Baptist church history will be a study looking for what Jesus promised.

Different Ways Of Looking At Baptist Origins

1. Some believe Baptists came from **English Separatism**. This is sometimes called the **English Descent Theory**. (See chapter eighteen.) This view suggests the Baptists came simply from the seventeenth century Separatist movement, which advocated separation from the Church of England. The claim is that the earliest Baptist church is traced to 1609 in Amsterdam, with John Smythe as pastor. ***Believer's baptism*** in Amsterdam became the defining moment which led to the first Baptist church. Shortly thereafter, Smythe left the group, and Thomas Helwys took over the leadership, leading the church back to England in 1611. However, evidence shows that Baptists were in England and Europe much earlier. This view insists that Baptists are simply another branch of Protestantism. Historians embracing this view include: William H. Whitsitt, Robert G. Torbet, Winthrop S. Hudson, Leon McBeth, William G. McLoughlin and Robert A. Baker.

2. Some believe Baptists descended from **the Anabaptists of Europe**. This outlook teaches that Baptists have their roots in the Anabaptist movement of the sixteenth century. This view would also teach that Baptists are another branch of Protestantism. However, history shows that the Anabaptist offspring from Europe were mostly Mennonite and the pacifist sects such as the Hutterites and Amish. Very few Baptists hold to this explanation of Baptist origins. The historians A.C. Underwood and William R. Estep basically follow this line of reasoning.

3. There are those that hold to a **Succession** of Baptist Churches. This viewpoint teaches that Baptist churches existed in an unbroken chain since the time of Christ and John the Baptist. Sometimes referred to as *Landmarkism* or the *Trail of Blood* theory, this view declares that those churches which stood outside the influence of the Roman Catholic Church at various times in church history were, in actuality although not in name, Baptist churches. Historians who share this viewpoint include James R. Graves, D. B. Ray, J. M. Carroll, G. H. Orchard, J. M. Cramp, and S. H. Ford.

4. There is a group of Baptist historians who believe that Baptist faith and practice or, a **Continuation of Biblical Teachings and distinctives** have existed since the time of Christ. This view has a large number of adherents, including a number of early Baptist historians. Some of these

Chapter 1—Distinctives of a New Testament Church

are: Thomas Crosby, Isaac Backus, A.H. Newman, David Benedict, Thomas Armitage and William Cathcart.

The scriptures and history point to numbers three and four as being nearest the truth. We will demonstrate this truth.

1. What are the four major views of Baptist origins?

2. Which is the correct view?

3. Give an example of a Baptist successional historian.

4. Write Matthew 23:34 twice.

5. Write the definitions above. You can limit the definition to 6 to 14 words.

6. The Old Testament commission became a what?
7. If we are going to understand the history of the true churches of Jesus Christ, we are going to have to identify what?

****

1.1.2

The following is background regarding the first century churches who sprang up after the resurrection of Christ. Carroll, quoting the Reformed historian Mosheim:•

> *What is a church?*
> A particular called out assembly of baptized believers who are organized to preach the Gospel to the lost, and teach the Word of God to the saved. It has officers and elders described in Eph. 4:11, I Tim. 5:17, is led by a bishop, (I Tim. 3:1) and has the Lord's Supper and Baptism as visible ordinances.

1. What we know today as Christianity or the Christian Religion, began with Christ, A.D. 25-30 in the days and within the bounds of the Roman Empire, one of the greatest empires the world has ever known in all its history.
2. This Empire at that period embraced nearly all of the known inhabited world. Tiberius Caesar was its Emperor.
3. In its religion, the Roman Empire, at that time, was pagan. Their religion had many gods, some material and some imaginary. There were many devout believers and worshipers. It was

---

• John Lawrence Mosheim, D.D., (1694-1775) German Reformed historian. He was born in Lubec, Germany and educated at the University of Kiev. Mosheim became professor of philosophy and filled the chair of divinity at Helmstadt for 22 years. He was chancellor of the University of Gottingen. Versed in German, Greek, Italian and English, his greatest work was his *Institutes of Ecclesiastical History*. He was not sympathetic to the Baptists.

a religion not simply of the people, but of the empire. It was an **established** religion, established by law and supported by the government.

4. The Jewish people at that period, no longer a separate nation, were scattered throughout the Roman Empire. They yet had their temple in Jerusalem, and went there to worship, and they were yet jealous of their religion. But it, like the pagan, had long since drifted into formalism and had lost its power (Mosheim, Vol. 1, *Ecclesiastical History*, P. 34).

5. The religion of Christ being a religion not of this world, its founder gave it no earthly head and no temporal power. It sought no establishment, no state or governmental support. It sought no dethronement of Caesar. Said its author, "Render unto Caesar the things that are Caesar's and to God the things that are God's." (See Matt, 22:19-22; Mark 12:17; and Luke 20:20.) Being a spiritual religion, it was a rival of no earthly government. Its adherents, however, were taught to respect all civil law and government Rom. 13:1-7; Titus 3:1; 1 Pet. 2:13-16; (J. M. Carroll, *The Trail of Blood*, Lecture 1, P. 7).

There were false prophets in those days. The book of Acts gives us an example: *Acts 5:36 For before these days rose up **Theudas**, boasting himself to be somebody; to whom a number of men, about four hundred, joined themselves: who was slain; and all, as many as obeyed him, were scattered, and brought to nought.*

There were even false baptizers with false baptism. If you think of the washing practices done by the Hindus in the Yangees River, in India, you get an idea how baptism can be corrupted. The Hindus believe the waters of the river cleanse them from sin, just as those who believe that the water of baptism in some kind of church ritual can wash away sins. This is known as *baptismal regeneration.*

Out of this age of paganism came the preaching ministry of **John the Baptist.** The Bible describes his ministry as unique:

David Benedict, the Baptist historian, was born in Norwalk, Conn., Oct. 10, 1779. His love for historical reading and investigation developed itself in early life. At twenty, he made a profession of his faith in Christ. Religion did for him what it has done for so many thousands of others, quickened his intellectual nature, and made him aspire after something elevating. He entered Brown University, where he graduated in 1806. Soon after, he was ordained as pastor of the Baptist church in Pawtucket, R. I., where he remained twenty-five years. During all this time he had been busy in gatherinng, from every part of the country, the materials out of which to form a comprehensive history of the Baptist denomination, and had sent to press several volumes relating to the subject of his investigations.

After retiring from his pastorate, he gave himself with great diligence to the work of completing the task he had undertaken. Among his published writings are the following: *History of the Baptists*, 1813; *Abridgment of Robinsons' History of Baptism*, 1817; *Fifty Years among the Baptists*, 1860. He wrote also *The History of the Donatists*, which was completed just before he was ninety-five years of age, and which, since his death, has been printed.

He was remarkably favored with good eyesight, and his vision was unimpaired to the last. At the time of his death he had been the senior member of the board of trustees of Brown University for sixteen years, and had been in the corporation for fifty-six years. Dr. Benedict died at Pawtucket, December 5, 1874 (William Cathcart, *Baptist Encyclopedia*, P. 39-40).

Benedict was one of the first American Baptist historians to connect the modern Baptists with the ancient Waldensians and Anabaptists. He took the suggestion of such a connection from Isaac Backus.

*Matt 11:12-13 And from the days of John the Baptist until now the kingdom of heaven suffereth violence, and the violent take it by force. For all **the prophets** and the law **prophesied until John**.*

Chapter 1—Distinctives of a New Testament Church

*Lu 16:16 The law and **the prophets were until John**: since that time the kingdom of God is preached, and every man presseth into it.*

John's place in history was unique. He was the last of the Old Testament prophets. He was the first of the New Testament prophets. He began a new practice by immersing hundreds, perhaps thousands of converts who repented of their sins and clung to the promise of the coming Messiah. **David Benedict** wrote:

> The manner in which the Messiah appeared, His ministry and death, and all the affairs of His kingdom and people, for many years after He ascended on high, are recorded in the New Testament. His disciples began to congregate into churches, soon after He left the earth. The church at Jerusalem was formed the evening of the glorious day of His ascension, in an upper room, and consisted of about a hundred and twenty believing men and women. The persecution, which arose about the time of Stephen's death, caused all the disciples of Jesus, except the apostles, to leave Jerusalem. They proceeded out every way like the radii of a circle from the center, and formed churches in many places, first in Palestine, then in other parts of Asia, next in the Asiatic islands, and lastly in Europe.

> ### *When did the church begin?*
> Many argue that the church, or the church *age* began on the day of Pentecost in Acts 1-3. However, it is more consistent to say that the church, or church age began with the ministry of Jesus. He was the first bishop, the church was organized and even was taught how to discipline according to Matthew 18. James became the next pastor of the church at Jerusalem. All of God's churches sprang from the church at Jerusalem.

> Mr. Robinson has shown that the apostles and primitive preachers gathered churches in between sixty and seventy different cities, towns, and provinces, and in many instances a number were gathered in each. These churches were all composed of reputed believers, who had been baptized by immersion on the profession of their faith. Their bishops and elders were merely overseers of their spiritual flocks; they claimed no right to lord it over God's heritage; every church was an independent body, and no one claimed a right to regulate the affairs of another. If they met in council, as they did at Jerusalem, it was to advise, not to give law.

> The church of Christ has always been taught by the conduct of the people of this world, that this is not her home. She was persecuted at first by the Jews, then by the pagans, and next by monsters under the Christian name.

> Christianity prospered greatly under the ministry of the apostles and primitive preachers, and in a short time was carried to most parts of the Roman empire, which extended in length above three thousands miles, from the river Euphrates in the east, to the western ocean; in breadth it was more than two thousand miles, and whole consisted of above sixteen hundred thousand square miles. This vast empire was an assemblage of conquered kingdoms and provinces, and comprehended, at the commencement of Christianity, most of the civilized world. And at this period, it is said to have contained one hundred and twenty millions of souls.

> It would be difficult to form any probable conjecture of the number of converts to Christianity in the early ages of the church, but it must have been immensely great, for it is supposed that three millions were sacrificed in the first three centuries, to the rage of pagan persecutors. In these three centuries there were ten general persecutions, fomented by so many cruel pagan emperors. They did not reign, however, in regular succession, and in the intervening spaces between their reigns, the empire was governed by princes, who entertained a great variety of opinions respecting Christianity. Some turned it into ridicule, others showed a degree of clemency towards the Christians; some repealed the persecuting laws of their

predecessors, while others left them to their destructive operation. But the pagan priests continually employed their malicious eloquence to defame the disciples of Christ, and to rouse the persecuting sword against them. They laid to their charge the earthquakes, famines, pestilences, and conflagrations, and all the national calamities which happened where they resided. And they persuaded the magistrates that the gods sent down these judgments to avenge their lenity towards the Christians (David Benedict, *History of the Baptists*, Vol. 1, P. 8-10).

1. Write Matthew 23:34 twice.

2. What was the religion of the Roman Empire at the time of Christ?
Paganism

3. What was the condition of the Jewish nation at the time of Christ?
Scattered

4. Name a false prophet that arose before the time of Christ?
Thudas

5. What is baptismal regeneration?
wash away your sin

6. Regarding David Benedict, he was the first American Baptist historian to do what? Connect modern baptists to previous baptists

7. What is a church? When did the church or church age begin?
an assembly of baptized believers

****

1.1.3
Satan's Devices

Consider this:

> 2 Corinthians 2:10-11 Lest Satan should get an advantage of us: for **we are not ignorant of his devices.**

The devil was using a device in the first days of the New Testament church age. That device was **martyrdom**. Satan's device in the first century was to KILL THE CHRISTIANS.

The sect of Christians was everywhere spoken against:

The Cruelty of the Romans
The Unheard-Of Cruelties Nero Practiced In Slaying the Pious Christians. In A.D. 66:

Touching the manner in which the Christians were tortured and killed at the time of Nero. A. Mellinus gives the following account from Tacitus and other Roman writers; namely: that four extremely cruel and unnatural kinds of torture were employed against the Christians:

Firstly that they dressed them in the skins of tame and wild beasts, that they might be torn to pieces by dogs or other wild animals.

Secondly, that they, according to the example of their Saviour, were fastened alive on crosses, and that in many different ways.

Thirdly, that the innocent Christians were burned and smoked by the Romans, with torches and lamps, under the shoulders and on other tender parts of their naked bodies, after these had been cruelly lacerated with scourges or rods.

Fourthly, that these miserable, accused Christian martyrs were used as candles, torches, or lanterns to see by them at night.

Of those who were burned, some were tied or nailed to stakes, and held still by a hook driven through the throat, so that they could not move the head when the pitch, wax, tallow, and other inflammable substances were poured boiling over their heads, and set on fire, so that all the unctuous matter of the human body flowing down made long, wide furrows in the sand of the theatre… And thus human beings were lighted as torches, and burned as light for the wicked Romans at night.

Juvenal and Martial, both Roman poets, and Tertullian, state this in a different manner, namely, that the Romans wrapped them in a painful burning mantle, which they wound around their hands and feet, in order to melt the very marrow in their bones…those mantles, that they made were made of paper or linen, and having been thickly coated with oil, pitch, wax, rosin, tallow, and sulphur, were wrapped around their whole body, and then set on fire.

For this spectacle Nero gave the use of his gardens, and appeared himself among the people in the garb of a charioteer, taking an active part in the Circusian game (Thieleman J. Van Braght, *The Bloody Theatre*, P. 79).

Chapter 1—Distinctives of a New Testament Church

Acts 28:22 But we desire to hear of thee what thou thinkest: for as concerning this sect, we know that every where it is spoken against.

Public opinion has never been favorable to the *baptized believers*. In the first century, pagan society turned violently against them and the devil's device against them was mayhem and murder. There were ten general persecutions in the first 100 years, and 14 altogether. **David Benedict** informs us:

> The first of these ten persecutions was begun by the abominable Nero. He was the first emperor who shed the blood of Christians, and it is said that Peter and Paul were of the number. The city of Rome took fire, and a considerable part of it was consumed. The perfidious Nero was thought to have kindled the fire, but that cruel prince accused the innocent Christians of the horrid crime, and avenged it upon them in a most barbarous manner. He caused some to be wrapped up in combustible garments, which were set on fire; others were fastened to crosses, others were torn to pieces by wild beasts, and thousands suffered death in the most horrid and cruel forms.
>
> The persecutions under all the ten emperors were similar in many respects; some of them were but short, and others of longer duration. The Christians suffered every privation, and were put to death by all the excruciating tortures, which infernal ingenuity could invent. Multitudes were confined in theatres, where wild beasts were let loose upon them, and they were worried and devoured, for the diversion of thousands of barbarous spectators, who sat elevated above the reach of harm.
>
> The third persecution was under Trajan, a prince renowned for many excellent qualities, but who was, nevertheless, a dreadful scourge to the disciples of Christ (David Benedict, *History of the Baptists*, Vol. 1 P. 10).

The first ten general persecutions of the first century are put into categories:
1. Tiberius
2. Claudius
3. Nero
4. Domician
5. Nerva
6. Trajan
7. Hadrian
8. Antoninus Pius
9. Marcus Aurelius
10. Commodius

The First Martyrs

The first martyr for the cause of Christ was John the Baptist. Then our lovely Saviour laid down His life for us. Quickly the **device of death** by the devil closed in. Stephen was stoned outside Jerusalem in A.D. 34. James the son of Zebedee and pastor of the church at Jerusalem was beheaded by order of Herod Agrippa A.D. 45. Philip was stoned in Phrygia in A.D. 54. James, the brother of Jesus, was beaten to death on the steps of the temple in Jerusalem in A.D. 63. Barnabas, the companion of Paul was burned on Cyprus in A.D. 64. John Mark, was dragged through the streets of Alexandria and died A.D. 64. Simon Peter was crucified under Nero in A.D. 69. The Apostle Paul was beheaded under the authority of Nero in A.D. 69.

The Collegiate Baptist History Workbook

All these met with death in A.D. 70: Aristarchus, companion with Paul, murdered at Rome; Epaphras, Priscilla, Aquila, Andronmicus, and Juna all friends of the Apostle Paul were martyred under Nero; Silas was beaten to death in Macedonia; Onesiphorus and Porphyrius were torn and dragged to death by horses at Hellespontus; Andrew was crucified in Patras, Achaia; Bartholomew was flayed alive in Armenia; Thomas, tormented with red-hot plates was stabbed to death by spears at Calamina; Also in or about A.D. 70: Matthew was nailed to the ground and beheaded at Nad-davar; Simon Zelotes and his brother Judas Thaddeus were crucified and beaten with sticks; Matthias was crucified and beheaded. Soon after, Luke was hanged in Greece in A.D. 93 and Antipas, the faithful witness, mentioned by Jesus himself to John at the Revelation, was roasted alive at Pergamos in A.D. 95.

Again, the great historian **David Benedict:**

From the New Testament account of the primitive Christians, we are led to think they were Baptists. But we will quote the accounts given of them by two authors, and then the reader may judge for himself. **Mosheim** (a Lutheran historian) was no friend to the Baptists, and yet he has made many important concessions in their favour; and in relating the history of the primitive church, he has given a description, which will not certainly apply to his own church, the Lutheran, nor to any sect in Christendom except the Baptists. "**Baptism**," he observes, "was administered in the first century without the public assemblies, in places appointed for that purpose, and **was performed by immersion** of the whole body in water." By this account it appears that the first Christians went "streaming away to some pond or river" to be baptized. Respecting church discipline, the same writer observes: "The churches in those early times were entirely independent, none of them subject to any foreign jurisdiction, but each one governed by its own rulers and laws. For though the churches, founded by the Apostles, had this particular difference shewn them, that they were consulted in difficult and doubtful cases, yet they had no juridical authority, no sort of supremacy over the others, nor the least right to enact laws for them. Nothing on the contrary is more evident than the perfect equality that reigned among the primitive churches," and so on.

A bishop, during the first and second century, was a person who had the care of one Christian assembly, which at that time was, generally speaking, small enough to be contained in a private house. In this assembly he acted not so much with the authority of a master, as with the zeal and diligence of a faithful servant," and so on.

"There was," says Robinson, [Robinson was an early English Baptist historian] "among primitive Christians, an uniform belief that Jesus was the Christ, and a perfect harmony of affection. When congregations multiplied, so that they became too numerous to assemble in one place, they parted into separate companies, and so again and again, but there was no schism; on the contrary all held a common belief, and a member of one company was a member of all. If any person removed from one place to reside at another, he received a letter of attestation, which was given and taken as proof; and this custom very prudently precluded the intrusion of impostors. One company never pretended to inspect the affairs of another, nor was there any dominion, or any shadow of dominion, over the consciences of any individuals."

Let any candid man compare the different denominations of Christians of the present day with these descriptions of the primitive church and he will, we think, be at **no loss** to determine which comes the nearest to it. But Mr. Robinson goes farther, and determines the matter just as a Baptist believes: "During the three first centuries, Christian congregations all over the east subsisted in separate, independent bodies, unsupported by government, and consequently without any secular power over one another. All this time they were Baptist churches, and though all the fathers of the four first ages down to Jerome were of Greece,

Chapter 1—Distinctives of a New Testament Church

Syria, and Africa, and though they gave great number of histories of the baptism of adults, yet there is **not one record of the baptism of a child** till the year 370, when Galates, the dying son of the emperor Valens, was baptized by order of a monarch, who sware he would not be contradicted. The age of the prince is uncertain, and the assigning of his illness as the cause of his baptism indicates clearly enough that infant baptism was not in practice (David Benedict, *History of the Baptists*, Vol 1, P. 99-100).

1. Write Matthew 23:34 twice.

2. What was the first device that Satan used on the first century Christians?
   "kill the Christians"

3. How many general persecutions were there?
   10

4. Name four martyrs from the first century.
   James

5. Mosheim, a Lutheran historian, admitted that primitive baptism was done a certain way. What way was that?
   Immersion

6. What was the duty of a Bishop in the first century?
   care of one local church

****

1.2.1
SECTION TWO

We have stated that there are distinctives among the Baptists. These are the earmarks of the New Testament church. The erosion of these distinctive doctrines and the struggle by believers to maintain them is our focus.

All of Christianity holds dear the *fundamentals* of our faith. **Those fundamentals are** obvious truths from scripture such as: **the inerrant inspiration of the Bible, salvation by grace through faith, the Deity of Christ, the Trinity, the blood atonement, and the great commission**. The wise student will understand, there are certain doctrinal differences between Baptists and other Christian groups. Our distinctives exist because of the strong desire of our forefathers to cling to Bible principles.

> ### Pivotal Points to Ponder
> Changing the nature of these *distinctives* changes the nature and purpose of the church, thereby taking away the right of the church to function as set up by Jesus. Read this verse to see the consequences of changing the *distinctives* of a church:
>
> *Revelation 2:4-5 Nevertheless I have somewhat against thee, because thou hast left thy first love. Remember therefore from whence thou art fallen, and repent, and do the first works; or else I will come unto thee quickly, and will remove thy candlestick out of his place, except thou repent.*

Baptist Distinctives

1. Independent churches
2. Regenerate church membership
3. Believer's baptism

The Collegiate Baptist History Workbook

4. Baptism by immersion
5. Soul Liberty

The defense of these distinctives provided the stage for the history of the churches in general and the Baptists in particular. Let us briefly discuss the distinctives.

1. Independent churches

Originally, the church had elders as leaders. The Bishop or pastor had charge of his own flock. In time, more powerful bishops began to exercise power over smaller congregations. These Bishops became known as *Metropolitans*. It was the beginning of the archbishop system of hierarchy.

In his famous booklet on Baptist history, *The Trail of Blood*, J. M. Carroll says this about the nature of the churches in the primitive era:

> The first of these changes from New Testament teachings embraced both policy and doctrine. In the first two centuries the individual churches rapidly multiplied and some of the earlier ones, such as Jerusalem, Antioch, Ephesus, Corinth, etc., grew to be very large; Jerusalem, for instance, had many thousand members (Acts 2:41; 4:4, 5:14), possibly 25,000 or even 50,000 or more. A close student of the book of Acts and Epistles will see that Paul had a mighty task even in his day in keeping some of the churches straight. (II Pet. 2:12; Acts 20:29-31. Rev. 2-3.)
>
> These great churches necessarily had many preachers or elders. (See Acts 20:17.) Some of the bishops or pastors began to assume authority

---

The Early System Of Elders And Deacons

Elders were leaders of God's people whose roots ex-tended to the Old Testament ministry of Moses.
  I. Moses' duties required help. His father-in-law suggested helpers or **elders** in Exodus 18:19-25.
  *II. God ordained His choice of seventy **elders*** to help Moses in Num. 11:14, 16, 24.
  *III. The Last mention of the Old Testament **elders*** was Acts 6:12, and the first mention of New Testament **elders** was Acts 11:30.

New Testament Elders
  1. Apostles and **elders** mentioned together. See Acts 15:2, 4, 6, 22; Acts 16:4.
  2. By Acts 17, **elders** alone mentioned. See Acts 20:17, 18; Acts 22:5.

Who were the New Testament Elders?
  1. They were God-called men of God who are publicly set apart for service by public ordination. See Acts 14:23, Acts 16:4, I Timothy 2:7, Titus 1:5.
  2. They were identified in Ephesians 4:11:
    Apostles
    Prophets: these two together formed the foundation of New Testament Christianity
    Evangelists
    Pastors and teachers

A **bishop** in a local church is the **elder** who is the pastor of the local congregation. He is an officer and his standards are given in I Timothy 3:1-7. He is to rule (I Tim. 5:17) and have all authority. (See Titus 2:1.) As overseer, he answers to God for the local church members. (See Hebrews 13:7, 17.) He oversees any other elder in the local assembly. (Such as assistant pastors, evangelists, God-called preachers, or missionaries.)

Equal elder rule or board run churches did not exist in the primitive church. Neither did any episcopacy rule any group of churches. The presbytery mentioned in I Timothy 4:14 is simply a group of God-called preachers (elders) who publicly set apart other men of God by ordination. *Metropolitans* or archbishops and synods did not appear until the second century.

What About the New Testament Deacons?
  They were officers of the New Testament church whose duties were to assist the bishop in any way the bishop may need them. Deacon is from the word "diaconas" which literally means a *dirt servant*. Deacons are not elders and do not rule. (See I Timothy 5:17.) In the Bible, they were not assigned until the church had thousands of members. (See Acts 6.)

---

not given them in the New Testament. They began to claim authority over other and smaller churches. **They, with their many elders, began to lord it over God's heritage. (See III John 9.)** Here was the beginning of an error which has grown and multiplied into many other seriously hurtful errors. Here was the beginning of different orders in the ministry running up finally to what is practiced now by others as well as Catholics. Here began what resulted in an

Chapter 1—Distinctives of a New Testament Church

entire change from the original democratic policy and government of the early churches. This irregularity began in a small way, even before the close of the second century. This was possibly the first serious departure from the New Testament church order (J. M. Carroll, *The Trail of Blood*, Lecture 1, P.12).

2. Regenerate church membership

The church is comprised of saved people. Acts 2:47 *"the Lord added to the church daily such as should be saved."* Since baptism was for those who were born again, water baptism became the requirement for church membership. Infant baptism muddied the waters on this issue confusing water baptism and regeneration.

In his writings, the *theologian* Augustine changed the text of Titus 3:5 which states: *"Not by works of righteousness which we have done, but according to his mercy he saved us, by **the washing of regeneration**, and renewing of the Holy Ghost;"* **Augustine changed the word *washing* to the word "laver,"** which changed the meaning of the passage. Instead of regeneration washing the Christian, a laver (baptismal pool or font) regenerated the Christian. This led to belief in ***baptismal regeneration***, a false doctrine that created infant baptism.

3. Believer's baptism

Only believers have a reason to be baptized. Believers only were baptized in the first century. Read Acts 8:36-37: *"And as they went on their way, they came unto a certain water: and the eunuch said, See, here is water; what doth hinder me to be baptized? And Philip said, If thou believest with all thine heart, thou mayest. And he answered and said, I believe that Jesus Christ is the Son of God."*

The debate over baptism has been repeated throughout history with great upheaval and terrible consequences. It *is* the question of baptism that makes a Christian what he is. It is debate about baptism that makes Christianity maintain its edge.

Did They Baptize Infants?

Historian S. H. Ford, writing in 1860 stated:

> We now make the bold, yet almost universally admitted assertion, that the primitive churches were in every distinguishing characteristic Baptist churches. We affirm that at the time of the departure of the great Tertullian, their Baptistic features were as yet uneffaced; and that, though lost in the development of the Man of Sin, they have preserved those lineaments intact in *the churches* to this day. Where shall we seek the proof of this? Whom shall we introduce as witnesses? Shall we let Baptists speak? Will their testimony be received? No; with all their research, and learning, and candor, we shall dismiss them as witnesses in the case. Let Pedobaptists speak; let Presbyterians and Episcopalians testify; and if a jury of rational men can be found, who, guided by their report, can give a verdict against our affirmation, we shall acknowledge that there is no confidence to be placed in testimony.

Ford continues, citing historical authorities:

> M. De la Roque:
>> The primitive churches did not baptize infants, and the learned Grotius proves it, in his annotations on the gospel. (In Stennett's answer to Russen, p. 188.)
>
> Salmasius and Suicerus:
>> In the two first centuries no one was baptized, except, being instructed in the faith, and acquainted with the doctrines of Christ, he was able to profess himself a believer; because of Epist. ad Tustum Pacium. Thesaur. Eccles. sub voce Evrazis, tom. ii, p. 1136.
>
> Curcelleus:
>> The baptism of infants, in the two first centuries after Christ, was altogether unknown, but in the third and fourth was allowed by some few. In the fifth and following ages it was generally received. The custom of baptizing infants did not begin before the third age after Christ was born in the former ages no trace of it appears, and it was introduced without the command of Christ. Epistle to the Churches of Galatia, chap. iii, verse 27 (2.) Annotat. ad Rom., v. 14.
>
> Venema:
>> **Tertullian** has nowhere mentioned Pedobaptism [child or infant baptism] among the traditions of the church, nor even among the customs of the church that were publicly received, and usually observed; nay, he plainly intimates that, in his time, it was yet a doubtful affair. Nothing can be affirmed with certainty concerning the custom of the church before Tertullian, seeing there is not anywhere, in more ancient writers, that I know of, undoubted mention of infant baptism. Justin Martyr, in his second apology, when describing baptism, mentions only that of adults. I conclude, therefore, that Pedobaptism can not be certainly proved to have been practiced before the times of Tertullian; and that there were persons in his age who desired their infants might be baptized, especially when they were afraid of their dying without baptism. Tertullian opposed, and by so doing he intimates that Pedobaptism [child or infant baptism] began to prevail. These are the things that may be affirmed with apparent certainty concerning the antiquity of infant baptism, after the times of the apostles; for more are maintained without solid foundation (Hist. Eccles., tom. iii, Secul. II, 108, 109).
>
> Episcopius:
>> Pedobaptism [child or infant baptism] was not accounted a necessary rite till it was determined so to be in the Milevitan Council, held in the year 418 (Institut. Theology, 1. iv, c. xiv).

Ford concludes:

> We close with the testimony of **Augustus Neander:**[*]
>> Baptism was administered at first only to adults, as men were accustomed to conceive baptism and faith as strictly connected. We have all reason for not deriving infant baptism from apostolic institution, and the recognition of it which followed somewhat later, as an apostolical tradition, serves to confirm this hypothesis. Irenaeus is the first church teacher in whom we find any allusion to infant baptism, and in his mode of expressing himself on the subject, he leads us at the same time to recognize its connection with the essence of the Christian consciousness; he testifies of the profound Christian idea, out of which infant baptism arose, and which procured for it at length universal recognition (Neander's *Ecclesiastical History*, Vol. I, P. 311).

---

[*] Augustus Neander, the Lutheran historian, finished his six-volume set on church history in 1843.

Chapter 1—Distinctives of a New Testament Church

Is there any possibility of denying this testimony? Is it not convincing, overwhelming, that the churches, previous to Tertullian, practiced but *one baptism,* and that it was adult baptism (S. H. Ford, *Origin of the Baptists*).

1. Write Matthew 23:34 twice.
   Wherefore behold, I send unto you Prophets, and wise men, and scribes: and some of them ye shall kill and crucify and some of them shall ye scourge in your synagogues and persecute
2. Name all 5 Baptist distinctives.
   Independent churches, regenerate church membership, believers baptism
3. What word did Augustine change in Titus 3:5? What word did he substitute for it?
   He changed the word washing to lather
4. What prerequisite for baptism did Philip give in Acts 8?
   If thou believest with all thine heart thou mayest
5. What were the Old Testament rulers called?
   elders
6. Name two New Testament kinds of elders.
   Apostles, Prophets / Pastors, bishops
7. Name at least two witnesses from the past that plainly state that baptism in the primitive church was for believers only.
   Venemous
8. What is pedobaptism?

****
1.2.2 *Infant baptism*

Baptist Distinctives Continued

4. Baptism by immersion

Baptism by immersion was a part of the first century church as evidenced by the following scriptures:

> Acts 8:38 And he commanded the chariot to stand still: and **they went down both into the water**, both Philip and the eunuch; and he baptized him.
>
> John 3:23 And John also was baptizing in Aenon near to Salim, **because there was much water there**: and they came, and were baptized.

The very meaning of the word baptize means *to immerse.* The scriptural evidence is great and so is the archeological evidence. Old baptismal pools have been excavated throughout the Middle East and Europe.

Again let us go to **Mr. Ford**, in *Origin of the Baptists*:

> We pause not now to argue the question of immersion. We simply wish to ascertain a fact. We ask historians what did the churches of the first and second centuries do when they performed that ordinance called baptism? Again we call on the most renowned, the most distinguished Pedobaptists, to answer, men who practiced and apologized for sprinkling, yet dared not, as scholars, garble or misrepresent the truth of history.

Following the lead of Mr. Ford, we invite you to hear the testimony of Augustus Neander, in his *History of the Christian Religion*:

The Collegiate Baptist History Workbook

> **In respect to the manner of baptizing:** in conformity with the original institution and the original import of the symbol, it was generally **administered by immersion**, as a sign of total baptism into the Holy Spirit, of being entirely penetrated by His grace. It was only in the case of the sick that any exception was made (Augustus Neander, *General History of the Christian Religion*, Vol. 1, P. 429).

And we quote John Mosheim, the German Reformed historian, in his *Ecclesiastical History*:

> In this century baptism was administered in convenient places, without the public assemblies and by **immersing the candidate wholly in water**. Twice a year, namely at Easter and Whitsuntide, baptism was publicly administered by the bishop or by the presbyters acting by his command and authority. The candidates for it **were immersed wholly in water** with invocation of the sacred Trinity. The baptized were signed with the cross and had renounced all their sins and transgressions…and finally directed to taste some milk and honey (Moshiem, *Ecclesiastical History*, Vol. 1, P. 313).

5. Soul Liberty

When the church began to deteriorate in the second century, infant baptism and baptismal regeneration began to be promoted as truth. This was protested by men like Justin Martyr and Tertullian, but it eventually became popular to baptize infants into regeneration and church membership. This removes the scriptural necessity of being *born again*. Infant baptism (sprinkling or christening), under the marriage of the "church" and Roman state, would come to mean *citizenship*. For refusing to have their child baptized, the people of Europe became subject to punishment, banishment and death. Baptist people resisted this *forced conversion*, and insisted upon **soul liberty**, the individual responsibility to turn to Christ. See these scriptures:

> *Matt 13:27-30 So the servants of the householder came and said unto him, Sir, didst not thou sow good seed in thy field? from whence then hath it tares? He said unto them, An enemy hath done this. The servants said unto him, Wilt thou then that we go and gather them up? But he said, Nay; lest while ye gather up the tares, ye root up also the wheat with them.* **Let both grow together until the harvest**: *and in the time of harvest I will say to the reapers, Gather ye together first the tares, and bind them in bundles to burn them: but gather the wheat into my barn.*

There would come a time when soul liberty would be buried under the crush of the church-state monstrosity. The state would take on the responsibility of uprooting the tares under the direction of "the church." It would ruin God's churches and scatter God's people.

Nevertheless, the first century church survived with their fundamentals and distinctives in place. The last apostle to die was John, around A.D. 100.

TIME TO THINK:

1. Write Matthew 23:34 twice.

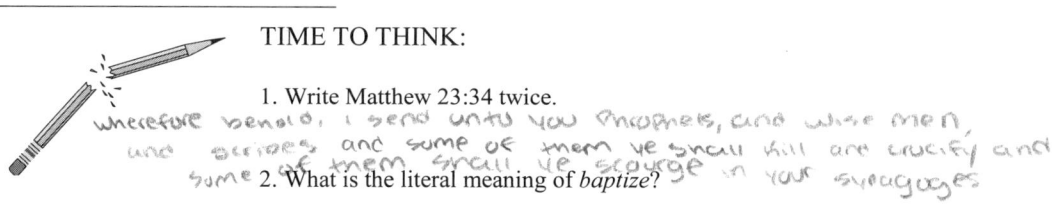

wherefore behold, I send unto you Prophets, and wise men, and scribes and some of them ye shall kill and crucify and some of them shall ye scourge in your synagogues

2. What is the literal meaning of *baptize*?

to immerse

Chapter 1—Distinctives of a New Testament Church

3. Of what is the church comprised?

saved baptized believers

4. What false doctrine led to the destruction of soul liberty?

church-state monstrosity | *Baptismal regeneration*

Special Assignment

Reformed theologians (sixteenth century) such as Zwingli and John Calvin, insisted that God dealt with Christians according to the same covenant relationship He had with Israel. They taught the *sign* of the conditional covenant in the Old Testament was circumcision and the *sign* of the covenant in the New Testament was baptism. John Calvin insisted that baptism indicated **ingrafting** into Christ (*Institutes* 4:15:1-6). Calvin's insistence on the sacerdotal power of infant baptism has confused the Reformed to this day. In our study we will discover the source of Calvin's infatuation with infant baptism.

The argument between Baptists and the "catholic Reformed" (a term the Reformed readily accept) has been about the conditional covenant relationship of God with Israel and the New Testament relationship of God with His churches. The catholic Reformed have a desire to keep the churches under the same covenant with Israel. An examination of the writings of the **church fathers of the first three centuries yields no mention of a a continued conditional covenant.**

Your assignment is to find two covenants defined in Galatians 3 and 4. Answer this question: Was the conditional covenant given to Israel in the Old Testament continued and binding for the New Testament churches? Give three verses to support your answer.

Catholic/Reformed/Covenant Theology Insists	Pauline/Baptist Theology Insists
1. The Old Testament conditional covenant with Israel continues with the churches. 2. The *sign* of the Old Testament conditional covenant is circumcism, the *sign* of the New Testament covenant is baptism. 3. Infant baptism regenerates and places you into the universal church. 4. The "church" rules the state in a church-state theocracy, just as Israel. 5. The church-state overcomes the world and since the "church" is Christ's body, there is no need for a literal return of Christ (amillennialism); or… 6. The church-state overcomes the world, then Jesus returns (postmillennialism).	1. Jesus fulfilled the Old Testament covenant of promise. The conditional covenant with Israel will be fulfilled in the future. (See Galatians 3 and 4.) 2. The New Testament is a new covenant of the heart. (See Hebrews 8, 9 and 10.) 3. The new covenant is individual, not patriarchal. 4. Baptism is immersion for believers only. 5. History is dispensational as Israel and the New Testament churches are not the same. 6. The tribulation period is Daniel's 70th week. 7. The first resurrection (rapture) occurs before the tribulation. This resurrection is imminent. 8. Christ return is premillennial. He returns, then establishes his millennial (1,000 year) kingdom.

Chapter Two
The Churches of the Second Century

Section One: The Transmission of the Text and the Beginning of the Corruption of the Ordinances.
Section Two: Apostolic Successors and Early Leaders

SECTION ONE

Time line of events in the first and second centuries:
  33. Descent of the Holy Ghost on the Day of Pentecost
  62. Martyrdom of St. James the Less
  64. Persecution by Nero begins
  68. Martyrdom of St. Peter and St. Paul
  70. Destruction of Jerusalem by Titus
  95. Persecution by Domitian
 100. Death of St. John
 116. Martyrdom of Ignatius
 166. Martyrdom of Justin and Polycarp
 168. Montanus publishes writings
 177. Persecution at Lyons and Vienne
 190. Tertullian flourishes

Transmission of the Text—Beginning of the Corruption of the Ordinances

In the previous chapter, we were introduced to Baptist principles and the Biblical makeup of the primitive church. We were also introduced to the **Satanic Device** of martyrdom. Along the trail, we also met a few Baptist historians, most notably, David Benedict. In this chapter, we will see how those principles which identified the primitive church came under attack, and how **Satan's Device** in the second century still operates among us. We will also meet two other great Baptist historians, Thomas Armitage and Henry D'Anvers.

Scripture to Memorize

> Jude 1:3 *Beloved, when I gave all diligence to write unto you of the common salvation, it was needful for me to write unto you, and exhort you that ye should earnestly contend for the faith which was once delivered unto the saints:*

Thomas Armitage wrote:

> It is estimated that at the opening of [the second] century, from two to three hundred churches had been gathered, some of them thousands of miles apart. When the Apostles died, their authority died with them and they lived only in their writings. Their office did not allow perpetuation, for they were the chosen witnesses of Christ's life and work, and could not bequeath their oral testimony to others. When these orphaned flocks were left alone in all their humanness, their only directory was the book by which the Apostles had transmitted their witness and revelations, under the infallible inspiration of the Holy Spirit.
>
> For the first time man was left on common ground, with the choice of making the unmixed authority of that book his guide to Christ, or of committing his soul to the lead of uninspired men. This fact alone put the Gospel to its severest test, and made the second century a most solemn period, as Christians had no alternative but to follow the New Book. How, then, did they bear themselves toward the Sacred Oracles?

Chapter 2—The Churches of the Second Century

Eusebius says, that they "Vied with each other in the preaching of Christ, and in the distribution of the Scriptures." The Epistle to the Thessalonians was written about twenty years after the crucifixion, and the last of the New Covenant books within fifty years thereafter. Probably Paul's Epistles were first collected into one volume; but within half a century after the death of John, the four Gospels were publicly read in the Churches of Syria, Asia Minor, Italy and Gaul, and all the New Testament books were collected about A.D. 150. The first translation appears to have been the Syriac, called Peshito, (literal) for its fidelity, rendered most faithfully into the common language of the Holy Land. Some think that our Lord's exact language is better preserved in this version than in the Greek manuscripts themselves. J. Winchelaus, who devoted much research to its history, says that it preserves the letter of sacred Scripture truly, and Michaelis pronounces it, "The very best translation of the New Testament that I have ever read."

The Peshito throws a strong light upon the act of baptism in that age. The word which expresses that act is *amad*, which the Syriac lexicons define by *immerse*. Bernstein uses these words: "He was

Thomas Armitage, D.D., was born in Yorkshire, England, in 1819. He is descended from the old and honored family of the Armitages of that section of Yorkshire, one of whom, Sir John Armitage, of Barnsley, was created a baronet by Charles I, in 1640.

Armitage lost his father a few years since, and his mother when five years old. The religious influence of his godly mother never forsook him. While listening to a sermon on the text, "Is it well with thee?" his sins and danger filled him with grief and alarm, and before he left the sanctuary his heart was filled with the love of Christ.

In his sixteenth year he preached his first sermon. His text was, "Come unto me all ye that labor and are heavy laden, and I will give you rest." The truth was blessed to the conversion of three persons. He declined pressing calls to enter the regular ministry of the English Methodist Church, but used his gifts as a local preacher for several years.

Like many Englishmen he imbibed republican doctrines, and these brought him in 1838 to New York. He filled many important appointments in the M. E. Church in New York, and he was pastor of the Washington Street church in Albany, one of its most important churches, where the Lord had given him a precious revival and eighty converts. At this period his influence in the M. E. Church was great, and its highest honors were before him. When he was first examined for Methodist ordination he expressed doubts about the church government of the Methodist body, and about sinless perfection, falling from grace, and their views of the ordinances. In 1839 he witnessed a baptism in Brooklyn by the Rev. S. Ilsley, which made him almost a Baptist, and what remained to be done to effect that end was accomplished by another baptism in Albany, administered by the Rev. Jabez Swan, of Connecticut.

An extensive examination of the baptismal question confirmed his faith, and placed him without a misgiving upon the Baptist platform in everything. Dr. Welsh baptized him into the fellowship of the Pearl Street church, Albany. Soon after a council was called to give him scriptural ordination. He was set apart to the Christian ministry in the winter of 1848. He was requested to preach in the Norfolk Street church, New York, in the following June. The people were charmed with the stranger, and so was the sickly pastor, the Rev. George Benedict. He was called to succeed their honored minister, who said to Mr. Armitage, "If you refuse this call it will be the most painful act of your life." In 1853-54, 140 persons were baptized, and in 1857, 152. The first year of his ministry in Norfolk Street the meeting-house was burned, and another erected. Since that time the church reared a house for God in a more attractive part of the city, which they named the "Fifth Avenue Baptist Church." In 1853, Mr. Armitage was made a Doctor of Divinity by Georgetown College, Ky. He was then in his 34th year.

Dr. Armitage is a scholarly man, with a powerful intellect; one of the greatest preachers in the United States; regarded by many as the foremost man in the American pulpit. Dr. Armitage completed his exhaustive *History of the Baptists* in 1889 (William Cathcart, *Baptist Encyclopedia*, Vol. 1, P. 39-40).

dipped, immersed: he dipped or plunged himself into something."

Michaelis declares, that this is the Syriac word which Jesus would use for baptism, in the vernacular language which he spoke. This version was read in the Christian assemblies, with the originals, and where they could not be understood by the people, interpreters rendered them into their mother tongue on the spot. In this age a Latin version was also made, which came into general use immediately. Woide ascribes the translation of the Sahidic, the dialect of Upper Egypt, and the Coptic, that of Lower Egypt, to this period. In the Latin, the word *taptizn* was rendered by the word *tingo*, to dip, or immerse; in the Sahidic it was transferred, evidently, because as a Greek term it was well understood in Upper Egypt; and in the Coptic it was translated by the word *amas*, to immerse or plunge. Augustine says: "Those who have translated the Bible into Greek can be numbered, but not so the Latin versions; for in the first ages of the Church, whoever got hold of a Greek Codex, ventured to translate it into Latin." **He also decides that the ancient Italic is the most literal of the Latin versions**. Irenaeus, too, speaks of many barbarous tribes who had "salvation in their heart without ink or paper;" alluding to the fact that the unlearned heard the Scripture read in their own tongue in the public assemblies.

These early Baptists decided all questions of doctrine by an appeal to their Sacred Books; being very jealous of forged books, which abounded very early. **Tertullian tells us where some of the inspired autographs could be found at that time. "The very images," he says, "of their voice and person are now recited and exhibited. Do you live in Achaia? There is Corinth. Are you not far from Macedonia? You have Philippi and Thessalonica. Are you nigh unto Asia? There is Ephesus. Or, if you border upon Italy, there is Rome."** And as late as the fourth century, Peter of Alexandria said that the Gospel of John, written with his own hand, was still preserved and venerated in the Church at Ephesus.

Before Christ, spurious Jewish writings purporting to be genuine, appeared; and an attempt was made to incorporate some of these manufactures with certain apocryphal gospels, into the Christian Scriptures. These false lights misled many of the primitive Christians, and have had a shameful influence in shaping current Christian history (Thomas Armitage, *History of the Baptists*, Vol. 1, P. 155-6).

In the above passage, Pastor Armitage brings to our attention the testimony of the great Christian writer, Tertullian, of whom we will learn more in our study. Tertullian said the word of God was still in existence *in its original form*, in the second century! As soon as the scriptures were completed, Satan attempted to destroy them. We introduce our second **Satanic Device**:

Satan's Devices

Satan's device in the first century was to KILL THE CHRISTIANS. His device in the second century was to DESTROY THE SCRIPTURES. Persecutions extended into the second century and copies of the scriptures were burned along with the martyrs. Tertullian purportedly said, "The blood of the martyrs is the seed of the church." No matter how vicious the attack on God's people, the more they multiplied in the Roman Empire.

Definitions

Apostle: Literally means, *to be sent out*. Apostles in the Bible knew and saw Jesus Christ personally. They were responsible for completing the revelation of the scriptures, and acted as *prophets* in that capacity.

Chapter 2—The Churches of the Second Century

Baptize: Literally means to *dip* or *immerse*.

1. Write Jude 1:3 twice.

2. Write the definition for apostle and for baptize. *to immerse*

3. According to the short biography of Thomas Armitage above, how did he eventually become a Baptist? *The doctrine of baptisim*
4. When was the last New Testament book written? *90-100*
5. When was the New Testament completed? *150*
6. What was Satan's Device in the second century? *destroy the scriptures*
7. What was the very first translation of God's Word? *Pesnito*

****

2.1.2

The Apostle Paul mentions grievous wolves would come into the local church. The earliest form of false doctrine involved the structure of the local church. Armitage wrote:

> Then, a pernicious tradition began to inject itself into the teaching of the Churches. By **tradition is meant,** from *traditio*, that which is delivered orally, **and is left unwritten, passing by word of mouth from one to another.** Of these, Eusebius calls **PAPIAS <u>the father.</u>** [Papias] died A.D. 163, leaving a collection of random, hearsay discourses and sayings of Jesus and his Apostles, called *Oracles of the Lord*. He tells us that this was made up of first-hand evidence only, and that he preferred oral testimony to written; hence, he details many ridiculous things, showing that he was fond of gathering up floating stories. He says that he made inquiry of the Elders, "What did Andrew or Peter, Thomas or Philip, or James, say?" Yet, it is doubtful whether he had seen any of them. **He had a great dislike for Paul**, beyond a few fragments. This turbid stream of tradition widened and deepened. Notwithstanding, Irenaeus says that the Christians came to salvation: "By the will of God delivered to us in writing, to be the foundation and pillar of our faith" (Thomas Armitage, *History of the Baptists*, P. 156).

From the above passage in Armitage's writing we can see that a man named Papias, had a following of people that accepted his writings above the scriptures. Notice that Papias had a *great dislike for Paul.* That is true of every false prophet. They will hate the man that God used to write most of His New Testament.

Corruption of the Distinctives

We stated the primitive church of the first century had distinctive marks that made it identifiable as a New Testament Baptist Church: 1. Independent churches 2. Regenerate church membership 3. Believers baptism 4. Baptism by immersion 5. Soul Liberty.

We shall now discuss the earliest corruptions of those distinctives.

1. The Corruption of Independent Churches

S. H. Ford, quoting Gibbon, the classic historian of Rome:

> Such was the mild and equal constitution by which the Christians were governed for more than a hundred years after the death of the apostles. Every society formed within itself a separate and independent republic, and although the most distant of those little states maintained a mutual, as well as friendly intercourse of letters and deputations, the Christian world was not yet connected by any supreme authority or legislative assembly. Toward the end of the second century the churches of Greece and Asia adopted **the useful institutions of provincial Synods**, and they are justly supposed to have borrowed the model of a representative council from the celebrated examples of their own country, the Amphictyons, the Achean league, and the assemblies of the Ionian cities (S. H. Ford, *Origin of the Baptists*, Ch. 15).

Synods, may have been *useful institutions* for the Greeks, but they proved to be disastrous for the New Testament churches, because **synods** created a non-Biblical structure that became the basis for the Roman Catholic institution.

2. The Corruption of Regenerate Church Membership

As believer's baptism became corrupt (see below), so did membership. The church became populated by unregenerate persons.

3. The Corruption of Believer's Baptism

On the corruption of baptism, Thomas Armitage wrote:

> But the most destructive error, which crept in, was that of **making baptism the channel of regeneration**. Before this, it was generally spoken of as *regeneration,* meaning, as the Scriptures teach, that the regenerated man, by baptism, put himself visibly under the new obligations which regeneration imposed. Now, they began to make it a *seal,* which bound the man to Christ with the effect of an oath; and they called it an *illumination,* confounding it with the light of the truth which it followed, and which sprang only from the Holy Spirit. As to the act of baptism itself, there was no change in this age. All ecclesiastical writers agree with Venema that: "Without controversy baptism, in the primitive Church, was administered by immersion into water, and not by sprinkling. Concerning immersion, the words and phrases that are used sufficiently testify, and that it was performed in a river, a pool or a fountain." Barnabas, A.D. 119: "Happy are they, who, trusting in the cross, go down, into the water full of sins and pollutions, but come up again bringing forth fruit, having in the Spirit hope in Jesus." Justin Martyr, A.D. 139, describes the baptized as those "who receive the bath in the water." Hermas, about A.D. 150, says, that they go down into the water devoted to death, and come up assigned to life; and that the Apostles went down into the water with them, and came up again. Guericke, Neander, Reuss, Kurtz, Weisa, Schaff, Dollinger, Pressonse, Farrar, Carr, Conybeare and Howson, Stanley, and many other historians, not Baptists, unite in like testimony. Stanley (*History of the Eastern Church*, P. 117) sums up the evidence in these words:
>
>> There can be no question that the original form of baptism, the very meaning of the word, was complete immersion in the deep baptismal waters; and that for the first four centuries, any other form was either unknown, or regarded, unless in the case of dangerous illness, as an exceptional, almost a monstrous, case. To this form the Eastern Church still rigidly adheres; and the most illustrious and venerable portion of it, that of the Byzantine Empire, absolutely repudiates and ignores any other mode of administration as essentially invalid. The Latin Church, on the other hand, doubtless in deference to the requirements of a northern climate, to the changes of manners, to the convenience of custom, has wholly altered the mode, preferring, as it would fairly say, mercy to sacrifice; and (with the two exceptions of the Cathedral of Milan, and the sect of the Baptists) a few drops of water are now the Western substitute for the three-fold plunge into the rushing rivers, or the wide baptisteries of the East (Thomas Armitage, *History of the Baptists, Vol. 1*, P. 160-2).

Chapter 2—The Churches of the Second Century

Evidence says *No* to *Infant* baptism

Sometime in the second century, a corrupt baptism was introduced. First, the mode (the way it is done) was corrupted. Then the subjects, (those who were to be baptized) were changed. But how did this happen?

One explanation may be that zealous persons wanting to save the lost took to baptizing before there was evidence of salvation. This would lead to earlier and earlier baptisms until eventually infants would be candidates for baptism. The other explanation would be, the reason for baptism would become confused. Instead of baptizing to remind witnesses of the resurrection, baptism would become a symbol of washing. Eventually, instead of it being a symbol of washing, it would become the washing itself!

And yet the Bible never says baptism is a washing or even a symbol of it. In fact the water symbolizes **dirt**, not a cleansing agent. Notice:

> *Romans 6:4 Therefore **we are buried** with him **by baptism** into death: that like as Christ was raised up from the dead by the glory of the Father, even so we also should walk in newness of life.*

So baptism was intended only for those that were already converted, and it symbolized the resurrection, not the cleansing of the soul. Tertullian, in his *De Baptismo*, declared:

> **We are not washed in order that we may cease from sinning, but because we have ceased, because we have already been washed in heart**.

That is why Neander (the Lutheran historian) declared:

> **Without the conscious participation of the person baptized, and his own individual faith, we have every reason for holding infant baptism to be no Apostolic institution, and that it was something foreign at that first stage of Christian development. At first, baptism necessarily marked a distinct era in life, when a person passed over from a different religious stand-point, to Christianity** (Augustus Neander, *Ecclesiastical History*, Vol. 1. P. 430).

4. The Corruption of the Mode of Baptism

Sometime during the second century, *clinic baptism* was first performed. *Clinic baptism* was given to the sick or invalid. It was done by *pouring* water upon the person. This is known as *effusion*. It became popular, because it was more convenient. Writers of the second century such as Justin Martyr testified that baptism was an ordinance delivered to believers by immersion, and that *clinic baptism* was a rarity.

5. The Corruption of Soul Liberty

We are aware of the fury of Rome, placed upon the head of the *baptized believers*. There was no *soul liberty*, that is, **the freedom to worship according to your own conscience**. Pagan Rome completely denied soul liberty and required her citizens to be pagan under penalty of death. The Christian of the second century would not persecute someone for conscience. However, here and there a strong bishop who fancied himself an emerging *Metropolitan* might publicly rebuke another church or preacher for heresy and bring shame upon them. Eventually, the powerful bishops would inflict far greater punishment.

The Collegiate Baptist History Workbook

Definitions

clinic baptism: baptism administered to the sick or invalid by pouring water
effusion: pouring water on the person for baptism (corrupted form)
Metropolitan: bishop who became a ruler over more than one church

STOP AND THINK

1. Write Jude 1:3 twice.

2. Give the definition for Clinic Baptism, effusion and Metropolitan.
- Was given to the sick or invalid.
- Pouring water upon the person
- Overseer of churches in a region

3. How is tradition different from scripture?
Scripture - written
tradition - vocal/oral

4. Who wrote *Oracles of the Lord* in the second century?
Papias the Farmer

5. The use of synods led to the corruption of what Baptist distinctive?
Independent churches

6. Thomas Armitage testified that the most destructive error was: ?

7. In Baptism, what does the water symbolize? channel of regeneration

8. What is Soul Liberty? freedom to worship to your own conscience

****
2.1.3

> **The story of Blandina,** Lyons, A.D. 177.
> She was a poor slave-girl, fifteen years of age, who was put to every torture, that her Christian mistress might be implicated. She was kept in a loathsome dungeon, and brought into the amphitheater every day to see the agonies of her companions as they were roasted in the iron chair, or torn to pieces by lions. Her spirit was clothed with superhuman endurance, for although racked from morning till night, so that her tormentors were obliged to relieve each other for rest, her constancy vanquished their patience, her only answer being: "I am a Christian, no wickedness is done by us." Then they took her into the circus and suspended her on a cross, within reach of the wild beasts, to frighten her fellow-confessors. The multitude howled for her life and a lion was let loose upon the poor child, but not a quiver passed over her frame. She looked into its mouth and smiled like a queen, and the monster did not touch her. Only a century before this, the first slave-girl was converted to Christ, at Philippi, and now her ennobled sister cast holy defiance at the empire, and serenely looked Europe in the face. Her calm soul told His great Power, that at last the weak were endowed with the omnipotence of the Gospel. Her intrepid spirit showed, for the first time, how Jesus could lift a worm into the empire of a human conscience; and could rebuke cruelty in the mute eloquence of love. The brightest page in the history of Rome was written that day, in the beams of that child's hope. Taken down from the cross she was removed to her dungeon, but finally brought back into the arena for execution. Her slender frame was a rare victim for the savage populace, and they gloated on her. But she flinched not, more than the angel in Gethsemane before the swords and staves of the Passover mob. She stepped as lightly as if she were going to a banquet. She was first scourged, then scorched in the hot chair, and at last cast before a furious bull, which tossed her madly. Even then a sharp blade was needful to take the lingering throb of life; and when her body was burnt to ashes it was cast into the Rhone. From that day, this harmless child-slave has been with her redeeming Master in Paradise (Thomas Armitage, *History of the Baptists*, Vol. 1, P. 186).

Corruption of the Ordinances of the New Testament Baptist Church

Every Christian should know that there are two ordinances in the church of God. One is **Baptism** and the other is **The Lord's Supper**. An ordinance is an act commanded by God to remind us of a key part of the Gospel. We have already discussed baptism as being that ordinance in the life of the church, which reminds us of the resurrection. The Lord's Supper is the ordinance that reminds us of the death and shed blood of Jesus Christ for our redemption. We have already seen how Satan began to corrupt baptism in the second century, let us examine corruption of the Lord's Supper. Thomas Armitage wrote:

Chapter 2—The Churches of the Second Century

> As to the Lord's Supper, the writers of this century use ambiguous language, invent new terms, and set forth new ideas concerning it, not found in the New Testament. They still call the elements bread and juice after consecration as well as before; and signs of Christ, "representing his body and blood," his "image," and "figure." Yet, they speak of the Supper as an "offering," a "sacrifice," of the table as an "altar," and of the administrator as a "priest." They also use many other florid words, which have led to corrupt uses in sanctioning the figments of real presence, **consubstantiation, and transubstantiation**. As yet, they had not fallen into the doctrine that the elements were Christ's literal flesh and blood; but they did hold that these were mystically in the bread and juice. Great efforts have been made to explain away their words, which opened a streamlet of error that has deluged nearly all Christendom, with the notion that the supper is something more than what the new testament makes it, a simple memorial (Thomas Armitage, *History of the Baptists*, P. 166).

Before a symbol can become corrupt, it is usually preceded by a name change.

Persecution During the Second Century

Armitage wrote:

> As the purity of Christian life was more and more felt, paganism became more violent, fierce and fanatical. The new issue which it had raised in the world was primary, relating to the rights of conscience in matters of faith. Most of the Christians were poor, and many were slaves who could not command their time, so they denied themselves of sleep, and met at each other's houses in the night. In using the pure but figurative language of their faith, they spoke of "passing from death to life," of being "one in Christ," and of "eating his flesh and drinking his blood" by faith; forms of speech which were seized upon and distorted in the most diabolical manner.
>
> They were pure, meek, loyal men; but all religions were tolerated except [that of love] a religion best fitted for torture, wild beasts and flame. Nor could it be otherwise, when Rome herself was a goddess, with the Emperor for high-priest. Sometimes the most odious of the emperors in morals persecuted the Christians the least, as they cared little for the gods or religion. Nero and Domitian were moved by caprice and cruelty largely, but as a rule, those most severe in their morals and devout in their spirit, were the sternest persecutors, because they were purely conscientious.
>
> Dean Milman ranks Marcus Aurelius as the rival of "Christians, in his contempt of the follies of life;" Gibbon calls him a model Emperor, and Guizot couples him with Louis IX of France, for sincerity and violence. The opposite of the selfish, sensual and reckless emperors, **he was ultra-conscientious**, even to blood-thirst. Called the "Philosopher," he made blood flow freely throughout his bitter reign; but when Commodus, his son, took the purple, he staunched every Christian artery which his father had opened. Yet, the Christians did not intend to overthrow the empire, nor did they complain of their political condition. The homes of Christians in the east and west were plundered; they were driven from the baths and streets they were dragged from dens and crypts: slaves were forced to charge their masters with cannibalism, incest and every kind of crime; and children were tortured to extort a criminating word against their Christian parents. Wherever a handful of them met for worship, brother after brother was taken from his home to death, and the few who escaped looked at the vacant places which were left. Then they drew a little nearer to each other, not knowing who would ascend in the fiery chariot before the little Church should meet again.
>
> They were burned with hot irons, tossed in nets by wild bulls, thrown to ravenous beasts in the arena, and their bones denied burial. Delicate and weak women passed through tortures unheard of, without complaint. An iron chair was devised, made red hot, and the martyrs fastened in it for the delight of the amphitheater. The public appetite was sharpened to all sorts

of horrors, and yet these children of God met their fate with a holy heroism (Thomas Armitage, *History of the Baptists*, P. 167-8).

Persecutions up to the year A.D. 300
There were General Persecutions under:
11. Tiberius
12. Claudius
13. Nero
14. Domician
15. Nerva
16. Trajan
17. Dadrian
18. Antoniinus Pius
19. Marcus Aurelius
20. Commodius
21. Caracalla
22. Decius Trajan
23. Valerian
24. Dioclesian in A.D. 284

Definitions

transubstantiation: The belief that the elements of the bread and juice of the Lord's Supper actually become the body and blood of Christ.

1. Write Jude 1:3 twice.

2. Give the definition for transubstantiation.
The elements of the lord's supper BECOME The body of Jesus
3. Of what was the Lord's Supper supposed to remind us? His death
4. What two ordinances began to change in the second century?
5. What happened to Blandina?
tortured and killed
6. How many general persecutions were there up until the year 284?
*************** 14

2.2.1

SECTION TWO

ordinance - commanded observance of my Church commemorating the Lord Jesus.

We have just read an overview of the transmission of the sacred text and reviewed some examples of the vicious persecution of Christians. Even with those pressures, some churches grew extensively, having many thousands in their membership. The church at Jerusalem was thought to have over 50,000 members. Some things happened to disrupt the growth of the churches: persecution and corruption. We shall examine the emerging corruptions in **church government** and then become aquatinted with some of **the people who followed the apostles** in leading the local churches.

Chapter 2—The Churches of the Second Century

What is Surely Believed?

The church government in the first and second century was an independent **Bishoprick.** It was governed by elders or *presbyters* sometimes called bishops or pastors. The local churches sent out missionaries to start churches and ordain elders. (See Titus 1:5.)

> **Acts 1:20** For it is written in the book of Psalms, Let his habitation be desolate, and let no man dwell therein: and his **bishoprick** let another take.
> **1Timothy 3:1** This is a true saying, If a man desire the office of a **bishop**, he desireth a good work.

There were four types of church governments that emerged in the second century.

1. **Bishoprick:** The bishop presided over the church and uniquely answered to God for its direction, progress and policy. The bishops of Paul's time ordained other elders (bishops) to fill the positions of leadership with the approval of the congregation. Bishops ruled only one church as pastor. All things were to be done "decently and in order" with the bishop *ruling*.
2. **Episcopalian**: An Archbishop (known as a Metropolitan in the first and second centuries) ruled a number of churches and installed pastors in local churches. This type of government became a powerful hierarchy of districts and regions. It led to the organization of the Holy Roman Catholic and Apostolic Church. Examples of this government are the Church of England, the Roman Catholic institution and Methodist societies.
3. **Presbyterian**: A board of elders (not usually the Biblical kind) within a church or *conference* or *assembly* or *synod* installs pastors, and the church answers to the conference or assembly or synod. This is *board run* government. Examples of this government are the Presbyterian Church, the Lutheran Church and some denominational Pentecostal churches. Some Baptist Churches are board run by the deacon board or *association*.
4. **Congregational**: The congregation chooses its pastor. The church is run democratically from the majority vote of the church membership. It is close to a Bishoprick, but not the same. Examples of this government: Brethren church, some Baptist churches, Congregational Churches.

The Rule of Faith by Irenaeus

There were several early summaries of the Christian faith which predated the creeds. One was the *Rule of Faith* as recorded by Irenaeus, which emphasized the trinity and the deity of Christ:

The Collegiate Baptist History Workbook

[margin note: Pre-millenial return of Jesus.]

This faith: in one God, the Father Almighty, who made the heaven and the earth and the seas and all the things that are in them; and in one Christ Jesus, the Son of God, who was made flesh for our salvation; and in the Holy Spirit, who made known through the prophets the plan of salvation, and the coming, and the birth from a virgin, and the passion, and the resurrection from the dead, and the bodily ascension into heaven of the beloved Christ Jesus, our Lord, and his future appearing from heaven in the glory of the Father to sum up all things and to raise anew all flesh of the whole human race.

HISTORIANS
When studying church history look for:
a: The opinions of a BELIEVER, he will have a love for the truth.
b: The view of a soul winner, he will have the correct perception.
c: Take into consideration the view of the historian as an enemy or lover of the truth.

Hippolytus's baptismal service:

When the person being baptized goes down into the water, he who baptizes him, putting his hand on him, shall say: "Do you believe in God, the Father Almighty?" And the person being baptized shall say: "I believe." Then holding his hand on his head, he shall baptize him once. And then he shall say: "Do you believe in Christ Jesus, the Son of God, who was born of the Virgin Mary, and was crucified under Pontius Pilate, and was dead and buried, and rose again the third day, alive from the dead, and ascended into heaven, and sat at the right hand of the Father, and will come to judge the living and the dead?"
And when he says: "I believe," he is baptized again. And again he shall say: "Do you believe in the Holy Spirit, in the holy church, and the resurrection of the body?"
The person being baptized shall say: "I believe," and then he is baptized a third time.

Both the Rule of Faith as recorded by Iranaeus and the baptismal service as recorded by Hippolytus are very close in wording to the Apostles' Creed which we shall soon investigate.

try these q's

1. Write Jude 1:3 twice.

Henry D'Anvers, first English Baptist Historian

Supposed to have been a very near relative of the Earl of Danby, D'Anvers was a soldier who distinguished himself in wars in Holland, France, and Ireland. D'Anvers was a colonel in the Parliamentary army. He was for a time governor of Stafford. He had such a reputation for integrity among the people over whom he exercised authority, that he was noted as one who would not take bribes. While governor, he adopted the sentiments of the Baptists, and notwithstanding his position, he was immersed by Henry Hagger, the minister at Stafford at that time. After the return of Charles II, his situation was very critical, he was a man of prominence by his family connections, by the respectable estate which he owned, and by his military service. A proclamation was issued offering Ł100 for his arrest; he was seized at length and sent a prisoner to the Tower of London; but his wife had great influence in the court of King Charles, and he was released on bail.

He was one of the ministers of a Baptist church near Aldgate, London. In this position he maintained a character so spotless that he greatly commended the truth which he proclaimed.

D'Anvers was the author a work which he called "Theopolis, or City of God," treating of the coming and personal reign of Christ in his millennial glory and triumphs. He also wrote a work on baptism, [*Treatise on Baptism*] which was the ablest on the subject publish by any Baptist till that time. It stirred up Richard Baxter (famous Reformed writer) most uncomfortably. David Russen abused Mr. D'Anvers and his book with a vehemence, which shows how powerfully he had been moved by it. Russen said, the book "is calculated for the meridian of Ignorance; that it is full of plagiary, prevarication, impertinencies, and manifold falsehoods; that no man of learning, but one designedly carries on a cause, will ever defile his fingers with such pitch." Mr. Russen…shows by his angry and slanderous words that Mr. D'Anvers had given him and other Pedobaptist sacramental warriors very heavy blows (William Cathcart, *Baptist Encyclopedia*, Vol. 1, P. 306).

D'Anvers' work paved the way for Thomas Crosby (1740) and Robert Robinson (1770), both English Baptist historians.

Henry D'Anvers supported the effort of the Duke of Monmouth to dethrone the Catholic tyrant James II. When the Duke was defeated at Sedgemore, D'Anvers fled England and died in Holland in 1686.

Chapter 2—The Churches of the Second Century

2. What was the true church government of the New Testament? *Bishoprick*
3. Name the four different types of church governments given in your text and give one example of church denomination that uses each type. *Bishoprick, Presbyterian, Episcopal, Congregational*
4. What did the *Rule of Faith* by Irenaeus emphasize? *Trinity and deity of Christ*
5. Name two of the three things you look for as you read the works of church historians. *The opinions of a believer / The view of a soul-winner*
6. What Reformed writer did D'Anvers stir by his *Treatise on Baptism*? *Richard Baxter*

****

2.2.2

The Apostles and Their Immediate Successors:

The Baptist historian, J. M. Carroll wrote:

> Following their Saviour in rapid succession fell many other martyred heroes: **Stephen** was stoned, **Matthew** was slain in Ethiopia, **Mark** dragged through the streets until dead, **Luke** hanged, **Peter** and **Simeon** were crucified, **Andrew** tied to a cross, **James** beheaded, **Philip** crucified and stoned, **Bartholomew** flayed alive, **Thomas** pierced with lances, **James**, the less, thrown from the temple and beaten to death, **Jude** shot to death with arrows, **Matthias** stoned to death and **Paul** beheaded.
>
> More than one hundred years had gone by before all this had happened. This hard persecution by Judaism and Paganism continued for two more centuries. And yet mightily spread the Christian religion. It went into all the Roman Empire, Europe, Asia, Africa, England, Wales, and about everywhere else, where there was any civilization. The churches greatly multiplied and the disciples increased continuously. But some of the churches continued to go into error (J. M. Carroll, *Trail of Blood*, P. 11).

Where Did the Apostles and their successors spread the Gospel?

According to Eusebius:

> That Paul preached to the Gentiles and laid the foundations of the churches from Jerusalem round about even unto Illyricum is evident both from his own words, and from the account which Luke has given in the Acts. And in how many provinces Peter preached Christ and taught the doctrine of the new covenant to those of the circumcision is clear from his own words in his epistle already mentioned as undisputed, in which he writes to the Hebrews of the dispersion in Pontus, Galatia, Cappadocia, Asia, and Bithynia. But the number and the names of those among them that became true and zealous followers of the apostles, and were judged worthy to tend the churches founded by them, it is not easy to tell, except those mentioned in the writings of Paul. For he had innumerable fellow-laborers, or "fellow-soldiers," as he called them, and most of them were honored by him with an imperishable memorial, for he gave enduring testimony concerning them in his own epistles. Luke also in the Acts speaks of his friends, and mentions them by name. **Timothy**, so it is recorded, was the first to receive the episcopate of the parish in **Ephesus**, Titus of the churches in Crete. But Luke, who was of Antiochan parentage and a physician by profession, and who was especially intimate with Paul and well acquainted with the rest of the apostles, has left us, in two inspired books, proofs of that spiritual healing art which he learned from them. One of these books is the Gospel, which he testifies that he wrote as those who were from the beginning eye witnesses and ministers of the word delivered unto him, all of whom, as he says, he followed accurately from the first. The other book is the Acts of the Apostles which he composed not from the accounts of others, but from what he had seen himself. And they say that Paul meant to refer to Luke's Gospel wherever, as if speaking of some gospel of his own, he used the words, "according to

my Gospel." Paul testifies that **Crescens** was sent to Gaul; but **Linus**, whom he mentions in the Second Epistle to Timothy as his companion at Rome, was Peter's successor in the episcopate of the church there, as has already been shown. Clement also, who was appointed third bishop of the church at Rome, was, as Paul testifies, his co-laborer and fellow-soldier. Besides these, that Areopagite, named Dionysius, who was the first to believe after Paul's address to the Athenians in the Areopagus is mentioned by another **Dionysius**, an ancient writer and pastor of the parish in Corinth, as the first bishop of the church at Athens (Eusebius of Caesarea, *Church History*, Book IV, P. 73-4).

The churches of the Mediterranean and Asia Minor can be found on examination of the Apostle Paul's journeys through the book of Acts. Paul wrote letters to these churches: Rome, Corinth, Galatia, Ephesus, Philippi, Colossi, and Thessalonica. He left Titus in Crete. We can also see the churches listed in Revelation 2:1-3:22 as recorded by John the beloved Apostle: Ephesus, Smyrna, Pergamos, Thyatira, Sardis, Philadelphia, and Laodicea.

According to the ancient account of Eusebius: "Thomas, according to tradition, received Parthia as his allotted region; Andrew received Seythia, and John, Asia; where, after continuing for some time, he died at Ephesus. **Peter** appears to have **preached in Pontus, Galatia, Bithynia, Cappadocia, and Asia** to the Jews that were scattered abroad (Eusebius of Caesarea, *Church History*, Book IV, P. 70). According to Neander, **Peter preached** to the **Parthians**, **Bartholomew** preached in Arabia, **Thomas to India, and Mark to Alexandria, Africa**, where the Gospel spread to Cyrene and Carthage. The Gospel was preached in **Rome by Paul** and from there the word of God flourished in Gaul (France), Italy, Germany and then by the hand of Paul, in Spain. Neander assumes the Gospel was taken to Britain by the missionary efforts of the churches of Asia Minor noted above.

Here are the words of Tertullian, writing in the third century, showing the tremendous success of the ancient church in obeying Matthew 28:19-20:

> In whom other than Christ, who has already come, do all the nations believe? For in him have believed the most diverse people; **Parthian, Medes, Elamites**; those who inhabit **Mesopotamia, Armenia, Phrygia, Cappadocia**; the dwellers of **Pontus, Asia** and **Pamphylia**; those occupying Egypt, and inhabiting the region of Africa beyond **Cyrene, Romans and natives**, even **Jews** dwelling in Jerusalem, and other nations; nay, the different tribes of the **Getulians**, and many territories of the **Moors**, all parts of **Spain**, the different peoples of **Gaul**, and part of **Britain** not reached by the Romans but subjugated by Christ. In all these the name of Christ who has already come, reigns.

Some Second Century Leaders:
- **Clement**: Clement of Rome is believed to have been the fourth bishop of Rome and served during the last decade of the first century. Around 96, he sent a letter from the Church of Rome to the Church of Corinth. This letter, known as Clement's *First Epistle to the Corinthians*, was a warning against the practices of prostitution connected with the Temple of Aphrodite. In the letter, Clement expresses his dissatisfaction with events taking place in the Corinthian Church and asks the people to repent. The letter is important because it seems to indicate that the author was trying to act as general head of the Christian Church centered in Rome. Clement was put to death under Emperor Domitian.

Chapter 2—The Churches of the Second Century

- **Ignatius**: Tradition says Ignatius was one of the little children who came to Jesus in the gospel account. He was a disciple of the apostles: his name is linked especially with those of John, Paul, and Peter. (He is listed as the second successor to Peter in Antioch.) Around 107, during Trajan's persecution, he was taken to Rome and sent to his death in the arena. Numerous letters have been attributed to Ignatius, and at least seven are authentic. These have sufficed to establish *the Godbearer*, as Ignatius is sometimes called, in the front rank of early Christian theologians.

> **People to Remember**
>
> **Tertullian** was a very brilliant scholar of the school at Alexandria. He was so disenchanted at the teachings that were coming out of the school that he joined with the Montanists and later formed his own congregation which continued for two hundred years.
>
> *Roberts History of the Baptists* P. 183 says Agrippinus, its first pastor with Tertullian, admitted members by examination and baptism, but all such as joined the Montanists from other communities were re-baptized.
>
> *Compton's Reference* says of Tertullian, A.D. 160-230. Roman theologian. A convert and a strong defender of Christianity, he later became a Montanist, and still later established his own sect, the Tertullians.

- **Justin Martyr**: Converted Greek philosopher began preaching Christ. He wrote an *apology*, (which is a defense of the faith) which was famous in his time. He was martyred in 166 at Rome.

- **Polycarp**: Bishop of Smyrna, who was put to death. He was a very old man; for it was almost ninety years since he had been converted from heathenism. He had known John, and is supposed to have been made bishop of Smyrna by that Apostle himself, and he had been a friend of Ignatius.

- **Marcion**: A wealthy Christian ship owner, came to Rome in about 139 and was **one of the first notable heretics**. He argued that there were moral contradictions between the Jewish scriptures and Christian belief. The religion based in retributive law of the Old Testament could have no similarity to the religion of love of the New Testament. **Marcion** identified these differences in a work called *Antitheses* which juxtaposed contradictory statements made about the God of the Hebrew scriptures and the Christian God. In 144 he was excommunicated from the Church in Rome and established a separate church. During the second century the Marcionites were seen as a serious rival to the mainstream church. However, the movement fell into rapid decline during the third and fourth centuries, and by the fifth century had largely disappeared in the west. In the east, particularly Syria, the church continued to flourish, surviving until the tenth century. **Marcion** and his followers *believed that there were two Gods: the God of wrath and vengefulness of the Hebrew scriptures and the God of love and mercy revealed through Jesus Christ.* Because Jesus could have nothing in common with the evil material world, his human body was apparent, not real. Marcion's followers were required to avoid, as far as possible, contamination with the material world. Baptist people have been accused of *Marcionism* because of our stand on separation and the new covenant.

- **Montanus** was a convert to Christianity who lived in Phrygia in Asia Minor during the 2nd half of the second century. He and two followers, Priscilla and Maximilla, were known for preaching the imminent premillennial return of Christ. When Tertullian was looking for a church, he united with a Montanist church. Though their teachings were condemned by the emerging catholic institution, they were puritans in their claim to return to the simplicity of the first Christians. Their critics claimed that the leaders of the movement were so-called "mouthpieces of the Holy Spirit proclaiming the end of the world.

The Montanists believed in the priesthood of all believers, strict discipline in the church, and in scriptural baptism and the imminent premillennial return of Christ.

1. Write Jude 1:3 twice.

2. Name four disciples who were martyred and how they died.

3. Write one sentence about: Tertullian, Clement and Marcion.

4. In the *Where is the Word of God* informational box at the left, what two things did Tertullian say you could actually see during his time by traveling to the original primitive churches?

5. What did Montanus believe about the Second Coming of Christ?
   Priesthood of believers

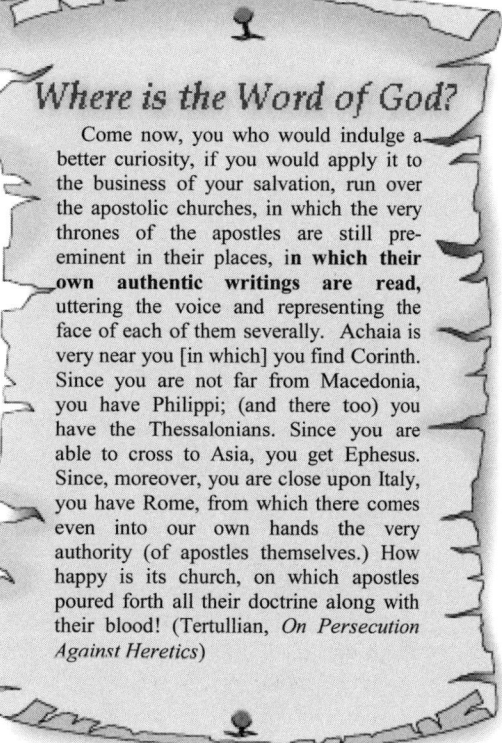

Where is the Word of God?

Come now, you who would indulge a better curiosity, if you would apply it to the business of your salvation, run over the apostolic churches, in which the very thrones of the apostles are still pre-eminent in their places, **in which their own authentic writings are read**, uttering the voice and representing the face of each of them severally. Achaia is very near you [in which] you find Corinth. Since you are not far from Macedonia, you have Philippi; (and there too) you have the Thessalonians. Since you are able to cross to Asia, you get Ephesus. Since, moreover, you are close upon Italy, you have Rome, from which there comes even into our own hands the very authority (of apostles themselves.) How happy is its church, on which apostles poured forth all their doctrine along with their blood! (Tertullian, *On Persecution Against Heretics*)

Chapter Three
The Churches of the Third Century
Section One: The Novatianists, The Apostle's Creed
Section Two: The Birth of the Sacraments

SECTION ONE
The Novatianists. The Apostle's Creed.

Third Century Time Line
202. Persecution by Severus begins
206. Martyrdom of Perpetua and her companions
248. Cyprian, bishop of Carthage
249. Persecution by Decius
251. Paul, the first hermit
----. Council at Carthage, Novatian excommunicated
253. Plague at Carthage
254. Death of Origen
----. Disagreement between Cyprian and Stephen of Rome
257. Persecution by Valerian
258. Martyrdom of Cyprian
260. Conversion of the Goths begins
261. Valerian prisoner; Gallienus tolerates Christians
270. Manes publishes his heresy
298. Diocletian requires idolatry from soldiers

Scripture to Memorize
Psalm 12:6-7 The words of the LORD are pure words: as silver tried in a furnace of earth, purified seven times. Thou shalt keep them, O LORD, thou shalt preserve them from this generation for ever.

The Identity of the New Testament Text

By the end of the second century, God's word was distinctively a work passing from the Apostles and through the soul winning, gospel preaching church at Antioch. (See Acts 11:26.) In the year 199 there existed:
1. The Original New Testament scriptures as testified by Tertullian.
2. The Syrian "Peshito" A.D. 150
3. The Old Latin *Itala Biblia* A.D. 150.

According to historians, the *Peshito* enjoyed great circulation among the Gospel preaching churches of Syria including Antioch, the greatest of all second century churches. It also held sway toward the east where a group of believers would emerge known as the **Paulicians**. We will learn more about them shortly. The *Itala Biblia* had great circulation and use in northern Italy and the highlands of central Europe, and among the fervent preachers of Gaul (France). The success and power of the word of God led to the third of **Satan's Devices** in our study of the church history of the *baptized believers*.

Chapter 3—The Churches of the Third Century

Satan's Devices

Satan's device in the first century was to KILL THE CHRISTIANS. His device in the second century was to DESTROY THE SCRIPTURES. The Bible bears testimony, and history reveals that Satan could accomplish neither. The more the Christians were persecuted the more they increased and the more the Scriptures were burned, the more they were copied. This brings us to the satanic device for the third century: CHANGE THE SCRIPTURES. This has become the adversary's most effective device.

The School at Alexandria and the Influence of Origen

Despite the warning of the Apostle Paul, "Beware lest any man spoil you through **philosophy** and vain deceit, after the tradition of men, after the rudiments of the world, and not after Christ."(See Col. 2:8.) A group of worldly Christian *scholars* sought out the ideas of the Greeks at the most prestigious college in the world at the time, the college at Alexandria, Egypt.

Alexandria was the most cosmopolitan city in the world at the turn of the second century. It had a diverse population, infamous for its decadence, and boasted a huge port on the Mediterranian. The port had one of the *ancient wonders of the world*, the 500 foot lighthouse in the harbor. The school at Alexandria was a type of *liberal arts* university for the ancient world. It had many branches, including a religious one.

The religious school was founded sometime in the early years of the ministry of Christ by none other than Philo himself, an apostate Jewish/Greek thinker for whom the word *philo-sophy* would spring. Philosophy was a word of which the Holy Spirit warned us to *beware*.

Here the New Standard Encyclopedia of 1990 about Alexandria:

> As the Christian Era began, the Alexandrian Jew, Philo, combining Jewish religious ideas with Greek philoshophy, emphasized the mystical quality of man's relationship to God. Philo influenced two late second century Greek fathers of the church, Clement of Alexandria, and his pupil, Origen. These two in turn headed Alexandria's catechetical (Christian) school, where both Christian and pagan (Greek) writings were studied, and where the philosophy later known as Neoplatonism evolved. Much of the mysticism of the Alexandrian school of theology was absorbed into Christian thinking.

This so-called "school of theology," which married the world's rudiments with God's word, produced a "Christian" but definitely *worldly* school of thought. It transpired in this fashion:

Clement of Alexandria was born about A.D.150 in Athens, Greece. His parents were party-line Roman pagans. He was supposedly led to Christ by Pantaenus, the pastor of the church at Alexandria. When Pantaenus died, Clement took the church and continued the college at Alexandria. He sought to merge the *philosophies* of Plato and Philo with Christ. His most dedicated student was Adamantius Origen.

After a period of persecution under Serverus, Clement abandoned the college and left it in the hands of **Origen** in 202. Origen went to work immediately collating texts of the Scriptures, adding and subtracting what he thought acceptable.

The Collegiate Baptist History Workbook

Origen was strange, yet his influence was great. He denied the inspiration of the book of Revelation, yet performed self mutilation in obedience to Mark 9:43. He had strange ideas about angels and denied the existence of Hell. He believed in the Roman doctrine of purgatory, and yet denied the existence of an eternal soul. He supposedly put together a six columned study of different versions of the Bible called the "Hexapla." His most in-fluencial deed was to preserve a group of Bible manuscripts which collectively have become known as the **"Alexandrian Text."**

Origen was actually excommunicated from the church at Alexandria. Afterwards, he brought his college and vast library to Caesarea in the mid third century. Upon his death, he left both the college and the library to his brightest pupil, **Pamphilus** (240-309). Pamphilus in turn gave all of the books,

---

THE NOVATIANISTS PART I BY WILLIAM CATHCART

Novatian, before he professed conversion, was a philosopher of remarkable ability, culture, eloquence, and powers of persuasion; he was a natural leader of men. When attacked by a dangerous disease, from which death was apprehended, in accordance with the opinion then commonly held by Christians, it was judged that he should be baptized to make heaven certain, and, as his weakness rendered immersion impossible without risking his immediate death, he was subjected, on his couch, to a profuse application of water. We are not informed that Novatian desired this ceremony himself, without any persuasions from his alarmed friends. The writer was once sent for to see a dying lady, and, after praying with her, was earnestly pressed by a follower of Irish Romanism, the perverted faith of St. Patrick the Baptist, to *regenerate* her; he declined to exercise the powers of the Spirit of God and the functions of a Pedobaptist minister; had he yielded, the lady was in a condition in which she could not be held responsible for the act. And it is not improbable that this was the situation of Novatian. He was spared by the providence of God for a mighty work in the churches, and when restored to health he became very active in advancing the interests of Christianity in Rome.

At that period, the church, in the capital of the world, as Eusebius records, had 46 presbyters, 14 deacons and subdeacons, 50 minor ecclesiastical officials, and widows and sick and indigent persons, numbering in all 1500, whose support had to be provided for. And partly to assist in bearing this burden, but chiefly through a lack of faith and of complete consecration to God, the door of the church was kept very wide for the admission of unconverted professors, and when these persons betrayed the Saviour by sacrificing to idols in times of persecution, their conduct was excused by their lax brethren; and the excommunication, necessarily pronounced upon them immediately after their apostasy, was speedily removed.

Cornelius, a Roman presbyter, with an eager eye to the support to be gathered from restored apostates, strongly advocated their forgiveness by the church. Novatian very strenuously resisted it; and when a successor to Bishop Fabianus was to be elected, Cornelius was properly made a predecessor of a long line of coming popes, who loved gold more than anything in the Christian religion.

After Cornelius became bishop, Novatian was elevated to the same office by three Italian bishops, and at once founded the purer community, for whose advancement he labored with great success until martyrdom removed him from the presence of wicked church members in full ecclesiastical standing.

Among the charges brought by Cornelius against Novatian, a list of which can be found in Eusebius, was an accusation of cowardice for refusing to per-form the duties of his ministerial office in a time of persecution. Novatian set up a new community in defiance of Cornelius and of nearly all the Christian bishops on earth; and in this he showed unusual courage. Opposition to the treachery, charged upon himself by Cornelius, was the chief instrument which he used to establish his pure church, and it is not in human nature to believe that any man could found a new community in Rome itself by denunciations of a cowardly crime of which he himself had given a conspicuous example. Besides, he left the world as a martyr (William Cathcart, *Baptist Encyclopedia*, Vol. 2, P. 861-3).

35

Chapter 3—The Churches of the Third Century

writings and student interest over to the famous **Eusebius** (260-340), the historian and bishop of Caesarea.

THE NOVATIANISTS, PART II BY WILLIAM CATHCART

It was customary in the time of Ambrose, when the minister distributed the Lord's Supper to the faithful, to say, "The body of Christ," and the recipient answered, "Amen." Cornelius, in the same calumnious letter in Eusebius, states that Novatian, when he gave a portion of the Eucharist to a communicant, instead of permitting him to say "Amen," according to the usage no doubt then in existence, seized his hand in both of his hands, before he partook of the symbolic bread, and made him "swear by the body and blood of our Saviour, Jesus Christ, that he would never desert him, nor turn to Cornelius." This story carries its own refutation; the idea that the founder of the purest Christian community then in existence should resort to such an infamous procedure is simply incredible. Cornelius, in the same connection, makes slanderous statements about the extraordinary ambition of Novatian, which have come down to us through the "Ecclesiastical History" of Eusebius; and his vanity is frequently given as the motive that led to his assumption of the bishop's office, and to the reformation inaugurated by Novatian."

The Novatians called themselves Kathari, or Puritans. The corner stone of the denomination was purity of church membership. Novatian charged Cornelius and his followers with dishonoring the church of God, and destroying its divine character by admitting apostates into its membership. He maintained that those who had sacrificed to the idols to save their lives should never be permitted to come to the Lord's table again. This theory became popular with the saintly heroes and heroines, who suffered terribly at the hands of Christ's persecuting enemies, but whose lives were spared. And all true Christians felt a strong leaning towards the holy religion advocated and exhibited by Novatian and his followers.

The general doctrines of the Novatians were in perfect harmony with those received by the church universal; they only differed from it on questions of discipline, and chiefly on the great subject of consecration to God.

Novatian himself was a man of fervent piety; and his life after his conversion was above reproach, unless when accusations came from a calumniator whose charges were incapable of proof. He was the author of works on "The Passover," "Circumcision," "The Sabbath," "High-Priests," "The Trinity," and on other subjects. He had many distinguished men among his disciples. His community spread very widely, and enjoyed special prosperity in Phrygia; but declined rapidly in the fifth century. The Novatians, as a people, were an honor to Christianity, and their teachings and example exercised a powerful restraint upon the growing corruptions of the old church.

The Novatians commenced their denominational life when the baptism of an unconscious babe was unknown outside of Africa; and there it had a limited, if not a doubtful, existence. These considerations, together with the holiness of life demanded by Novatian churches, have led many persons to regard them as Baptists. Of the truth of this opinion in the early history of this people there can be no doubt; and that the majority of their churches baptized only instructed persons (William Cathcart, *Baptist Encyclopedia*, Vol. 2, P. 862).

To understand the influence of the *Clement-Origen-Pamphilus-Eusibius* connection, let us remember that Emperor Constantine asked for copies to be made of the Bible. He requested them from his friend **Eusebius**. **Eusebius** supplied the Alexandrian Text for **Jerome** to copy for the Emperor.

The Novatianists

After the bitter persecutions of the second century, the churches had some rest. The Christians enjoyed peace from their enemies for about 40 years. However in 249, the emperor Decius required all Roman citizens to conform to pagan worship. Because of the soft and lax attitude of believers, large numbers denied the Lord during this persecution. They were called *traditores*. After the Decius persecution, some of the *traditores* wanted back into the churches. You may imagine after watching loved ones and pastors brutally murdered at the hand of pagan Rome, some of the faithful church members would be hesitant to welcome the *traditores* into regular fellowship with the persecuted church.

The Collegiate Baptist History Workbook

What transpired was pivitol. The *traditores* had been given letters of mercy from those that suffered during the persecution, beseeching the churches to allow them to re-enter. (This was the beginning of prayers to the saints!)

From 200-250, the purity of the local church had begun to erode. The Bishoprick degenerated into central governments headed by new, more powerful bishops. These bishops did not rule in one local church, they ruled several, and appointed priests to care for the local assemblies. This was not a universal structure, but it was popular in the largest of the Asian and European cities. As some of the *traditores* attempted to re-enter the local churches, a great controversy occurred at the most powerful of all metropolitan churches, the church at Rome.

The church at Rome had just lost its pastor, and in the process of securing a new bishop a young preacher named Novatian voiced his concerns about the admission of *traditores* back into fellowship. By now, a Roman synod (not found in the Bible) had evolved and began their self-appointed process of locating a new pastor for the church. The synod decided upon Cornelius to be the next Bishop of Rome. Novatian opposed the appointment. Novatian was so convinced that his cause was correct that he began a separate church apart from the authority of the Roman Synod. G. H. Orchard, English Baptist historian explains:

> The flagrancy of some apostates occasioned an opposition to their re-admission. In the time of peace, many had entered the church without calculating on trials, and when persecution arose such persons revolted easily to idolatry, and on trials subsiding, gained but too easy admittance again to communion. One **NOVATIAN**, a presbyter in the church of Rome, strongly opposed the re-admission of apostates, but he was not successful. The choice of a pastor in the same church fell upon Cornelius, whose election Novatian opposed, from his readiness to re-admit apostates. Novatian consequently separated himself from the church, and from Cornelius's jurisdiction. Dupin's Hist., c. 3, p. 125, &. (G. H. Orchard, *A Concise History Of Foreign Baptists: taken from the New Testament, etc.,* P. 53)

Evil and good came out of this battle. The evil included the arrogance of the new Roman Synod (also called a *See*), which ruled that the new breakaway church did not have a right to exist. As a by-product of the public repentance of the traditores, **confession** began to be practiced by preacher/priests, who heard penitent speeches and judged whether they were adequate.

The good thing that came from the break was the display of courage on the part of those who separated from tyranny to follow God's leading into independency.

A council of 60 bishops called by Cornelius, excommunicated Novatian in 251. However, a large number of bishops, disgusted at the growing control of Rome and her *See*, withdrew to form their own independent congregations. Novatian became the first bishop or pastor at the new Novatianist church at Rome. These people collectively became known as the *Novatianists*, and their independent churches existed well into the fifth century.

1. Write Psalm 12:6-7 twice.

37

Chapter 3—The Churches of the Third Century

2. Which Bible translation was used widely in Syria in the first two centuries? _Peshito_
3. Which Bible translation was used widely in Northern Italy and in Gaul in the first two centuries? _Italic_
4. What was Satan's third device used on Christianity? _Change the scriptures_
5. Who were the *traditores*? _believers who did not stay true to Christ during persecution_
6. What man protested receiving the *traditores* back into the church at Rome? _Novatian_
7. Novatian became the new bishop of what church?

*************** _The Novationist church at Rome_

3.1.2

What is Surely Believed?

Remember the "Rule of Irenaeus" from chapter two? It was an early creed in the primitive church. In the third century, the churches often recited the *Apostles' Creed*.

The Apostle's creed as commonly written and recited before A.D. 325:

> I believe in God, the Father Almighty,
> the Creator of heaven and earth,
> and in Jesus Christ,
> His only Son, our Lord:
> Who was conceived of the Holy Spirit,
> born of the Virgin Mary,
> suffered under Pontius Pilate,
> was crucified, died, and was buried.
> He descended into hell.
> The third day He arose again from the dead.
> He ascended into heaven
> and sits at the right hand of God the Father Almighty,
> whence He shall come to judge the living and the dead.
>   I believe in the Holy Spirit,
> the holy church,
> the forgiveness of sins,
> the resurrection of the body,
> and life everlasting.
> Amen.

Definitions:

Archbishop: the eventual position of authority assumed by the metropolitans
bishop: originally meant the pastor of one local church
elder: a God called man set apart (ordained) publicly for the work of the ministry
deacon: a servant in the church publicly commended for service (not ordained)

pastors and teachers: one of the duties of the bishop in the church, may be assigned by him to others in assistance to the benefit of the church.

sacramentum: the public oath of allegiance made by Roman soldiers, often accompanied by a token or badge.

sacerdotal: having to do with an outward action used to convey grace or salvation, dependent upon the administrator's position.

sacrament: a religious act that is thought to confer, bestow or be a means to grace

ordinance: a symbolic act in a Bible believing church that reminds us of God's grace. In a Baptist church the ordinances are Baptism and the Lord's Supper.

The Birth of the Sacraments

One of the most stunning blows of the third century came from the writings of one of the best men of the age. Tertullian wrote that baptism was *similar* to the act of a Roman soldier receiving his **badge** of service from the Roman government. The **badge** or medallion was an emblem of service to his country and was known in the Latin language as a ***sacramentum.*** (In English the word is *sacrament*.) When a soldier enlisted for military service, he received his badge (*sacramentum*) which identified him with the Roman military.

Even though the sacramentum was meant to be a simple illustration, the Latin word sacramentum became nearly synonymous with baptism. Baptism became a sacramentum, and a sacramentum became a way to be spiritual or do spiritual things. Sacramentum eventually became a way to achieve grace, even a way to achieve salvation. This way of salvation is known as ***sacerdotal***.

In *Roman Catholicism, Yesterday and Today*, Loyola University Press, Chicago, Illinois, P. 133, author Robert A. Burnes makes this amazing statement in defense of sacerdotal salvation:

> In the third century, the Christian writer Tertullian referred to baptism as a **sacrament** in order to emphasize the commitment one made to Jesus when one was baptized. By means of the **sacraments**, a Christian is helped to "put on a new man," that is, take up a new life-style dedicated to Christ.

MARCELLUS REJECTION OF THE ROMAN BADGE

Marcellus had been a centurion in the Roman army, but in 298 A.D. took the initiative and insisted on resigning from his office. On the occasion of the Emperor's birthday, he cast off his military belt before the standards, and called out: "I serve Jesus Christ, the eternal king." Then he threw down his vine staff and arms, and added: "I cease from this military service of our Emperors, and I scorn to adore your gods of stone and wood, which are deaf and dumb idols. If such is the position of those who render military service, that they should be compelled to sacrifice to gods and emperors, I renounce the standards, and this badge, and I refuse to serve as a soldier."

There is no evidence in ANY of Tertullian's writings that he was **sacerdotal.** Yet Burnes, and all Roman Catholic writers before him, insist Tertullian supported baptism as a SACRAMENT, which he did not. Tertullian very powerfully illustrated that baptism by immersion, in the audience of others, was a grand statement of allegiance to Christ. The public display of obedience reminded Tertullian of the Roman soldier's public oath and emblem of service.

Chapter 3—The Churches of the Third Century

The New Testament church never had *sacraments*. What Jesus instituted were **ordinances**, not sacraments. The two ordinances of the local New Testament church are **Baptism** and the **Lord's Supper**. These ordinances do not give anyone grace, they are simply reminders of grace already given.

Today, in Catholic, Greek Orthodox, Presbyterian, Lutheran, Anglican, and Methodist churches, Baptism and the Lord's Supper are mistakenly called **sacraments**. Baptist churches have never referred to the **ordinances** as **sacraments**.

Definitions

traditores: believers who did not stay true to Christ during the persecutions
baptismal regeneration: the belief that the act of baptism regenerates the soul
infant baptism: practice of baptizing or pouring water on babies instead of those who professed faith in Christ. Made popular by Cyprian in the third century.
hierarchy: a group of persons who exist in a chain of command
metropolitan: a bishop in the second and third century who exercised power over several pastors and churches at the same time.

STOP AND THINK

1. Write Psalm 12:6-7 twice.

2. Find four doctrines stated in the Apostle's creed.
   [handwritten]: The resourrection, the trinity, belief in heaven and hell, the virgin birth
3. Write the definition for: deacon, sacramentum, sacerdotal, ordinance.
   [handwritten]: servant of the church
4. What is a *sacramentum*, literally?
   [handwritten]: a badge/medallion
5. What is the difference between an ordinance and a sacrament?
   [handwritten]: Ordinance - symbolic act reminding us of God's bread. Sacrament - Gives/Conveys Grace

****

3.2.1
Changing the Churches of the Third Century

To sum up the first three centuries of church history, Carroll wrote:

> During the first three centuries, congregations all over the East subsisted in separate independent bodies, unsupported by government and consequently without any secular power over one another. All this time they were baptized churches, and though all the fathers of the first four ages, down to Jerome (A.D. 370,) were of Greece, Syria, and Africa, and though they give great numbers of histories of the baptism of adults, yet there is not one of the baptism of a child till the year 370 (J. M. Carroll *The Trail of Blood*, P. 13).

Carroll continues summing up the findings of the Lutheran historian Mosheim:

> Let it be remembered that changes like these here mentioned were not made in a day, nor even within a year. **They came about slowly and never within all the churches. Some of the churches vigorously repudiated them. So much so that in A.D. 251, the loyal**

churches declared non-fellowship for those churches which accepted and practiced these errors. And thus came about the first real official separation among the churches.

Thus it will be noted that during the first three centuries three important and vital changes from the teachings of Christ and His Apostles had their beginnings. And one significant event took place, Note this summary and recapitulation:

(1) The change from the New Testament idea of bishop and church government. This change grew rapidly, more pronounced, and complete and hurtful.

(2) The change from the New Testament teachings as to regeneration to baptismal regeneration.

(3) The change from believers' baptism to infant baptism. (This last, however, did not become general nor even very frequent for more than another century.)

Baptismal regeneration and infant baptism. These two errors have, according to the testimony of well-established history, caused the shedding of more Christian blood, as the centuries have gone by, than all other errors combined, or than possibly have all wars, not connected with persecution, if you will leave out the recent *World War*. Over 50,000,000 Christians died martyr deaths, mainly because of their rejection of these two errors during the period of the *dark ages* alone, about twelve or thirteen centuries:

Three significant facts, for a large majority of the many churches, are clearly shown by history during these first three centuries.

(1) The separateness and independence of the churches.

(2) The subordinate character of bishops or pastors.

(3) The baptism of believers only (J. M. Carroll, *The Trail of Blood*, P. 13-14).

How significant that Mr. Carroll* should mention the deaths of 50 million during the dark ages across Europe. These are not flippant figures. The figures are based on the writings of the enemies of God's people.

What this means is that more people were murdered for the cause of Christ concerning simple faith and the rejection of the sacraments than any other calamity known to man. May God forgive us of our complacency in forgetting these pitiful martyrs.

Third Century Leaders

- **Cyprian**: Bishop at Carthage, an opponent of Novatian. He attended the Council of Carthage, in Africa, A. D. 251. In writing to Fidus, Cyprian took the ground that infants should be baptized as soon as they are born. William Cathcart, the Baptist historian, believes that this *Epistle of Cyprian* may be a fraud. Cyprian is the father of the invisible church theory, which gave rise to Roman Catholicism.

- **Felicissimus**: Ordained elder of Novatian's independent church. He argued for the existence of the independent church in Rome at the Council of Carthage in 251. He lost the argument with Cyprian and the rest of the Bishops from North Africa, but his independent church lived.

---

* We find the criticism of Carroll in our day unfounded, for our research has found that Carroll used the most respected pedobaptist historians as sources in his *Trail of Blood* lectures.

Chapter 3—The Churches of the Third Century

- **Clement of Alexandria**: Date of birth unknown; died about the year 215. St. Clement was an early Greek theologian and head of the catechetical school of Alexandria. He passed his work of Bible revision on to Origen.

- **Origen**: Born in 185, Origen was barely 17 when a bloody persecution of the Church of Alexandria began. He assumed of his own accord, the direction of the catechetical school on the withdrawal of Clement, and in the following year was confirmed in his office by the patriarch Demetrius. Origen's school, which was frequented by pagans, soon became a nursery of neophytes, confessors, and self-afflicted martyrs. After being banished from Alexandria, Origen moved his school to Caesarea in Palestine (232), and founded a new school there. Origen was the original Bible corrector, allegorizing the portions of the Bible he could not believe, and omitting portions he could not explain. (He considered the entire book of Revelation non-inspired.) He supposedly put together the HEXAPLA, a side by side comparison of six versions of the Bible. He died in 254.

- **Pamphilus**: Martyred in 309 and went to Alexandria where his teacher was Pierius, then the head of the famous Catechetical School. He eventually settled in Cæsarea where he was ordained a priest, collected his famous library, and established a school for theological study. He became a student and apologist for Origen, and took over what was left of Origin's writings and library. Pamphilus' scripture editions were given to Jerome in anticipation of the *New Latin Vulgate*, (printed about the year 400) the corrupted revision of the old *Italia Biblia*.

- **Dionysius**: Bishop of Corinth about 170. The writer of many encouraging letters to other churches.

- **Methodius**: Bishop of Olympus in Lycia and martyr (311) he wrote several works against Origen, among which was a treatise "On the Resurrection."

- **Arius**: born 250, Libya **died** 336, Constantinople (now Istanbul, Turkey). He was a Christian priest of Alexandria, Egypt, whose teachings gave rise to a theological doctrine known as *Arianism* or, denying the Deity of Christ. By declaring that Christ was finite and created, *Arianism* was denounced by the early church as a major heresy. His views led to the calling of the council of Nicea in 325.

> **Where is the Word of God?**
>
> By the end of the third century, God's word was distinctively a work from the Apostles and through the Gospel preaching church at Antioch. (See Acts 11:26.)
>
> In the year 199 there existed:
> 1. The Original New Testament scriptures as testified by Tertullian
> 2. The Syrian *Peshito* A.D. 150
> 3. The Old Latin *Itala Biblia*. around A.D. 150.

The Collegiate Baptist History Workbook

1. Write Psalm 12:6-7 twice.

2. According to J. M. Carroll, how many people lost their lives because of the baptismal controversy through the centuries? *50 million*

3. Cyprian takes the ground that infants should be baptized as? *they are born*

4. Who was **Felicissimus?** *an ordained member of Novatian's independent church*

5. Name three things wrong with Origen's beliefs.
   1. *Changed the scriptures*
   2. *rejected the book of revelations*
   3. *he denied the resurrection*

6. Origen took over the school at Alexandria from whom? *Clement*

7. After Origin was banished from Alexandria, where did he go and who assumed leadership of his new school after he died? *Caesarea, Palestine*

8. By the year 199, where was the word of God and its first translations?

****

3.2.2

The Gospel Arrives in Britain—Second and Third Century

We have concerned ourselves mainly to the spread of the Gospel from Jerusalem to the east, south and north. We will now briefly look at the progress of New Testament Christianity to the extreme west, to the Islands of Britain. Before *Briton*, as it was called, was conquered by the Angles (English) in the fifth century, she enjoyed a blessed revival and saw scores of her people saved and baptized by immersion. Most historians believe that the Gospel was originally preached in Briton by missionaries from Antioch and by friends of Pudence and Claudia, both of

---

> **PERPETUA AND FELICITAS, OF TURURBI IN MAURITANIA, AND OTHERS, VIOLENTLY PUT TO DEATH, FOR THE FAITH OF THE SON OF GOD, ABOUT THE YEAR 201. As related by Tertullian**
>
> Perpetua and Felicitas were two very pious and honorable Christian women, at Tururbi, a city in Mauritania, a providence of Africa. Both were very untimely apprehended, to suffer for the name of Christ, as Felicitas was very far advanced in pregnancy, and Perpetua had recently given birth to a child, which she was nursing. But this did not make them fainthearted, nor so surprised them that they forsook Christ, nor did it prevent them from going on in the way of godliness; but they remained equally faithful disciples of Christ, and became steadfast martyrs.
>
> According to the Roman laws, they waited with the pregnant woman, until she was delivered, before they sentenced her and put her to death. When the pains of labor seized her in prison, and she cried aloud for fear and anguish, the jailer said to her: "Thou are so much afraid and distressed now, and criest aloud for pain; how then wilt thou behave, when, tomorrow, or the day after, thou will be led to death?" Felicitas replied thus:
>
> "Now I suffer as a poor woman the punishment which God on account of sin has laid upon the female sex; but tomorrow I shall suffer as a Christian woman for the faith and the confession of Jesus Christ." By these words she sufficiently indicated that she had firmly immovably founded her faith upon Christ, who never forsakes His own, even though they be in the midst of the fire, and are consumed, God also specially strengthened her, that she might be able to endure her sufferings. With reference to this, Tertullian says: "Perpetua, the very strong and steadfast martyr, had a revelation or vision of the heavenly paradise, on the day of her sufferings, in the which she saw none but her fellow martyrs. And why no others? Because the fiery sword which guards the door of paradise gives way to none but those who die for Christ."
>
> In the meantime, these two pious heroines of Christ were martyred, that is, they died a violent death, for the name of their Saviour; for which they will afterwards be crowned with the unfading wreath of immortality, as a triumph over the foes they overcame, namely, the cruelties and pains of death.
>
> The names of their fellow martyrs are Revocatus, Satyrus, Saturninus, and Serundulus. It is supposed that the last-mentioned one of these died in prison from extreme hardship, but the others were all thrown before the wild beasts, such as bulls, lions, bears, leopards, ect., to be torn by them. Thus these exchanged their dear lives for death, for Christ's sake. They were buried in Carthage (Tertullian, *de Anima*, Ch. 5).

Chapter 3—The Churches of the Third Century

Welch decent, as early as A.D. 63. Note this from the *History of the Welch Baptists*, by Jonathan Davis, written in 1835:

> About fifty years before the birth of our Savior, the Romans invaded the British Isles, in the reign of the Welch king Cassebellun; but having failed, in consequence of other and more important wars made peace with them, and dwelt among them many years. During that period many of the Welsh soldiers joined the Roman army, and many families from Wales visited Rome; among them there was a certain woman named Claudia, who was married to a man named Pudence. At the time, Paul was sent a prisoner to Rome, and preached there in his own hired house, for the space of two years, about the year of our Lord 63. Pudence and Claudia his wife, who belonged to Caesar's household, under the blessing of God on Paul's preaching, were brought to the knowledge of the truth as it is in Jesus, and made a profession of their Christian religion. These together with other Welshmen, among the Roman soldiers, who had heard that the Lord was gracious, exerted themselves on behalf of their countrymen in Wales, who were at that time idolaters.

William Cathcart writing about the advance of the Gospel into Britain:

William Cathcart was born in the County of Londonderry, in the north of Ireland, Nov. 8, 1826; his parents, James Cathcart and Elizabeth Cously, were of Scotch origin (the stock known as Scotch-Irish in the United States). He was brought up in the Presbyterian Church, of which, for some years, he was a member. The Saviour called him into his kingdom in early life, and taught him that he should preach the gospel. He was baptized by Rev. R. H. Carson, of Tubbermore, in January, 1846. He studied Latin and Greek in a classical school near the residence of his father. He received his literary and theological education in the University of Glasgow, Scotland, and in Horton, now Rawdon College; Yorkshire, England.

He was ordained pastor of the Baptist church of Barnsley, near Sheffield, England, early in 1850. From political and anti-state church considerations he determined to come to the United States in 1853, and on the 18th of November in that year he arrived in New York. In the latter part of the following month he became pastor of the Third Baptist church of Groton, in Mystic River, Conn. In April 1857, he took charge of the Second Baptist church of Philadelphia, Pa., where he has since labored.

In 1873, the University of Lewisburg (present-day Bucknell) conferred on Mr. Cathcart the degree of Doctor of Divinity. In 1876, on the retirement of Dr. Malcom from the presidency of the American Baptist Historical Society, Dr. Cathcart was elected president, and has been re-elected at each annual meeting since. In 1875, in view of the Centennial year of our national independence, the Baptist Ministerial Union, of Pennsylvania, appointed Dr. Cathcart to prepare a paper, to be read at their meeting in Meadville in 1876, on *The Baptists in the Revolution*. This paper, by enlargement, became a duodecimo volume, entitle *The Baptists and the American Revolution*. Dr. Cathcart has also published a large octavo, called *The Papal System*, and *The Baptism of the Ages and of the Nations*.

The Christian religion was introduced into Britain in the second century, and it spread with great rapidity over the ancient inhabitants, this is over the Britons, or Welsh, not over the English, who came to their present home as pagans in the fifth century, and afterwards gave it their name. The ancient Britons, unlike the English, were not converted by missionaries from Rome, but apparently by ministers from the East, like Irenaeus, the Greek bishop of Lyons, in France. The Britons refused obedience to the commands of the pope, and they observed some customs in opposition to the usages of the Romish church. As the Britons had no relations with Africa, the birthplace of infant baptism, and no religious ties with Rome, and little intercourse with the distant East at that period, it is most likely that the infant rite was wholly unknown among them. The Irish and Scotch in that day were in perfect harmony with the ancient Britons in wholly rejecting papal authority, and most probably infant baptism (Willam Cathcart, *Baptist Encyclopedia*, Vol. 1, P. 373).

While the Roman Catholic re-writers of history would have you believe Britian was an un-evangelized country until the time of *Saint* Patrick sometime after the year 400, the evidence proves otherwise. English Baptist historian Joseph Ivimey wrote:

> It is generally supposed that the gospel was introduced at a very early period into this country (England), which, at the commencement of the Christian era was like other heathen nations, full of the habitations of cruelty. Our forefathers were, if their own historians may be credited, gross idolaters, and were accustomed to offer up their prisoners taken in war, as sacrifices to their gods. It is said they made a statue, or image of a man of a prodigious size, whose limbs consisted of twigs woven together after the manner of basketwork; this they filled with living men, and setting it on fire, burned them to death!
>
> There are different opinions respecting the time when the gospel was first preached in Britain, and also by whom the message of salvation was at first proclaimed. Bishop Newton says, "There is some probability that the gospel was preached here by Simon the apostle; there is much greater probability that it was preached here by St. Paul; and there is absolute certainty that Christianity was planted here in the times of the apostles, before the destruction of Jerusalem."
>
> Tacitus says that "Pomponia Greacina, wife of Pautius; and Claudia Ruffina, a British lady, are supposed to be of the saints that were in Caesar's household, mentioned by Paul, Phil. 3:22." Pautius was in Britain, A.D. 45: it is probable Claudia may have returned with him; and it has been thought, from this statement of Tacitus, that this lady was the first British Christian. Claudia is celebrated by Martial for her admirable beauty and learning, in the following epigram:
>
> "From painted Britons how was Claudia [2 Tim. 4:21] born!
> The fair barbarian! how do arts adorn!
> When Roman charms a Grecian soul commend,
> Athens and Rome may for the dame contend." [Rapin, vol. i, p. 14]
>
> Speed, a very ancient British author, says that "Claudia sent Paul's writings, which he calls spiritual manna, unto her friends in Britain; to feed their souls with the bread of life: and also, the writings of Martial, to instruct their minds with those lessons best fitting to produce moral virtues which Speed thinks was the occasion of this line in Martial's works."
>
> Gildas, the most ancient and authentic British historian, who wrote about A.D. 564, in his book called *De Vict. Aurelli Ambrossii*, **affirms, that the Britons received the gospel under Tiberius, the emperor under whom Christ suffered**; and that many evangelists were sent from the apostles into this nation, who were the first planters of the gospel, and which, he elsewhere says, continued with them until the cruel persecution of Dioclesian the emperor, about A.D. 290.
>
> Fuller, in his *Ecclesiastical History*, says, "It is generally agreed, that about the year 167, many pagan temples in Britain had their property altered, and that they were converted into Christian churches; particularly that dedicated to Diana in London, and another near it formerly consecrated to Apollo, in the city now called Westminster" (*Ecclesiastical History*, Book 1. p. 13).
>
> This account is corroborated by Fox, the English martyrologist, who says, "Out of an ancient book of the antiquities of England, we find the epistle of Eleutherius, written to Lucius king of Britain, A.D. 169, who had written to Eleutherius for the Roman laws to govern by: in

Chapter 3—The Churches of the Third Century

answer to which, Eleutherius says, 'You have received, through God's mercy, in the realm of Britany, the law and faith of Christ; you have with you both the parts of the scripture; out of them, by God's grace, with the council of your realm, take ye a law, and by that law, by God's sufferance, rule your kingdom of Britain'" (Joseph Ivemy, *History of the English Baptists*, Ch. 1).

---

1. Write Psalm 12:6-7 twice.

2. Where were Perpetua and Felicitas martyred and where were they buried?
   Turinal, Carthage

3. When was the Gospel first brought to Briton and who brought it? *63, missionare friends of Pudence and Claudia*

4. What group invaded Briton in the fifth century and conquered it?
   Anglo-Saxons

5. What couple was converted to Christ under Paul's preaching and had a hand in bringing the Gospel to Briton? *Claudia and Pudence*

6. Where was William Cathcart born? Name a book he authored.
   Londenberry, Ireland, The baphst and the american revaution

7. What pagan temple was altered in London to use for Christian service?
   temple of Diana

Chapter Four
The Churches of the Fourth Century

Section One: The Century of Corruption.
The Apostle's Creed vs. The Nicene Creed
Section Two: The Donatists. How the Dark Ages began.

SECTION ONE
The Century of Corruption

Scripture to Memorize

> John 16:2 They shall put you out of the synagogues: yea, the time cometh, that whosoever killeth you will think that he doeth God service.

At the dawn of the fourth century, the churches of Christ had not only survived grievous torture and mayhem, but had succeeded in dumbfounding the pagan legions of Rome. The martyrs of Christ's churches had won the admiration, and in many cases, the souls of those that observed their steadfastness in the face of the demonic debauchery of pagan Rome.

The body of Christians was by no means perfect, and the local churches had decisions to make concerning the *lapsed* or the back-slidden. As we have seen, the *lapsed*, and the *traditores* turned their backs on God while others were faithful unto death. What to do about these *lapsed* church members, and more importantly, what to do about the preachers who turned *traditore* continued to draw lines and break the invisible unity of the so-called universal church.

The Gospel had spread to the East as far as India, and into the Middle East. It was in Africa, and Europe, and the British Isles. The churches were fairly united in belief: the Trinity, Deity of Christ, salvation by grace through faith, and baptism for believers only. The universal beliefs were known as *Catholic* and this Catholic group of churches was ***Baptist*** in its practices.

Fourth Century Time Line
303. The last general persecution of pagan Rome
305. Council of Elvira or Grenada
311. Separation of the Donatists from the apostate church
313. End of the persecution by pagan Rome
314. Council of Arles about the Donatists
319. Arius begins to publish his heresy
324. Emperor Constantine defeats Licinius, and declares himself Christian
325. The First General Council held at Nicaea. Arius condemned. The Nicene Creed
326. Athanasius, bishop of Alexandria
335. Council of Tyre
----. Athanasius banished to Treves
336. Death of Arius
337. Death of Constantine
338. Athanasius restored to his See
341. Second banishment of Athanasius
343. Persecution in Persia

Chapter 4—The Churches of the Fourth Century

347. Defeat and banishment of the Donatists
348. Ulfilas, bishop of the Goths
349. Second return of St. Athanasius
356. Third exile of Athanasius
----. Death of Antony the hermit
360. Council of Laodicea
361. Julian emperor, Paganism restored
362. The Donatists recalled
----. Athanasius restored, but again banished
----. Attempt to rebuild the Temple of Jerusalem
363. Death of Julian
370. Basil, bishop of Caesarea, in Cappadocia
372. Gregory of Nazianzum consecrated bishop of Sasima
373. Death of Athanasius
374. Ambrose, bishop of Milan born
378. Gregory of Nazianzum goes to Constantinople 379. Theodosius, emperor
380. Gregory, bishop of Constantinople, Death of Basil
381. The Second Ecumenical Council condemned Apollinarius for preaching **chiliasm**, or millennialism. (Chiliasm is from the Greek *chiliasmos*, meaning "one thousand.")
385. Execution of Priscillian
387. Baptism of Augustine
----. Sedition at Antioch
390. Massacre at Thessalonica, repentance of Theodosius
391. Destruction of the Temple Of Serapis
395. Death of Theodosius
----. Augustine made bishop of Hippo
397. Death of Ambrose
----. Chrysostom, bishop of Constantinople
398. Council of Carthage, A. D.
400. Pelagius teaches at Rome

Definitions:

chiliasm: belief in the 1,000 year reign of Jesus Christ on the earth
catechumen: someone who has made a profession of faith and is awaiting baptism
lapsed: backslidden Christian
catholic: universal or generally accepted

Constantine's "Conversion"

Until the time of Constantine, every Roman emperor was a practicing pagan. Belief in the Roman system of gods and sub-gods was a way of life. Every citizen was required to live and believe in the gods. That is why Christians suffered under the emperors. In the year 312, the emperor Constantine marched against Maxentius, who had usurped the government of Italy and Africa. Constantine seems to have been brought up by his father to believe in one God, although he did not know who this God was, nor how He had revealed Himself in Holy Scripture. But as he was on his way to fight Maxentius, he saw in the sky an appearance, which seemed like the figure of a cross, with words around it, "By this conquer!" He then caused the cross to be put on the standards (or colours) of his army. When he had defeated Maxentius, he set up at Rome a statue of himself, with a cross in its right hand, and with an inscription, which declared that he owed his victory to that saving sign.

The Collegiate Baptist History Workbook

About the same time that Constantine overcame Maxentius, Licinius put down Maximin in the East. The two conquerors now had possession of the whole empire, and they joined in publishing laws by which Christians were allowed to worship God freely according to their conscience. (A.D. 313) This was called the *Edict of Constantine*.

Constantine defeated Licinius in battle (A.D. 324,) and the whole empire was once more united under one head. This action was both good and bad for Christianity. The good part was that it gave some peace to the persecuted. The bad part was that it brought together the church and the state of Rome. Constantine declared Christianity the official state religion of Rome, thereby marrying the church of Jesus Christ to the world.

We do not have solid evidence that Constantine was ever converted. He delayed his baptism until just before his death.

Satan's Devices

Satan's device in the first century was to KILL THE CHRISTIANS. His device in the second century was to DESTROY THE SCRIPTURES. His device in the third was to CHANGE THE SCRIPTURES. Satan's device for the fourth century was to CHANGE THE NATURE OF THE CHURCH. We shall see this plan in action in the pages following.

1. Write John 16:2 twice:

2. What does it mean to be *lapsed*?
   a blacksidden Christian
3. Write the definitions for catechumen, lapsed, and Catholic.
   Pg. 48
4. True or False: the Catholic churches of the fourth century were Baptist in their practices.
   True
5. What religion were the Romans required to practice before Constantine?
   Paganism
6. What caused Constantine's conversion? Was he really a saved man?
   a "vision", no (he wanted to win)
7. How did Constantine unite the whole empire and how was that bad for Christians?
   Through Christianity. It brought together the state and church of Rome.
8. What was Satan's device against Christians in the fourth century?
   Change the nature of the church

****
4.1.2

What Is Surely Believed?

The Arian Controversy

Remember Arius?

Arius was born in 250 in Libya and died in 336 in Constantinople (now Istanbul, Turkey). **He was** a Christian priest of Alexandria, Egypt, whose teachings gave rise to a

Chapter 4—The Churches of the Fourth Century

theological doctrine known as Arianism (denying the Deity of Christ). Arius affirmed the created, finite nature of Christ and was denounced by the early church as a major heretic. His views led to the council of Nicea in 325.

Arius denied the Trinity and the Deity of Christ. He was the first Jehovah's Witness in that he denied the existence of the Trinity. His heresy was much revived in the nineteenth century among American Congregationalists (who became the Unitarians.)

Nicene Council and Creed A.D. 325
- ✓ The Nicene Council was called *the First General Council* and was held in reaction to the Arian controversy about the Deity of Christ.
- ✓ 318 bishops attended.
- ✓ It was called by Emperor Constantine
- ✓ It was held in Bythynian Nicea.

The Apostle's Creed was an unofficial statement of faith read in many churches across Europe and Asia. The Council of Nicea took the informal creed and made it into an official document. In its finished form it revealed subtle changes that **were perverting the nature of the church:**

Let's look at the differences between the Apostle's Creed and the Nicene Creed:
Here are the creeds, placed side by side:

Apostle's Creed:	*Nicene Creed:*
I believe in God, the Father Almighty, the Creator of heaven and earth, and in Jesus Christ, His only Son, our Lord: Who was conceived of the Holy Spirit, born of the Virgin Mary, suffered under Pontius Pilate, was crucified, died, and was buried. He descended into hell. The third day He arose again from the dead. He ascended into heaven and sits at the right hand of God the Father Almighty, whence He shall come to judge the living and the dead. I believe in the Holy Spirit, the holy church, the forgiveness of sins, the resurrection of the body, and life everlasting. Amen.	I believe in one God the Father Almighty; Maker of heaven and earth, and of all things visible and invisible. And in one Lord Jesus Christ, the only-begotten Son of God, begotten of the Father before all worlds [God of God], Light of Light, very God of very God, begotten, not made, being of one substance [essence] with the Father; by whom all things were made; who, for us men and for our salvation, came down from heaven, and was incarnate by the Holy Ghost of the Virgin Mary, and was made man; and was crucified also for us under Pontius Pilate; He suffered and was buried; and the third day He rose again, according to the Scriptures; and ascended into heaven, and sitteth on the right hand of the Father; and He shall come again, with glory, to judge both the quick and the dead; whose kingdom shall have no end. (This last paragraph was added in A.D. 381.) And [I believe] in the Holy Ghost, the Lord and Giver of Life; who proceedeth from the Father [and the Son]; who with the Father and the Son together is worshiped and glorified; who spake by the Prophets. And I believe in **one Holy Catholic and Apostolic Church**. I acknowledge one **Baptism for the remission of sins**; and I look for the resurrection of the dead, and the life of the world to come. Amen.

The Nicene creed is much more *wordy* than its predecessor. Some of the terms of the earlier creed had to be defined in reaction to the heresy of Arius (denying the Deity of Christ) and Origen (denying the bodily resurrection). There are two main differences in the creeds, making this a *pivotal point* in church history.

1. The Phrase: "one Holy Catholic and Apostolic Church"

The council at Nicea is giving approval to the hierarchy of church organization, therefore wiping out the independent nature of Christ's churches.

2. The Phrase: "**one Baptism for the remission of sins**"

Nicea declares a universal (catholic) belief in baptismal regeneration.

An Emerging Controversy

As we have seen, the Synods began to control the churches, so much so that an independent group sprang up in the Novatians. Baptism was beginning to be corrupted and the seeds of baptismal regeneration were growing into a killer weed. Now that Christianity was the official state church, the Catholic belief system could be enforced as law.

Another group was about to break from the Catholics and when it did, it brought the Catholic church its first theologian, who virtually sealed the fate of the churches called Catholic, by teaching them what to believe, most of it corrupt. This theologian would fulfill an awful prophecy and plunge the world into the ***dark ages***.

The Donatists

The majority of the Catholic bishops believed it acceptable to receive the *traditores* into full fellowship. In 311, a *traditore* named Felix consecrated a new bishop in Carthage, Africa, Caecilian. A number of bishops in Africa (called the Numidians) did not want Caecilian because Felix was thought to be an unworthy consecrator. The Numidians consecrated their own bishop, Majorinus. An intense battle ensued over the church at Carthage. Majorinus died in 315 and the Numidians installed Donatus to be the new pastor at Carthage.

Two organizations were now in existence: The Catholic institution was pastored by Caecilian and the true New Testament church by Donatus. The independent church did not want to be ruled by the Catholic bishops. Thus, a pattern began: ***a pattern of believers separating from apostate churches***. This pattern has continued to this day.

Donatus (as did the Novatianists) argued that not only should the members of the church be trustworthy, but the bishops should be without spot. **The ordinances administered by bishops who were either traitors or in sin were not valid**. A good number (but not the majority of bishops) agreed. Those that sided with Donatus were called *Donatists*. The catholic bishops maintained that the church needed to maintain order and doctrine through the hierarchy that had been forming. The Donatists didn't think so. To them, the scriptures gave no ground for a so-called universal church governed by a hierarchy of Bishops and bureaucracy. The only way for Christ's body to remain pure was for them to remain independent of each other. The bishop was to rule one church alone.

David Benedict wrote:

Chapter 4—The Churches of the Fourth Century

In the year 340, the emperor (Constans) directed his two commissioners, Urascius and Leontius, to endeavor by the distribution of money under the name of alms to win over the Donatist churches; and the said Emperor at the same time issued an edict whereby he called upon the North African Christians to return back to the unity of the church.

Of the failure of this convert scheme for gaining the Donatists, forcible measures were the next resort. The Donatist now were to be deprived of their churches, and they were actually fallen upon by armed troops while assembled in them for the worship of God. **Hence followed the effusion of blood**, [starting in 347] and the martyrdoms so often complained of their adversaries. Those who fell victims in these persecutions, says Neander, were honored by their party as martyrs, and the annual celebration of the days of their death furnished new means of enkindling the enthusiasm of the Donatist party (David Benedict, *History of the Donatists*, p. 32).

We maintain that the *effusion of blood*, described by Benedict, was a catastrophic event, predicted by Jesus in *John 16:2: "They shall put you out of the synagogues: yea, the time cometh, that whosoever killeth you will think that he doeth God service."* We mark the year 347, as the unofficial beginning of **the dark ages**, lasting for 1,000 years, 347-1347.

The Donatists Part 1 by William Cathcart

In North Africa, during the fierce persecution of Diocleasian, many Christians courted a violent death. These persons, without the accusation, would confess to the possession of the Holy Scriptures, and on their refusal to surrender them, they were immediately imprisoned and frequently executed. While they were in confinement they were visited by throngs of disciples, who bestowed upon them valuable gifts and showed them the highest honor.

Mensurius, bishop of Carthage, disapproved of all voluntary martyrdoms, and took steps to hinder bloodshed. And if he had gone no farther in this direction he would have deserved the commendation of all good men. But by zealous Christians in North Africa he was regarded as unfriendly to compulsory martyrdom, and to the manifestations of tender regard shown to the victims of tyranny. And by some he was supposed to be capable of a gross deception to preserve his own life, or to secure the safety of his friends. When a church at Carthage was about to be searched for copies of the Bible, he had them concealed in a safe place, and the writings of heretics substituted for them. This removal was an act of Christian faithfulness, but the works which he put in the church in their stead were apparently intended to deceive the heathen officers. Mensurius seems to us to have been too prudent a man for a Christian bishop in the harsh times in which he lived. In his own day his conduct created a most unfavorable opinion of his religious courage and faithfulness among multitudes of the Saviour's servants in his country. Secundus, primate of Numidia, wrote to Mensurius, giving utterance to censures about his conduct, and glorifying the men who perished rather than surrender their Bibles. Caecilian was the arch-deacon of the bishop of Carthage, and was known to enjoy his confidence and share his opinions.

Mensurius, returning from a visit to Rome, became ill, and died in the year 311. Caecilian was appointed his successor, and immediately the whole opposition of the enemies of his predecessor was directed to him. In his own city a rich widow of great influence, and her numerous friends, assailed him; a synod seventy Numidian bishops excommunicated him for receiving ordination from a traitor (one who had delivered up the Bible to be burned to save his life); and another bishop was elected to take charge of the church of Carthage. The Donatist community was then launched upon the sea of its stormy life.

Bishop Donatus, after whom the new denomination was named, was a man of great eloquence, as unbending as Martin Luther, as fiery as the great Scotch Reformer, whose principles were dearer to him than life, and who was governed by unwearied energy. Under his guidance the Donatists spread all over the Roman dominions on the African coast, and for a time threatened the supremacy of the older Christian community. But persecution laid its heavy hand upon their personal liberty, their church property, and their lives. Again and again this old and crushing argument was applied to the Donatists, and still they survived for centuries. Their hardships secured the sympathy of numerous hands of armed marauders called Circumcelliones, men who suffered severely from the authorities sustained by the persecuting church, "free lance" warriors who cared nothing for religion, but had a wholesome hatred of tyrants. These men fought desperately for the oppressed Donatists. Julian the Apostate took their side when he ascended the throne of the Caesars, and showed much interest in their welfare, as unbelievers in modern times have frequently shown sympathy with persecuted communities in Christian lands.

There were a few Donatist churches outside of Africa, but the denomination was almost confined at that continent. They suffered less from the Vandals than their former oppressors, but the power of these conquerors was very injurious to them; and the victorious Saracens destroyed the remaining churches of this grand old community.

The Collegiate Baptist History Workbook

STOP AND THINK
1. Write John 16:2 twice:

2. Who was the first Jehovah's Witness? *Arius*
3. Would you say that Arius had a large or small following? *large*
4. Who were the Unitarians? *denied trinity and deity of Christ*
5. Who was the *traditore* that consecrated Caecilian? *Felix*
6. What was the group of African bishops who rejected Caecilian? *Numidians*
7. Who did the bishops install instead of Caecilian? *Majorinus*
8. Donatus became pastor of what church? *Independent church at Carthage*
9. When the Donatists did not expel their Bishop from Carthage, Emperor Constans did what? *they used forcible measures (even death)*
10. What marked the beginning of the dark ages and how long did it last? *347*
11. According to Cathcart, who were the marauders who helped the Donatists? *Circumcelliones*
12. What are the two main differences between the Apostles' and the Nicene Creeds? *Apostolic and holy Catholic Church. one baptism and remission of sins*

****
4.2.1

SECTION TWO
The Macarean War

An all out war against the Donatists began in 347. David Benedict wrote:

After Constantine the Great, the Roman empire was divided into two parts, which were called the eastern and western, from the geographical positions. The western portion, in which North Africa was included, fell to Constans, who, says Neander, "instead of forcible measures in the early part of his reign, simply employed those means which were then frequently resorted to on the part of the court for the purpose of making proselytes, in the times under consideration Gratius had succeeded Caecilian as bishop of Carthage." Both he and the emperor Constantius (Constans), says Robinson, "persecuted the Donatists with great severity." The Macarian war against the Donatists began in 347. This followed the unsuccessful experiments with the royal bounty, [bounty was a cash offer made by the military commander Macarus to come back to the Catholic church] which was rejected by the Donatists. According to Mosheim, after the repulse of Macarius with the royal bounties, he no longer used the soft voice of persuasion, but that of authority, [in the beginning.] Macarius was without a military force, he sought one of count Sylvester, from whom he obtained a company of armed horseman, who came equipped with the death-dealing arms of the age, that is, quivers filled with arrows. Macarius, surrounded with his military aid, proclaimed the Catholic union; in other words, he commanded the Donatists to go into the Catholic church, unite with them in worship, and adopt the Catholic' faith (David Benedict, *History of the Donatists*, P. 31-35).

Chapter 4—The Churches of the Fourth Century

The Rise of Augustine

Augustine, (354-430) was born on November 13, 354, in Tagaste, Numidia (Algeria.) His father, Patricius (died about 371,) was a pagan (later converted to Christianity,) but his mother, Monica, was a devout Christian who labored untiringly for her son's conversion. She was canonized by the Roman Catholic institution. Augustine was educated as a rhetorician in the former North African cities of Tagaste, Madaura, and Carthage.

Between the ages of 15 and 30, he lived with a Carthaginian woman whose name is unknown; in 372 she bore him a son, whom he named Adeodatus, which is Latin for *the gift of God.*

Augustine came under the influence of Ambrose in Milan in 387 and *embraced* Christianity. He was soon afterward baptized. He became bishop of Hippo (now Annaba, Algeria) in 395, an office he held until his death.

Augustine systemized the theology of the sacraments and devised a works salvation based on the ordinances, which he falsely called sacraments. The sacraments according to Augustine were a *means or way to obtain grace.*

The idea of working the sacraments came from a reckless translation of the Greek word *mysterion* which the apostle Paul used to describe the soul winning work of the

---

> **The Donatists Part II by William Cathcart**
>
> The Donatists were determined to have only godly members in their churches. In this particular they were immeasurably superior to the Church Universal (Catholic), even as represented by the great Augustine of Hippo. They regarded the Church Universal as having forfeited her Christian character by her inconsistencies and iniquities, and they refused to recognize her ordinances and her ministry. Hence they gave the triple immersion a second time to those who had received it in the great corrupt church. Every town, in all probability, had its bishop, and if there were two or more congregations, these formed but one church, whose services were in charge of one minister and his assistants. The Donatists held boldly the doctrine that the church and the state were entirely distinct bodies. Early in their denominational life, Constantine the Great, for the first time in earthly history, had united the church to the Roman government, and speedily the Donatists arose to denounce the union as unhallowed, and as forbidden by the highest authority in the Christian Church. No Baptist in modern times brands the accursed union between church and state with more appropriate condemnations than did his ancient Donatist brother. Soul liberty lived in their day.
>
> It is extremely probable that they did not practice the baptism of unconscious babes, at least in the early part of their history. It is often urged that Augustine, their bitter enemy, would not fail to bring this charge against them if they had rejected his favorite rite. His works now extant do not directly bring such an accusation against them, and it is concluded that they followed his own usage. This argument would have great weight if it were proved that all the Catholics of Africa baptized unconscious babes. But there is no evidence of such universal observance. Outside of Africa, in the fourth century, the baptism of an unconscious babe was a rare occurrence. Though born of pious parents, Augustine himself was not baptized till he was thirty-three years of age. His works are bristling with weapons to defend infant baptism; they are the arsenal from which its modern defenders have procured their most effective arms, and if the custom had been universally accepted, he would have seen no cause to keep up such a warfare in its defense. The frequency with which Augustine treats of infant baptism is striking evidence that its observance in his day and country was often called in question, and that had he directly pointed out this defect in the observances of the Donatists he would have been quickly reminded that he had better remove the opposition to infant baptism from his own people before he assailed it among the Donatists. This fact would account for the supposed silence of Augustine on this question. The second canon of the Council of Carthage, where the principles of Augustine were supreme, "Declares an anathema against such as deny that children ought to be baptized as soon as they are born." (Du. Pin. i. 635. Dublin.) If this curse is against the Donatists, it shows that they did not practice the infant rite; if it is against other Africans, it gives a good reason why Augustine should be cautious in bringing charges against the Donatists on this account. Augustine wrote a work *On Baptism, Against the Donatists*, in which, speaking of infant baptism, he says, "And if any one seek divine authority in this matter, although, what the whole church holds, not as instituted by councils, but as a thing always observed, is rightly held to have been handed down by apostolical authority." (Et si quisquam in hac re autoritatem divinam quaeret. Patrol. Lat., vol. xlii. p. 174, Migne Parisiis.) This book is expressly written against the views of baptism held by the Donatists; it was designed to correct their errors on that subject. And he clearly admits that some of them doubted the divine authority of infant baptism, and he proceeds to establish it by an argument from circumcision. Augustine was a powerful controversialist; to have charged the Donatists directly with heresy for rejecting infant baptism…and he boastfully and ignorantly, or falsely speaks of it as always observed by the whole church, while one of his own African councils pronounces a curse upon those who "denied that children ought to be baptized as soon as they are born" (William Cathcart, *Baptist Encyclopedia*, Vol. 1, P. 341-2).

New Testament local church. It is properly translated *mystery* in the received text of scripture used by the first four century of Bible believers. The corrupt Latin Vulgate mistranslated it *sacramentum*. Sacramentum as we have learned, refers to the oath of allegiance taken by the soldiers who filled the ranks of the Roman Legion. How *mysterion*, which is "a hidden plan that becomes revealed," can become *sacramentum*, "an open oath of allegiance," is a *mysterion* all by itself.

Augustine engaged in two great theological conflicts. One was with the Donatists, a sect that believed the ordinances were not valid unless they were administered by worthy elders. The other conflict was with the Pelegians, followers of a British monk who denied the doctrine of original sin. In the course of these debates, Augustine developed his doctrines of original sin, divine grace, divine sovereignty, and predestination. **He also approved of *Christians* persecuting Christians,** fulfilling John 16:2: *"They shall put you out of the synagogues: yea, the time cometh, that whosoever killeth you will think that he doeth God service."* Augustine said:

> Better that men should be brought to serve God by instruction, than by fear of punishment, or by pain. But because the former means are better, the latter must not therefore be neglected. Many must often be brought back to their Lord, like wicked servants by the rod of temporal suffering. (See Jean Plaidy, *The Rise of the Spanish Inquisition*, P. 20.)

Jean Plaidy wrote:

> He (Augustine) firmly believed that heretics should die, as their presence among believers was dangerous (Jean Plaidy, *The Rise of the Spanish Inquisition,* P. 20).

Salvation is by grace through faith in Jesus alone, without works, and baptism is a work that follows belief and salvation. Based on your knowledge of salvation, compare Augustine's chapter titles about baptism with the Bible plan of salvation:

Augustine to His Friend Marcellinus. (Selected chapter titles.)
Chapter 21 Unbaptized Infants Damned, But Most Lightly.
Chapter 24 Infants Saved as Sinners.
Chapter 25 Infants Described as Believers and as Penitents. Sins Alone Separate Between God and Men.
Chapter 26 No One, Except He Be Baptized, Rightly Comes to the Table of the Lord.
Chapter 27 Infants Must Feed on Christ.
Chapter 35 Unless Infants are Baptized, They Remain in Darkness.
Chapter 55 Unbaptized Infants Will Be Involved in the Condemnation of the Devil.

Borrowing from the doctrines of Cyprian in the second century, Augustine forever sealed ***infant baptism*** into the theology of the Catholic institution. If Augustine believed that baptism saves (see chapter 25 above), enlightens (see chapter 35 above), and overcomes the condemnation of the Devil (see chapter 55 above), then he died outside of Christ and is in Hell today.

The Unbelievable Fate of the Donatists

The Donatists were condemned by the Synod of Arles in A.D. 314.

The Macarian war against them followed in A.D. 347. In derision, the Donatists from that point forward referred to the Catholics as *Macarians*. For the next 42 years, they were hunted down, murdered or banished. For a brief period, they were welcomed back

Chapter 4—The Churches of the Fourth Century

by the Emperor Julian, but then put in danger by **the code of Emperor Theodosius**. Theodosius' code against heretics was enforced in 395. It was a death knell against the Donatists.

Councils of the Fourth Century Which Declared Against Infant Baptism

Acceptance of infant baptism was not universal. The first world wide council was Nicea, but there were other councils in the fourth century. The early councils of the church were all *against* infant baptism. The Council of Elvira or Grenada, A. D. 305, required the delay of baptism for two years. (See Hefele, *History of the Councils*, 1.155. Edinburgh, 1871.) The Council of Laodicea held in 360, demanded that those who are "to be baptized must learn the creed by heart and recite it." The Council of Constantinople decreed that persons should "remain a long time under Scriptural instruction before they receive baptism." And the Council of Carthage in 398, decreed that "catechumens shall give their names, and be prepared for baptism." (See DuPin, *Bibliotheque Universelle*, c. 4.282.)

> *Pivotal Points to Ponder*
> **AUGUSTINIAN WORLDVIEW**
>
> **Augustine** created a theological system based on:
> 1. Original sin
> 2. Infant baptism and baptismal regeneration.
> 3. Sacerdotal salvation only through the Holy Roman Catholic and Apostolic Church.
> 4. Predestination and Election before being born or born again.
> 5. Covenant theology, theocracy and postmillennialism. He rejected *chiliasm*, or premillennialism in accordance with the ecumenical council in Constantinople in 381.
> 6. Capital punishment upon heretics.
> His opponents were called "dualists" or "Manichæan."

> *Pivotal Points to Ponder*
> **PAULINE WORLDVIEW**
>
> **Baptists** are **not Augustinian**, but **Pauline** in Theology
> 1. Our sin condemns us individually.
> 2. Regeneration is by the Holy Spirit at conversion.
> 3. Each man must be born again, not by the will of any other person (John 1:12-13). Individually we are to be the salt of the earth (Matthew 5:13).
> 4. Predestination is the condition of man before the fall and the destination of man *after* conversion (Romans 8:29-30.)
> 5. Israel and the local churches are **not** one and the same.
> 6. The church is a local exclusive assembly separate from the world (II Cor 6:17). She is a garden enclosed, a little flock, an elect lady, and the virgin bride of Jesus Christ. She is in the world but not of it (I John 2:15). She does not rule the world, for Jesus said in John 18:36, "My kingdom is not of this world." We do not marry the church with the state.
> 7. Christ return is premillennial. History is dispensational with the Old Testament and New Testament rightly divided (II Tim. 2:15).
> 8. We await Christ's return, not the antichrist (I Thess. 1:10), for Jesus return is imminent (Matt 24:42, Matt 25:13 Titus 2:13).

1. Write John 16:2 twice:

2. What was the royal bounty offered by Macarius to the Donatists?

3. What did the Donatists call the Catholics after the war against them?

4. According to Cathcart, how did the Donatists regard the state of the Church Universal?

5. What word in the old text of the Bible was changed to sacramentum?

6. What is a mysterion?
7. According to his own writings, was Augustine a saved man?
8. True or False: Augustine was opposed to corporeal and capital punishment of heretics.
9. The Elvira, Laodicia, Constantinople and Carthage councils were all opposed to what?

****

4.2.2

Third Century Leaders

- **Donatus:** Second bishop of the independent New Testament Church at Carthage. Was installed by Numidian bishops at Carthage in 315.
- **Athanasius:** Bishop of Alexandria 350-366 Chief defender of the Nicene Creed. Warned against the teaching of Arius. There was a creed based on the Apostles' Creed and quoted prior to the Nicene Creed that emphasized the Deity of Christ and the Trinity. It was attributed to Athanasius and called the *Athanasian Creed.* It was nearly identical to the Apostle's Creed and probably was just a variation in tribute to Athanasius' stand of the doctrine of God. He died in the year 373, at the age of seventy-six.
- **Basil:** (329-380) Bishop of Cappadocia, who protested the Emperor Valens acceptance of Arianism. Withstood the emperor's threats of torture and death to defend the Trinity and Deity of Christ.
- **Gregory of Nazianzum:** (329-) Was given a mission to Constantinople in 378 to preach the Gospel and defend the Deity of Christ. Constantinople had been a city conquered by Arianism. Gregory held services in a home of a friend. His orthodox church became influential. When Emperor Theodosius came into power he visited Constantinople in the year 380. He turned the Arian bishop and his clergy out of the churches, and gave Gregory possession of the cathedral. Theodosius then called a council (the second Council of Nicea) which was held by Gregory and met at Constantinople in the year 381.

> *People to Remember*
>
> **Donatus:** Heart and soul of the Donatist movement. Donatus was the successor to Majornus in the fight for the Carthage church. The Donatist (independent) church was the result. In every way a Bible believing Baptist church, the church pastored by Donatus brought into question the nature and credibility of the emerging Roman Catholic hierarchy and system.

- **Ulfilas, bishop of the Goths:** Taken captive by the Goths in a raid on Asia Minor in 267, Ulfilas led many Goths to Christ and birthed churches. He translated the Bible from the received text of the Greek, and it became one of the base translations for the translation of the King James in English. Ulfilas has been accused of being an Arian, however his confession, written before the Nicene Creed, shows strong belief in the Deity of Christ.
- **Ambrose:** (340-?) Ambrose himself was brought up as a lawyer, and rose to be governor of Liguria, a large country in the north of Italy, of which Milan was the chief city. He became the bishop of Milan.
- **Theodosius:** (335?-395) The bloodthirsty "Christian" emperor. Responsible for the infamous *code* that sent untold thousands to their deaths. His friendship with Ambrose was a disgrace and reproach to the cause of Christ. Theodosius ordered the deaths of over 5,000 Thessalonians in revenge of their governor's death. They were invited to an amphitheatre for entertainment and all men, women and children were clubbed, bayoneted and stabbed to death by Roman soldiers. Theodosius was allowed back into communion by Ambrose into the Catholic Church after a period of *repentance*. He never revoked his code.

Chapter 4—The Churches of the Fourth Century

- **Augustine:** Bishop of Hippo. First Roman Catholic Theologian and father of the predestinarian school of theology.
- **Parmenian**: Successor to Donatus, was elected in 350 as Bishop of Carthage of the Donatists**.**
- **Chrysostom:** (347-407) His name meant *golden-mouthed,* for his preaching ability. He was Archbishop of Constantinople. Promoted the use of the Litany and Antiphons in the 390's.

The Advancement of the Word of God and a Corruption

In chapter three we outlined how Clement of Alexandria started the College at Alexandria, passed his *scholarship* to Origen, who moved to Caesarea and passed his scholarship to Pamphillus, who passed the books, scholarship and Bible tampering to Eusebius. Now, in the fourth century, the Christian emperor Constantine made a request to Eusebius to give his scholarship to a scribe named Jerome to revise and copy 50 Latin Bibles for the empire. Jerome was instructed to *revise* the old Latin Bible, which was the beloved *Itala Biblia*. Jerome finished his revision and the 50 copies in A.D. 382.

Time and research have proven Jerome's Latin Vulgate (Latin for vulgar or common) was corrupted by the scholarship of Alexandria. The Bible believers of the Alpine regions of Europe, and the soul winning churches of Asia Minor and Britain held onto their old Itala Biblia for the next 1,000 years, while the emerging *Holy Mother Roman Catholic Church* held forth the corrupt Latin Vulgate of Jerome. This is where the stream of Bible texts divides with the persecuted Bible believers copying their Itala Biblia and *Peshito* and the Roman institution their *Vulgate*. From this point on, the two streams are easy to identify: the **Antiochian text**, or received text which was the basis for the Old Latin (Itala Biblia,) Peshito, and the Gothic Bible of Ulfilas, and **the Alexandrian text** which was the basis for the Latin Vulgate of Jerome.

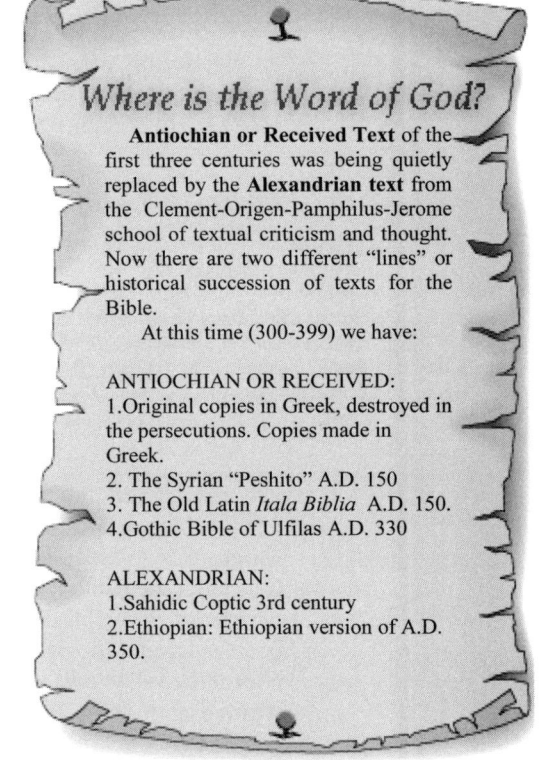

Where is the Word of God?

Antiochian or Received Text of the first three centuries was being quietly replaced by the **Alexandrian text** from the Clement-Origen-Pamphilus-Jerome school of textual criticism and thought. Now there are two different "lines" or historical succession of texts for the Bible.

At this time (300-399) we have:

ANTIOCHIAN OR RECEIVED:
1. Original copies in Greek, destroyed in the persecutions. Copies made in Greek.
2. The Syrian "Peshito" A.D. 150
3. The Old Latin *Itala Biblia* A.D. 150.
4. Gothic Bible of Ulfilas A.D. 330

ALEXANDRIAN:
1. Sahidic Coptic 3rd century
2. Ethiopian: Ethiopian version of A.D. 350.

Definitions:

sacrament: a means or a way to obtain grace
sacramentalism: a system of doctrines or outward duties designed to obtain grace
code of Theodosius: the law created by Theodosius to destroy heretics
anabaptism: to re-baptize, a name of scorn. A Baptist does not re-baptize; if a baptism is non-scriptural or illegitimate, it is no baptism.

The Collegiate Baptist History Workbook

Anabaptist: name given to those who baptized upon profession of faith-name of scorn
litany: written instructions and repetitions in a church service
antiphons: responsive readings made popular by Chrysostom.

 1. Write John 16:2 twice:

2. What was the litany? What is an antiphon?

3. True or False: Athanasius, Gregory and Ambrose were Arians.
4. What ridiculous thing did Ambrose allow Theodosius to do?

5. Ulfilas translated the Greek Bible into the Goth language in what year?
6. What two lines of texts came to the surface in the fourth century?

7. Jerome got his text from where?

8. What translation came from the Antiochian line during the fourth century?

9. If Baptists are not Augustinian, then what may they be rightfully called?
10. Contrast the Augustinian/Catholic and the Pauline/Baptist view of the millennium.
11. Can Baptists be rightfully called "dispensational?" For what reason?

Identifying Marks of True Baptist Christianity

1. Salvation by grace
2. Baptism by immersion upon a profession of faith
3. Believe the Bible to be without error
4. Regenerate church membership
5. Rejection of church-state control
6. Liberty of conscience
7. Rejection of any form of Catholic or Catholic Reformed baptism

Chapter Five
The Churches of the Fifth and Sixth Centuries
Section One: The Dark Ages in Full Fright
Section Two: Soul Winning Churches of the Fifth and Sixth Centuries

SECTION ONE
Fourth Century Time Line
400. Pelagius teaches at Rome
403. Death of Telemachus at Rome
----. Council of the Oak, Chrysostom banished, recalled
404. Chrysostom banished to Cucusus
405. Patrick begins his ministry in Ireland (Hibernia)
407. Death of Chrysostom
409. The Romans withdraw from Britain
410. Rome taken by Alaric
----. Pelagius and Celestius in Africa
411. Conference with the Donatists at Carthage
412. Ninian bishop of Whithorn
415. Councils in the Holy Land as to Pelagius
416. Infant Baptism becomes compulsory
429. Pelagianism put down in Britain by German & Lupus
430. Death of Augustine of Hippo
431. Third General Council held at Ephesus. Condemnation of Nestorius. Further condemnation of chiliasm.
432. Death of Ninian
449. Landing of the Saxons in England
451. Fourth General Council held at Chalcedon. Condemnation of Eutyches
----. Attila the Hun in France, Deliverance of Orleans
452. Attila in Italy
455. Rome plundered by Genseric
465. Death of Patrick
476. End of the Western Empire
484-519. Schism between Rome and Constantinople, split off of the Greek Orthodox
496. *Conversion* of Clovis

Scripture to Memorize

1Thessalonians 5:5 Ye are all the children of light, and the children of the day: we are not of the night, nor of darkness.

The Dark Ages in full fright

With the ***Dark Ages*** continuing on, the hierarchy of Catholic institution exercised tremendous authority over the population. The Catholic institution was recognized as the official church of the Roman Empire and "The Church" was enjoying its power. The fourth century ended with the authorization of the *new* Latin Vulgate, translated by Jerome from texts edited by the scholarship of the Clement-Origen-Pamphilus-Eusebius Alexandrian school of texts. This new bible was an attempt to replace the ancient *Itala*.

Augustine Advances

Theology also took the center stage as Augustine began a series of written denunciations of the British preacher, Pelegius. Pelegius believed in *free will,* that is, he

Chapter 5—The Churches of the Fifth and Sixth Centuries

taught that man was his own moral agent and must make his own decisions for right or wrong. Pelegius took this to the extreme in that he believed some could overcome sin and merit salvation. However, Augustine took predestination to the extreme. Those not predetermined (predestined) were created for the express purpose of being damned to hell. Pelegius came to Rome to preach the gospel, bringing about public debate concerning these things.

J. M. Carroll wrote:

23. Remember that we are now noting the events occurring between the years A.D. 300 and 500. The hierarchy organized under the leadership of Constantine, rapidly developed into what is now known as the Catholic Church. This newly developing church, joined to a temporal government, no longer simply an **executive** to carry out the completed laws of the New Testament, began to be **legislative**, amending or annulling old laws or enacting new ones utterly unknown to the New Testament.

24. One of the first of its legislative enactments, and one of the most subversive in its results, was the **establishing by law of *infant baptism*.** By this new law, Infant Baptism becomes compulsory. This was done A.D. 416. Infants had been infrequently baptized for probably a century preceding this. Insofar as this newly enacted law became effective, two vital New Testament laws were abrogated believers baptism and voluntary personal obedience in Baptism.

25. **As an inevitable consequence of this new doctrine and law, these erring churches were soon filled with unconverted members.** In fact, it was not very many years until probably a majority of the membership was composed of unconverted members. So the great spiritual affairs of God's great spiritual kingdom were in the hands of an unregenerate temporal power. What may now be expected?

26. Loyal Christians and churches, of course, rejected this new law. Believer's baptism, of course, New Testament baptism was the only law for them. They not only refused to baptize their own children, but believing in the baptism of believers only, they refused to accept the baptizing done by and within the churches of this unscriptural organization. If any of the members from the churches of this new organization attempted to join any of the churches which had refused to join in with the new organization, a Christian experience and a rebaptism was demanded.

27. The course followed by the loyal churches soon, of course, incurred the hot displeasure of the state religionists, many, if not most of whom, were not genuine Christians. The name *Christian*, however, was from now on denied those loyal churches who refused to accept these new errors. They were robbed of that, and called by many other names, sometimes by one and sometimes by another, *Montanist Tertullianists, Novationists, Paterines,* etc., and some at least because of their practice of rebaptizing those who were baptized in infancy, were referred to as *Ana -Baptists.*

28. A.D. 426, just ten years after the legal establishment of infant baptism, the awful period known as the *Dark Ages* had its beginning. What a period! How awfully black and bloody! From now on, for more than a decade of centuries, the trail of loyal Christianity is largely washed away in its own blood. Sometimes these names [above were] given because of some specially heroic leader and sometimes from other causes, and frequently names for the same people vary in different countries and even in different centuries.

29. **It was early in the period of the dark ages when real Popery had its definite beginnings. This was by Leo II, A.D. 440 to 461**. This, however, was not the first time the title was ever used. This title, similar to the Catholic Church itself, was largely a development. The name appears, as first applied to the Bishop of Rome 296-304. **It was formally adopted**

by Siricius, bishop of Rome 384-398. Then **officially adopted by Leo II, 440-461. Then claimed to be universal, 707.**

    30. Now to sum up the most significant events of this first five-century period:

        (1) The gradual change from a democracy to a preacher-church government.
        (2) The change from salvation by grace to Baptismal Salvation.
        (3) The change from believers' baptism to infant baptism.
        (4) The Hierarchy organized. Marriage of church and state.
        (5) Seat of empire changed to Constantinople.
        (6) Infant baptism established by law and made compulsory.
        (7) Christians begin to persecute Christians.
        (8) The Dark Ages.
        (9) The sword and torch rather than the gospel become the power of God unto salvation.
        (10) All semblance of *Religious liberty* dies and is buried and remains buried for many centuries.
        (11) Loyal New Testament churches, by whatever name called, are hunted and hounded to the utmost limit of the new Catholic temporal power. Remnants scattered over the world are finding uncertain hiding places in forests and mountains, valleys, dens and caves of the earth.

Carroll continued:

    1. We closed the first Lecture with the close of the fifth century. And yet a number of things had their beginnings back in those early centuries, which were not even mentioned in the first Lecture. We had just entered the awful period known in the world's history as "The Dark Ages." Dark and bloody and awful in the extreme they were. The persecutions by the established Roman Catholic Church are hard, cruel and perpetual. The war of intended extermination follows persistently and relentlessly into many lands, the fleeing Christians. A Trail of Blood is very nearly all that is left anywhere. Especially throughout England, Wales, Africa, Armenia, and Bulgaria. And anywhere else Christians could be found who were trying earnestly to remain strictly loyal to New Testament teaching.

    2. **We now call attention to these Councils called *Ecumenical*,** or Empire wide. It is well to remember that all these Councils were professedly based upon, or patterned after the Council held by the Apostles and others at Jerusalem; (Acts 15:1) but probably nothing bearing the same name could have been more unlike. We here and now call attention to only eight, and these were all called by different Emperors, none of them by the Popes. And all these were held among the Eastern or Greek churches. Attended, however, somewhat by representatives from the Western Branch or Roman Churches.

    3. **The first of these Councils was held at Nice or Nicea, in A.D. 325**. It was called by Constantine the Great, and was attended by 318 bishops.

    The second met at Constantinople, A.D. 381, and was called by Theodosius the Great. There were present 150 bishops. (In the early centuries, bishops simply meant pastors of the individual churches.) **The third was called by Theodosius II, and by Valentian III. This had 250 bishops present. It met at Ephesus, A.D. 431. The fourth met at Calcedon, A.D. 451**, and was called by Emperor Marian; 500 or 600 bishops or Metropolitans (Metropolitans were city pastors) were present. During this council the doctrine of what is now known as **Mariolatry** was promulgated. This means the worship of Mary, the mother of Christ. This new doctrine at first created quite a stir, many seriously objecting. But it finally won out as a permanent doctrine of the Catholic Church. **The fifth of these eight councils was held at Constantinople (which was the second to be held there.) This was called by Justinian,**

Chapter 5—The Churches of the Fifth and Sixth Centuries

A.D. 553, and was attended by 165 bishops. This, seemingly, was called mainly to condemn certain writings (J. M. Carroll, *The Trail of Blood*, P. 20-21).

The Roman Catholic Apostasy 400—599

With no one to stop her, the Holy Roman Catholic and Apostolic Church went into a tailspin. Basing her doctrine on experience and tradition rather than the word of God, the Catholic institution began a freefall of false doctrine. Here is a sample of her apostasy during the fifth and sixth centuries:

1. The worship of relics (by 400). The churches had papers, testimonials, and even the bones of the martyrs, which were looked upon and eventually thought to have spiritual powers. Some priests of the Catholic institution spoke out against this practice, but they were in the vast minority.

2. Infant baptism became compulsory in A.D. 416. What began as an experiment and a convenience was now a doctrine, and because of the union of Mother Church and the Roman State, this doctrine was put upon the people by force. With the acceptance of the Infant Baptism/Predestinarian scheme of theology, baptism became a weapon to control the population.

3. Graveyard (and later in the sanctuary) candle lighting—a custom from the pagans. Because the gravesites of the martyrs were visited frequently, graveside services were conducted until they became ritualistic. The lighting of candles was an invention borrowed from pagan practices and made its way into the Roman religion.

4. Celibacy of the clergy:

> Innocent I was fain to write, AD 405, to Exuperius, the Bishop of Toulouse, upon the same subject of the celibacy of the Clergy; so much opposition did that business everywhere meet at the same time (Peter Allix, *History of the Albigenses*, P. 31).

5. The worship of the Eucharist. The bread from the Lord's Supper was blessed and became an object of worship. The clergy even carried it in the streets for people to bow down to it. This still takes place in Roman Catholic countries today.

6. Prayers to the saints (fourth century).

7. Belief in unleashed spirits from the dead. Jerome, the translator of the Latin Vulgate believed this (Peter Allix, *History of the Albigenses,* P. 35-36).

8. The rise of Monasticism. Because the state of spirituality was so low, sincere people gravitated toward the monasteries. The consecration eventually grew to be bizarre, as self-inflicted wounds and self-starvation became common.

9. Observance of Lent (a forced fast):

> We are to know that as long as the perfection of the primitive Church remained unattained, there was no such observation of Lent—Cassian, pastor from the fifth century and a convert of John Crysostom (Peter Allix, *Ancient Churches of the Albigenses*, P. 55).

10. Prohibition of Marriage for the pastors/priests (fifth century). This practice has led to much abuse and filthy behaviour on the part of priests. The influences of this unscriptural practice are still felt today in the Roman Catholic Institution.

11. Prayers for the dead (fifth century). Borrowed from pagan practices.

12. Transubstantiation (fifth century). A belief that the bread and juice of the Lord's Supper became the actual body and blood of the Lord Jesus. This cannibalistic practice came directly from heathen and satanic ritual.

13. Purgatory (fifth century). A make believe place where God holds captive those who need further penance for their sins. It was a way for Holy Mother church to control people.

14. The Necessity of *Intent* (fifth century). In order for the sacraments to effectively to convey grace, the priest must be holy and sincere.

15. Bible Reading forbidden (sixth century). Only the clergy should read the scriptures. Only "the Church" can interpret the scriptures.

16. Auricular Confession (sixth century). The practice of confessing sin to your priest or *confessor* comes directly from the pagan Romish practices of controlling the people. If I know your secrets, I can control you. It violates *1Timothy 2:5 "For there is one God, and one mediator between God and men, the man Christ Jesus."*

---

1. Write 1Thessalonians 5:5 twice.

2. What was the scholarship behind the New Latin Vulgate? Clement - Origin - Pamphilus - Eusebius
2. What Bible did the New Latin Vulgate replace? Itala
3. What is *free will*? Man can choose
4. According to Augustine if you were not predestined for eternal life, why were you born? Damnation to hell
5. What year was infant baptism made compulsory? What was the inevitable consequence of the infant baptism law? 416, the destruction of soul liberty
6. What title did Leo II officially adopt? Pope
7. At which counsel was the worship of Mary promoted? fourth (Calcedon)
8. How did candle lighting start? graveside church services
9. What is transubstantiation? What is Auricular Confession? confessing sins to a Priest/confessor

****
5.1.2

Time Line Sixth Century:
527. Justinian, emperor
529. The heathen schools of Athens shut up
----. Benedict draws up his Rule for monks
541. Jacob leader of the Monophysites
553. Fifth General Council held at Constantinople
565. Columba settles at Iona
----. Death of Justinian
589. Third Council of Toledo, Catholic Church in Spain renounces Arianism
----. Columbanus' mission to France
590. Gregory the Great, bishop of Rome
596. Mission of Augustine II to England
597. Conversion of Ethelbert

Chapter 5—The Churches of the Fifth and Sixth Centuries

Definitions:

catholic: a universally accepted belief or assertion, in the first three centuries the Catholic belief was salvation by grace through faith, and baptism for believers only by immersion. The Catholic belief system had changed by the fifth century.
heretic: someone who denies the basics of the faith resulting in the rejection of salvation.
predestinarianism: extreme belief in predestination which removes necessity of the new birth.

What Is Surely Believed?

As the pages turned in the fifth century, several shifts away from the primitive design of the New Testament church became firmly entrenched in the apostate Roman Catholic Institution. Infant baptism, which became law in A.D. 416, destroyed the basis of believers' baptism and predestinarianism took away the necessity of the new birth. Infants became *christened* or initiated into the "Christian" religion by baptism and confirmed by a series of sacraments. There was now no need for anyone to be a *catechumen* (someone who is saved but not yet baptized).

These practices had challengers. The brave group of Christians who stood against the new Catholic institution were labeled as *heretics*. They rejected infant baptism and insisted on a baptism for believers only and regeneration as a prerequisite for being a member of a church. Here are some of those **brave voices** that opposed the decaying practices of Holy Mother Church:

FOURTH CENTURY
- **Vigilantius**: Pastor of Barcelona, wrote against Jerome about the year 400. Was suspicious of Jerome's acceptance of Origen's writings. (See Jerome's 75th epistle.) Vigilantius desired to bring into force the forgotten Council of Elvira, which was convened around the year 300. He fought Jerome's worshipful attitude toward relics.

FIFTH CENTURY
- **Exuperius**: Bishop of Toulouse, carried the Eucharist in a wicker basket in protest of the Catholic church worshipping the bread host. This he did to the horror of the pope.
- **Sulpitius Serus**: Monk of Primuliacum in Guienne. Opposed popery. Distinguished the second commandment from the first as the Massoretic text of the Old Testament reveals. He refused to split the last commandment into two as the Roman church did in their catechism in order for the second commandment to disappear. (Exodus 20 and Deut. 5.) Serus opposed Bishop Ithacus who persecuted the Pricillianists, a dissident sect in Spain. Criticized the worship of the saints and martyrs, opposed the use of force against heretics and opposed the worship of the Eucharist. Severus said, "It was the custom of the country people of Gaul to carry madly about their grounds the images of demons, covered over with a white veil" (Peter Allix, *Ancient Churches of the Piedmont*, P. 45).
- **Vincentinus of Lerins**: Wrote *Commontorium*. Asserted that the church can make progress in the knowledge of the truth but not a change of faith.
- **Salvan of Marseilles**: Asserted faith must be based only on scripture, Salvan opposed the prohibition of marriage and prayers for the dead. He preached repentance, writing:

    > They have only changed their garments, not their minds, for they do almost all things in such a manner, that you would not so much think that they had repented of their former crimes…A new kind of conversion this is: what is lawful they do not do, and commit what is unlawful. They abstain from woman but not from rapine (theft) (Peter Allix, *Ancient Churches of the Piedmont*, P. 55-56).

Salonius, Bishop of Gallia Narbonensis: Rejected the Apocrypha and purgatory. He opposed transubstantiation on the grounds that Christ could not "eat His own flesh."

Prosper, a layman from Aquitain: A writer who rejected the idea of *intent,* writing that if the intentions of the minister are necessary for the salvation of the person being baptized, then salvation would not be freely of grace.

Faustus, Bishop of Rietz: Faustus said:

> Though we endeavor with all labors of soul and body; though we exercise ourselves with all the might of our obedience; yet nothing of all this is sufficient worth to be rendered or offered up by us as a deserving recompense for heavenly good things (Peter Allix, *Ancient Churches of the Piedmont*, P. 61).

SIXTH CENTURY

Caesarius(502), Bishop of Arles: Taught that the Eucharist was symbolic. Encouraged the reading of the Bible.

Ferreolus, Bishop of Uzez (553): Required the monks to read the scriptures.

Fortunas, pastor at Poictiers (575-600): Rejected prayers to the saints and said, "All bishops were vicars of St. Peter's chair."

Serenus, Bishop of Marseilles (590): Broke the images the people were worshipping.

1. Write 1Thessalonians 5:5 twice.

2. Define heretic and predestinarian. *pg. 66*

3. What happened to the catechumen status by the fifth century? *not needed*

4. What does predestinarianism take away? *new birth / salvation*

5. Which of the brave voices above opposed the pope? *Sulpitius Serus*

6. Which of the brave voices above opposed purgatory? Which one opposed the worship of relics? *Salonius, Serenus*

Look up articles in an encyclopedia on *St.* Augustine and John Calvin and tell us at least two things where they are similar in their beliefs. Make your answer at least three paragraphs long.

SECTION TWO
****
5.2.1
Gospel Preaching Churches Defying Roman Control — *belief in the same things as the apostles*

There existed at least three places of primitive belief in the fifth and sixth centuries. The Christians in those places did what Christ commanded in Matthew 28:19-20: they preached the Gospel to *every* creature, and baptized those that believed by immersion. This put them on a collision course with the Holy Roman Catholic and Apostolic Church. Especially when those heretics sent their missionaries to **Rome**.

Chapter 5—The Churches of the Fifth and Sixth Centuries

Asia Minor

The information on the Gospel preaching churches of Asia Minor is sketchy and buried under sands of time. Remember that the word of God went out from Antioch, Syria and settled in the east. A group of soul winning churches sprang from the area of Asia Minor along with the original churches Jesus spoke of in the book of Revelation. Many of these churches were known as Armenian, for the country of Armenia, and from their roots would spring the missionary minded **Paulicians** of which we will learn in another chapter.

The Alps

This group of soul winning Christians was known by various names including *Cathari* and *Paterines.* They used the *Itala Biblia* for their rule of faith and they flourished in spite of excommunications, banishments, imprisonments, torture and death.

The Cathari were the ancestors of the famous *Waldenses* whose *written* history begins in the early 1100's. It is an accepted fact that the Waldenses and the ancient Cathari were one and the same. They were Baptist in doctrine and practice.

The Islands of Briton

Perhaps the most astounding testimony for primitive Christianity in the fifth and sixth centuries has to do with the Spirit-filled ministry of Patrick, the Briton who won the nation of the Scots to Christ and turned the Emerald Island of Ireland into "the Island of the Saints."

"Saint Patrick"

The true story of St. Patrick is quite different from the Roman Catholic tale of a green clad lad who "christened" thousands of Irish heathen into the arms of Holy Mother church. The truth is that Britain had a rich Christian history long before the invasion and conquest by the Catholic institution.

> Ireland was always the true home of the Scots. The name of the country was changed around 1200 A.D. St. Patrick in his confession mentions the sons of the Scotti and the daughters of the chieftains, especially one blessed Irish princess that he baptized (una benedicta Scota!) All writers up to the 12th century refer to the inhabitants of Hibernia as the Scottish Tribes. The Scotland of today was then called Caledonia and was inhabited by a people called *Picts*. When God's chosen people were taken captive to Babylon in the Old Testament, the *first thing* the King of Babylon did was to change their names! (See J. A. Wylie, *History of the Scottish Nation*.)

Patrick was a Briton and was born in either present day England or Scotland around the year 387. At age 16, he was kidnapped by pirates and sold to an Irish prince. This led to his conversion to Christ. After a second imprisonment, he answered the call of God to preach the gospel to the people who had imprisoned him. His call was to preach the Gospel to the *Emerald Island*. His successes were nearly total. He baptized thousands of adult believers by immersion by the year of his death in 493. Here is J. A. Wylie's account of Patrick:

> Around the beginning of the fourth century the mighty Roman Empire began to crumble and fall, the lamp of civilization was about to go out and the long dark shadows of the approaching night of the Dark Ages began to appear. It was at that time that God raised up a small nation in the West, at the ends of the earth, to keep the torch burning and be a light to the nations. That island, far from Rome, was Ireland, and the man chosen by God to begin this glorious work was St. Patrick.

St. Patrick was born in the year 373, along the banks of the River Clyde in Roman Britain, now a part of the country called Scotland. He was descended from a family, which for two generations had publicly professed the Gospel. His father Calpurnius, was a deacon, and his grandfather, Potitus, was a presbyter in the Christian Church. His father was an important official holding the rank of "decur," a member of the council of magistracy in a Roman provincial town. As a youth Patrick ignored the spiritual instructions of his father and mother.

One day a little fleet of strange ships suddenly made their appearance in the Clyde. Patrick, with others was at play on the banks of the stream, and they remained watching the new arrivals, not suspecting the danger that lurked under their apparently innocent and peaceful movements. In an instant, Patrick was a captive and on his way to Ireland. He was a youth of 16 at that time.

The pirates who had borne him across the sea, had no sooner landed him on the Irish shore than they proceeded to put him up for auction on the slave block. Patrick was purchased by a chieftain and sent to herd his master's cattle and swine on the mountains. Was ever a metamorphosis so complete or so sudden? Yesterday the cherished son of a Roman magistrate, today a slave and a swine herder. Pinched with hunger, covered with rags, soaked with the summer's rain, bitten by the winter's frost, or blinded by its snowdrifts, he is the very picture of the Prodigal son who was sent into the fields to keep swine. Like the proud King Nebuchadnezzar, he had to learn the hard way that the Most High rules. (See Daniel 4:33-37.)

After several years Patrick likewise lifted up his eyes to Heaven. He called on the name of the Lord, was born again into the kingdom of God, and indeed excellent majesty was added to his name. He was able to escape and found a ship which carried him back home. Discouraged by his parents and friends, he tried to ignore the plight of the Irish, but the Lord spoke to him by dreams for many years. One such dream he records:

In the dead of the night I saw a man coming to me as if from Hiberio, whose name was Victoricus, bearing innumerable letters, He gave one of them to me to read, It was entitled, "The Voice of the Irish" (Vox Hibernicæum.) As I read I thought I heard at that same moment the voice of those that dwell at the wood of Foclut, near the western ocean; and thus they cried, as with one mouth, "We beseech thee, holy youth, come and walk still among us." I felt my heart greatly stirred in me, and could read no more, and so I awoke.

Patrick received his Divine Commission, not from the Seven Hills, but from the Mount of Olives. Attended by a few companions and humble men like himself, he crossed the sea and arrived in Ireland. He was now just over 30 years of age. The story of Patrick is so much like the story of Joseph in the *Book of Genesis*. Both were sold into slavery as teenagers. Both were given special dreams and both began their ministry at about 30. Joseph fed Egypt with bread; Patrick fed Ireland with the *living bread;* both were a great blessing to the whole world!

[He arrived around A.D. 405.] All the medieval writers of his life, save the very earliest, and even his modern biographers, date his arrival in Ireland 27 years later, making it fall about 432. The reason for this is that Celestine, Bishop of Rome, sent a bishop named Palladius to Ireland about the year 431. The monkish biographers of Patrick had Palladius on their hands, and being careful of his honor, and of his master in Rome, they adjusted the mission of Patrick so as to harmonize with the mission of Palladius. It was to the converts of Patrick that Palladius was sent as their bishop.

Patrick's first sermon was preached in a barn! The use of this humble edifice was granted to him by the chief of the district, whom, the legend says, was his former master Milchu. In later years a church was built on the site where Patrick began his ministry and won his first converts to Christ. It was called *Sabhal Padriuc*, that is Patrick's Barn. It faced north to south. It never dawned on Patrick that a church had to face east to west in order for the sacraments to be effective (Dr. J. A. Wylie, *History of the Scottish Nation*).

Chapter 5—The Churches of the Fifth and Sixth Centuries

Evidence indicates that missionaries from the churches of Asia Minor labored in the British Isles and established churches in the first two centuries after Christ. A missionary training school was established on the westerly island of **Hy, now known as Iona**. What a tremendous lighthouse this station became! In fact there really was a lighthouse in the harbour. But instead of the 500 foot "wonder of the world" in Alexandria, Egypt, the lighthouse off the Island of Hy was the real thing, and Iona was a real missionary training center. Missionaries were sent all over Europe, Asia and Africa. The gospel was preached and because of the need, missions were started in the old citadels of Christianity such as Lyons, Alexandria, Carthage and **Rome**!

> THE COURAGE OF PATRICK AND HIS PREACHERS
>
> The great annual festival of Tara called "Baal's fire" was at hand. No other occasion or spot in Ireland, Patrick knew, would offer him an opportunity of lifting his mission out of provisional obscurity and placing it fully in the eyes of the nation. All Ireland would be there. Mixing with the multitudes of all ranks which were crowding to the scene of the festival, Patrick pursued his journey, and arrived in the neighborhood of Tara without attracting attention. He and his attendants immediately began their preparations. Like the Prophet Elijah of old, Patrick decides to fight fire with fire. Ascending the hill of Slane, the little party collected the broken branches and rotten wood which were lying about, and piling them up on the summit of the hill, they applied the torch and set the heap in a blaze. The flames shot high in the air. On that night the fire on every hearth in Ireland must by law be extinguished. If even a solitary lamp were seen to burn, the rash or profane man was surely to be burned alive. Patrick was arrested and brought to the royal court. He preached Christ to the king. The simple message of the Gospel, the one sacrifice of Christ, was all that was required to overthrow the Druid human sacrifice and convert Ireland from paganism to Christianity.
>
> After his victory at Tara, Patrick was given an "open door" to the entire nation. The king realized that true Christianity was not a threat to *his* throne. He did not have to have a Papal Nuncio, nor submit to *any* foreigner. His ministry covered a period of 60 years. He founded 365 churches, and a school arose beside each church. The schools were frequently called monasteries. The monasteries of St. Patrick's day were *nothing* like the Roman Catholic monasteries of later years. They were not isolated from the world, the retreat of the idle and ignorant, no vows were taken and the clergy were always allowed to marry. The monasteries were associations of studious men, who occupied their time in transcribing the Scriptures, in cultivating such sciences as were then known, and instructing the young. They were *colleges* in which the youth were trained for the work of the home ministry and the labors of the foreign mission-field. Patrick died near the place where he began his ministry 60 years earlier, an old man and full of days. He did not perform miracles as his later biographers claim, except the conversion of an entire nation! (Dr. J. A. Wylie, *History of the Scottish Nation*)

1. Write 1 Thess. 5:5 twice.

2. Name three places where primitive belief and soul winning still existed during the fifth and sixth centuries.
Briton, The Alps, Asia Minor

3. What were many of the true churches of the east known as?
Paulicians

4. The churches of the Alps were the ancestors of what famous group of Christian churches?
Waldenses

5. According to Wylie, Ireland was always the home of the whom? The Scots

6. Patrick was a ___Briton___ by birth.

7. By what method or mode did Patrick baptize his converts in Ireland?
Immersion

8. Approx. how many did Patrick baptize?

thousands

9. According to Dr. Wylie, how many churches did Patrick found? In how many years?

365 churches in 60 years

****

5.2.2

Columba and Columbanus

In the year 565, the Irish Churches sent forth a famous missionary named **Columba**, who with twelve companions, went into Scotland. He preached among the Northern Picts, and founded a school in one of the Western Islands, which from him got the name of Icolumbkill [this was the island of Hy, that is to say, the Island of Columba of the Churches.] From that little island the light of the Gospel afterwards spread, not only over Scotland, but far towards the south of England.

For hundreds of years the schools of Ireland continued to be in great repute. Young men flocked to them from England, and even from foreign lands, and many Irish missionaries laboured in various countries abroad. The chief of these who fall within the time, was **Columbanus**. He left Ireland with twelve companions, in the year 589, preached in the East of France for many years, and afterwards in Switzerland and all Italy, and died in 615.

More Information on Ireland, Scotland and England

Dr. William P. Grady wrote:

> Historians will generally point to the attendance of three British bishops (those of London, York and Lincoln) at the Council of Arles in A.D. 314 as the earliest recorded presence of Christianity in England. The British monk Pelagius (c. 360-c. 420) is also recognized as the earliest proponent of man's free will (as opposed to the systems of his contemporary, Augustine and Reformation-era Calvin). However, in his *Ecclesiastical History of the English Nation*, the Venerable Bede acknowledges a distinct evidence of British Christianity as early as A.D. 156.
>
> Scholars agree that the English congregations radiated a more primitive brand of Christianity than that practiced on the Continent. The factor most responsible for this dual standard was the obvious geographical contribution made by the English Channel. This natural barrier of Providence (a persistent hindrance to as recent a victim as Adolph Hitler) enhanced Britain's spiritual climate. While Europe was succumbing to the leavening effects of Roman Catholicism, the insulated British Isles were experiencing revival under such spiritual giants as Piranus (325-430), Patrick (389-461), Servanus (450-543), Drostan (470-540), Finbar (490-578), Columba (521-597) and Columbanus (543-615).
>
> Patrick personally testified of having immersed thousands of adult men from the over 300 local assemblies which he started (This is why Ireland means "Island of the Saints.") Numbers of these preachers became fruitful missionaries (William P. Grady, *Final Authority*, P.118).

The Insane Jealousy of "Holy" Mother Church

Toward the Paulicians:

> The earlier persecutions of the Paulician sect had promoted its spread; had tended, in particular, to further its extension beyond the then limits of the East Roman empire into districts where it met with a favourable reception from the most formidable enemies of that

Chapter 5—The Churches of the Fifth and Sixth Centuries

empire, the Saracens; and the same was the result when these persecutions were revived and pushed to a more violent extreme by the fanatical zeal of the empress Theodora. Military officers were sent to the districts of Armenia, to extirpate the Paulicians; and multitudes were hung, beheaded, drowned, and their property confiscated. The number of the victims to this outrage is reckoned at not less than **a hundred thousand** (Augustus Neander, *Ecclesiastical History*, Vol. VI. P. 340).

Toward the Cathari: (Baptists of the Alps, called Waldenses), Ford wrote:

The Roman Catholic scholar Hosius, writing in the year 1524, said, "Were it not that the Baptists have been grievously tormented and cut off with the knife during the past twelve hundred years, they would swarm in greater number than all the Reformers. (See page 121.)

That acknowledged fact, set forth by an enemy of the baptized believers, puts the ancient Baptists in existence around 323 A.D., at the time of the rise of the Cathari in and around Rome, Italy and the Alps (Samuel H. Ford, *Origin of the Baptists*).

Toward the British and Irish Churches:

Roman Catholicism did not arrive in Ireland until at least 100 years after Patrick died. And Roman Catholicism was sent as a conquering force to subdue the Irish churches to submission to the Pope of Rome. Please note this incredible turn of events in history occurring in 597:

The sword of Edelfrid drew near. The magnitude of the danger seemed to recall the Britons to their pristine piety; not to men, but to the Lord Himself will they turn their thoughts. Twelve hundred and fifty servants of the living God, calling to mind what are the arms of Christian warfare, after preparing themselves by fasting, met together in a retired spot to send up their prayers to God. A British chief, named Brocmail, moved by tender compassion, stationed himself near them with a few soldiers; but the cruel Edelfrid, observing from a distance this band of kneeling Christians, demanded: "Who are these people, and what are they doing?" On being informed, he added: "They are fighting, then, against us, although unarmed;" and immediately he ordered his soldiers to fall upon the prostrate crowd. Twelve hundred of them were slain. They prayed and they died.

The Saxons forthwith proceeded to Bangor, the chief seat of Christian learning, and razed it to the ground. Romanism was triumphant in England. The news of these massacres filled the country with weeping and great mourning; but the priests of Romish consecration (and the venerable Bede shared their sentiments) beheld in this cruel slaughter the accomplishment of the prophecy of the 'holy pontiff' Augustine; and a national tradition among the Welsh for many ages pointed to him as the instigator of this cowardly butchery (James D. McCabe Jr., *Cross and Crown*, P. 402-403).

Referring to the above outrage, Grady wrote:

Prior to their eventual "miraculous conversion" under Pope Gregory's invading "missionaries," (armed with literal "swords of the spirit") these humble believers differed with Rome in several outstanding particulars: they denied the doctrines of transubstantiation, Mariolatry, infant sprinkling, and prayers for the dead; they refused the vow of celibacy; and they rejected the ecclesiastical monstrosity of apostolic succession.

This satanic subjugation of Britain was facilitated by the marriage of King Ethelbert to a Roman Catholic woman from Paris named Bertha.

Thus when the Benedictine Abbot, Augustine, arrived to do a little "witnessing" for Gregory, he found Ethelbert's fields "white unto harvest." Ten thousand Englishmen were sprinkled during the Christmas season of A.D. 597. Of course, the official Bible of

"Christianized" England would now become Jerome's Latin Vulgate (William P. Grady, *Final Authority*, P. 118).

The Earliest Attempts to Translate the Bible to English

Grady wrote:

The ensuing centuries witnessed an ebb-and-flow relationship between the two religious factions with the light of true Christianity nearly extinguished by the 14th century. By this time, the English language was in its second major stage of development known as Middle English (the Old English period ushered in by the 5th century Germanic invasions of the Angles, Saxons and Jutes promptly concluded with the conquest in 1066 by the Danish/French-speaking Normans.)

Throughout these many centuries, very little Scripture was translated into the tongue of the common man. The earliest, effort of any kind was a selection of Bible stories communicated by poetry. Referring to one Caedmon as the "unlettered poet of Whitby," Bede says that he:

Where is the Word of God?

Columba esteemed the cross of Christ higher than the royal blood which flowed in his veins, and that precious manuscripts were brought to Iona, where a theological school was founded and the Word was studied. "Ere long a missionary spirit breathed over this ocean rock, so justly named *the light of the Western world* (J. N. Andres and L. R. Conradi, *History of the Sabbath*. P. 581-582).

The old Waldensian liturgy which they used in their services down through the centuries contained "texts of Scripture of the ancient Version called **the Italick**" (Peter Allix, *Ancient Churches of Piedmont*, P. 37).

"The Reformers held that the Waldensian Church was formed about 120 A.D., from which date on, they passed down from father to son the teachings they received from the apostles." Ibid, P. 177.

There was a long and bitter struggle between the Bible of the British Christians and the Bible which was brought later to England by the missionaries of Rome. And as there were really only two Bibles, the official version of Rome, and the Received Text. We may safely conclude that the Gallic (or French), as well as the Celtic (or British), were translations based on the Received Text (David Otis Fuller, *Which Bible?* P. 203).

Sang the creation of the world, the origin of man, and the history of Genesis, and made many verses on the departure of the children of Israel out of Egypt, and their entering into the promised land, with many other histories from Holy Writ; the Incarnation, Passion, and Resurrection of our Lord, and His ascending into heaven; the coming of the Holy Ghost, and the preaching of the apostles; also the terror of judgment to come, the horror of the pains of hell, and the joys of heaven.

This token effort was followed by several partial translations such as *the Psalms by Aldhelm* (A.D. 640-709); *the Gospels by Egbert* (d.766); the *Ten Commandments and portions of Exodus and Acts by Alfred the Great, King of England* (A.D. 849-901); and various Old Testament selections by Aelfric. It is interesting that Aelfric's translation selections were limited by King Ethelred II to the Bible's warlike books to invigorate his English subjects with a fighting spirit in

Chapter 5—The Churches of the Fifth and Sixth Centuries

the wake of Danish invasion (978-991) (William P. Grady, *Final Authority*, P. 119).

_____

1. Write 1Thessalonians 5:5 twice.

2. Describe briefly the ministry of Columba, where he came from and when he preached the Gospel: He came from Ireland, preached the gospel in Scotland, and preached in 565

3. What greatly used evangelist/missionary followed the ministry of Columba?
   Colombanus

4. How many Paulicians died during persecutions according to Neander?
   not less than a hundred/thousand

5. Describe briefly the incredible turn of events in Ireland in A.D. 597.
   Persecution of Christians

6. From what island were the missionaries of Briton sent?
   Ireland

7. Name the Irish city in which the missionary training center was located:
   Iona

* Most word of the root name busr

74

Chapter Six
Churches of the Seventh, Eighth and Ninth Centuries

Section One: The Rise of the Waldenses (Cathari), Albigenses and Paulicians

Section Two: The Kingdom of Charlemagne. Mohammed and Islam

SECTION ONE

The Christians of the east (in Armenia) were called *Paulicians*, because of their affection for the apostle to the Gentiles and their Gospel-preaching-church planting zeal. Bear in mind that the Donatists were still in existence at this time in the seventh century, though struggling to stay alive. One of the places the Donatists preached the gospel was Asia Minor, into Bulgaria. There the Holy Ghost gave rise to the ancient *Bogomils*. Another place was east into Arabia, where the *Paulicians* sprang from those missionary endeavors.

Time Line Seventh and Eighth Century:
589-615. Missionary labours of Columban
604. Deaths of Gregory and Augustine of Canterbury
612. Mahomet (Mohammed) begins to publish his religious sentiments
627. Jerusalem taken by the Muslims
632. Death of Mahomet. (Mohammed)
635. Settlement of Scottish missionaries in the Holy land
664. Council of Whitby
724. Beginning of controversy as to images
----. Victory of Charles Martel over the Saracens
734. Death of the Venerable Bede
715-755. Missionary Labours of St Boniface
752. Pipin becomes king of the Franks
787. Second Council of Nicea
794. Council of Frankfort

Scripture to Memorize

> Revelation 2:10 *Fear none of those things which thou shalt suffer: behold, the devil shall cast some of you into prison, that ye may be tried; and ye shall have tribulation ten days: be thou faithful unto death, and I will give thee a crown of life.*

The Testimony of the Paulicians

Until 1893, the history of the Paulicians could only be obtained by reading accounts written by their bitter enemies. While keeping in mind the devilish opinions of those that polluted the Gospel, we can determine the way of life of these courageous Bible-believers of the seventh, eighth and ninth centuries.

Ch. 6—Churches of the Seventh, Eighth and Ninth Centuries

Around the year 660, an Armenian man named Constantine gave a place of hospitality in his home to a persecuted Christian deacon. This deacon presented Constantine with a portion of the New Testament, which Constantine began to read with interest. His study of the New Testament, coupled with the observance of the testimony of this Christian lodger, caused Constantine to reject his affiliation with Manichaeism (see box) and receive Christ. J. T. Christian, the Baptist historian from the early twentieth century wrote this about the Paulicians:

> This young Armenian sheltered a Christian deacon who was flying from Mohammedan persecutions. In return for his kindness, he received a copy of the New Testament. "These books became the measure of his studies and the rule of his faith, and the Catholics, who disputed his interpretation, acknowledged that his life was genuine and sincere. The name of *Paulicians* is derived by their enemies from some unknown leader; but I am confident that they gloried in their affinity to the apostle to the Gentiles" (Gibbon, *The Decline and Fall of the Roman Empire*, V. P. 386).
>
> Constantine felt that he was called upon to defend and restore primitive Christianity; being greatly impressed by the writings of Paul, he took the name of one of his followers, Silvanus; and the churches founded by him received names from the primitive congregations. The entire people were called Paulicians from the apostle. These statements of the apostolic simplicity of these devout Christians tell more of the manners, customs and doctrines than volumes of prejudiced accounts left by their enemies. With Paul as their guide, they could not be far removed from the truth of the New Testament (J. T. Christian, *History of the Baptists*, P. 50).

The Historical Slander of the Paulicians and Their Alleged Manichaeism

Non-Baptist and Baptist histories alike throughout the eighteenth and nineteenth centuries accused the Paulicians of Armenia of embracing the heresy of Manichaeism. **Manichaeism was an eastern mystical belief that a dual supreme deity existed—God and Satan, good and evil. God created and ruled the spiritual world, and Satan the material.** Baptist historians such as J. M. Cramp would warn readers of the apparent heretical views of the Paulicians believing their enemies must have been at least somewhat truthful in their criticisms of this robust Baptist group of people.

However, in the late nineteenth century a discovery was made in Armenia, which J. T. Christian brought to light in his 1922 **Baptist History**. Christian wrote:

> The second source of information in regard to the Paulicians is Armenian in its origin and has recently been brought to light and illustrated. There was **an old book of the Paulicians** called the ***Key of Truth***, mentioned by Gregory Magistos, in the eleventh century. Fortunately, Mr. Fred C. Conybeare, M. A., formerly Fellow of University College, Oxford, was much interested in the affairs in Armenia. He was a second time in that country in 1891, in quest of documents illustrative of the history of the Paulicians. He fell upon a copy of the *Key of Truth* in the Library of the Holy Synod at Edjmiatzin. He received a copy of it in 1893; and the text with an English translation was printed by Mr. Conybeare in 1898. He also accompanied the text with important data received from Armenian histories and from other sources. As may be judged this is not only a new but a very important source of information. The Paulicians are at length permitted **to plead**, in a measure, **for themselves**. We are able, therefore, practically **to reconstruct the Paulician history** (J. T. Christian, *History of the Baptists*, P. 49).

J. T. Christian wrote of Constantine:

> Manichæism, by which he had been deluded, was immediately renounced. His Manichæan books were thrown aside, and the sacred writings were exclusively studied. Shortly afterwards he removed to Cibossa, where he lived and laboured for twenty-seven years. He was a diligent and successful preacher. Great numbers received the truth.
>
> Professor Wellhausen, in his life of Mohammed (Encyclopedia Britannica, XVI. 571, 9th Edition) gives a most interesting account of the Baptists of the Syro-Babylonian desert. He says they were called Sabians, Baptists, and that they practiced the primitive forms of Christianity. Indeed, "Sabian" is an Arabized word meaning "Baptist." They literally filled,

with their members, Syria, Palestine, and Babylonia (Renan, Life of Jesus, chap. XII.) They were of the line of the main advance of Christianity, and were left untouched in their primitive simplicity. From them Mohammed derived many of his externals. The importance of this must not be undervalued. "It can hardly be wrong to conclude," continues Prof. Wellhausen, "that these nameless witnesses of the Gospel, unmentioned in church history, scattered the seed from which sprung the germ of Islam." These Christians were the Paulicians.

This bit of history will account for a fact that heretofore has been hard to understand. The emperors had determined to drive the Paulicians from their dominions. They took refuge in the Mohammedan dominions generally, where they were tolerated and where their own type of belief never ceased to be accounted orthodox. This we learn from John the Philosopher. The Arabs had since the year 650 successfully challenged the Roman influence in Armenia. The same protection, probably, preserved the Paulician churches through many ages. It is certain that the Paulicians were true to the Arabs, and that the Mohammedans did not fail them in the hour of trial.

The number of the Paulicians constantly increased, and they soon attracted the attention of their enemies. In the year 690 Constantine, their leader, was stoned to death by the command of the emperor; and the successor of Constantine was burned to death. **The Empress Theodora instituted a persecution** in which **one hundred thousand Paulicians** in Grecian Armenia are said to have lost their lives.

The Paulicians, in the ninth century, rebelled against their enemies, drove out Michael III, and established in Armenia, the free state of Teprice. This is a well-known site, some seventy miles from Sivas, on the river Chalta. **They gave absolute freedom of opinion to all of its inhabitants**. From the capital of this free state, itself called **Teprice**, went forth a host of missionaries to convert the Slavonic tribes of Bulgaria, Bosnia, and Servia to the Paulician faith. This is positively stated by Sikeliotes. Great was their success, so great that a large portion of the inhabitants of the free state migrated to what were then independent states beyond the emperor's control. The state of Teprice lasted one hundred and fifty years, when it was overcome by the Saracens. All around them were persecutions for conscience sake. They themselves had lost one hundred thousand members by persecutions in the reign of Theodora, yet here was a shelter offered to every creed and unbeliever alike. This is a striking Baptist peculiarity. The Baptists have always set up religious liberty when they had opportunity. Conybeare, speaking of the Paulicians, justly remarks:

> And one point in their favor must be noticed, and it is this, Their system was, like that of the European Cathars, [with] its basic idea and conception alien to persecution; for membership in it depended upon baptism, voluntarily sought for, even with tears and supplications, by the faithful and penitent adult. Into such a church there could be no dragooning of the unwilling. On the contrary, the whole purpose of the scrutiny, to which the candidate for baptism was subjected, was to ensure that his heart and intelligence were won, and to guard against the merely outward conformity, which is all that a persecutor can hope to impose. It was one of the worst results of infant baptism, that by making membership in the Christian church mechanical and outward, it made it cheap; and so paved the way of the persecutor. (See Conybeare, *The Key of Truth*.)

In the year 970 the Emperor, John Tzimisces, transferred some of the Paulicians to Thrace and granted them religious liberty; and it is recorded to their credit that they were true to his interests. In the beginning of the eighth century their doctrines were introduced and spread throughout Europe, and their principles soon struck deep into foreign soil.

It was in the country of the Albigenses, in the Southern provinces of France, that the Paulicians were most deeply implanted, and here they kept up a correspondence with their brethren in Armenia. The faith of the Paulicians "lived on in Languedoc and along the Rhine

Ch. 6—Churches of the Seventh, Eighth and Ninth Centuries

as the submerged Christianity of the Cathars, and perhaps also among the Waldenses. In the Reformation, this Catharism comes once more to the surface, particularly among the so-called Anabaptists and Unitarian Christians. The *Key of Truth* and the *Cathar Ritual of Lyons* supply us with the two great connecting links.

They were persecuted by the popes; and all literary and other traces of them, as far its possible, were destroyed. But "the visible assemblies of the Paulicians, of Albigeois, were extirpated by fire and sword; and the bleeding remnant escaped by flight, concealment, or Catholic conformity. In the state, in the church, and even in the cloister, a latent succession was preserved of the disciples of St. Paul, who protested against the tyranny of Rome, and embraced the Bible as the rule of faith, and purified their creed from all the visions of the Gnostic theology" (Gibbon, *Decline and Fall of The Roman Empire*, V. 398).

Many historians, besides Gibbon, such as Muratori and Mosheim, regard **the Paulicians as the forerunners of the Albigenses** and in fact, as the same people. One of the latest of these, already frequently quoted, is Professor Conybeare, one of the highest authorities in the world on Paulician matters. He affirms that the true line of succession is found among Baptists. He says:

> The various sects of the Middle Ages which, knowing themselves simply as, Christians, retained baptism in its primitive form and significance, steadily refused to recognize as valid the infant baptism of the great orthodox or persecuting churches; and they were certainly in the right, so far as doctrine and tradition count for anything. Needless to say, the great churches have long ago lost genuine baptism, can have no further sacraments, no priesthood, and, strictly speaking, no Christianity. If they would reenter the Pale of Christianity, they must repair, not to Rome or Constantinople, but to some of the obscure circles of Christians, mostly in the East, who have never lost the true continuity of the baptismal sacrament. These are the Paulicians of Armenia, the Bogomil sect round Moscow whose members call themselves Christ's, the adult Baptists (those who practice adult baptism) among the Syrians of the upper Tigris valley, and perhaps, though not so certainly, the Popelikans, the Mennonites, and the great Baptist communities of Europe. This condemnation of the great and so-called orthodox churches may seem harsh and pedantic, but there is no escape from it, and we place ourselves on the same ground on which they profess to stand. Continuity of baptism was more important in the first centuries of the church than continuity of order (J. T. Christian, The *History of the Baptists*, P. 50-3).

1. Write Rev. 2:10 twice.
2. What were the Christians of the east called? *Paulicians*
3. Why were they given their nickname? *Paul*
4. How was Constantine (of Armenia) converted to God? *Gave place to a deacon in his home*
5. What false belief system were the Paulicians accused of believing? What is Manichaeism? *Manichaeism, the belief that God and Satan are equals*
6. What ancient book clears up the confusion about the Paulicians? *Key of truth 1891*
7. What name did Constantine take after his salvation? *Sylvanius*
8. What does the Arabian name *Sabian* mean? *baptist*
9. What happened to Constantine? *he was stoned to death - 690*
10. What was one of the first things the Paulicians did when they established Teprice? *they gave freedom of speech to its inhabitants*

The Collegiate Baptist History Workbook

****

6.1.2

Rise of the Vaudois (Waldensians)

The authority of the Bishop of Rome was still not received universally. In the Alps and the valleys of Italy and Switzerland, a group of primitive churches formed. They were called the Vaudois, meaning people of the Valley, or later, *Waldenses,* after one of their preachers, Peter Waldo:

Seemingly they took no share in the great struggle which was going on around them in all parts of Europe, but in reality they were exercising a powerful influence upon the world. Their missionaries were everywhere, proclaiming the simple truths of Christianity, and stirring the hearts of men to their very depths. In Hungary, in Bohemia, in France, in England, in Scotland, as well as in Italy, they were working with tremendous, though silent power. Lollard, who paved the way for Wycliffe in England, was a missionary from these Valleys. The Albigenses, whose struggle with Rome forms one of the most touching episodes of history, owed their knowledge of the truth to the Vaudois missions. In Germany and Bohemia the Vaudois teachings heralded, if they did not hasten, the Reformation, and Huss and Jerome, Luther and Calvin did little more than carry on the work begun by the Vaudois missionaries (James D. McCabe, Jr., *Cross and Crown*, P. 32).

> **What is in a nickname?**
> *Vaudois, people of the Valley* comes from *Vaud* or *low life.* From whence sprang the name *Vaudville* a term for entertainment, made popular in nineteenth century America.
> The Vaudois were also known as:
> **Waldenses**
> **Lyonists**
> **Poor men of Lyons**

The inquisitor Reinerius wrote about the Waldensians:

Among all sects that have hitherto existed there has none been more pernicious to the [Roman] church than of the Lyonists. First because this sect reaches back the farthest, for some say that it exists since the time of Sylvester (Reinerius in the year 1259).

If Reinerius is to be believed, the Lyonists, Vaudois or Waldenses had their start sometime in the third century. The power of this group of believers was felt across Europe for over 1000 years. What was the origin of the Vaudois? **G. H. Orchard**, Baptist historian who wrote *the Concise History of the Baptists* tells us:

The catholic party, now accumulating power, saw, in other churches' rebaptizing, **a virtual renunciation of the baptism** they had conferred upon those who went over to the other party; as understood by the paedobaptists of the present day: consequently a spirit of persecution was raised against all those who rebaptized catholics. In the fourth Lateran council, canons were made to banish them as heretics, and these canons were supported by an edict in 413, issued by the emperors, Theodosius and Honorius, declaring that all persons rebaptized, and the rebaptizers, should be **both punished with death**. Accordingly, Albanus, a zealous minister, with others, was punished with death, for rebaptizing. The edict was probably obtained by the influence of **Augustine, who could endure no rival**, nor would he bear with any who questioned the virtue of his rites, or the sanctity of his brethren, or the soundness of the Catholic creed; and these points being disputed by the Novatianists and Donatists, two powerful and extensive bodies of dissidents in Italy and Africa, they were

79

Ch. 6—Churches of the Seventh, Eighth and Ninth Centuries

consequently made to feel the weight of his influence. **These combined modes of oppression led the faithful to abandon the cities, and seek retreats in the country, which they did, particularly in the valleys of Piedmont, the inhabitants of which began to be called Waldenses.** (See G. H. Orchard, *History of the Baptists*.)

William Cathcart, in speaking of the Waldenses:

> The Waldenses are the most interesting people in Europe. Their history reaches back to the period when popes gathered armies without difficulty to desolate prosperous Albigensian regions of what is now the French republic, when the Bible was almost an unknown book, and when the intellect and liberties of Europe were in shackles, except in the case of heretical heroes, who were treated as outlaws by the banded priests and tyrants of the Old World. We speak of this people with reverence, and think of their long records of fidelity and suffering with tender affection.
>
> Saccho, (the man who turned his back on the Albigenses-ed.) states about the Waldenses that, "They say a man is then first baptized when he is received into the sect. Some of them hold that baptism is of no use to little children, because they are not yet actually able to believe (William Cathcart, *Baptist Encyclopedia*, Vol. 2, P. 1200).

The Character of the Waldenses:
The Waldenses loved the Scriptures, could repeat entire books with ease, sometimes the whole New Testament, and were extremely anxious to circulate Bibles, and to read them to men. Reinerius (Saccho), the apostate and papal inquisitor, gives the well-known representation of the Waldensian peddler, who, after selling articles to ladies in splendid homes, tells them about a richer jewel, which, if the situation is favorable, he presents; and they see and speedily hear the Scriptures read and expounded. The business of the traveling merchant is undertaken only to make known the teachings of the Bible. According to the testimony of their greatest enemies they were humble, truthful, self-sacrificing Bible Christians (William Cathcart, *Baptist Encyclopedia*, Vol. 2, P. 1200).

Many denominations attempt to trace their history back to the Waldenses. The Lutherans claim them to be early reformers and the Presbyterians claim them as their own. The Baptists also have shown that the Waldenses believed the primitive way. All of these groups claim the Waldenses because of the widespread influence of their doctrines in opposition to Rome and because of the large number of their converts across Europe.

Some Opposition to the Powers of Rome, 600-899

SEVENTH CENTURY
At **The Council of Toledo 633** these principles were noted:
1. We read that there are divers flocks, where each Bishop is the pastor, to every Bishop is given the title *Summas Pontifex*
2. In the Gallican Liturgy, the Eucharist is presented as symbolic, not actual. Transubstantiation was not a part of that liturgy. This was changed when Pope Adrian I had Charlemagne abolish the Gallic Liturgy.

Opposition to popery in Gaul (France) will bring about the birth of the Albigenses, a Bible-believing group of baptized believers.

EIGHTH CENTURY

The Collegiate Baptist History Workbook

Alcuin: In the 790's this British preacher condemned the Second Council of Nicea. The Second Council of Nicea was the seventh such *ecumenical* council. It was called by Pope Adrian in 787. The councils had gotten so bad that most of the strange beliefs of the Catholic institution began to be approved with little or no opposition. The worst thing about the Second Council of Nicea, was the approval and regulation of the "veneration of holy images." That is what Alcuin opposed. In essence, the Catholic institution now not only approved idol worship, but also had rules on how to go about venerating.

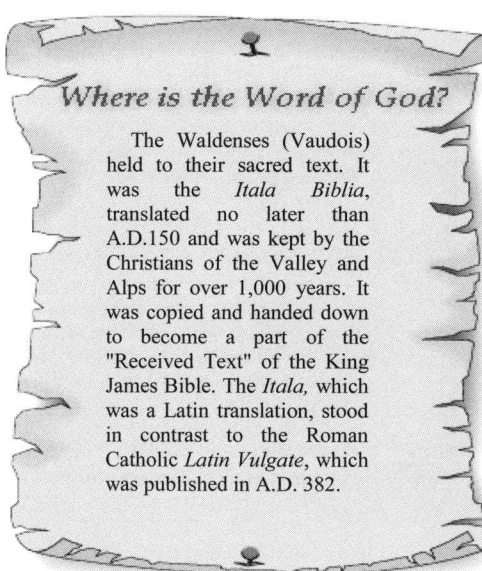

Where is the Word of God?

The Waldenses (Vaudois) held to their sacred text. It was the *Itala Biblia*, translated no later than A.D. 150 and was kept by the Christians of the Valley and Alps for over 1,000 years. It was copied and handed down to become a part of the "Received Text" of the King James Bible. The *Itala*, which was a Latin translation, stood in contrast to the Roman Catholic *Latin Vulgate*, which was published in A.D. 382.

Definitions:

Vaudois: people of the Valley
the Eucharist: the bread used in the Lord's Supper. Holy Mother Church gave it a "mystic" aura.
the Apocrypha: extra set of books supposedly for the Bible, but rejected by the early church and writers.
purgatory: place of departed spirits who must *burn off* some of their sins before entering into eternal life.
transubstantiation: belief that the bread and juice from the Lord's supper actually become the body and blood of Christ, still a doctrine in the Catholic institution.

STOP AND THINK

1. Write Rev. 2:10 twice.

2. True or False: the authority of the Catholic institution was universally received by the seventh century. False

3. The Vaudois were from where?
   The valleys of Italy and Switzerland

4. What is meant by the word: *Vaudois*?
   People of the valley

Ch. 6—Churches of the Seventh, Eighth and Ninth Centuries

5. Define purgatory.

6. Name the preacher from Britain who opposed the Roman Catholic Second Council of Nicea:

7. What bad thing happened at the second Council of Nicea?

8. What is the Apocrypha?

****

6.1.3
The Rise of the Albigensians

The Albigensians were named for the southern French town of Albi. This part of Europe was home to Lyons, a city known for dissent and resistance to "Holy Mother Church." History records flickers of light that came from the area of France and Spain which gave rise to the people known as the Albigensians. J. T. Christian's account of the Albigensians:

> **About John Taylor Christian**
>
> A prominent young minister of Columbus Association, Miss., was born in Kentucky in 1854, began to preach in 1874, graduated at Bethel College, KY., in 1876, became pastor at Tupelo, Miss., in 1877, and supplied Verona at the same time; after two years he removed to West Point and engaged in his present work. At the last commencement at Bethel College he received the degree of A.M. (William Cathcart, *Baptist Encyclopedia*, Vol. 1, P. 222).
>
> **William Cathcart**, writing in 1880, could not have known that **J. T. Christian** would go on to pastor great churches and write the great Baptist history of 1922. Christian corrected the criticisms of the Paulicians, Waldenses and Petrobrussians and gave compelling evidences of the practice of baptism by immersion throughout the centuries.

> It has already been indicated that the Paulicians came from Armenia, by the way of Thrace, settled in France and Italy, and traveled through, and made disciples in, nearly all of the countries of Europe. The descent of the Albigenses has been traced by some writers from the Paulicians (Encyclopedia Britannica, I. 454. 9th edition). Recent writers hold that the Albigenses had been in the valleys of France from the earliest ages of Christianity. Prof. Bury says "it lingered on in Southern France," and was not a "mere Bogomilism, but an ancient local survival." Mr. Conybeare thinks that it lived on from the early times in the Balkan Peninsula, "where it was probably the basis of Bogomilism" (Gibbon, *History of Rome*, VI. 563).
>
> They spread rapidly through Southern France, and the little city of Albi, in the district of Albigeois, became the center of the party. From this city they were called Albigenses. In Italy the Albigenses were known by various names, like the Paulicians, such as "Good Men," and others. It is difficult to determine the origin of all of the names; but some of them came from the fact that they were regarded as vulgar, illiterate and low bred, while other names were given from the purity and wholesomeness of their lives. It is remarkable that the inquisitorial examinations of the Albigenses did not tax them with immoralities, but they were condemned for speculations, or rather for virtuous rules of action, which the Roman Catholics accounted heresy. They said a Christian church should consist of good people; a church had no power to frame any constitutions; it was not right to take oaths; it was not lawful to kill mankind; a man ought not to be delivered up to the officers of justice to be converted; the benefits of society belong alike to all members of it; faith without works could not save a man; the church ought not to persecute any, even the wicked; the law of Moses was no rule for Christians; there was no need of priests, especially of wicked ones; the sacraments, and orders, and ceremonies of the church of Rome were futile, expensive, oppressive, and wicked. They baptized by immersion and rejected infant baptism (Jones, *The History of the Christian Church*, I. 287).
>
> They were decidedly anti-clerical.

The Collegiate Baptist History Workbook

"Here then," says Dr. Allix, "we have found a body of men in Italy, before the year one thousand and twenty-six, five hundred years **before the Reformation**, who believed contrary to the opinions of the Church of Rome, and who highly condemned their errors." Atto, Bishop of Vercelli, had complained of such a people eighty years before, and so had others before him, and there is the highest reason to believe they had always existed in Italy (Ibid, I. 288.) The Cathari themselves boasted of their remote antiquity.

In tracing the history and doctrines of the Albigenses it must never be forgotten that **on account of persecution they scarcely left a trace of their writings**, confessional, apologetical, or polemical; and the representations which Roman Catholic writers, their avowed enemies, have given of them, are highly exaggerated. The words of a historian who is not in accord with their principles may here be used. He says:

> It is evident, however, that they formed a branch of that broad stream of sectarianism and heresy which rose far away in Asia from the contact between Christianity and the Oriental religions, and which, by crossing the Balkan Peninsula, reached Western Europe. The first overflow from this source were the Manichaeans, the next the Paulicians, the next the Cathari, who in the tenth and eleventh centuries were very strong in Bulgaria, Bosnia, and Dalmatia. Of the Cathari, the Bogomils, Patoreni, Albigenses, etc., were only individual developments (See C. Schmidt, Schaff-Hersog, I. 47.), (J. T. Christian, The *History of the Baptists*, P. 50-3).

J. T. Christian continues about the Albigensians:

> That is to say, these parties were all of the same family, and this connection is rendered all the more forceful on account of the terms of reproach in which this writer clothes his language.
>
> It has already been indicated that the Paulicians were not Manichaeans, and the same thing may probably be said of the Albigenses. The Albigenses were oppressed on account of this sentiment, which accusation was also made against the Waldenses. Care must be taken at this point, and too prompt credence should not be given to the accuser. The Roman Catholic Church sought diligently for excuses to persecute. Even **Luther was declared by the Synod of Sens to be a Manichaean**. The celebrated Archbishop Ussher says that the charge "of Manichaeanism on the Albigensian sect is evidently false." It would be difficult to understand the Albigenses from this philosophical standpoint. They were not a metaphysical people. Theirs was not a philosophy, but a daily faith and practice, which commended itself to the prosperous territory of Southern France.
>
> They held to the division of believers into two classes, the perfect and the imperfect. This was the common classification of the Paulicians, Waldenses and Anabaptists. The most elaborate accounts are given of the initiation of the *perfecti* by a single immersion into the body of believers (John T. Christian, *History of the Baptists*, P. 62).

The Albigenses have one of the saddest stories in the history of the New Testament Churches. The greater part of them shed their blood for the cause of Christ.

1. Write Rev. 2:10 twice.

2. How did the Albigenses get their name?
   From the city of Albi

Ch. 6—Churches of the Seventh, Eighth and Ninth Centuries

3. According to the Encyclopedia Britannica, from whom did the Albigenses descend?
   Vadois / Paulicians
4. Give four things the Albigenses believed.
   * bold section pg. 82 *

****

6.2.1

SECTION TWO
Seventh, Eighth, and Ninth Century Leaders

- **Mohammed:** Arab leader who unified the Arabic tribes under the god "Alla." His followers conquered all of the Middle East including Jerusalem.
- **Charles Martel:** Frankish prince who defeated the Muslims at the battle of Poitiers in 732.
- **the Venerable Bede:** English bishop and early historian of Britain
- **Boniface (Winfrid)** The so-called "Apostle of Germany." Winfrid was born near Crediton, in Devonshire, about the year 680. He became a monk at an early age. Went to Germany and baptized thousands of "converts" for the Roman Catholic Institution.
- **Charlemagne:** First emperor of the Holy Roman Empire, crowned by Pope Leo III.
- **Alcuin:** Preacher from Britain who advised Charlemagne and opposed the worship of images.

The seventh, eighth and ninth centuries were filled with intrigue and political maneuvering. The Arabs, beginning with Mohammed in A.D. 612, united under the Muslim belief system, overran the Middle East, gained control of Jerusalem, and would have conquered all of Europe had they not been turned back by Charles Martel at Poitiers in 732.

Boniface, an English missionary of the Catholic institution, began his ministry to the German tribes at this time. Boniface supposedly baptized many "converts," but Irish missionaries in Germany opposed him. It is evident that these Irish missionaries were opposed to Roman Catholic idolatry.

The Birth of Islam

The so-called prophet of Islam, Muhammad was born in Mecca, Arabia in 570. His parents both died before he reached the age of seven. Muhammad began traveling in caravans and learning the ways of trade in the Arabian peninsula.

He married at age 25 and in the year 610 he claimed to have his first revelation from the Angel Gabriel, which began his transmission of the Koran, the Muslim holy book.

Reasons for the Rise of Islam:
1. The decline of the true church.
2. Lack of soul winning zeal in the Arab peninsula.
3. The outlawing of the Paulicians by the catholic church. If the Paulicians would have been allowed to flourish, perhaps their zeal for the Bible and for souls would have had a greater impact on the Arabs.

What about Islam?
1. "Islam" means "peaceful," or "peaceful path."
2. The Koran gives instruction on how to kill unbelievers. The forcible conversion of the world is one of the tenants of the Koran.
3. Islam is one of the fastest growing religions in the world with over **one billion** adherents world-wide.
4. Islam is distinctly a "works" religion. Salvation is rewarded for service to Allah.
5. Allah is not God. Allah is just one god of many Arabian deities.
6. Some strange things:
   a) Because of the Koran's attitude toward unbelievers, rape of unbelieving women has long been a standard act for conquering Islamic armies.
   b) Muhammad got several revelations from Allah to kill dogs lots of them, especially black ones.

84

Muhammad began his public ministry and in the beginning was largely rejected by the Arabs. In 621 he was "transported by Gabriel" to Jerusalem and back in one night where he met Abraham, Moses, Jesus, etc. and yes, even taken to heaven where he saw the signs of God.

After being warned by Gabriel that his kinsmen, the *Quraysh* were plotting to kill him, Muhammad escaped by night and began to lead his nomad band of *Muslims*. Over a period of five years Muhammad married several more women, fought with Mecca and collected goods and money plundered from his raids on traveling caravans.

In 630 Muhammad marched on Mecca where the Meccans surrendered to the "messenger of God" without a fight. He destroyed the idols around the **Kabah** (believed to have been built by Adam, rebuilt by Abraham and Ishmael) rededicated it to Allah, and gave the old pagan rites of the **hajj** (pilgrimage to Mecca) an Islamic significance. Muhammad died in 632 and Abu Bakr was elected as his **caliph** (prophet in his place).

In the next 12 years, under the next two caliph's, the religion captured Jerusalem, Syria, Egypt, Persia, and Mesopotamia, all by warfare. The next two caliph's continued as their predecessors. They took the areas of North Africa, parts of India, and Spain. The caliph's line continued, and wars continued unabated. France, Germany and the rest of Europe would have surely fallen, if it had not been for Charles Martel's victory in 732 at the Battle of Poitiers. There was 110 years of Islam and 110 years of Islamic warfare against the rest of the world. Their plan of action has not changed. All the lands from Turkey to India, from North Africa to Spain, are in the hands of Islam, including the Arabian Peninsula, Mid-east and Persia.

Charles Martel's Victory over the Muslims

Martel was a Frenchman who gathered an Army and formed a line to stop the onslaught of the Muslim forces. Charles Martel (*Martel* means "the Hammer") was the son of Pepin II, Mayor of the Palace of Austrasia. On the death of Pepin II in 714, the succession was passed to an infant grandson A faction between Austrasian nobles who supported the grandson and those that supported Martel developed over who would lead Austrasia. Charles secured his power through a series of military victories and by winning the loyalty of several important priests and bishops of the catholic institution. He did it partly by donating lands and money for the founding of abbeys and monasteries. In any event, Charles Martel was waiting for the Muslims when they invaded France. Martel's army defeated the Muslims at the Battle of Poitiers in 732.

Charles Martel had a son named Pipin, (Pepin III) who sat as a governor in France. He was crowned King of the Franks and Germans by the pope and in exchange, Pipin granted the church a large tract of land that he had taken from the Lombards. This began a long history of donations given to the Roman Catholic institution and instilled the idea of ***The Divine Right Of Christian Kings*** to confiscated lands of conquered nations.

STOP AND THINK
1. Write Rev. 2:10 twice.

Ch. 6—Churches of the Seventh, Eighth and Ninth Centuries

2. When did Muhammad first receive his revelation from God and when was he supposedly transported to Jerusalem? 1. 610, 621
3. Name one strange belief of Islam. kill dogs
4. How many Muslims are there today? one billion (over)
5. What did the Paulicians have to do with the rise of Islam? They were outlawed by the catholic church
6. What difference did Charles Martel make to the history of Europe? Victory of the battle
7. What bad thing did Pipin put into action that has been repeated throughout history? The divine right of christian kings
8. Whom did Leo III crown? Charles The Great
9. Would you say that the Holy Roman Empire became tremendously strong? no
10. What notable British preacher was opposed to the second council of Nicea? Alcuin

****

6.2.2

Time Line Nineteenth Century:
800. Charles the Great crowned as emperor
----. Forgery of Constantine's donation (approx.)
814. Death of Charles the Great
826-865. Missionary labours of Anskar
846. Forgery of the False Decretals (approx.)
860-870. "Conversion" of Bulgarians, Moravians, Bohemians

Charlemagne

Pipin died in 768 and his son Charles the Great became the new king. Pope Leo III successfully defended his office of supreme pontiff with the help of Charles the Great. And in the year 800, in a huge ceremony at St. Peters church in Rome, Leo III surprisingly crowned Charles the Great, placing a golden crown on the king's head, while the people shouted, "Long life and victory to our **emperor** Charles!" Now, after a long time, an emperor was again set up in the West. Charles the Great was from then on known as **Charlemagne**. He died in 814, his empire, known as the **Holy Roman Empire**, was never as strong as the old emperors, but the idea of a vast European empire under the charge of a great king has never died. One day the empire will be revived under the **Antichrist's kingdom**.

Alcuin was a British preacher who aided Charlemagne in the education of his own children and the children of the privileged in Germany. Alcuin was opposed to the worship of idols as outlined in the second council of Nicea.

The advance of the true Christian faith in the seventh, eighth, and nineteenth centuries is obscure. All writings and histories of Christ's true and persecuted church were destroyed while the lives of untold thousands were broken, scattered and slaughtered.

The Collegiate Baptist History Workbook

The Donation of Constantine

One of the most embarrassing situations the Holy Roman and Apostolic Church found itself in involved the infamous ***Donation of Constantine***. There had always been some embarrassing things involving the relics and the remains of the saints. This particular embarrassment involved forgery and thievery of the most grotesque nature:

> **The Skull of John the Baptist**
> One of the biggest farces in the history of the "relics" of the Catholic institution involved the skull of John the Baptist. As the bishops would gather the relic side shows to entertain and control the people, several skulls of John the Baptist kept appearing at the showings. On one occasion, two of the John the Baptist skulls appeared in a public show. This was explained to the gullible public by telling them the smaller skull was the skull of John the Baptist when he was a boy.

In A.D.756 the Italian Papal States (much of the city of Rome and major areas in western Italy) were officially acquired by the Catholic Church. This land transfer was legitimated on the basis of a document supposedly written by the Roman Emperor Constantine I in A.D.337, which granted all of these regions to Pope Sylvester I (Pope from A.D.315-335,) and his successors.

For many centuries the authenticity of **the Donation of Constantine** was not questioned. However, in 1440 Lorenzo Valla published his *Declamitio de falso credita et ementia donatione Constantini (Discourse on the Forgery of the Alleged Donation of Constantine)*. In this declamation, Valla argued that the donation was a fraud. He noted that not only was there no record indicating that Pope Sylvester I had been aware of such a gift, but also that the text of the Donation contained a number of historical anachronisms. For instance, it referred to Byzantia as a province when in the fourth century it was only a city. It referred to temples in Rome that did not yet exist; and finally, it referred to "Judea," which also did not yet exist.

It is now believed that **the Donation of Constantine** was actually written around A.D.750 shortly before the Catholic "Church" acquired the Papal States (and long after Constantine's death.) Its true author is unknown. The Catholic Church ceded the Papal States back to Italy in 1929 (Gordon Stein, *The Encyclopedia of Hoaxes*, 66-67).

1. Write Rev. 2:10 twice.

2. Who crowned Charlemagne as an emperor? Pope Leo III
3. By what name was Charlemagne's empire known? Holy Roman Empire
4. Describe the "Donation of Constantine," in a paragraph.
   a fraud which allowed the church to steal land.
5. What happened to the "Donation of Constantine" in 1929?
   The catholic church ceded the Papal states back to Italy
6. How many skulls did John the Baptist have?
   1

87

Chapter Seven
Churches of the Tenth, Eleventh and Twelfth Centuries

Section One: The Freefall of the Papacy
Section Two: The Crusades, Henricians, Petrobrussians

SECTION ONE
The Freefall of the Papacy

Time Line Tenth and Eleventh Century:
912. Foundation of the Order of Clugny
962. Otho I, emperor
988. "Conversion" of Basil of Russia
999. Sylvester II, pope
994-1030. "Conversion" of Norwegians.
1048. Pope Leo IX., Beginning of Hildebrand's influence over the papacy
1073. Hildebrand elected pope (Gregory VII)
1074. Foundation of the Carthusian Order
1085. Death of Gregory VII
1098. Foundation of the Cistercian Order
1099. Jerusalem taken back in the First Crusade

It was in the tenth century that the papacy became the monster which its critics had feared. Even the historians of that time such as Genebrard, and Baronius, who belonged to the Church of Rome, admitted the terrible and gross errors of the Popes. (See Peter Allix, *The Churches of the Piedmont*, Ch. 10.)

Scripture to Memorize

Matthew 5:44 But I say unto you, Love your enemies, bless them that curse you, do good to them that hate you, and pray for them which despitefully use you, and persecute you.

The Persecution of the Paulicians

We met the Paulicians in the previous chapter. We begin this chapter by relating the persecution of the Paulicians. The effect of these missionaries from the east was significant.

The Paulicians had a profound effect on the Catholic institution. They were the reason for the birth of the **Clugny order**. The Clugny order was founded in response to the corruption of the Popes, and to train men for a sincere ministry. The first supervisor of the order of Clugny (or Cluny) was Odo, and it is evident from his writings that he rejected special powers of the Eucharist and did not receive Extreme Unction at his death.

Clugny was in northern France in the diocese of Rheims, which in 991 received Gerbertus to be archbishop. Two historians, **Peter Allix** (1821), and **Alexis Muston** (1852), did extensive research in Europe and concluded that Holy Mother institution had serious problems with the diocese (district) of Clugny in northern France. It was evident that Rheims, Clugny, and the Alpine region were influenced by the testimony of the Paulicians, as well as the Vaudois.

Ch. 7—Churches of the Tenth, Eleventh and Twelfth Centuries

The Paulicians denied image worship, the office of the Papacy, baptismal regeneration, and the veneration of the saints. They believed in *believer's baptism* and paid a price for their separation from Rome. As mentioned in chapter six, many thousands lost their lives. Augustus Neander wrote:

> The earlier persecutions of the Paulician sect had promoted its spread; had tended, in particular, to further its extension beyond the then limits of the East Roman empire into districts where it met with a favourable reception from the most formidable enemies of that empire, the Saracens. And the same was the result when these persecutions were revived and pushed to a more violent extreme by the fanatical zeal of **the empress Theodora**. Military officers were sent to the districts of Armenia, to extirpate the Paulicians; and multitudes were hung, beheaded, drowned, and their property confiscated. **The number of the victims to this outrage is reckoned at not less than a hundred thousand** (Augustus Neander, Ecclesiastical History, Vol. VI. P. 340).

The Incredible Saga of the Three (or four) Popes

In 999, King Otho III received disturbing news that Pope John XV had been committing adultery. No longer able to defend the Pope's infidelity, King Otho III deposed the Pope, and Sylvester II was installed in his place.

That would have been the end of the story, but in 1033, the dukes of Tuscoli, not preferring Sylvester II, elected Pope Benedict IX. He was 12 years old. Now there were two popes. We suppose that both were "the vicar of Christ" on earth, and that both were "infallible in their judgments in church affairs." After 10 years of this insanity, another party of bishops elected Sylvester III to be pope. Now there were three popes.

To add to this comedy, within a year of the pope trilogy, Benedict IX, now at the wise old age of 23, decided he didn't want the responsibility of popedom upon him. To remove himself from being "the Holy Father," he SOLD HIS POSITION to arch bishop John Gratian, who became Gregory VI. However, Benedict IX, did not want to rid himself of his title, so he remained *The Pope*!? Now in essence, there were four popes.

In 1046, King Henry III deposed all four.

The Progeny of the Novatianiss, the Paterines

G. H. Orchard, the English Baptist historian, found evidences for the descendents of the old Novatian protest of the third century alive and well in Italy during the tenth century. These people were called the Paterines, a name meaning *sufferers* for patient suffering in the face of persecution:

> We have given the outlines of these suffering people, under the denomination of Novatianists, and endeavored to trace their history till penal laws compelled them to retire into "caves and dens," to worship God. While oppressed by the catholic party, they obtained the name of Paterines; which means sufferers, or what is nearly synonymous with our modern acceptation of the word *martyrs*, (See Peter Allix's *Rem. on the Anc.*, ch. 3, P. 25; and Jones's *Hist. of the Christ. Ch.*, v. ii., P. 107.) and which indicated an afflicted and poor people, trusting in the name of the Lord; and which name was, in a great measure, restricted to the dissenters of Italy, where it was as common as the Albigenses in the south of France, or Waldenses in Piedmont.
>
> We left off our narrative of the Novatianists at the end of the sixth century; yet it is very evident Dissenters continued in Italy, as is proved by the complaints of the clergy, (See Robinson's. Res. P. 408.) which point is ceded to us by Dr. Mosheim. (See Mosheim's Hist.

The Collegiate Baptist History Workbook

Cent. 12, pt. 2, ch. 5,-4, note.) "It was by means of the Paterines," says Dr. Allix, "that the truth was preserved in the dioceses of Milan and Turin" (G. H. Orchard, *A Concise History Of Foreign Baptists: taken from the New Testament, etc.*, P. 141-2).

> The public religion of the **Paterines** consisted of nothing but social prayer, reading and expounding the gospels, baptism once, and the Lord's supper as often as convenient. Italy was full of such Christians, which bore various names, from various causes. They said a Christian church ought to consist of only good people: a church had no power to frame any constitutions, i.e., make laws; it was not right to take oaths; it was not lawful to kill mankind, nor should he be delivered up to the officers of justice to be converted; faith alone could save a man; the benefit of society belonged to all its members; the church ought not to persecute; the law of Moses was no rule for Christians. The Catholics of those times baptized **by immersion**; the Paterines, therefore, in all their branches, made no complaint of the action of baptism; but when they were examined, they objected vehemently against the baptism of infants, and condemned it as an error.
>
> Atto, bishop of Vercilli, complained of these people in 946, as other clergy had done before; but from this period, until the thirteenth century, Baptists continued to increase and multiply. The wickedness of the clergy considerably aided the cause of dissent (G.H. Orchard, *Concise History of the Baptists*, P.142-3).

Orchard, continuing:

The PATERINES were, in 1040, very numerous and conspicuous at Milan, which was their principal residence: and here they flourished at least two hundred years. **They had no connection with the (catholic) church, nor with the Fathers, considering them as corrupters of Christianity**. They called the cross [the crucifix, worshipped as an image] the abomination of desolation standing in the holy place; and they said it was the mark of the beast. Nor had they any share in the state, for they took no oaths, and bore no arms. The state did not trouble them, but the clergy preached, prayed, and published books against them, with unabated zeal. (See Robinson's Research, P. 405.) **The Paterines were decent in their deportment, modest in their dress and discourse, and their morals were irreproachable.** In their conversation there was no levity, no scurrility, no detraction, no falsehood, no swearing. Their dress was neither fine nor mean. **They were chaste and temperate, never frequenting taverns or places of public amusement. They were not given to anger or violent passions.** They were not eager to accumulate wealth, but were content with a plain plenty of the necessaries of life. They avoided commerce, because they thought it would expose them to the temptations of collusion, falsehood, and oaths; and they chose to live by labor or handicraft. They were always employed in spare hours, either in giving or receiving instruction.

Their churches were divided into sixteen compartments, such as the English Baptists would call associations. Each of these was subdivided into parts, which would here be called churches or congregations. In Milan there was a street called Pararia, where it is supposed they met for worship. Their bishops and officers were mechanics, weavers, shoemakers, who maintained themselves by their industry. They had houses at Ferrara, Brescia, and in many other cities and towns. One of their principal churches was that of Concorezzo, in the Milanese; and the members of churches, in this association, were more than 1500. During the kingdom of the Goths and Lombards, the Anabaptists, as the Catholics called them, had their share of churches and baptisteries, during which time they held no communion with any hierarchy. The language of the Paterines is very strongly expressed against infant baptism. See Gregory and Muratori, with others, quoted in Robinson's Research 408, note 9; and History Baptists, P. 211, note 4 (G. H. Orchard, *A Concise History Of Foreign Baptists: taken from the New Testament, etc.*, P. 145-7).

Definitions:

Ch. 7—Churches of the Tenth, Eleventh and Twelfth Centuries

Papacy: anything pertaining to the Pope or his office
Extreme Unction: Roman Catholic doctrine that teaches there can be an anointing of a person ready for death which is said to remove sin

---

1. Write Matthew 5:44 twice:

2. Name two historians who researched the Christian history of Clugny. *Alexis Muston, Peter Allix*
3. According to Neander, how many Paulicians perished during the dark ages? *not less than 100,000*
4. What is "Extreme Unction?" *ceremony to prepare someone for heaven before death*
5. Why was the order of Clugny begun? *The popes (corruption)*
6. What four men where "Pope" at the same time? *Benedict, Sylvester III, Sylvester II, Gregory VI*
7. From whom were the Paterines descended, and what does the name *Paterine* mean? *Novatianists, sufferers*
8. Give four characteristics of the Paterines. *modest, marials, no bear arms, decent in proportions*

****
7.1.2

Time Line Twelveth Century:
1113. Order of St John (or Hospitallers) founded
1116. Order of the Templar Knights founded
        Henry of Clugny begins his ministry. Henricians begin their ministry.
1123. Agreement between pope and emperor at Worms
1126. Peter de Bruys burned at the stake in St. Gilles. Petrobrussians begin their ministry.
1147-1149. The Second Crusade
1153. Death of St. Bernard
1155. Arnold of Brescia burned at the stake.
1154. Nicolas Breakspeare, an Englishman, chosen pope (Adrian IV)
1170. Murder of Archbishop Thomas Becket
1189. The Third Crusade
1198. Innocent III elected pope

The Crusades: the first three parts

The first Crusade to win back the Holy Land from the hand of the Moslems began in 1099. At this time military/religious orders were formed. These orders were actually military groups fighting for Holy Mother church. The first of these orders was the famous Templar Knights. The knights were bound by their rules: to remain unmarried, to be regular and frequent in their religious exercises, to live plainly, to devote themselves to the defense of the Christian faith and of the Holy Land.

For the sake of the work, emperors, kings, and other wealthy persons bestowed lands and other gifts on them, so that they had large estates in all the countries of Europe. But as they grew rich, they forgot their vows of poverty and humility and inevitably became vicious mercenaries.

The Crusades part 2

This crusade was conducted in the years 1147-1149. The crusade was led by "Saint" Bernard and resulted in gaining back lost ground from the Muslims.

The Crusades part 3

Held in 1189.

During this time there emerged several Baptist parties. They were all spiritual descendents of the Novatians, Paulicians, Vaudois, and Paterines. There were three major Baptist communities during the tenth, eleventh and twelfth centuries and great men of God led all three.

The Henricians

Henry, a monk of Clugny, preached against the sins of the clergy. As we have seen, Clugny was a city that was known for its purity of doctrine and practice. It is not a surprise that Henry should come forth from that place. In 1116, Henry entered the city of Mans on the first day of Lent. He preached for weeks *against* the worship of saints, infant baptism, works salvation and the corruption of the clergy. Revival broke out. He preached with the same results in different towns across Europe. He was imprisoned in Clugny but escaped. He was arrested at Rheims and imprisoned for life. William Cathcart wrote of him:

> **Monks?** The hermit lifestyle, which started among pagan religions, began among Christians in the third century in the midst of the rampant worldliness in the churches. The first official monk was "St." Anthony, whose followers drew up the first orders for a "monk." Anthony built the first "abbey" in the fifth century followed by Benedict in the sixth.

> Henry, a monk in the first half of the twelfth century, became a great preacher. He was endowed with extraordinary powers of persuasion, and with a glowing earnestness that swept away the greatest obstacles that mere human power could banish. He had the grace of God in his heart. He denounced prayers for the dead, the invocation of saints, the vices of the clergy, the superstitions of the church, and the licentiousness of the age, and he set an example of the sternest morality. He was a master-spirit in talents, and a heaven-aided hero, a John Knox, born in another clime, but nourished upon the same all-powerful grace.
>
> When he visited the city of Mans the inferior clergy became his followers, and the people gave him and his doctrine their hearts, and they refused to attend the consecrated mummeries of the popish churches, and mocked the higher clergy who clung to them. In fact, their lives were endangered by the triumph of Henry's doctrines. The rich and the poor gave him their confidence and their money, and when Hildebert, their bishop, returned, after an absence covering the entire period of Henry's visit, he was received with contempt and his blessing with ridicule. Henry's great arsenal was the Bible, and all opposition melted away before it.
>
> He retired from Mans and went to Provence, and the same remarkable results attended his ministry; persons of all ranks received his blessed doctrines and forsook the foolish superstitions of Rome and the churches in which they occupied the most important positions. At and around Thoulouse his labors seem to have created the greatest indignation and alarm among the few faithful friends of Romanism, and Catholics in the most distant parts of France heard of his overwhelming influence and his triumphant heresy with great fear. In every direction for many miles around he preached Christ, and at last Pope Eugene III, sent a cardinal to overthrow the heretic and his errors. He wisely took within him, in 1147, the

Ch. 7—Churches of the Tenth, Eleventh and Twelfth Centuries

celebrated St. Bernard. This abbot had the earnestness and the temper of Richard Baxter, whom he resembled in some respects. He was a more eloquent man, and he was probably the most noted and popular ecclesiastic in Europe. He [St. Bernard] speaks significantly for the state of things which he found in Henry's field: "The churches (Catholic) are without people, the people without priests, the priests without due reverence, and, in short, Christians are without Christ; the churches were regarded as synagogues, the sanctuary of God was not held to be sacred, and the sacraments were not reckoned to be holy, festive days lost their solemnity, men died in their sins, souls were snatched away everywhere to the dread tribunal. Alas! Neither reconciled by repentance nor fortified by the communion. The life of Christ was closed to the little children of Christians, whilst the grace of baptism was refused, nor were they permitted to approach salvation, although the Saviour lovingly proclaims before them, and says, *Suffer the little children to come to me.*"

Elsewhere, St. Bernard, speaking of Henry and other heretics, says, "They mock us because we baptize infants, because we pray for the dead, because we seek the aid of *glorified* saints."

That Henry had a great multitude of adherents is beyond a doubt, and that he was a Bible Christian is absolutely certain, and that he and his followers rejected infant baptism is the testimony of St. Bernard and of all other writers who have taken notice of the Henricians and their founders. We include to the opinion of Neander that Henry was not a Petrobrusian. **We are satisfied that he and his disciples were independent witnesses for Jesus raised up by Baptists**, and their founder perished in prison (William Cathcart, *Baptist Encyclopedia*, Vol. 1, P. 518).

1. Write Matthew 5:44 twice:

2. When was the first crusade? 1099
3. Name the first order formed to fight for the Holy Roman Empire: Templar Knights
4. For what was Clugny known? Purity of doctrine and practice
5. Name the monk from Clugny that preached against the practices of the Catholic institution? Henry
6. What happened in the city of Mans when Hilderbert returned? recieved with contempt
7. What kind of Christians were the Henricians according to Cathcart? independent witnesses for Jesus raised by baptists
8. True or False: Henry died at the stake. false, he died in prison

****

7.2.1

SECTION TWO

The Petrobrussians

John Horsch wrote:

> The sect of the **Petrobrussians, followers of Peter de Bruys**, spread widely in southern France. In doctrine and practice there was close agreement between them and the Waldsenses. Peter de Bruys was an eloquent evangelist, preaching against the foremost doctrines of Romanism. In 1126 he was burned at the stake as a heretic in St. Gilles. Like the Waldenses,

the Petrobrussians rejected infant baptism, the oath, prayers to the saints, prayers for the dead, adoration of images, and veneration of relics. They agreed with the Waldenses and earlier evangelical parties in giving a strong testimony against all forms of worldliness (John Horsch, *Mennonite History*, P. 4).

Of Peter de Bruys, and the Petrobrussians, William Cathcart wrote:

Peter de Bruys was the Catholic priest of an obscure parish in France, which he left, early in the twelfth century, when he became a preacher of the gospel.

He taught that baptism was of no advantage to infants, and that only believers should receive it, and he gave a new baptism to all his converts; he condemned the use of churches and altars, no doubt for the idolatry practised in them; he denied that the body and blood of Christ are to be found in the bread and wine of the Supper, and he taught that the elements on the Lord's table are but signs of Christ's flesh and blood; he asserted that the offerings, prayers, and good works of the living could not profit the dead, that their state was fixed for eternity the moment they left the earth. Like the English Baptists of the seventeenth century, and like the Quakers of our day, he believed that it was wrong to sing the praises of God in worship; and he rejected the adoration of crosses, and destroyed them wherever he found them.

It is said that on a Good-Friday the Petrobrusians once gathered a great multitude of their brethren, who brought with them all the crosses they could find, and that they made a large fire of them, on which they cooked meat, and gave it to the vast assemblage. This is told as an illustration of their blasphemous profanity. Their crucifixes, and along with them probably the images of the saints, were the idols they had been taught to worship, and when their eyes were opened they destroyed them, just as the converted heathen will now destroy their false gods. Hezekiah did a good thing in destroying the serpent of brass, which in the wilderness had miraculous powers of healing, when the Israelites began to worship it as a god.

Peter's preaching was with great power; his words and his influence swept over great masses of men, bending their hearts and intellects before their resistless might. "In Provence," says Du Pin, "there was nothing else to be seen but Christians rebaptized, churches profaned or destroyed, altars pulled down, and crosses burned. The laws of the church were publicly violated, the priests beaten, abused, and forced to marry, and all the most sacred ceremonies of the church abolished."

Peter de Bruys commenced his ministry about 1125, and such was his success that in a few years in the places about the mouth of the Rhone, in the plain country about Thoulouse, and particularly in that city itself, and in many parts of "the province of Gascoigne" he led great throngs of men and women to Jesus, and overthrew the entire authority of popes, bishops, and priests.

Peter and his followers were decided Baptists, and like ourselves they gave a fresh baptism to all their converts. They reckoned that they were not believers when first immersed in the Catholic Church, and that as Scripture baptism required faith in its candidates, which they did not possess, **they regarded them as wholly unbaptized**; and for the same reason they repudiated the idea that they rebaptized them, confidently asserting that because of the

> Had the life of this illustrious man been spared, the Reformation probably would have occurred four hundred years earlier under **Peter de Bruys** instead of Martin Luther, and the Protestant nations of the earth would not only have had a deliverance from four centuries of priestly profligacy and widespread soul destruction, but they would have entered upon a godly life with a far more Scriptural creed than grand old Luther, still in a considerable measure wedded to Romish sacramentalism, was fitted to give them (William Cathcart, *Baptist Encyclopedia*, Vol. 2, P. 912).

Ch. 7—Churches of the Tenth, Eleventh and Twelfth Centuries

lack of faith they had never been baptized (William Cathcart, *Baptist Encyclopedia*, Vol. 2, P. 912).

The enemies of the Petrobrussians accused them of:
1. Denying that little children under years of responsibility can be saved by the baptism of Christ; and that the faith of another could benefit those who were unable to exercise their own.
2. Of saying that temples or churches should not be built.
3. Requiring holy crosses [crucifixes used for idol worship] to be broken and burned. They urged their destruction as a Christ-dishonoring idol.
4. Denying the reality of the body and blood of the Lord, as offered daily and constantly in the sacrament (Eucharist) [That is, they denied transubstantiation.]
5. Their enemies further accused them of demanding Scripture for everything and not just the sayings of the fathers.

STOP AND THINK

1. Write Matthew 5:44 twice:

2. From where did the term "Petrobrussian" come?
   followers of Peter de Bruys

3. Why did the Petrobrussians "re-baptize?"
   believed in believers baptism, no advantage in infant baptism

4. What was the name of Peter de Bruys' closest disciple?
   Henry of Telluz

5. What was the fate of Peter de Bruys?
   burned at the stump in St. Giles

PETER BRUIS, BURNT AT ST. GILES; HENRY OF TOULOUSE APPREHENDED AND PUT OUT OF THE WAY, BY THE POPE'S LEGATE; AND MANY OTHER PERSONS PUT TO DEATH AT PARIS, ABOUT THE YEARS 1145, 1147.

P. J. Twisck gives the following account in his *Chronijck*, for the year 1145: About this time there were famous in France, Peter Bruis, formerly a priest, and his disciple, Henry of Toulouse; both had been monks, were learned men, and great not small. They called the pope the prince of Sodom, and the city of Rome the mother of all unrighteousness, abomination, and execration. They spoke against the mass, images, pilgrimages, and other institutions of the Roman church. They renounced infant baptism, saying that none but the believing were entitled to baptism.

When Peter had preached about twenty years, namely, from before the year 1126 until 1145, the people flocked to him in great numbers, he was finally publicly burnt in the city of St. Giles, also called St. Aegidius.

His disciple Henry, who followed him in the doctrine, was intercepted and apprehended some time after by the legate of the pope, and put out of the way, so that his fate is not known. This is held to have occurred two years after the death of Peter Bruis, namely A.D. 1147.

After their death **a cruel persecution arose against all those who had followed their doctrine**, many of whom went joyfully to meet death. In short, however assiduously the popes with all their shaved heads aided by princes and secular magistrates, exerted themselves to exterminate them, first, by disputations, then by banishment and papal excommunications and anathemas, proclamation of crusades, indulgences, and pardons to all those who should do violence to said people, and, finally by all manner of torment, fire, gallows, and cruel bloodshedding, yea, so that the whole world was in commotion on account of it; yet, could they not prevent this persuasion from spreading everywhere. And going forth into every country and kingdom, holding their worship secretly as well as openly, with great or small numbers, according to the tyranny, cruelty or persuasion of the times, and continuing until the year 1304; of whom over a hundred persons were put to death, or burnt, at Paris. Thus their descendants, as history states, continued, though under much tribulation, until this time. P. J. Twisck, Chron., page 450, from Philip Marnix Tafer, 3d part, cap. 12, fol. 141, 142. Merula, fol. 748, 853. Hist. Mart. Doopsg., fol. 15. Also, Introduction, page 49. (Thieleman J. Van Braght *Martyr's Mirror, or Bloody Theatre of the Defenseless Christians*, P. 293).

The Collegiate Baptist History Workbook

6. What happened to the Petrobrussians after Bruys' death?

Cruel persecution

****

7.2.2

As we have said, there were three major Baptist groups during the tenth, eleventh and twelfth centuries and great men of God led all three. We have briefly examined the Henricians and the Petrobrussians. We will now look at the Arnoldists and their leader, Arnold of Brescia.

Arnold of Brescia and the Arnoldists

G. H. Orchard wrote:

> **A reformer now appeared in Italy**, and one who proved himself a powerful opponent to the church of Rome, and who in fortitude and zeal was inferior to no one bearing that name, while in learning and talents he excelled most. This was **ARNOLD of BRESCIA**; a man allowed to have been possessed of extensive erudition, and remarkable for his austerity of manners; he traveled into France in early life, and became a pupil of the renowned Peter Abelard. On leaving this school, he returned into Italy, and assumed the habit of a monk, began to propagate his opinions in the streets of Brescia, where he soon gained attention. He pointed his zeal at the wealth and luxury of the Roman clergy. The eloquence of Arnold aroused the inhabitants of Brescia. They revered him as the apostle of religious liberty, and rose in rebellion against the bishops. The church took an alarm at his bold attacks; and in a council, (113) he was condemned to perpetual silence (M'Crie's *History of the Reform. in Italy*, p. 3, &c).
>
> Not only were great fees required by the clergy for every duty to the living and the dead, but when any malady prevailed in a nation, as in France, A.D. 996, the afflicted were taught to propitiate heaven, by giving their property to the clergy, and as the tenth century drew to a close (999), a general panic prevailed throughout the catholic world, from Rev. 20:2-4, that the last judgment was approaching. Arnold left Italy, and found an asylum in the Swiss canton of Zurich. Here he began his system of reform, and succeeded for a time, but the influence of Bernard made it necessary for him to leave the canton. This bold man now hazarded the desperate experiment of visiting Rome, and fixing the standard of rebellion in the very heart of the capitol. In this measure, he succeeded so far as to occasion a change of the government, and the clergy experienced for ten years a reverse of fortune, and a succession of insults from the people. The pontiff struggled hard, but in vain, to maintain his ascendancy. He at length sunk under the pressure of the calamity. Successive pontiffs were unable to check his popularity. Eugenius III withdrew from Rome, and Arnold,

> "Arnold," says Gibbon, "presumed to quote the declaration of Christ, that his kingdom was not of this world. The abbots, the bishops, and the pope himself, must renounce their state, or their salvation." The people were brave, but ignorant of the nature, extent, and advantages of a reformation. The people imbibed, and long retained the color of his opinions. His sentiments also were influential on some of the clergy in the Catholic church. He was not devoid of discretion, he was protected by the nobles and the people, and his services to the cause of freedom; his eloquence thundered over the seven hills. He showed how strangely the clergy in vice had degenerated from the primitive times of the church. He confined the shepherd to the spiritual government of his flock. It is from the year 1144 that the establishment of the senate is dated, as a glorious era, in the acts of the city (G. H. Orchard, *A Concise History Of Foreign Baptists: taken from the New Testament, etc.*, P. 150).

Ch. 7—Churches of the Tenth, Eleventh and Twelfth Centuries

taking advantage of his absence, impressed on the minds of the people the necessity of setting bounds to clerical authority; but the people, not being prepared for such liberty, carried their measures to the extreme, abused the clergy, burnt their property, and required all ecclesiastics to swear to the new constitution. Arnold maintained his station above ten years, while two popes, either trembled in the Vatican, or wandered as exiles in the adjacent cities. [Ro. Hist. ch. 69] The pope having mustered his troops, and placing himself at their head, soon became possessed of his official dignity. Arnold's friends were numerous, but a sword was no weapon in the articles of his faith.

Who can question the necessity of a reform? From the immense wealth of the (Catholic) church, idleness and every evil was found among the clergy. Religion was a jest! A dispute existed as to which liturgy, the Gothic or Roman, should be used in the church, this was decided by single combat (Mosheim v. ii. p. 220). The festivals of fools and [donkeys] were established in most churches. On days of solemnity, they created a bishop of fools; and a [donkey] was led into the body of the church, dressed in a cape and four-cornered cap, When the people were dismissed, it was by the priests braying three times like a [donkey,] and the people responded in an asinine tone. (See Jones's Lect. v. i. p. 534).

Yet, for his efforts, Arnold, in the eyes of clergymen, and state writers, was a sad heretic (Moshiem. Hist. v. ii. P. 318).

In 1155, this noble champion was seized, crucified, and burnt. His ashes were thrown into the river. The clergy triumphed in his death; with his ashes, his sect was dispersed; his memory still lives in the minds of the Romans. Though no corporeal relic could be preserved to animate his followers, the efforts of Arnold in civil and religious liberty were cherished in the breasts of future reforming spirits, and inspired those mighty attempts, in Wickliff, Huss, and others. (See Jones's Lect., v. ii. p. 211. Hist., v. ii. P. 318.)

Arnold's memory was long and fondly cherished by his countrymen, and his tragical end occasioned deep and loud murmurs; it was regarded as an act of injustice and cruelty, the guilt of which lay upon the pope and his clergy, who had been the occasion of it. The disciples of Arnold, who were numerous, obtained the name of ARNOLDISTS; these separated from the communion of the church of Rome, and long continued to bear their testimony against its numerous abuses. (See Allix's *Churches of the Piedmont* P. 170.)

> **MANY CHRISTIANS BURNT IN FLANDERS, A.D. 1183 AND VERY MANY PUT TO DEATH IN OTHER PLACES**
>
> For the year 1183 we read of many more such people, who were called publicans (of which name we have already spoken) and whom Philip, Count of Flanders, and William, Archbishop of Rheims, caused, most unmercifully, to be burnt.
>
> Concerning this, Rigordus, an ancient historian of those times, writes as follows for said year: "At this time, very many heretics (thus this papistic writer calls the true Christians), were burnt in Flanders, by the reverend bishop of Rheims, cardinal priest of the title of Sancta Sabina, Legate of the Pope, and by Philip, the illustrious count of Flanders, *rig. p. 168, edit. Wechelian.*
>
> "The same year," says the above author, "over seven thousand Cottarelli (Thus he calls the pious witnesses of Jesus, also called Waldenses and Albigenses), were slain in the province of Bourges, by the inhabitants of the land, who all united against them, as against the enemies of God.
>
> Notice here, that they must all have been defenseless people, since so great a number suffered themselves to be put to death by so few people as there were at that time in the small province of Bourges; however, we leave this to God.
>
> The same writer adds also this: "In the same year, Pope Lucius condemned as heretics those who in Italy were called Humilitani, and in France, Poor Men of Lyons (the Albigenses and Waldenses), whereupon, as may well be supposed, no small persecution took place in those hot times."
>
> This decree, it seems, was the first published, or else renewed, A.D. 1184, or, as others state A.D. 1885, according to the account of Mellinus, *2d book, fol. 443, col. 2.* (T. J.Van Braght, *Martyr's Mirror*, P. 297).

[Arnold] considered the clergy should be divested of all their worldly possessions, and live on the contributions of the people. The Arnoldists condemn the (catholic) sacraments, particularly baptism, which they administer only to the adult. They do not believe infant baptism, alleging that place of the gospel, whoever shall believe and he baptized shall be saved. (See Wall's *Hist.*, P. 2, and Allix' *Churches of the Piedmont* P. 140.)

Arnold was condemned by the Lateran council of 1139 for rejecting infant baptism. Arnold had laid to his charge, that he was unsound in his judgment about the sacrament of the altar and infant baptism. He is said to have held the opinion of Berengarius, and that from him the Waldenses were (sometimes) called Arnoldists. Arnold denied that baptism should be administered to infants (G. H. Orchard, *A Concise History Of Foreign Baptists: taken from the New Testament, etc.*, P. 150-3). _____

1. Write Matthew 5:44 twice:

2. What were the three Baptist groups of the tenth, eleventh and twelfth centuries?
   Henricians, Petrobrussians, Arnoldists
3. Where did Arnold first begin to preach?
   Brescia
4. Against what did he preach?
   Authoritative structure
5. According to Cathcart, who protected Arnold in the beginning of his ministry?
   Nobles and people
6. When Arnold left Italy, where did he go?
   Zurich
7. True or False: Arnold was hanged for his beliefs.
   False - burned at the stake

Chapter Eight
Churches of the Thirteenth and Fourteenth Centuries

Section One: The Lateran Councils. The War on the Albigenses.
Section Two: Wycliff

SECTION ONE

Time Line Thirteenth Century:
1198. Innocent III elected pope
1203. Constantinople taken by Crusaders
1208. England put under an interdict
1208-1238. War against the Albigenses
1215. Fourth Council of the Lateran. Innocent sanctions the Dominican and Franciscan Orders of Mendicant Friars
1229. The Council of Toulouse. The Reading of the Bible forbidden. The oath of allegiance to "Holy Mother Church" was instigated. The oath had to be repeated every two years.
1240. First Crusade of St. Louis
1270. Second Crusade and death of St. Louis
1274. Second Council of Lyons
1294. Election of Pope Celestine V
-----. Election of Pope Boniface VIII

The Lateran Councils—Permission to Murder

As the dark ages grew even darker, the Roman church began to call councils to help put out the fires started by the Bible-believing independent churches. The greatest of these churches was collectively known as the Albigenses.

The Albigenses differed from the Waldenses in that they did not descend from the people of the mountains and valleys of the Alps, but from the Paulicians of the east. The Albigenses made plain their opposition to infant baptism. (See Pivotal Points to Ponder.) For this, the Albigenses were condemned in council in 1119, 1139, and again in 1176. The most devilish of all councils, the Council of Toulouse, was held in 1229. J. M. Carroll wrote:

> The first of these Lateran or Western Councils, those called by the popes, was called by Calixtus II [in A.D. 1119]. There were present about 300 bishops. At this meeting **it was decreed that Roman priests were never to marry**. This was called the *celibacy of the priests.* We of course do not attempt to give all things done at these meetings.
>
> Years later, A.D.1139, Pope Innocent II, called another of these Councils especially to condemn two groups of very devout Christians, known as Petro-Brussians and Arnoldists.
>
> Alexander III called yet another [in 1176], just forty years after the last. In that was condemned what they called the "Errors and Impieties" of the Waldenses and Albigenses.
>
> Another was called by Pope Innocent III. This was held in A.D. 1215, and seems to have been the most largely attended of possibly any of these great councils. According to the historical account of this meeting, "there were present 412 bishops, 800 Abbots and priors, Ambassadors from the Byzantine court, and a great number of Princes and Nobles." From the very make-up of this assembly you may know that spiritual matters were at least not alone to be considered.

Ch. 8—Churches of the Thirteenth and Fourteenth Centuries

At that time was promulgated the new doctrine of "**Transubstantiation**," the intended turning of the bread and wine of the Lord's Supper into the actual and real body and blood of Christ, after a prayer by the priest. This doctrine among others, had much to do with stirring up the leaders of the Reformation a few centuries later. This doctrine, of course, taught that all those who participated in the supper actually ate of the body and drank of the blood of Christ. **Auricular confession**: confessing one's sins into the ear of a priest—was another new doctrine seemingly having its beginning at this meeting. But probably the most cruel and bloody thing ever brought upon any people in all the world's history was what is known as the "**Inquisition**," and other similar courts, designed for trying what was called "heresy." The whole world is seemingly filled with books written in condemnation of that extreme cruelty, and yet it was originated and perpetuated by a people claiming to be led and directed by the Lord. For real barbarity there seems to be nothing, absolutely nothing in all history that will surpass it. I would not even attempt to describe it. I will simply refer my readers to some of the many books written on the "Inquisition" and let them read and study for themselves.

And yet another thing was done at this same meeting, as if enough had not been done. It was expressly decreed to extirpate all "heresy." What a black page, yea, many black pages were written into the world's history by these terrible decrees. In A.D. 1229, just 14 years after the last awful meeting, still another meeting was held. (This seems not to have been ecumenical.) It was called the council at Toulouse. Probably one of the most vital matters in all Catholic history was declared at this meeting. At this **it was decreed, the Bible, God's book, should be denied to all laymen, all members of Catholic churches other than priests or higher officials**. How strange a law in the face of the plain teaching of the Word, "Search the scriptures; for in them ye think ye have eternal life: and they are they which testify of me." (See John 5:39.)

Yet another Council was called to meet at Lyons. This was called by Pope Innocent IV, in 1245 A.D. This seems to have been mainly for the purpose of excommunicating and deposing Emperor Frederick I of Germany. The Church, the adulterous bride at the marriage with the State in 313, in the days of Constantine the Great, has now become the head of the house, and is now dictating politics of State government, and kings and queens are made or unmade at her pleasure (J. M. Carroll, *The Trail of Blood*, P. 27-29).

In reviewing the results of the infamous councils let us examine the four most heinous fruits:

1. Celibacy of the Priests.

> *Pivitol Points to Ponder*
>
> **Infant Baptism: from the testimony of Justin Martyr**
>
> There is not a single recorded case in the first two ages of Christian history of the baptism of an unconscious babe. Men have searched this period with a scrutiny and a measure of learning never surpassed to find one undeniable instance of the kind, but the literature of Christianity has been examined in vain, and it ever will be. Justin Martyr gives a full account of the manner of conferring baptism in the later half of the second century: "As many," says he, "as are persuaded and believe that the things which we teach and declare are true, and promise that they are determined to live accordingly, are taught to pray to God, and to beseech him with fasting to grant them the remission for their sins, while we also pray and fast with them. We then lead them to a place where there is water" (**William Cathcart**, *Baptist Encyclopedia*, Vol. 1, P. 578).
>
> It is obvious from this account, that no candidate for baptism would have been an infant, for what infant could be persuaded of anything, or fast with someone, or be led to a place of water to be baptized?

This requirement of the Catholic clergy was in direct violation of I Timothy 4:3. The enforcement of such an unjust law has led to years of heartache and sin within the priesthood of the Roman Catholic Institution. Scandal upon scandal has disgraced the "Church" and rocked her to her foundation and yet she persists in this direct violation of scripture.

2. Transubstantiation.

The simple commemorative Lord's Supper was transformed into a works-salvation sacrament at this time. The bread and juice are simply symbols of the death of Jesus.

3. The Inquisition.

The institutionalizing of persecution is an undeniable fact of history. We will deal with the inquisition later in this chapter.

4. Denial of Access to the Word of God.

This devilish thing has cursed the Catholic institution. Its enforcement was designed to keep "the Church" from following the scriptural practices of the Albigenses.

Scripture to Memorize

Revelation 2:10 Fear none of those things which thou shalt suffer: behold, the devil shall cast some of you into prison, that ye may be tried; and ye shall have tribulation ten days: be thou faithful unto death, and I will give thee a crown of life.

Definitions:

Celibacy: "forbidding Roman Catholic Priests to marry"

Transubstantiation: "the supposed turning of the bread and wine of the Lord's Supper into the actual and real body and blood of Christ"

Inquisition: a cruel system of dealing with "heretics" that included torture, dismemberment and many kinds of satanic death rituals.

1. Write Revelation 2:10 two times.

2. Write the definitions above.

Ch. 8—Churches of the Thirteenth and Fourteenth Centuries

3. The first of the Lateran or Western Councils created a bad situation for the priests, what was it? To what kind of sin do you think it led? *Celibacy of Priests; fornication*

4. How does Justin Martyr's account of baptism in the second century refute infant baptism? *Not able to be persuaded of anything, or led to water*

5. Why were "Catholic" church members denied access to the Word of God? *designed to keep church from following practices of Anabaptists*

6. Name two terrible errors put into effect by the council of 1215. *Transubstantiation, Auricular confession*

****

8.1.2

The Albigenses were known by various names. One of most prominent was *the Cathari*, a nickname that meant *pure* or *holy*. The war against the Albigenses lasted for 30 years, 1208-1238. The war was aggravated by **The council of Toulouse,** which was **held in 1229**. The council called for the extermination of the Albigenses.

The Inquisition

Infamous throughout history, the story of the inquisition should make us weep, cause us anger, and make us sober to serve God in the face of hatred.

The first of three general Inquisitions was instigated by Pope Gregory IX in 1231. It was known as the **Papal Inquisition** for the apprehension and trial of heretics. The name Inquisition is from the Latin verb *inquiro* meaning simply to inquire. The

---

The War on the Albigenses (the Cathari)

The Albigenses received this name from the town of Albi, in France. in and around which many of them lived. The Albigenses were called Cathari, Paterines, Publicans, Paulicians, Good Men, Bogomiles, and they were known by other names. They were not Waldenses. They were Paulicians, either directly from the East, or converted through the instrumentality of those who came from the earlier homes of that people.

Such a host had they become that in 1238 Coloman, the brother of the king of Hungary entered Bosnia to destroy the heretics. Gregory IX congratulated him upon his success, but lived to learn that the Bogomiles were still a multitude. A second crusade led to further butchery, but the blood of martyrs was still the seed of the church, and they continued a powerful body until the conquest of their country by the Turks, in 1463. There was direct communication between these Bogomiles and the Albigenses in France. Matthew Paris++ tells us that the heretic Albigenses in the provinces of Bulgaria, Croatia, and Dalmatia elected Bartholomew as their pope, that Albigenses came to him from all quarters for information on doubtful matters, and that he had a vicar who was born in Carcassone, and who lived near Toulouse.

Reinerius Saceho belonged to the Cathari (not the Waldenses, he was never a member of that community) for seventeen years. He was afterwards [in a terrible betrayal] a Romish inquisitor, and he describes his old friends [the Albigenses], in 1254, in these words:

"Heretics are distinguished by their manners and their words, for they are sedate and modest in their manners. They have no pride in clothes, for they wear such as are neither costly nor mean. They do not carry on business in order to avoid falsehoods, oaths, and frauds, but only live by labor as workmen. Their teachers also are shoemakers and weavers. They do not multiply riches, but are content with what is necessary, and they are chaste, especially the Leonists. **They are also temperate** in meat and drink. They do not go to taverns, dances, or other vanities."

Reinerius mentions several causes for the spread of heresy. His second is that all the men and women, small and great, day and night do not cease to learn, and they are continually engaged in teaching what they have acquired themselves. His third cause for the existence and spread of heresy is the translation and circulation of the Old and New Testaments into the vulgar tongue. These they learned themselves and taught to others. Reinerius** was acquainted with a rustic layman who repeated the whole book of Job, and with many who knew perfectly the entire New Testament. He gives an account of many schools of the heretics, the existence of which he learned in the trials of the Inquisition. Assuredly these friends of light and of a Bible circulated everywhere were worthy of the curses and tortures of men like Reinerius and lordly bigots like St. Bernard. In a council held at Toulouse in 1229 the Scriptures in the language of the people were first prohibited. The Albigenses, surviving the horrid massacre of the Pope's murderous crusaders were forbidden to have the "books of the Old or New Testament, unless a Psalter, a *Breviary*, and a *Rosary*, and they forbade the translation in the vulgar tongue." No doubt many of the members of the council supposed that the Breviary and Rosary were inspired as well as the Psalter (William Cathcart, *Baptist Encyclopedia*, Vol. 1, P. 20).

*Evan's Bosnia, pp 36. 37, 42
++Matthew Paris, at A.D. 1223
**Bibliotheca Patrum, tom 4 p. ii, Coll. 746

Inquisitors went looking for what they condemned as heresy. Although the Inquisition was created to hunt down the "heretical" Cathari, later it extended its devilish activity to include Jews, witches, diviners, blasphemers, and other so-called sacrilegious persons.

If they persisted in their heresy, the offensive heretics were handed over to civil authorities and submitted to mind numbing torture and death. Since the church and state were a perfect union of one mind, this does not dismiss "Holy Mother Church" from blood guiltiness. The inquisitors were largely from the Fransician and Dominican orders.

A second variety of the Inquisition was the infamous **Spanish Inquisition**, authorized by Pope Sixtus IV in 1478. Pope Sixtus tried to establish harmony between the inquisitors and the ordinaries, but was unable to maintain control of the desires of King Ferdinand V and Queen Isabella. Sixtus agreed to recognize the independence of the Spanish Inquisition. This institution survived to the beginning of the nineteenth century, and then was permanently suppressed by a decree on July 15, 1834.

A third variety of the Inquisition was the **Roman Inquisition**. Alarmed by the spread of Protestantism and especially by its penetration into Italy, Pope Paul III in 1542 established in Rome the Congregation of the Inquisition. This institution was also known as the Roman Inquisition and the Holy Office. Six cardinals constituted the original inquisition whose powers extended to the whole church. In its first twelve years, the activities of the Roman Inquisition were restricted almost exclusively to Italy. This meant that in the 1500's the Roman Inquisition turned its wrath on the Waldenses. The Inquisition is still an official office of the Roman Catholic institution.

The War on the Albigenses (the Cathari) Part 2

At the great trial in Toulouse in 1176 they (the Albigenses) would not accept anything as an authority but the New Testament. Throughout their widespread fields of toil from Armenia to Britain, and from one end of Europe to the other, and throughout the nine hundred years of their heroic sufferings and astonishing successes, they have always shown supreme regard for the Word of God. If these men, coming from the original cradle of our race, journeying through Thrace, Bulgaria, Bosnia, Italy, France, and Germany; and visiting even Britain, were not Baptists, they were very like them.

If all the wicked slanders about them were discarded it would most probably be found that some of them had little in common with us, but that the majority, while redundant and deficient in some things as measured by Baptist doctrines, were substantially on our platform.

Reinerius+++ says that the Cathari had 16 churches, the church of the Albanenses, or of Sansano, of Contorezo, of Bagnolenses, or of Bagnolo, of Vincenza, or of the Marquisate, of Florence, of the Valley of Spoleto, of France, of Toulouse, of Cahors, of Albi, of Sclavonia, of the Latins at Constantinople, of the Greeks in the same city, of Philadelphia, of Bulgaria, and of Dugranicia. He says, 'They all derive their origin from the two last.' That is, they are all Paulicians, originally from Armenia. He says that 'the churches number 4000 Cathari, of both sexes, in all the world, but believers innumerable.'

By churches we are to understand communities of *the Perfect* (Albigenses) devoted to ministerial and missionary labor. The believers in the time of Reinerius were counted by millions (William Cathcart, *Baptist Encyclopedia*, Vol. 1, P. 20).

+++Du Pin's Eccles. Hist., ii. 456. Dublin.

STOP AND THINK

1. Write Rev. 2:10 two times.

Ch. 8—Churches of the Thirteenth and Fourteenth Centuries

2. Who were the Albigenses and from where did they come?
   Albi, France - Paulicians
3. What council ordered the extermination of the Albigenses? *- Toulouse in 1229*
4. By what other names were the Albigenses known?
   Bosomiens, Publicans, Patennes, Paulicians
5. Who turned his back on the Cathari (Albigenses) and became a Romish inquisitor?
   Meinerius Sansono
6. Name five characteristics of the Albigenses as described by Saceho:
   No pride in clothes

7. Name the three Inquisitions:
   Romans, Spanish, Papal Inquisitions
****
8.1.3

The War on the Albigenses continued

The valleys of Albi, the region around Toulouse, yea, all France, England, and other kingdoms, furnish us during the thirteenth century, many martyrs, who, were pitiable and most miserable. Yet they suffered with good cheer and even with joy, because of their great confidence in the Lord as being their shield and their life.

According to Van Braght:

> **The persecutions that occurred in this century, by far surpass all other** persecution of which we read in the preceding centuries; for it seemed now as if the very furies of hell, so to speak, had broken loose, to destroy all believers, yea, almost the whole earth.
>
> In the years 1209-12, 1225, 1234, yea, throughout the entire thirteenth century, crusades, or so-called holy, voluntary preparations of war were preached, by order of the pope, for the extermination of the Waldenses and Albigenses, all over the world, but more particularly in the Kingdom of France.
>
> But that they might acquit themselves the more courageously and intrepidly, in exterminating the Albigenses, yea, that they might suffer none of them to remain alive, but kill them by fire, sword, gallows, and other means, the pope most solemnly promised to all who by so doing should meet death, or fall by the weapons of the princes seeking to protect the Albigenses and Waldenses, **full remission of all their past sins**, yea, that they should straightway go to heaven. [This is the same doctrine of atonement taught in Islam.]
>
> This had the effect, that countless multitudes flocked together, as it were, to the honor of God, and for the extirpation of the so-called heresies, in order to obtain forgiveness of sins, and thus dying find salvation; and having, under certain chieftains, been formed into armies they marched forth and engaged alone in murdering, burning, desolating and tyrannizing among the Waldenses and Albigenses, sparing not even the infant in the cradle. It is impossible to relate how great a multitude of these innocent people perished, and under what severe torments, simply on account of their true faith (Thieleman J. Van Braght, *Martyrs Mirror*, P. 304).

All of this suffering was because the Albigenses would not *save their children by baptism*. The Albigenses stood for the truth of the scriptures and refused their infant children to be baptized. That meant a death sentence. One has to wonder if Baptist believers of our day would care to stand for anything under pain of death, much less for believer's baptism.

William Cathcart came to the right conclusion about the Albigenses when he wrote:

> Throughout the nine hundred years of their heroic sufferings and astonishing successes, they have always shown supreme regard for the Word of God. If these men, (the Albigenses, ancestors of the Paulicians) coming from the original cradle of our race, journeying through Thrace, Bulgaria, Bosnia, Italy, France, and Germany, and visiting even Britain, were not Baptists, they were very like them (William Cathcart, *Baptist Encyclopedia*, Vol. 1. P. 20).

As you may read in the informational box, the history of the Inquisition has been called into question. Some historians refuse to believe plain facts. There are Catholic and secular re-writers who have simply changed the facts. How awful are we to allow this history to be rewritten without answer! The Mennonite historian **Thieleman J. Van Braght,** writing in 1660, sensed what might happen to the history of the martyrs and carefully documented their deaths. **Those that killed them recorded their sufferings**. Van Braght lists no less that eight sources who recorded (bragged about?) their part in the Inquisition. Did the Inquisition happen? Van Braght records:

A look at Modern Re-Write

The Fordham University web site has this to say about the Inquisition:

"Inquisitors worked in cooperation with the local bishops. Sentence was often passed in the name of both . The overwhelming majority of sentences seem to have consisted of penances like wearing a cross sewn on one's clothes, going on pilgrimage, etc. The inqusitor's goal was not primarily to punish the guilty but to identify them, get them to confess their sins and repent, and restore them to the fold. **Only around ten percent or less of the cases resulted in execution**, [not according to historians like Van Braght] a punishment normally reserved for obstinate heretics (those who refused to repent and be reconciled) and lapsed heretics (those who repented and were reconciled at one time but then fell back into error)."

The *matter of fact* way the Inquisition is referred to at the Fordham web site is typical of modern historians. The Inquisition never happened, or if it did, it wasn't so bad. Yet we know, appearing before an Inquisition meant you were guilty until proven innocent. According to the record of Arnold, Henry, Peter de Bruys and John Huss, NO DEFENSE WAS ALLOWED. An accused person was only allowed to admit he was wrong.

We wonder how Fordham University would feel about a government that treated its people that way? What do you think?

> One hundred and eighty persons called Albigenses, burnt without the castle Minerve, 1210.
> Sixty persons called Albigenses, burnt for the faith, at Casser, 1211.
> About one hundred person called Albigenses or heretics, burnt for the faith in a tower at Caassas, 1211.
> Fifty persons called Abigenses, burnt for the faith at Chastelnau D'ari, at the close of the year 1211.
> Over four hundred persons called Induti, or Albigenses, burnt for their faith, at Lavaur, or Vaurum, A.D. 1211 (Thieleman J. Van Braght, *Martyrs Mirror*, P. 305-309).

We shall close this section by repeating just one of the martyr stories from the thirteenth century as related by Van Braght:

Ch. 8—Churches of the Thirteenth and Fourteenth Centuries

Previously we stated, that the Albigenses, whose confession we showed both to be good and Scriptural were called by various names. Besides those names already explained, they were also called Induti or Vestiti, that is, the *clothed*, or *covered*.

This, at least, is certain, that they are compared by Mellinus, 2d book, page 433, col. 3, to the Albigenses, called Perfecti; who were also styled, as he shows, *Boni hominess*, that is, *good men*, because they, as it seems, were good and upright in their walk.

Nicholas Bertrand quotes the following from the papistic chronicle of William de Podio Laurentii: "Simon, count of Montfort, hastened with the Lord's (the Roman Pope's) army, to lay siege to the fortress or city, of Vaurum, which Amerius, lord of Montreal and Larack, brother of the lady Geralda, had undertaken to defend for her sake. Within there was no small number of those heretics called Induti, who did not always reside there, but had congregated at that time from distant countries."

"The army of God, therefore," he writes, (the army of the pope) "encompassed the fortress, or city, and gave the besieged no rest night and day."

He then goes on to relate how they dealt with those who had guarded the city, or fortress, "the heretics called Induti, that is, *clothed*, about three hundred, others write, over four hundred, he caused to be burned alive." Nich, Bertrand de Gest. Tholosan., fol. 27.

"A large fire was made of wood," says Robert Altissiodorensis, "and the choice was given to all, either to turn from their errors, or to be burnt alive; whereupon a great number, **over four hundred**, as stated, were found who were so obstinate in their error (as he calls their true faith) that they would rather be burnt than confess the Roman Catholic faith (Thieleman J. Van Braght, *Martyrs Mirror*, P. 309).

---

1. Write Rev. 2:10 two times.

2. What did Van Braght say about the persecutions of the thirteenth century?
   Worst time of history
3. What unbelievable thing did the pope promise to those who lost their lives fighting for the Roman Catholic Church against the defenseless Albigenses? *Absolution — taken away*
   Eternal life and forgiveness of sin
4. What was Cathcart's conclusion about the Albigenses?
   If they were not baptists - they were like them
5. Who carefully documented the deaths of the Albigensian heretics?
   Theilemon J. Van Bragnt
6. What is modern scholarship's attitude toward the Inquisition, the way Fordham University views it? *It was not that bad*
7. What nickname given to the Albigenses meant *clothed* or *covered*?
   induti or vestiti

****

8.2.1
SECTION TWO
Time Line Fourteenth Century:

1300. Boniface celebrates the first jubilee
1303. Death of Boniface
1310. The popes settle at Avignon
1312. Council of Vienne; The Templars dissolved
1330. Walter Lollard burned at the stake
1377. Gregory XI moves the papacy from Avignon to Rome
1378. Beginning of the Great Schism of the West
1384. Death of John Wyclif

Walter Lollard and The Lollards

The Waldenses who migrated into Bohemia had descendents who were Bible believers known as the *Picards*, or sometimes called the *Beghards*. In 1315, a great preacher named **Walter Lollard** became a "barb" or pastor, among them of great favor and usefulness. Lollard brought revival to the Albigenses also by his powerful preaching. He seemed to be everywhere and had great influence with the Waldenses, and took their doctrines into England, where they prevailed all over the kingdom.

Mosheim remarks that Walter was a "Dutchman, and was a chief among the *Beghards*, or brethren of the free Spirit. He was a man of learning and of remarkable eloquence, and famous for his writings. Walter Lollard was in unity of views in doctrine and practice with the Waldenses."

Lollard was also a great success among the Baptists along the Rhine River according to Peter Allix, and his converts flooded England which led to a revival among the baptized believers of the islands. The Lollards vehemently denied infant baptism, which led to their severe persecution.

In 1320, Walter Lollard was apprehended and burnt. With that, the Beghards (Picards) on the Rhine in Germany lost their chief leader. Around 1330, the Lollards were placed under the persecuting punch of **Eachard**, a *Jacobian monk*. The people faced terrible oppression as only the Inquisition could bring. However, after torturing and inflicting pain upon the Lollards of Germany for a certain length of time, Eachard had to face the truth. He began to investigate seriously the grievances and errors of which the Lollards (Picards) preached. He began to see their reasons for separation from Rome as true. **He embraced the doctrines of salvation by grace** and openly rejected infant baptism and joined the communion of the Lollards! As you might imagine, the Inquisition went in hot pursuit of their converted inquisitor. They caught up with him in Heidelberg, where he was burned at the stake for the faith of Jesus Christ.

The Lollards spread throughout Europe, and became notorious defenders of the faith:

> That the denial of the right of infants to baptism was a principle generally maintained among the **Lollards**, is abundantly confirmed by the historians of those times (Daniel Neal, *History of the Puritans*, Vol. II, P. 354).

The truths that the Lollards lived and preached thrived. Their churches and societies increased and influenced all of Europe and most importantly, England. These missionary-minded people went to England to preach the Gospel and stir the truth of the word of God. One of their own would be the first of a mighty chain of men who would bring the word of God to the English speaking world, and as Providence would have it, from there the word of God would circle the globe.

Ch. 8—Churches of the Thirteenth and Fourteenth Centuries

The Twelve Conclusions of the Lollards

The Twelve Conclusions of the Lollards are preserved in their original English form in Roger Dymok's Against the Twelve Heresies of the Lollards, an elaborate refutation of each of the heresies, written in 1396-97 for Richard II.

We poor men, treasurers of Christ and his Apostles, denounce to the Lords and the Commons of the Parliament certain conclusions and truth for the reformation of the Holy Church of England, the which has been blind and leprous many years by the maintenance of the proud prelacy, borne up with flattering of private religion, the which is multiplied to a great charge and onerous [to] people here in England.

The First Conclusion: State of the Church
When the Church of England began to dote in temporality after her stepmother, the great Church of Rome, and churches were slain by appropriation to diverse places. Faith, Hope, and Charity began for to flee out of our Church. For Pride with his sorry genealogy

of deadly sins challengeth it by title of heritage. This conclusion is general and proved by experience, custom, and manner, as you shall after hear.

The Second Conclusion: The Priesthood
The Second Conclusion is this: Our usual priesthood, the which began in Rome feigned of a power higher than angels, is not the priesthood the which Christ ordained to his Apostles. This conclusion is proved: for the priesthood of Rome is made with signs, rites, and bishops' blessings, and that is of little virtue.

The Third Conclusion: Clerical Celibacy
The Third Conclusion, sorrowful to hear, is: That the law of continence annexed to priesthood, that in prejudice of women was first ordained, induces sodomy in the Holy Church;

The Fourth Conclusion: Transubstantiation
The Fourth Conclusion that most harms the innocent people is this: That the sacrament of bread induces all men but a few to idolatry, for they [believe] that Christ's body, that never shall out of heaven, by virtue of the priest's word should be essentially enclosed in a little bread, that they show to the people

The Fifth Conclusion: Exorcisms and Hallowings

The fifth conclusion is this: that exorcisms and hallowings, made in the church, of wine, bread, and wax, water, salt, oil and incense, the stone of the altar, upon vestment, miter, cross, and pilgrim staffs be the very practice of necromancy rather than of the holy theology.

The Sixth Conclusion: Clerics in Secular Offices

[margin note: Separation of church and state]

The sixth conclusion that maintaineth much pride is: that a king and a bishop all in one person, a prelate and a justice in temporal cause, a curate and an officer in worldly service, make every realm out of good rule. This conclusion is openly showed, for temporality and spirituality be two parts of Holy Church and therefore he that hath taken him to the one should not meddle him with the other

The Seventh Conclusion: Prayers for the Dead

The Seventh conclusion that we mightily affirm is: that special prayers for dead men's souls made in our church, preferring one by name more than another, this is the false ground of alms deeds, on the which all alms houses in England be wickedly grounded.

The Eighth Conclusion; Pilgrimages

The eighth conclusion needful to tell the people beguiled is the pilgrimage, prayers, and offerings made to blind and deaf images of tree and stone be near kin to idolatry and far from alms deeds.

The Ninth Conclusion: Confession

The ninth conclusion that holdeth the people low is, that the articles of confession that is said necessary to the salvation of man, with a feigned power of absolution enhanceth priests' pride, and giveth them opportunity of calling other than we will not say.

The Tenth Conclusion: War, Battle, and Crusades

The tenth conclusion is that manslaughter by battle or law of righteousness for temporal cause or spiritual with out special revelation is express contrary to the New Testament, the which is a law of grace and full of mercy.

The Eleventh Conclusion: Female Vows of Continence and Abortion.

The eleventh conclusion is shameful for to speak: that a vow of continence made in our church of women, the which be fickle and imperfect in kind, is the cause of bringing in of a most horrible sin possible to man kind. For though slaying of children ere they be christened, abortion, and destroying of kind by medicine be full sinful.

The Twelfth Conclusion: Arts and Crafts.

The twelfth conclusion is that the multitude of crafts not needful used in our church nourisheth much sin in waste, curiosity, and disguising.

Ch. 8—Churches of the Thirteenth and Fourteenth Centuries

Definitions:
Lollard: nickname given to the followers of Walter Lollard and later John Wycliff
Beghards: Bohemian name for the Waldenses, sometimes called "Picards"

---

1. Write Revelation 2:10 two times.

2. Write the definition for Lollard and Beghards.
   brethren of the free spirit

3. Who were the Picards? *Beghards - Waldenses of Bohemia*
4. Name the original leader of the Lollards. *Walter Lollard*
5. What member of the Inquisition converted to Christ? What happened to him after he embraced the Lollards? *Eachard → Burned at the stake*

6. Name three Roman Catholic practices condemned by the Lollard conclusions.
   The state of the church, transubstantiation, celibacy
7. How is abortion (the murder of the unborn) described in the Lollard conclusions?
   sinful slaying

****
8.2.2

John Wycliffe

The fourteenth century introduced a group of men who paved the way for the Reformation. We shall look at the Reformation in the next chapters, but the events surrounding these men ushered in the great changes of the Reformation.

Our first key man leading to the Reformation was **John Wycliffe**. He was from England, (1329-1384) and came under the influence of the Lollards early in his ministry. He then became their leader, being forever associated with them.

Courtney, when bishop of London, was strenuous in his opposition to Wyckliff, he was afterwards appointed to the See of Canterbury; and as [Wycliffe] himself was protected from the effects of his power, [Courtney] engaged in persecuting [Wycliffe's] followers, who were called the *Lollards*; one of those names of reproach by which the followers of Christ have been reviled in all ages. It is supposed to have been derived from Walter Lollardus, one of the teachers of these truths on the continent, or from a German word 'lollen,' which signifies psalm-singers. Many of them, who were preachers, traveled about the country, in the simplest manner, barefoot and in common frieze gowns, preaching in the market-places, and teaching the doctrines of truth with great zeal and much success. In a few years, their numbers were very considerable; it was calculated that at least one fourth of the nation were really or nominally inclined to these sentiments.

Wycliffe was born in Hipswell, England of Saxon descent. He received the Doctor of Theology degree from Oxford University in 1372. He served as an envoy to France, and represented his native England in a dispute with the Pope. Upon his return, he wrote against the secular power of the papacy. He was threatened by the Vatican, but continued to write against its abuses. He argued against the infallibility of the Pope.

Wycliffe's great struggle was to get the Gospel to the common people. His messages were to bring a simplicity to the Gospel that he felt had been complicated by the religious institutions. He became a confrontational preacher, yet his messages were filled with hope.

In answer to the question, "How must the Word of God be preached?" Wycliffe once answered, "Appropriately, simply, directly, and from a devout, sincere heart."

When the Bishop of London prohibited him from preaching, Wycliffe confined himself to writing and translating the Bible from Latin to English.

Persecutions were poured out upon the followers of Wycliffe and upon other Bible-believing Christians from the time of **Henry IV**, who reigned from 1399 to 1413. (Interestingly, Henry IV was the son of John of Gaunt, Duke of Lancaster, the man who protected Wycliffe some two decades prior to Henry's ascension to the throne.) From the time of Henry, "Their blood flowed in a stream for nearly two centuries with slight respite" (Thomas Armitage, *A History of the Baptists*, Vol. 1, P. 323).

Wycliffe died in 1385. It is said in England that ten years after he was dead, if you met two men on the street, one of them was a Lollard. Thirty-one years after his death, the Roman Catholic institution ordered all his books burned, his bones dug up and burned, and his ashes scattered on the Thames River. In the city of Prague there was a great riot because of the influence of Wycliffe 50 to 70 years after he was dead. **He was known as *the Morning Star of the Reformation*.** A hundred and forty-five years later, the Bishop of London wrote to Erasmus and explained to him that the New Testament of William Tindale (who was influenced by Wycliffe) was adding great fuel to the fires of **the Lollards**; meaning that they existed a 145 years after the death of their leader.

In 1401, Henry IV condemned "divers false and perverse people of a new sect; they make unlawful conventicles, they hold and exercise schools, and make and write books." Henry IV's law was called, "The Orthodoxy of the Faith of the Church of England Asserted, And Provision Made Against Oppugners Of The Same, With The Punishment Of Heretics." This meant total control by the Bishops, as if they needed more power. Now, a simple decree of a bishop was enough to send a man to the stake. (See Eadie, *History of the English Bible*, I, P. 84-85.)

In 1400 William Sawtree was burned at the stake, and in 1409 Bradbe was roasted alive in a barrel. And so the persecution ran on. Joseph Ivimey wrote:

> The Lollard's Tower still stands as a monument of their miseries, and of the cruelty of their implacable enemies. This tower is at Lambeth palace, and was fitted up for this purpose by Chicheley, Archbishop of Canterbury, who came to his See in 1414. It is said that he expended two hundred and eighty pounds to make this prison for the Lollards. The vast staples and rings to which they were fastened, before they were brought out to the stake, are still to be seen in a large lumber-room at the top of the palace, and ought to make protestants

Ch. 8—Churches of the Thirteenth and Fourteenth Centuries

look back with gratitude upon the hour which terminated so bloody a period (Joseph Ivimey, *History of the English Baptists*, P. 71-2).

1. Write Revelation 2:10 two times.

2. Where did Wycliff preach? London, England
3. Did Wycliff suffer martyrdom? What unusual thing happened to his writings?
   no   they were burned

4. Who prohibited Wycliff from preaching?
   Bishop of London
5. What was the prison in London called?
   Lollards tower

Chapter Nine
The Churches of the Fifteenth Century
Section One: Sawtree, Huss, Savonarola
Section Two: Evidences of Baptist people in Europe and England

SECTION ONE
Time Line Fifteenth Century:
1414-1418. Council of Constance
1415. Pope John XXIII deposed
----. John Huss burnt by order of the Council
1417. Election of Pope Martin V and end of the Schism
1418. Religious war of Bohemia breaks out
1431. Council of Basel opened
1438. Council of Ferrara and Florence
1453. The Turks, under Sultan Mahomet II, became masters of Constantinople.
1455. Invention of Printing
1464. Pope Pius II vainly attempts a crusade
1498. Death of Savonarola

Scripture to Memorize

2 Corinthians 4:4 In whom the god of this world hath blinded the minds of them which believe not, lest the light of the glorious gospel of Christ, who is the image of God, should shine unto them.

If ever the dark ages were dark, they were darkest in the fifteenth century.

We three (or four) Popes (again)

In 1378 the College of Cardinals elected a new pope, an Italian who was called **Urban VI**. He held himself vastly above the cardinals, wishing to reform them violently, and to lord it over them in a style which they had not been used to. By such conduct he provoked them to oppose him. They objected that he had not been freely chosen, and also that he was not in his right mind, and a party of them met at Fondi and chose another pope, **Clement VII**, a Frenchman, who settled at **Avignon**.

Thus began what is called **the Great Schism of the West**. There were now two rival popes: one of them having his court at **Rome**, and the other at **Avignon**; At length, it seemed as if the breach were to be healed by a council held at Pisa in 1409, which set aside both the rivals, and elected **a new pope, Alexander V**. But it was found that the two old claimants would not give way; and thus the council of Pisa, in trying to cure the evil of having two popes, had saddled the "Church with a third."

Alexander did not hold the papacy quite eleven months (June 1409 to May 1410.) He had fallen wholly under the power of a cardinal named Balthasar Cossa; and this cardinal was chosen to succeed him, under the name of **John XXIII**. John was one of the worst men who ever held the papacy. It is said that he had been a pirate, and that from this he had got the habit of waking all night and sleeping by day. He had been governor of Bologna, where he had indulged himself to the full in cruelty, greed, and other vices. He was even suspected of having poisoned Alexander; and, although he must no doubt have been a very clever man, it is not easy to understand how the other cardinals could have chosen one who was so notoriously wicked to the papacy.

Ch. 9—The Churches of the Fifteenth Century

When Pope John had been got rid of, Gregory XII, the most respectable of the three rival popes, agreed to resign his claims. But the third pope, Benedict VIII, would hear of no proposals for his resignation, and shut himself up in a castle on the coast of Spain, where he not only continued to call himself pope, but after his death two popes of his line were set up in succession. The council of Constance, however, finding Benedict obstinate, did not trouble itself further about him, and went on to treat the papacy as vacant. (See Robinson's *Church History*.)

Of Sawtree, Huss and Savonarola

William Sawtre

William Sawtre, a *Lollard* or follower of Wycliff, was the first English martyr burned alive for opposing the abominations of Popery. He was priest of St. Osyth's in the city of London; and although at one time he had been induced to renounce before the bishop of Norwich the sentiments he held, yet he was enabled, by the grace of God, to see his error and again openly to profess the truths of the gospel.

On February 12, 1401, he was summoned to appear before the archbishop of Canterbury and accused of holding heretical opinions. The principal articles against him were that he had said, "He would not worship the cross on which Christ suffered, but only Christ that suffered upon the cross; (In this he opposed the worshipping of relics or images) that every priest and deacon is more bound to preach the word of God than to say particular services at the canonical hours; and that after the pronouncing of the sacramental words of the body of Christ, the bread remaineth of the same nature that it was before, neither doth it cease to be bread." In this he opposed transubstantiation. He was also in favor of re-distribution of the enormous wealth of the Catholic institution (an idea that did not sit well with the bishops, abbots, friars, priests, etc.) He was hated, not only because he believed those things, but also because he was an impassioned preacher of the truth.

Because the Lollards and William Sawtre had condemned the idolatry of Holy Mother church, the English government moved against them. In 1401 a church war was declared against them, and the law, *De Heretico Comburendo*, was passed against them. This law permitted the burning of heretics, a humane and just form of capital punishment in their perverted eyes. William Sawtre, the fiery rector of Lynn, was the first one committed to the flames.

John Huss

John Huss was ordained to the priesthood of the Roman Catholic Church in 1401 after receiving the Bachelor's and Master's degrees at the University of Prague. He preached against the evils of the church and gained popular acceptance. He was the confessor for the Queen of Bohemia. He was a powerful preacher of Roman doctrine until he translated some of the sermons of John Wycliffe into the Bohemian language. These sermons moved him to cry out for reform in the church and a return to the authority of the Scriptures as the sole source of faith and doctrine for the believer.

Huss maintained that Christ, not Peter, was the foundation of the Church and that some Popes had been heretics. At once Huss was branded a heretic, ex-communicated, and his writings suppressed. He found refuge outside Prague, where he continued to preach, write and study. The chief product of John Wycliffe's pen, *Concerning the Church,* developed Huss' teachings concerning the universal priesthood of all believers, emphasizing that Christ is the only Head of the Church. Because of this, some credit Huss with beginning the reformation that Martin Luther carried to full bloom one hundred years later.

In 1414, Huss was promised safe conduct by the Pope and Emperor Sigismund to the Council of Constance to present his views. Instead of hearing Huss, the council had him arrested, gave him a mock trial without the benefit of a hearing, and condemned him to death as a heretic. He was kept in prison for seven months before he was burned. As Huss stood before the stake he said, "In the truth of the gospel which I have written, taught, and preached, I die willingly and joyfully today." Then the fire was kindled, and as the red tongues of flame driven by the wind from Lake Boden rose high around the body of the martyr, Huss sang, "Jesus Christ, the Son of the Living God, have mercy on me." The Pope dismissed his own broken promise of safe conduct to Huss with, "When dealing with heretics, one is not obligated to keep his word."

> **John Huss and Jerome of Prague by David Benedict:**
>
> Bohemia received the gospel from the Eastern Church, and not from the Church of Rome. Popery, however, was introduced into this kingdom in the ninth century by two Greek monks, but it was not fully established here till the fourteenth century, and then not by the consent of the Bohemians, but by the power and artifice of the emperor Charles IV. About this time, it appears there was an attempt made for a reformation by two of the emperors' chaplains, whose names were Milicius and Janovius. But the attempt proved unsuccessful, and the reformers were suppressed with disgrace. But from this period multitudes withdrew themselves from the public places of worship, and followed the dictates of their own consciences by worshipping God in private houses, woods, and caves. Here they were persecuted, dragooned, drowned, and killed, and thus they went on till the appearance of John Huss and Jerome of Prague.
>
> The names of John Huss and Jerome of Prague are generally mentioned in connection, and Bohemia is rendered famous in ecclesiastical history, on account of their labours. Under the ministry of Huss and Jerome, a work commenced in this kingdom, more than a hundred years before the rise of Luther and Calvin, which, in some respects, was similar to the reformation under them; for it began upon spiritual principles, and arose to a thing of a political consequence. Both Huss and Jerome were destroyed by the council of Constance, in 1415. Jerome is said to have been a far more distinguished man than his friend Huss; but, for what reason I have not learnt, the followers of both were called Hussites.
>
> Huss was professor of divinity in the university of Prague, a preacher in one of the largest churches in the city, and a man of eminent abilities and more eminent zeal. He taught much of the doctrine of Wickliff. His talents were popular, his life was irreproachable, and his manners the most affable and engaging. He was the idol of the people, but execrated by the priests. He was not a Baptist, but as his sermons were full of what are called Anabaptistical errors, Wickliffites, Waldenses, and all sorts of hereticks became his admirers and followers, and as he, in the spirit of a true Bohemian, endeavoured to curb the tyranny of the churchmen (who the nobles knew were uniting with the house of Austria to enslave the state) he was patronized by the great, and all Bohemia was filled with his doctrine and his praise.
>
> The cruel fate of these two eminent men produced very astonishing effects in Bohemia. The news of their death flew like lightning all over the kingdom, and it was soon all in an uproar.
>
> The barbarous conduct of the council of Constance was considered (as all other events are) in very different lights by different people, according to their various interests and passions. The pious mourned the loss of these two eminent servants of God, while others were filled with resentment for the insult to their nation (David Benedict, *History of the Baptists*, Vol. 1, P.153-4).

Ch. 9—The Churches of the Fifteenth Century

The martyrdom of Huss kept the hope for reformation going for a hundred years. It also served as a warning. A century later Martin Luther was warned against going to Leipzig even when promised a safe conduct by the Pope.

The influence of Huss lived on through his preaching and the godly example of his death. The Bible believing sect of the *Moravians* sprang from him.

Definitions:

Moravians: a group of Bible believers in Bohemia who sprang from the ministry of John Huss.

1. Write 2 Corinthians 4:4 twice.
2. Who became pope at the same time? *Alexander VI, Urban VI, Clement VII*
3. Who was the first English martyr to be burned for opposing the Pope? *William Sawtre*
4. True or False: Sawtre was a Lollard. *True*
5. What was the name of the law that allowed the burning of heretics? *De Heretico Comburendo*
6. Name the University John Huss attended. *University of Prague*
7. Who offered safe conduct to Huss so that he might present his views? *The Pope*
8. What Bible believing group sprang from Huss and his ministry? *Moravians*

****

9.1.2

Savonarola

Savonarola was born in 1452 at Ferrara, where his grandfather had been physician to the duke; and his family wished him to follow the same profession. But Jerome was set on becoming a monk, and from this nothing could move him. He therefore joined the Dominican friars, and after a while he was removed to St Mark's, at **Florence**, Italy a famous convent of this order. He found things in a bad state there; but he was chosen prior (or head) of the convent, and reformed it, so that it rose in character, and the number of the monks was much increased. He also became a great preacher, so that even the vast cathedral of Florence could not hold the crowds, which flocked to hear him. He was especially fond of preaching on the dark prophecies of the Revelation, and of declaring that the judgments of God were about to come on Florence and on all Italy because of sin. (See Robinson's *Church History*.)

Savonarola became an early reformer. He was not thorough, but turned the mind of Europe toward reform. He was arrested when a dispute with a friar carried on too long for the public to endure. They turned on both men and arrested them.

Savonarola had a long trial, during which he was often tortured; but whatever might be wrung from him in this way, he afterwards declared that it was not to be believed, because the weakness of his body could not bear the pain of torture, and he confessed whatever might be asked of him. This trial was carried on under the authority of the wicked Pope Alexander VI.

The Collegiate Baptist History Workbook

Although no charge of error as to the faith could be made against Savonarola, in 1498, his enemies were bent on his death; and he with two of his companions were sentenced to be hanged and burnt in the city of Florence.

The Vaudois (Waldenses) Revisited, The Christmas Tragedy of 1400

Dr. J. A. Wylie wrote:

The closing days of the year 1400 witnessed a terrible tragedy, the memory of which has not been obliterated by the many greater which have followed it. The scene of this catastrophe was the Valley of Pragelas, one of the higher reaches of Perosa, which opens near Pinerolo, and is watered by the Clusone. It was the Christmas of 1400, and the inhabitants dreaded no attack, believing themselves sufficiently protected by the snows which then lay deep on their mountains. They were destined to experience the bitter fact that the rigors of the season had not quenched the fire of their persecutor's malice. Borelli, at the head of an armed troop, broke suddenly into Pragelas, meditating **the entire extinction of its population**. The miserable inhabitants fled in haste to the mountains, carrying on their shoulders their old men, their sick, and their infants, knowing what fate awaited them should they leave them behind. In their flight a great many were overtaken and slain. Nightfall brought them deliverance from the pursuit, but no deliverance from horrors not less dreadful. The main body of the fugitives wandered in the direction of Macel, in the storm-swept and now ice-clad valley of San Martino, where they encamped on a summit which has ever since, in memory of the event, borne the name of the Alberge or Refuge. Without shelter, without food, the frozen snow around them, the winter's sky overhead, their sufferings were inexpressibly great. When morning broke what a heartrending spectacle did day disclose! Some of the miserable group lost their hands and feet from frostbite; while others were stretched out on the snow, stiffened corpses. Fifty young children, some say eighty, were found dead with cold, some lying on the bare ice, others locked in the frozen arms of their mothers, who had perished on that dreadful night along with their babes. In the Valley of Pragelas, to this day, sire recites to son the tale of that Christmas tragedy (J. A. Wylie *The History Of The Waldenses*, P. 26-27).

> Innocent resolved that the Vaudois should no longer exist, and, in 1487, he proclaimed a general crusade against them, and summoned all the Catholic powers of Europe to take up arms for their extermination, absolving beforehand all who should take part in this crusade from all ecclesiastical penalties, general or special, setting them free from the obligation of vows which they might have made, legitimating their possession of goods which they might have wrongfully acquired, and concluding with a promise of the remission of all sins to every one who should slay a heretic. Moreover, he annulled all contracts subscribed in favor of the Vaudois, commanded their domestics to abandon them, forbade anyone to give them any assistance, and authorized all and sundry to seize upon their goods.

1. Write 2 Corinthians 4:4 twice.
2. Savonarola preached in what city? *Florence*
3. What was Savonarola put in charge of in Florence? *Covenant; Dominican St. Marks*
4. What Pope carried on Savonarola's trial? *Alexander VI*
5. Who headed the troop that pushed the Waldenses of Pragelas into the snows the Christmas of 1400? *Borelli*
6. What was the name of the Pope that ordered the extermination of the Vaudois in 1487? *Pope Innocent*

Ch. 9—The Churches of the Fifteenth Century

****

9.2.1
SECTION TWO

At this time, the Reformation was beginning in Europe, which began "Protestantism." The reformers pushed to reform the Roman Catholic institution, but not to separate from it. However separation at different levels occurred all over Europe. Yet, it must be remembered that the Protestants never separated from Rome's *baptism*.

Baptist people were not looking to reform. They had never been a part of Rome throughout the dark ages. Those who were not a part of "Holy Mother Church" were in the ever present terrible valley of decision concerning infant sprinkling.

Some of the Reformers rejected baptismal regeneration, in theory, while others retained it. Baptist people taught scriptural baptism *after* a profession of faith in Christ. To receive believers' baptism was an offense that usually carried the death penalty as punishment.

Evidence of the Baptists in Europe and Great Britain during the Fifteenth Century

We turn our attention to the nineteenth century pastor and author **S. H. Ford**. Ford was the editor of the Christian Repository, and wrote various books and pamphlets defending the ancient origin of the Baptists. From 1860-1890, a great controversy raged between Protestant and Baptist churches over their origins and their baptism. Ford wrote a book entitled *Baptist Origins*:

Samuel Howard Ford by William Cathcart

The son of Thomas H. Ford, was licensed in 1840, passed through the classes in the State University of Missouri, and was ordained in 1843, at Bonne Femme church, in Boone Co., Mo. He became pastor at Jefferson City, Mo., and in two years after of the North church in St. Louis for two years; also at Cape Girardeau, Mo., and the East Baptist Church in Louisville, Kentucky. In 1853 he was associated with Dr. John L. Waller in the editorship of the *Western Recorder and Christian Repository*. Of the latter he is still the editor. (Ford was still living when Cathcart wrote this) His talented wife has written *Grace Truman*, *The Dreamer's Blind Daughter*, and other works of great value. At the breaking out of the war, Dr. Ford went to Memphis, where he preached for some time. For two years he was in Mobile as pastor of the St. Francis Street church. At the close of the war he accepted the pastorate of the Central Baptist church of Memphis, where he preached for seven years, till ill health caused him to resign.

While in this church he was instrumental in building a capacious and splendid house of worship, upon which $75,000 were expended during his pastorate, and in increasing the membership from 75 to 450. Dr. Ford has received the honorary degree of LL.D. He preaches without manuscript, is earnest and eloquent, and many hundreds have been converted under his ministry. He is a firm Baptist, and he has had discussions with Alexander Campbell, Bishop Spaulding, of the Catholic Church, and Dr. N. L. Rice. Dr. Ford is a Hebrew and Syriac scholar; he is well read in general literature, and is specially familiar with the Romish controversy.

In the past twenty-seven years he has written upon almost every subject bearing on the religious issues of the times. He is now sixty years of age, and is as active, energetic, and laborious as ever. Baptists in all parts of our country and the British provinces, and in the British islands, wish length of years to the learned editor of the *Repository*, and to his cultured and talented wife (William Cathcart, *Baptist Encyclopedia*, Vol. 1, P. 404-5).

> The true origin of that sect which acquired the denomination of Anabaptists, by their administering anew the rite of baptism to those who came over to their communion, and derived that of Mennonites, from that famous man to whom they owe much of their present felicity, is hidden in the depths of antiquity, and is of consequence difficult to be ascertained. This uncertainty will not appear surprising when it is considered that this sect started up suddenly in several countries at the same point of time, under leaders of different talents and different intentions, and at the very period when the first contests of the Reformers with the

Roman pontiffs drew the attention of the world, and employed all the pens of the learned in such a manner as to render all other objects and incidents almost matters of indifference.

Mosheim wrote, "the Mennonites (Anabaptists) not only considered themselves descendants of the Waldenses, who were so grievously oppressed and persecuted by the despotic heads of the Romish Church, but pretend, moreover, to be the purest offspring of the respectable sufferers, being equally opposed to all principles of rebellion on the one hand, and all suggestions of fanaticism on the other."

"It may be observed," continues **Mosheim**, "that they are not entirely in an error when they boast of their descent from the Waldenses, Petrobrussians, and other ancient sects, who are usually considered as witnesses of the truth in times of general darkness and superstition. *Before the rise of Luther and Calvin*, there lay concealed in almost all the countries of Europe, particularly in Bohemia, Monrovia, Switzerland, and Germany, many persons who adhered tenaciously to the doctrine, etc., which is the true source of all the peculiarities that are to be found in the religious doctrine and discipline of the Anabaptists." (See Mosheim's *History of the Mennonites or Anabaptists*, *Eccl. Hist.* (New York: Harper Bros., V 2, 1871), P 128.) These words of the learned Pedobaptist (Lutheran) historian we have given in full, for all ought to know them. (See S. H. Ford, *Origin of the Baptists*.)

Mr. Ford points out the fact that the great Lutheran historian, Mosheim, testified to the existence of Baptist people throughout the dark ages.

S. H. Ford gives evidences of Baptist presence in Wales from the Fifteenth Century

The vale of Carleon is situated between England and the mountainous parts of Wales, just at the foot of the mountains. It was for centuries the Piedmont of the Welsh. The Welsh Alps, Mount Merthyn and Tydfyl, the recesses and caverns, were the hiding-places of

> Testimonials of ancient Baptist presence from non-Baptist scholarship
>
> "There shall be no faythe more certayne and true, then is the Anabaptistes, seeing there be none nowe, or have bene before time fore ye space of these thousand and two hundred years, who have bene more cruelly punished." Stanislaus Hosius, **President of the Council of Trent of the Catholic Church,** writing in 1565, *Treatise of the Begynnyng of Heresyes*, (Yorkshire, England: The Scholar Press Ltd., 1970), P. 44.
>
> "The Baptists are the only body of known Christians that have never symbolized with Rome." **Sir Isaac Newton**
>
> "It must have already occurred to our readers that the Baptists are the same sect of Christians that were formerly described as Anabaptists. Indeed this seems to have been their leading principle from the time of Tertullian to the present time."
>
> From the *Edinburg Cyclopedia* **(Presbyterian).**

Christ's lambs. In this vale, as in other portions of Wales, the ordinances of Christ had been administered since the time of the Apostles. So soon as the Reformation occurred in England, and spread into Wales, communication was at once opened between the obscure followers of Christ in the mountain fortresses, and the awakened clergy of the establishment. Of the latter, three distinguished men adopted the sentiments held by those Welsh "heretics," who claimed descent from the Apostles. Their names were Perry, Wroth and Ebury. These henceforth were called the Baptist Reformers, because they were of the Reformation, and had joined with the Baptists. We will now let the **History of the Welsh Baptists** present the facts in the case:

It is no wonder that Perry, Wroth, and Ebury, commonly called the first Baptist Reformers in Wales, should have so many followers at once, when we consider that the field of their labors was the vale of Carleon and its vicinity. As they were learned men belonging to that religion established by law, and particularly as they left that establishment and joined the poor Baptists, their names are handed down to posterity, not only by their friends, but also by their foes, because more notice was taken of them than of those scattered Baptists on the mountains of the

Ch. 9—The Churches of the Fifteenth Century

principality (Wales). If this denomination had existed in the country since the year 63, and so severely persecuted, it must be, by this time, an old *thing*. But the men who left the Popish establishment were the chief objects of their rage, particularly as they headed the sect everywhere spoken against, and recognized Baptist churches. **The vale Olchan**, [the Baptists of the valley of Olchan were called *the Olchan*] also, is situated between mountains almost inaccessible. How many hundred years it had been inhabited by Baptists before William Ebury, it is impossible to tell. It is a fact that cannot be controverted, that there were Baptists here at the commencement of the Reformation; and no man upon earth can tell when the church was formed, and who began to baptize in this little Piedmont. Whence came these Baptists? It is universally thought to be the oldest church, but how old none can tell. We know that, at the separation, they had a minister named HOWELL VAUGHAN, quite a different sort of Baptist from Ebury. Vavasor Powell, and others, had come out from the Established Church. And this is not to be wondered at; for they had dissented from the Church of England, and had, probably, brought some of her corruptions with them. But **the mountain Baptists were not Protestants** or dissenters from the establishment. We know the Reformers were for mixed communion, but **the Olchan received no such practice.**

These are most conclusive evidences that **William Tyndale**, who translated the Bible into the English language, and the four books of Moses into the Welsh language, in 1536, was a Welsh Baptist of that plain, strict, apostolic order. He lived most of his time in Gloucester, England; but Llewellyn Tyndale and Hezekiah Tyndale were members of the Baptist Church in Abergavenny, South Wales. (See J. Davis, *History Welsh Baptists*, P. 21.) The text of Mosheim is thus fully illustrated by facts. Baptists lay concealed in almost all the countries of Europe before the rise of Calvin and Luther. (See S. H. Ford, *Origin of the Baptists*.)

STOP AND THINK

1. Write 2 Corinthians 4:4 twice.

2. What was the penalty for believer's baptism in the fifteenth century? Death
3. What controversy was raging in 1860 when Ford wrote his book *Baptist Origins*? Wether or not baptist churches came from the protestant reformation
4. What did the Lutheran historian Moshiem say about the Anabaptist people? Baptist were hidden all over Europe before the reformation
5. What astounding thing did the scientist Sir Isaac Newton say about the Baptists? Baptists are only body of christians not a part of rome
6. Who were the three so-called Baptist reformers of Wales? P.P. Erebury
7. The Baptists of the valley of Olchan were called what? The Olchan
8. What famous man, known for translating the Bible in English, is thought to be an ancient Welsh Baptist? William Tyndale

****

9.2.2

Definitions:

Paedobaptist: one who practices the baptism of infants or unbelieving children.

The Collegiate Baptist History Workbook

Evidence of the Baptists in Europe and Great Britain during the Fifteenth Century continued:

Ford described the situation in Bohemia:

> A deep forest, extending three hundred miles in length, and two hundred in breadth, was, in the days of Roman triumph, settled by a tribe of Celts called Boii, who fled to its shelter to avoid the Roman yoke. Hence the word "Bohemia," under which are now included the countries of Silesia and Moravia. A short time before the birth of Christ, Caesar described this Hercynian Forest thus:
>
> It is nine day's journey over. It begins on the confines of the Helvetii, Nemetes, and Rauraci, (that is, Switzerland, Basil, and Spires,) and extends along the Danube to the borders of the Daci and Anartes, (that is, Transylvania,) there turning from the river to the left, it runs through an infinite number of countries. No one could ever yet come to the end of it or know its utmost extent, though some have gone sixty days journey into it.
>
> **This was the Hercynian Forest**, of which the Black Forest was then a part. Amid its depths, Paul tells us he preached the gospel of Christ, and its tribes were visited by Titus (Rom. XV:19, 28; 2 Tim. iv:10). In this wilderness, before the rise of Luther, Mosheim tells us, were Baptists. Thousands of them claim to have been sheltered there in the wilderness from the wrath of the dragon. Is it true? In 1519, six years before Luther appeared before the Diet of Worms, a letter was addressed to Erasmus from Bohemia, thus describing this people:
>
>> These men have no other opinion of the Pope, cardinals, bishops, and other clergy than of manifest Antichrists. They call the Pope sometimes the beast, and sometimes the whore, mentioned in the Revelation. Their own bishops and priests, they themselves do choose for themselves, ignorant and unlearned laymen that have wife and children. They mutually salute one another by the name of brother and sister. They own no other authority than the Scriptures of the Old and New Testament. They slight all the doctors, both ancient and modern, and give no regard to their doctrine. Their priests, when they celebrate the offices of mass, (or communion,) do it without any priestly garments; nor do they use any prayer, or collects on this occasion, but only the Lord's Prayer, by which they consecrate bread that has been leavened. They believe, or own, little or nothing of the sacraments of the church. Such as come over to their sect, must every one be *baptized anew in mere water*. They make no blessing of salt, nor of water; nor make any use of consecrated oil. They believe nothing of divinity in the sacrament of the Eucharist; only that the consecrated bread and wine do, by some occult signs, represent the death of Christ; and, accordingly, that all that do kneel down to it, or that that sacrament other purpose but to worship, are guilty of idolatry; was instituted by Christ to no renew the memory of his passion, and not to be carried about or held up by the priests to be gazed on. For Christ himself, is to be adored and worshipped, sits at the right of God, as the Christian Church confesses in the Creed. Prayers to saints, and for the dead, they count a vain and ridiculous thing; as likewise auricular confession and penance enjoined by the priest for sins. Eves and fast-days are, they say, a mockery and disguise of hypocrites.

> Consider the testimony of the "Men of the Hercynian Forest"!!!

> Every word in this description points out Baptists. Two of these brethren waited on Erasmus at Antwerp, to congratulate him on his bold statements of truth. He declined their congratulations, and reproached them as *Anabaptists*. Luther and the German Reformers, whom they joyfully welcomed into the light, turned from them with antipathy and cheerlessly they returned to their concealment in the depths of their native forests to tell their brethren, "They are adverse to us because of our name - i.e. *Anabaptists*." (Erasmus's answer is in Camerarus de Eccl. Fratrum, P. 125.) They acknowledged the charge; they owned themselves Baptists. But their concealment, their principles, and their numbers were known. Entreaty, sophistry, and threats were used in vain to influence, pervert, or intimidate them. They appealed to God's word, and were unwavering.

Ch. 9—The Churches of the Fifteenth Century

Their destruction was planned and brutally executed. An edict for their banishment was obtained from the Emperor, **and Protestants and Catholics** rejoiced in its enforcement. About forty thousand Baptists were proscribed. His majesty, in the edict, expresses his astonishment at the number of Anabaptists, and his horror at their principal error, which was, that they would submit to no human authority on matters of religion. The edict was published just three weeks before the harvest and vintage came on, that these poor people might not be able to carry away the produce of their toil. Their lands were to be forfeited to the emperor, and they were banished to beggary. And three weeks after the proclamation of the edict, death would be inflicted on any of them found in the borders of the country.

And thus is the scene described:

> It was autumn, the prospect and the pride of husbandmen. Heaven had smiled on their honest labors. Their fields stood thick with corn; and the sun and the dew were improving every moment to give them their last polish. The yellow ears waved an homage to their owners; and the wind, whistling through the stems and the russet herbage, softly said, *Put in the sickle, the harvest is come*. Their luxuriant vine leaves, too, hung aloft by the tendrils, mantling over the clustering grapes, like watchful parents over their tender offspring; but all were fenced by an imperial edict, and it was instant death to approach. Without leaving one murmur upon record, in solemn, silent submission to the power that governs the universe and causes *all things to work together for good* to his creatures, they packed up and departed. In several hundred carriages they conveyed their sick, the innocent infants, and their decrepit parents, whose work was done, and [those] whose silvery locks told every beholder that they wanted only the favor of a grave. At the borders they filed off, some to Hungary, others to Transylvania, some to Wallachia, others to Poland, far greater for their virtue, than Ferdinand for all his titles and for all his glory.
>
> Ah, me! What a sad pilgrimage was that! Sad! No, it was sublime. And when the triumphal march of bannered legions, flushed with victory and crowned with glory, shall have been forgotten, the memory of these men, their pilgrimage, their tears, their sublime trusting silence will be held in everlasting remembrance. Bohemian Baptists, forty thousand of them, who sent messengers to cheer the German Reformers at the first dawn of the Reformation; who lay concealed in the dark forests of Dalmatia, "before the rise of Calvin and Luther." *Where did they come from*? (See S. F. Ford, *Origin of the Baptists*.)

Ford, continuing, wrote:

> **Luther**, in his strugglings into light, had boldly written at the commencement of his career as a Reformer, these words:
>
> The term "*baptism*" is Greek, and may be rendered "*dipping*," as when we dip anything all over, so that it is covered all over; and although the custom is now abolished among many, (for they do not dip children, but only pour on a little water) yet **they ought to be wholly immersed**, and immediately taken out; the etymology of the word seems to require this. The Germans call baptism *tauff* from *tieff*, depth, signifying that to baptize is to plunge into the depth. And, indeed, if we consider the design of baptism, we shall see that this is requisite. (See Martin Luther, *De Pedobaptism*, P. 71.)
>
> He [Luther] had also said: "If you receive the sacraments without faith, you bring yourselves into great difficulty, for we oppose against your practice the saying of Christ, 'He that believeth and is baptized shall be saved.'" (See Luther's *Works*, tome vii.)
>
> What wonder that from their concealment came forth the banished, enfeebled, downtrodden Baptists, to hail him as a brother. And so they did. "The drooping spirits of these people," says Mosheim, "who had been dispersed through many countries, and persecuted everywhere, were revived when they were informed of Luther's course. Then they spoke with openness and freedom." But some years afterward **he became their foe**, and notwithstanding what he had said about dipping, persecuted them as re-dippers or Anabaptists. Among these German Baptists was one MUNZER, on whose noble efforts to break the fetters of political

slavery so much insult and falsehood have been heaped. But Munzer was a Popish priest. He followed Luther in his reforming projects. "Thomas Munzer," says D'Aubigné, "was not without talent. Certain mystical writings, which he had read in his youth, had given a false direction to his thoughts. He made his first appearance at Zwickau; quitted Wittenberg on Luther's return thither; and, not willing to hold a secondary place in general esteem, became pastor of the small town of Alstadt." (See D'Aubigné, vol. iii p. 148.) He was then a reforming parish priest, and not till years after was he known or named as an Anabaptist. So before Munzer left Rome and joined the political party engaged in the Munster Rebellion, Luther and Erasmus, as well as the Pope, had denounced and persecuted the thousands of Baptists scattered through Europe.

Is the statement of the **Paedobaptist historian** sustained? [remember Moshiem?] Let it be repeated: *"Before the rise of Luther and Calvin there lay concealed in almost all the countries of Europe many persons who adhered tenaciously to the doctrines of the Anabaptists."*

Thousands upon thousands in the mountain fastnesses, amid the sheltered valleys of the Alps, in the deep forests of Illyricum, and the obscure glens of England, were Baptists. The torch of truth, which lit their places of concealment, revealing the blackness of the deep rayless night which surrounded them, flashed unnoticed into the cell of the hermit and the monk, and, under God's guiding eye, directed priests and scholars to His holy word. That torch, which these Baptists had borne steadily aloft and handed down along their blood-tracked path, at length lit up the world in the blaze of splendor, which burst forth at the Reformation! That became an epoch, a milestone, in the march of Christ's witnesses. Beyond it, before it, we have found these witnesses, these Baptists. (See S. H. Ford, Origin *of the Baptists*.)

1. Write 2 Corinthians 4:4 twice.

2. Mosheim was what kind of historian? *Lutheran*
3. According to Moshiem, who came first, the reformers or the Baptists?
4. Are Baptists Protestants? *no*
5. According to Robinson's researches, how were the men of the Hercynian Forest (Bohemia) described in a letter to Erasmus? (Give 4 characteristics.)
Celibate, Antichrist, no authority other than scripture
6. What is the German word for Baptism, and what does it mean?
tauff / Tieff

Chapter Ten
The Churches of the Sixteenth Century
Section One: The Reformation in Europe. The Anabaptists
Section Two: The Reformation Debate on Baptism

SECTION ONE
Time Line Sixteenth Century:
1481. Hubmaier born in Bavaria
1483. Luther born
1484. Ulrich Zwingli born
1503. Death of Pope Alexander VI
1517. October 31, Martin Luther, German Reformer, wrote 95 theses and tacked them to the door at Wittenberg, Germany
1515. Ministry of Zwingli begins in Switzerland
1520. Emergence of the Anabaptists in Switzerland
1528. Hubmaier and his wife martyred in Austria
1530. Augsburg Confession (Lutheran) presented to the Imperial Diet
1536. Menno Simons joins the Anabaptists in Germany
1538. Henry the VIII's decree
1551. Joan of Kent burned at the stake in England
1559 Royal edict was published, declaring the crime of heresy (any person holding to the Reformed faith or to *Anabaptism*) punishable by death. Extermination of the Huguenots begun.
1559. John Calvin published his *Institutes of the Christian faith*

Scripture to Memorize

Titus 3:7 That being justified by his grace, we should be made heirs according to the hope of eternal life.

The Reformation and the Rise of the Anabaptists of Europe

The reformation is that time in history where scholars, theologians, and preachers openly questioned the doctrines and practices of the Roman Catholic institution. Certainly *reformers* had always been present, but with the invention of the printing press and faster means of communication, the Reformation, the reforming of "Holy Mother Church" began to flourish. The "catholic Reformed" churches such as the Church of England and the Presbyterian Church were the result.

Inquisition Part III

Pope Paul IV ordered the leaders of the Catholic institution to draw up a list of books which offended the "Catholic" faith. This resulted in the first *Index of Forbidden Books* (1559). The Inquisitors, with great zeal, hunted and burned these books. Although succeeding popes tempered the zeal of the Roman Inquisition, many viewed the institution as the accepted enforcer of the Pope's government used in keeping the "faithful" in order. The Inquisition part III put the scientist Galileo on trial.

Luther and Zwingli

Martin Luther in Germany, and **Ulrich Zwingli** in Switzerland, are given credit for igniting the Reformation in Europe. But as we have already seen, Baptist people in

Chapter 10—The Churches of the Sixteenth Century

different areas of the world had carried on the work of God at their own peril in the years before the Reformation. However, it is important to know something about the lives of these two men.

Martin Luther was born a peasant in Eisleben on November 10, 1483. In 1501, at the age of 17, he enrolled at the University of Erfurt, receiving a bachelor's degree in 1502 and a master's degree in 1505. In the summer of 1505, he entered the **Augustinian** monastery in Erfurt. Luther made his profession as a monk in the fall of 1506, and his superiors selected him for the priesthood. He was ordained in 1507.

> The end result of Luther's theology was **the Augsburg Confession of Faith**. Luther and Melanchthon were the authors. Having been signed by the Protestant princes and leaders, it was presented to the emperor and imperial diet in Augsburg, A.D.1530.

After his ordination, Luther was asked to study theology in the hope that he might become a professor. In 1508 he was assigned by Johann von Staupitz, vicar-general of the *Augustinians* to the new University of Wittenberg to give introductory lectures in moral philosophy. He received his bachelor's degree in theology in 1509 and returned to Erfurt, where he taught and studied (1509-1511). In November 1510, on behalf of seven **Augustinian** monasteries, he made a visit to Rome, where he was shocked by the worldliness of the Roman clergy and began to reject the reliance of works for salvation as he climbed/crawled the stairs at the Vatican. In 1512 he received his doctorate and took over the chair of Biblical theology at Wittenberg, which he held until his death.

Sometime during his study of the New Testament in preparation for his lectures, he came to believe that Christians are saved not through their own efforts but by the gift of God's grace, which must be accepted by faith. He came to this conclusion by thinking of the verse "the just shall live by faith." This turned him decisively against some of the major tenets of the Catholic institution.

Luther became a public and controversial figure when he published (October 31, 1517) his *Ninety-Five Theses*. These were propositions opposing the manner in which indulgences (release from the temporal penalties for sin through the payment of money) were being sold in order to raise money for the building of Saint Peter's church in Rome. Luther nailed these theses to the door of the Castle Church in Wittenberg.

Summoned to appear before Emperor Charles V at the Diet of Worms in April 1521, he was asked before the assembled secular and ecclesiastical rulers to recant. He refused firmly, asserting that he would have to be convinced by Scripture and clear reason in order to do so and that going against conscience is not safe for anyone, saying, "Here I stand, I cannot do otherwise."

In 1534, Luther's translation of the Bible from the original Hebrew was published. Luther never broke from Rome completely and continued to believe baptism and the Lord's Supper were sacraments that conveyed, or were a "means to grace."

He wrote a violent booklet against the Jews, as well as booklets against the papacy and the Anabaptists. He died on February 18, 1546, in Eisleben. (See *Martin Luther, Microsoft Encarta Encyclopedia 1999*.)

Ulrich Zwingli was born in 1484 just seven weeks after the birth of Martin Luther. In 1506 he graduated from the University at Basel and became a priest. He moved to the

Grossmünster church and became the people's priest in Zurich, Switzerland in 1519. After a plague hit the city, in which 30% of the population perished, Zwingli began to preach the Gospel only, and in its simplicity. After a careful study of the scripture, Zwingli attacked Roman Catholic belief and practice. In 1521, Zwingli found himself in conflict with the bishop of the diocese because of his attack on the regulations pertaining to Lent. The Zurich city council defended Zwingli, but the effect of this was to begin a process that resulted in the city council removing itself from the Episcopal authority of the Roman Catholic institution.

In November 1521, he began a study group. This group began with ten men. Some in that group were Simon Stumpf, George Binder, Conrad Grebel, Valentine Tsuchude, J. J. Amman, and Felix Mantz. At least two of these men would eventually become the core of the Anabaptist movement in Switzerland. In all probability Reublin, George Blaurock, Brotli, and Balthazar Hübmaier were also in the study group.

The Zurich Bible study began very seriously to question the validity of infant baptism and most of the *Zurich Ten* would come to embrace believer's baptism. For this, some would pay the ultimate price. History record that Zwingli himself came to view infant baptism as invalid and believer's baptism the correct view. However, Zwingli never took a stand for it. We shall see what happened to these *Brethren* in their crisis of belief in just a while.

The Anabaptists of Europe and their Sufferings

This quote is from S.H. Ford:

> Truly great men were these Reformers, these founders of the present Protestant Churches. From the monk of Wittenberg, from the valleys of the Alps, from the plains of France, the notes of soul-freedom rung forth. These notes were heard amid the mountain glens, in the forest depths, by thousands sheltered in remote obscurity who came forth at the cheering call and owned themselves; BAPTISTS. Is this so? Let their opponents decide. Mosheim (the Lutheran historian) says this:
>
> The true origin of that sect which acquired the denomination of Anabaptists, by their administering anew the rite of baptism to those who came over to their communion, and derived that of Mennonites, from that famous man to whom they owe much of their present felicity, is hidden in the depths of antiquity, and is of consequence difficult to be ascertained. This uncertainty will not appear surprising when it is considered that this sect started up suddenly in several countries at the same point of time, under leaders of different talents and different intentions, and at the very period when the first contests of the Reformers with the Roman pontiffs drew the attention of the world, and employed all the pens of the learned in such a manner as to render all other objects and incidents almost matters of indifference. (The Anabaptists) not only **considered themselves** descendants of the **Waldenses**, who were so grievously oppressed and persecuted by the despotic heads of the Romish Church, but pretend, moreover, to be the purest offspring of the respectable sufferers, being equally opposed to all principles of rebellion on the one hand, and all suggestions of fanaticism on the other.

> The Anabaptist or Baptists sprang up in Germany, Holland, and Switzerland, and organized independent congregations. **They thought that the Reformers stopped halfway**, and did not go to the root of the evil. They broke with the historical tradition, and constructed a new church of believers on the voluntary principle. Their fundamental doctrine was, that baptism is a voluntary act, and requires personal repentance, and faith in Christ. They rejected infant-baptism as an antiscriptural invention. (Philip Schaff, *History of the Christian Church*, Vol. VII. p. 607).

Chapter 10—The Churches of the Sixteenth Century

"It may be observed," continues Mosheim, "that **they are not entirely in an error when they boast of their descent from the Waldenses, Petrobrussians, and other ancient sects**, who are usually considered as witnesses of the truth in times of general darkness and superstition." ((See Mosheim's *History of the Mennonites or Anabaptists, Eccl. Hist.* (New York: Harper Bros., V 2, 1871), P 128.)

The Baptists "started up suddenly in several countries at the same point of time, at the very period the Reformers drew attention of the world." **They came not from these Reformers**, for they started up at the same point of time, and according to Mosheim, "they were not satisfied with the reformation proposed by Luther. They looked upon it as much beneath the sublimity of their views, and, consequently, undertook a more perfect reformation; or, to express more properly their visionary enterprise, *they proposed to found a true church, entirely spiritual, and truly divine.*" The Baptists did not begin with Menno Simons, for when first he attended the Anabaptist assemblies, says Mosheim, "he was a Popish priest; and not till 1536 did he throw off the mask and publicly embrace their communion." They did not come from Rome. They had not received baptism from her priests, and attempted no reformation of her dead, corrupting form. (See S. H. Ford, *Origin of the Baptists*, Ch. 3.)

1. Write Titus 3:7 twice.

2. When was the first index of forbidden books put together? 1559

3. Name the two men who are given credit for igniting the reformation in Europe.
Luther and Zwingli

4. True or False: there were numbers of Baptist reformers in Europe and Britain many years before the "Reformation." true

5. Luther was saved thinking of what verse? The just shall live by faith; Romans 1:17

6. Luther continued to believe Baptism and the Lord's Supper were sacraments that conveyed or were a "means to grace." Is that true or false? True

7. What was Zwingli a part of in Zurich that made him examine his views on Baptism? Zurich ten

8. What view did Zwingli come to in his study on infant baptism? invalid

9. Are Baptists reformed? no

****

10.1.2

The Anabaptist Movement in Switzerland

The little study group of ten led by Zwingli came to the conclusion that infant baptism was not scriptural. When they made their findings public by preaching, the city turned on them. Zwingli recanted and embraced infant baptism again. In fact, Zwingli now became an avowed enemy of the *Anabaptists*.

> **Anabaptist**: a name of scorn and ridicule.
>
> The term *Anabaptist* meant: "ana," (again); "Baptist," (baptize). In other words, an *Anabaptist* is a re-baptizer. However, Baptists **do not re-baptize** because immersing or christening of unbelievers (infants cannot believe) is **no** baptism.

The Collegiate Baptist History Workbook

The City Council of Zurich had decided to suppress the small company of people in Zurich under the leadership of **Conrad Grebel, Felix Manz, and George Blaurock**, who had refused to have their children baptized and who insisted that a thorough going reformation should take place in accordance with Zwingli's original promise. Before taking radical measures, however, the City Council had decided to give the Brethren a chance to defend themselves in public in a debate in which Zwingli and his friends were to refute the arguments against infant baptism. As soon as the debate was over, the City Council issued strict decrees forbidding them to meet, to teach, and to have fellowship together. **The little group of devoted Brethren who felt in their hearts deeply convinced that they should follow the teachings of the New Testament completely, and who endeavored to set up a church according to the pattern of Christ** and the apostles, were faced with tragic alternatives. If

> The demand of rebaptism [believer's baptism] virtually unbaptized and unchristianized the entire Christian world, and completed the rupture with the historic church. It cut the last cord of union of the present with the past (Philip Schaff, *History of the Christian Church*, Vol. VIII, P. 77).

they surrendered their position, they would be untrue to their conscience, but if they refused to obey **the edict of the Council, they would be subject to persecution and arrest. In their extremity they met together for prayer, seeking guidance from God, the date being about January 21, 1525.** They found the guidance they sought and were convinced that they should institute a brotherhood of believers upon the basis of baptism and confession of faith. In that meeting they baptized one another, Conrad Grebel baptizing George Blaurock, and Blaurock baptizing the remainder of the group. From that meeting they went forth with joyful conviction that they should continue their fellowship, and should teach and preach their faith, and summon men everywhere to become members of the body of Christ.

During the following months and years, the witness and life of the Brethren and their aggressive missionary endeavor's led to a rapid and far-reaching spread of the new church. The Swiss government authorities of Zurich and neighboring cantons tried every means to stop the movement short of the death penalty, but they failed. Imprisonment, exile, torture, fine, all were of no avail. Finally, in January, 1527, **they imposed the death penalty**, the first of the martyrs in Zurich being Felix Manz. Conrad Grebel had died a few months before of the plague. George Blaurock was burned at the stake two years later in Tyrol, after his exile from Zurich. But still the movement grew, and for almost a hundred years there was a strong and vigorous church in the country round about Zurich. The last martyr of this district was Hans Landis, who was executed in the year 1614. (See Harold S. Bender, *The Origin of the Mennonites, and the Mennonites of Europe*.)

Remember this verse? *John 16:2 "They shall put you out of the synagogues: yea, the time cometh, that whosoever killeth you will **think that he doeth God service**."* The Reformers now joined Rome and **"doeth God service"** by executing the Anabaptists:

> The only dissenters in Zurich were a small number of Romanists and Anabaptists, who were treated with the same disregard of the rights of conscience as the Protestants in Roman Catholic countries, only with a lesser degree of severity. The Reformers refused to others the right of protest which they claimed and exercised for themselves, and the civil magistracy **visited the poor Anabaptists with capital punishment** (Philip Schaff, *History of the Christian Church, Vol. VIII*, P. 67).

Some Swiss Anabaptist Leaders
Balthasar Hubmaier 1481-1528

Chapter 10—The Churches of the Sixteenth Century

Born in Fiedburg, Bavaria, Hubmaier earned his master's degree from the University of Friedburg in 1511. Around 1520 he went to pastor a church in Waldshut, just over into Austria from Switzerland. In 1523, Hubmaier went to Zurich and began a close relationship with Zwingli.

[Zwingli] was in the beginning of his career as a reformer, and voiced often the desire to do all of what the scriptures say. This led those in the *Zurich ten* (the ten men that met with Zwingli to study) to reject infant baptism, which Zwingli also rejected in the beginning. In his writings and sermons of this period **Zwingli clearly denounced infant baptism**. But within a few months, Zwingli could not bring himself to reject the baptism of his childhood. Hubmaier acted on what he believed, but **Zwingli completely backpedaled** on the controversy.

Hubmaier was expelled from Waldshut in December of 1524 after he submitted his eighteen articles of faith and began preaching and reading the Bible in native German to his congregation. He had been baptized by William Rueblin and the Austrian authorities demanded Hubmaier for trial. He fled to Zurich Switzerland for protection but got none from Zwingli. It seems that Hubmaier's book, *Concerning the Christian Baptism of Believers*, was not well received by Zwingli or Zurich. Hubmaier, Grebel, Manz, and Blaurock were all imprisoned. Under extreme torture, Hubmaier recanted his beliefs about baptism, but upon his release he publicly repudiated his weak confession. He went to Moravia to preach the Gospel. Under his leadership, the number of Anabaptists (they called themselves *Brethren* or *Disciples*) grew. Hubmaier baptized over 12,000 converts by immersion *in three years.*

In September of 1527, Hubmaier and his wife were deported to Vienna, Austria to be tried for heresy. On March 10, 1528 Hubmaier was publicly strangled, his body burned and the ashes thrown into the waters of the Danube. Three days later, his devoted wife was drowned under those same waters.

Menno Simons 1496-1561

Menno Simons was born in the little town of Witmarsum, a few miles from the North Sea in Friesland, Holland. He came from a peasant family, but being set apart for the "Catholic" priesthood, he received the usual training for that office and by 1524 entered upon his career in the church. For twelve years he served as parish priest, 1524-36, first for seven years in the town of Pingjum and then for five years in his hometown of Witmarsum. About April 1535, he surrendered to God, and pledged his life henceforth to the Gospel.

Shortly thereafter he found his way to the Obbenite group in Leeuwarden, where he was baptized in January 1536. He accepted the call to serve as an elder or bishop, receiving ordination to this office at the hands of Obbe Philips in 1536. He at once gave himself unreservedly to the shepherding of the brethren, to the defense of the Gospel, and to the preaching of the faith to all men. He used his gifts of writing effectively and became widely known "through his books." The Mennonite Church descended from his influence.

STOP AND THINK
1. Write Titus 3:7 twice.

2. Should Baptists be called "Anabaptists?" If not, why not? *not*
   no. because they are not rebaptizers
3. Concerning the Baptists, the reformers joined Rome by doing what?
   persecuting the baptists
4. Who was the first Ana-Baptist martyred in Zurich? *Felix Manz*
5. How many did Hubmaier baptize in the space of three years? What became of Hubmaier and his wife? *12,000; Hubmaier was publicly strangled and his wife drowned*
6. What group of Christians descended from Menno Simmons?
   mennonites

****

10.1.3

The Vaudois Revisited to Near Total Destruction

Wylie wrote:

Only two years after the synod; that is, in 1534, wholesale destruction fell upon the Vaudois Churches of Provence; in the valleys of Piedmont events were from time to time occurring that showed that **the inquisitor's vengeance had been scotched, not killed.** While the Vaudois as a race were prosperous, their churches multiplying, individual Vaudois were being at times seized, and put to death, at the stake, on the rack, or by the cord.

Three years after the persecution broke out anew, and raged for a short time, Charles III of Savoy gave his consent to 'hunting down' the heretics of the Valleys. The commission was given Bersour, a man of savage disposition, who collected a troop of 500 horse and foot, and attacked the Valley of Angrogna. He was repulsed, but the storm which had rolled away from the mountains fell upon the plains. Turning to the Vaudois who resided around his own residence, he seized a great number of persons, whom he threw into the prisons and convents of Pinerolo and the Inquisition of Turin. Many of them suffered in the flames.

In 1536, the Waldensian Church had to mourn the loss of one of the more distinguished of her pastors. Martin Gonin, of Angrogna, a man of public spirit and rare gifts, who had gone to Geneva on ecclesiastical affairs, was returning through Dauphine, when he was apprehended on suspicion of being a spy. He cleared himself of that charge, **but the gaoler searching his person, and discovering certain papers upon him, he was convicted of what the parliament of Grenoble accounted a much greater crime, heresy.** Condemned to die, he was led forth at night, and drowned in the river Isere. He would have suffered at the stake had not his persecutors feared the effect of his dying words upon the spectators.

There were others, also called to ascend the martyr-pile, whose names we must not pass over in silence. Two pastors returning from Geneva to their flocks in the Valleys, in company

> One of these martyrs, Catalan Girard, taught the spectators a parabolic lesson, standing at the pile. From amid the flames he asked for two stones, which were instantly brought him. The crowd looked on in silence, curious to know what he meant to do with them. Rubbing them against each other, he said, "You think to extinguish our poor Churches by your persecutions. You can no more do so, than I with my feeble hands can crush these stones" (J. A. Wylie, *The History Of The Waldenses*, P. 65).

Chapter 10—The Churches of the Sixteenth Century

of three French Protestants, were seized at the Col de Tamiers, in Savoy, and carried to Chambery. There all five were tried, condemned, and burned.

The martyr who died thus heroically at Aosta was a youth, the one we are now to contemplate was a man of fifty. **Geofroi Varaile** was a native of the town of Busco, in Piedmont. His father had been a captain in that army of murderers who, in 1488, ravaged the Valleys of Lucerna and Angrogna. The son in 1520 became a monk, and possessing the gift of a rare eloquence, he was sent on a preaching tour, in company with another cowled ecclesiastic, yet more famous, Bernardo Ochino of Sienna, the founder of the order of the Capuchins. The arguments of the men he was sent to convert [to the Romish faith] staggered **Varaile**. He fled to Geneva, and in the city of the Reformers he was taught more fully the "way of life." Ordained as a [Reformed] pastor, he returned to the Valleys, where "like another Paul," says Leger, "he preached the faith he once destroyed." After a ministry of some months, he set out to pay a visit of a few days to his native town of Busco. He was apprehended by the monks who were lying in wait for him. He was condemned to death by the Inquisition of Turin. His execution took place in the castle-piazza of the same city, March 29th, 1558. **He walked to the place where he was to die with a firm step and a serene countenance; he addressed the vast multitude around his pile in a way that drew tears from many eyes; after this, he began to sing with a loud voice, and so continued till he sank amid the flames.**

Two years before this, the same piazza, the castle-yard at Turin, had witnessed a similar spectacle. Barthelemy Hector was a bookseller in Poictiers. A man of warm but well-tempered zeal, he travelled as far as the Valleys, diffusing that knowledge that maketh wise unto salvation. In the assemblage of white peaks that look down on the Pra del Tor is one named La Vechera, so called because the cows love the rich grass that clothes its sides in summer-time. **Barthelemy Hector** would take his seat on the slopes of the mountain, and gathering the herdsmen and agriculturists of the Pra round him, would induce them to buy his books, [and Bibles] by reading passages to them. Portions of the Scriptures also would he recite to the grandames and maidens as they watched their goats, or plied the distaff. His steps were tracked by the inquisitor, even amid these wild solitudes. He was dragged to Turin, to answer for the crime of selling Genevese books. His defense before his judges discovered an admirable courage and wisdom:

"You have been caught in the act," said his judge, "of selling books that contain heresy. What say you?"

"If the Bible is heresy to you, it is truth to me," replied the prisoner."

"But you use the Bible to deter men from going to mass," urged the judge.

"If the Bible deters men from going to mass," responded Barthelemy, "it is a proof that God disapproves of it, and that mass is idolatry."

The judge, deeming it expedient to make short shrift with such a heretic, exclaimed, "Retract!"

"I have spoken only truth," said the bookseller, "can I change truth as I would a garment?"

The smoke of these martyr-piles," as was said with reference to the death of Patrick Hamilton, "was infecting those on whom it blew." But the constancy of Barthelemy compelled his persecutors to disregard these prudential considerations. At last, despairing of his abjuration, they brought him forth and consigned him to the flames. His behaviour at the stake "drew rivers of tears," says Leger, "from the eyes of many in the Popish crowd around his stake, while others vented reproaches and invectives against the cruelty of the monks and the inquisitors" (J. A. Wylie, *The History Of The Waldenses*, P. 65-8).

And yet a far greater persecution was on the horizon, the infamous massacre of 1655 was a hundred years into the future.

The Collegiate Baptist History Workbook

_____

1. Write Titus 3:7 twice.

2. What noble gave consent to hunt down the Waldenses?
   Charles III of savoy
3. Name the monk who was converted by the Waldenses and became a Vaudois missionary:
   Gefroi varaile
4. What man was caught "selling" (distributing) Bibles?
   Barthelemy Hector

****

10.2.1

SECTION TWO

John Calvin 1509-64

Born to an upper middle class family in France, John Calvin emerged as one of the most important figures of the Reformation. Having studied for the priesthood at Paris in his youth, Calvin turned his attention to civil and canon law in Orleans when his father became dissatisfied with the priests. Calvin showed an early interest for theology and for the study of Greek and Hebrew. Exposed to the ideas of Luther while he was still in Paris, Calvin's writings indicate that he had definitely moved into the Protestant camp by 1533. On November 1 of that year, he preached a sermon in which he attacked the established church and called for reforms.

Calvin's ideas, rather than bringing about the reforms he sought, elicited a wave of Roman Catholic sentiment that forced him to flee for his own safety. During the next few years, he sought refuge in various cities, most notably in Basel, Switzerland. It was also during this period that he began work on his theology book, *Institutes in the Christian Religion*. This was the work that would consume a good deal of his energy for the next three decades.

During Calvin's flight, he happened to stay the evening in Geneva with a man named Farel. Farel used all his power to persuade Calvin to remain in Geneva working in support of the Protestant cause there. Reluctantly, Calvin agreed. In 1541, pro-Protestant forces gained control of the city.

> **The Canons of the Synod of Dort** in 1619 were the most important statements of Calvin's theology. The Confession made at Dort, Holland was received by all the Reformed Churches as true, accurate, and eminently authoritative. It was the first concise exhibit of the Calvinistic system of theology.

For the remainder of his life, Calvin stood as the dominant figure in Geneva. The city became a place of refuge for persecuted peoples from all over Europe, including a soon to be reconstructed remnant of the Vaudois. Yet for all his benevolence, Calvin was never a friend to the Baptists.

Chapter 10—The Churches of the Sixteenth Century

Calvin's main work was his theology, which has been greatly influential in many Protestant denominations. As we have mentioned earlier, **the invention of the printing press and faster means of communication** was a great aid in the Reformation. So it was that Calvin's beliefs were distributed more quickly and widely than any man before him.

The primary tenets of Calvinism include a belief in the primacy of the scripture as the authority for doctrinal decisions, a belief in predestination, a belief in salvation wholly accomplished by grace with no influence from works, and a rejection of the episcopacy. The tenants of Calvinism are thought of in the acrostic TULIP: T-the total depravity of man, U-unconditional election, L-limited atonement, I-irresistible grace, P-the perseverance of the Saints. Along with *the Institutes* in 1559, Calvin also produced commentaries on the books of the Bible. He died on May 27, 1564.

Reformation Debate over the Baptists

Phillip Schaff wrote about the so-called *radical* Baptists of the Reformation:

Radicalism was identical with the ana-Baptist movement.

The Reformers aimed to reform the old church by the Bible, the Radicals attempted to build a new Church from the Bible. The former maintained the historic continuity; the latter went directly to the apostolic age, and ignored the intervening centuries as an apostasy.

They [the ana-Baptists] raised a protest against Protestantism. They denounced the state-church as worldly and corrupt. They were cruelly persecuted by imprisonment, exile, torture, fire and sword, and almost totally suppressed in Protestant as well as in Roman Catholic countries (Phillip Schaff, *History of the Christian Church,Vol. VIII*, P. 70-72).

The mode of Baptism was not an article of controversy at that time; for the Reformers either preferred immersion (Luther), or held the mode to be a matter of indifference (Calvin). [However] Luther agreed substantially with the Roman Catholic doctrine of baptism. His *Taufbuchlein* of 1523 is a translation of the Latin baptismal service, including the formula of exorcism, the sign of the cross, and the dipping (Phillip Schaff, *History of the Christian Church, Vol. VII.* P. 607-8).

He [Zwingli] regarded the sacraments as signs and seals of a grace already received rather than as means of a grace to be received. He [Zwingli] rejected the doctrine of baptismal regeneration and of the corporal presence. Luther adhered to both (Phillip Schaff, *History of the Christian Church, Vol. VIII.* P. 86).

The Anabaptist or Baptists sprang up in Germany, Holland, and Switzerland, and organized independent congregations. They thought that the Reformers stopped half-way, and did not go to the root of the evil. They broke with the historical tradition, and constructed a new church of believers on the voluntary principle. Their fundamental doctrine was, that baptism is a voluntary act, and requires personal repentance, and faith in Christ. They rejected infant-baptism as an anti-scriptural invention (Phillip Schaff, *History of the Christian Church,, Vol. VII.* P. 607).

The Absorption of the Waldenses into the Reformed Movement

The Waldenses were Baptist, and one of the tenets of the Vaudois was rejection of infant baptism. Yet, the Waldensian church eventually became a part of the Reformed and Protestant body, the Presbyterians. How did it happen? Horsch wrote:

The Collegiate Baptist History Workbook

[In] 1530 the Walsenses sent two of their ministers, George Morel and Pierre Masson, to Switzerland and South Germany to confer with Zwinglian leaders and to ask for their instruction and counsel. [A] letter was written by Morel in the name of the Zwinglian party among the Waldenses in France and Italy. The letter stated the Waldensian position on various points of doctrine and practice. Among the statements made in this letter is the mention of objections raised by the Waldenses to the denial of free will and to the doctrine of predestination, as taught by Luther and Zwingli. "Nothing has brought us such consternation," the writer of the letter states, "as this doctrine." He adds that they had supposed that divine grace is offered freely to all, and that man himself is responsible for spurning or accepting the offer of grace (John Horsch, *Mennonite History*, P. 6).

Some Waldensian "barbes" began to receive their training in Geneva. Due to extended persecution, the number of preachers was drastically reduced. The number of Waldenses was reduced to hundreds. For the protection of their homes and families the remaining leadership of the Waldenses began to seek protection by identifying themselves with the rising Reformed churches of Europe. They began to embrace infant baptism.

The Huguenots

A group of Reformed churches emerged in France. Known as the Huguenots, they were descendents of the Albigenses and Waldenses. They were not true Baptists due to their continuation of infant sprinkling, yet they nonetheless believed in salvation by grace, and rejected the mass, relics, sacraments, and idolatry of the Catholic institution. Their sufferings were also recorded:

> The priests and their adherents exerted themselves to the utmost to inflame the king against the Huguenots. They appealed to his bigotry and superstition, and also declared to him that the Reformed were becoming so powerful that they would surely seek to overthrow the throne itself. "If the secular arm," said the Cardinal de Lorraine to Henry II, who had succeeded his father, Francis I, "fails in its duty, all the malcontents will throw themselves into this detestable sect. They will first destroy the ecclesiastical power, after which it will be the turn of the royal power." Such arguments had the desired effect. The brief respite which had followed the death of King Francis came to an end, and Henry II became a cruel persecutor of the Reformed.
>
> In 1559 a royal edict was published, declaring the crime of heresy punishable by death. The judges were forbidden to remit or mitigate the penalty. The former persecutions were instantly revived in all parts of France, and the monks took good care that the civil officers were not remiss or lenient in the performance of their dreadful duties. The last year of Henry's reign and the entire period of that of his successor, Francis II, were marked by the most dreadful cruelties. The Huguenots were driven from their churches and places of meeting, their religious edifices were destroyed, and they were forced to assemble at night in subterranean vaults, in the forests, in the mountains, and in caves. Those who possessed Bibles were obliged to conceal them with the utmost care. When they undertook to read them, they did so at the risk of their lives. In spite of the care taken to conceal their movements, they were often surprised at their meetings by the royal troops, and were slain on the spot or captured. But few of the captives escaped punishment.
>
> The Protestant towns of Cabrieres and Merindol, in the South of France, were utterly destroyed. Every house was leveled to the ground, and the people of all ages and both sexes, were ruthlessly butchered in the streets. Four hundred women and children who had sought

Chapter 10—The Churches of the Sixteenth Century

refuge in a church were killed without mercy in the sacred place. Twenty-five women took refuge in a cave. The Papal Legate kindled a fire at the entrance with his own hands, and smothered them all. An entire congregation of Protestants was captured in Paris. They were imprisoned in the terrible Chatelet, and were offered pardon and freedom if they would desert the Reformed faith, and go to hear the Mass. They unanimously refused. After a long and dreary imprisonment, the most prominent of the captives were taken to the Place Maubert, in September, 1558, and executed in the presence of a large and applauding crowd, the king himself looking on from a neighboring window. The tongues of the victims were first cut out, they were strangled, and their bodies burned. One of these victims was Philippa de Lunz, a young, beautiful, and wealthy widow of twenty-two years. (See James D. McCabe, Jr., *Cross and Crown*.)

1. Write Titus 3:7 twice.

2. Give two reasons why the Reformation began to flourish.
   1. The Printing Press. 2. Faster means of communication

3. Calvin's theology can be summed up by what "acrostic?"
   TULIP (P. 136)
4. If the Protestants were protesting the Catholics, who were the Baptists protesting? *Reformers / both*
5. What happened to the Waldenses? *were reduced to hundreds / merged into reformation /*
6. Who were the Huguenots descended from and were they Baptist people? *absorbed*
   Albigenses and Waldenses, No

****

10.2.2

The Old Black Book

1. The Antiochian text came from the original churches of Asia Minor.
2. Evidences of the **Antiochian** or **Received Text**:
   From Apostolic Fathers:

   > To illustrate the contributing value of the church fathers, the writings of Tertullian, Irenaeus, Hippolytus, Origen, and Clement of Alexandria have supplied us with 30,147 scripture citings alone. When we consider that the great majority of their quotations agree with the *Textus Receptus*, their worth is even more appreciated (William P. Grady, *Final Authority*, P. 26).

   From Lectionaries:
   Over 2,000 existing manuscripts of lectionaries testified of the widespread usage of the Antiochian text.

   From Early translations:
   The Syrian *Peshito* A.D. 150, Old Latin A.D. 150, *Itala Biblia* of the Waldenses fourth to sixteenth century, Gothic Bible of Ulfilas A.D. 330, Armenian Bible of A.D. 400 of Mesrob (there are over 1200 existing copies of this Bible,) Old Syriac A.D. 400, Harclean Syriac A.D. 616.

3. The Alexandrian text.

Examples of early translations:
Egyptian: Sahidic Coptic third century, Boharic Coptic 6th century
Ethiopian: Ethiopian version of A.D. 350.
European: Jerome's Latin Vulgate of A.D. 382

4. Two definite lines of texts come out of early church history: **Antiochian and Alexandrian.**

Which text was used for the English Bibles of the Reformation period?

Wycliffs' English translation had been available since 1380, and the Reformers used it as a reference along with other translations of the Received Text. Luther used the **Antiochian/ Received Text** as did the translators of the King James Bible.

The Growth of the Reformation

Carroll writes of this time:

Before the close of the Sixteenth Century, **there were five established churches, churches backed by civil governments**, the Roman and Greek Catholics counted as two; the Church of England; the Lutheran, or Church of Germany; the Church of Scotland, now known as the Presbyterian. All of them were bitter in their hatred and persecution of the people called Baptists, and all other non-established churches, churches that never in any way had been connected with the Catholics. Their great help in the struggle for reformation had been forgotten, or was now wholly ignored. Many more thousands, including both women and children were constantly perishing every day in the yet unending persecutions. The great hope awakened and inspired by the Reformation had proven to be a bloody delusion. Remnants now found an uncertain refuge in the friendly Alps and other hiding places over the world.

These new organizations, separating from, or coming out of the Catholics, retained many of their most hurtful errors, some of which are as follows:

> With the printing of the Guttenburg Bible in 1456, Holy Mother church sensed the danger to their territory. In 1535 Rowland Phillips said, **"We must root out printing or printing will root us out."**

(1) Preacher-church government (differing in form).
(2) Church Establishment (Church and State combination)
(3) Infant BAPTISM
(4) Sprinkling or Pouring for Baptism.
(5) Baptismal Regeneration
(6) Persecuting others.

In the beginning, all these established Churches persecuted one another as well as every one else, but at a council held at Augsburg in 1555, a treaty of peace, known as the *Peace of Augsburg* was signed between the Catholics on the one hand, and the Lutherans on the other, agreeing not to persecute each other. You let us alone, and we will let you alone. For Catholics to fight Lutherans meant war with Germany, and for Lutherans to fight or persecute Catholics meant war with all the countries where Catholicism predominated.

But persecutions did not then cease. The hated Ana-Baptists (called Baptists today), in spite of all prior persecutions, and in spite of the awful fact that fifty million had already died martyr deaths, still existed in great numbers. It was during this period that along one single European highway, thirty miles distance, stakes were set up every few feet along this highway,

Chapter 10—The Churches of the Sixteenth Century

the tops of the stakes sharpened, and on the top of each stake was placed a gory head of a martyred Ana-Baptist. Human imagination can hardly picture a scene so awful! And yet a thing perpetrated, according to reliable history, by a people calling themselves devout followers of the meek and lowly Jesus Christ (J. M. Carroll, *The Trail of Blood*, P. 35).

1. Write Titus 3:7 twice.

2. Name the two lines of texts that came out of early church history.
   Peshito, and recieved text

3. What did Rowland Phillips say about printing?
   "We must root out printing or printing will rule us out"

4. Name the 5 established denominations that existed by the end of the Reformation.
   Lutheran, presbytirian, ~~lutheran~~ Greek, roman catholic, Church of england

5. Name 3 of the 6 hurtful errors left in place by the Reformers.
   infant baptism, Church establishment, baptismal regeneration

Chapter Eleven
The Churches of the Sixteenth Century Part II
Section One: The Reformation in England
Section Two: The Baptists Presence Revealed

SECTION ONE
Time Line Sixteenth Century II:
1530. Jesuits founded
1531. Henry VIII recognized as head of the English Church
1539. Henry's decree of death to those denying infant baptism
1551. Joan Boucher burned at Smithfield
1553. "*Bloody*" Mary begins her reign of death in England
1559. "Puritanism" begins in England
1572. St. Bartholomew's Day Massacre. Huguenots murdered in France by the Roman Catholic institution.
1579. Brownist (Congregationalist) movement started in England, led by Robert Browne.
1580. Classical movement begins in England

Scripture to Memorize

    2 Corinthians 6:17 *Wherefore come out from among them, and be ye separate, saith the Lord, and touch not the unclean thing; and I will receive you*

The Reformation and The Discovery of the Baptists in England

England was far distant and isolated from the rest of Europe. While Protestantism tore apart European society, it took a far different form in England, and the Church of England retained much of the doctrine and the practices of Catholicism. England also experienced the greatest wavering between the two religions as the monarchs of England passed from one religion to the other.

England had for several centuries, an uncomfortable relationship with Rome. Some of the most strident and successful Reformers in the Middle Ages were English; the first translation of the Bible from Latin into the common language was made in England. There were **two major influences** in England: the Wycliff rebellion against the church and the spread of northern independence. These prepared the foundation for the English Reformation.

The adoption of Protestantism in England however, was in the beginning, a political rather than a religious move. King Henry VIII had married Catherine of Aragon. Since she had been previously married to his brother, Henry had to get special permission from the pope for the marriage. The marriage, however, produced no male children to occupy the throne at Henry's death. In the mid-1520's, Henry fell in love with Ann Boleyn, a lady in waiting to Catherine. He wished to annul his marriage to Catherine and marry Ann because he feared leaving the throne of England without a male heir.

In order to marry Ann, the marriage with Catherine had to be annulled by the pope. The pope refused Henry's request for annulment.

Henry VIII fired Cardinal Wolsey, the Lord Chancellor of England, who was against the annulment and replaced him with Thomas Cranmer and Thomas Cromwell. Both these men were sympathetic to the new ideas of Martin Luther. They gave the king some radical advice: if the pope does not grant the annulment, then split the English "church"

Chapter 11—The Churches of the Sixteenth Century Part 2

from the Roman "church." Rather than the pope, the king would be the spiritual head of the English church. And so it came to pass, in 1531, the clergy of England recognized Henry as the head of the church.

Henry VIII's children reigned after him. First, Edward IV, who established Puritan Calvinism to be the theology of the English church, died in 1553. Then Mary (Bloody Mary) re-established Catholicism and burned both Protestants and Baptists. She died in 1558.

Elizabeth I reigned queen from 1558-1603. She returned England somewhat to Protestantism, but was mild toward the "catholics."

The Counter-Reformation

In answer to the growth of the Protestants, the Catholic institution began its own series of reforms. This movement was called the **Counter-Reformation**. The most important of the reactionary movements was the **Society of Jesus** or **the Jesuits**, founded by **Ignatius of Loyola** in the 1530's.

The history of the Jesuits is filled with intrigue and espionage. It was the Jesuits that planned the murder of King James during what was called the *Gunpowder Plot*. Jesuits led in the forced conversion of the aboriginal peoples of North and South America.

The Jesuits became so out-of-control that the pope himself outlawed them just before the turn of the nineteenth century. They were reinstated in 1805, and many believe them to be the cause of much evil in the world.

The Puritans

The Puritan movement was a broad trend toward a militant, biblically based Calvinistic Protestantism. It emphasized the *purification* of church and society from the remnants of corrupt and unscriptural papist ritual and dogma. **It advocated a state controlled by an Augustinian church, just as its Roman mother had controlled Europe.** Puritanism first manifested itself in Presbyterian and Congregational (Independent) circles.

The Puritans became dissatisfied with the compromises inherent in the religious settlement carried out under Queen Elizabeth in 1559. They sought a complete reformation both of religious and secular life, and advocated, in consequence, attacks upon the Anglican establishment. To their credit, they emphasized a disciplined, godly life, and energetic evangelical activities (preaching the new birth).

The Rise of the Separatists in the Church of England

Cambridge University became the focal point of a new theological movement from 1569-70. A milder form of Calvinism was taught by Thomas Cartwright based on the Acts of the Apostles. Cartwright had been a professor at Cambridge under previous reigns.

> **The Puritans verses the Separatists**:
> The Separatists wanted separation from the Church of England to form independent churches. The Puritans wanted to reform the Reformed Church of England.

Along with milder Calvinism, Cartwright and his friends preached for a change in church government, and an independent church polity. In 1571, Cartwright was removed and went to Geneva in search of the right church government. In 1573, a Royal Proclamation was issued against dissenters, and dissident groups.

A group of mild Calvinists came to the surface during the 1580's, under the leadership of John Field (1545-88) who proclaimed himself a *Puritan* clergyman. This group attempted to put into place a Presbyterian structure within the existing Church of England. It was known as the Classical Movement (1580-90), and it collapsed in 1591. The leaders of the movement were arrested and brought to trial by the Star Chamber.

The Classical Movement (1580-90) was somewhat a failure. It did not establish any new government nor replace the Calvinism imported from Geneva at the beginning of the Reformation.

> **The Star Chamber** was not really a chamber filled with stars, the "Star Chamber" was a British court established in 1487 and authorized to torture defendants to compel confessions. The Star Chamber also administered an oath requiring individuals to answer any questions asked of them, including those that might demonstrate guilt. Parliament abolished the Star Chamber in 1641.

The early Puritan effort laid the groundwork for the birth of the *Separatists* within the Church of England.

Men such as Robert Browne, Henry Barrow, John Greenwood, Francis Johnson, John Smythe, and John Robinson would further expound Separatism and Separate views. To those men the message of reform and separation meant a separation from the communion (and later baptism) of the Church of England.

This Presbyterian wing of the Puritan party was eventually defeated in Parliament, and after suppression of nonconformist ministers in 1583, a minority moved to separate from the church and sought refuge; first in the Netherlands, and later in New England.

The Brownists

Many of these young Cambridge graduates became *Separatists*. One of those graduates was Robert Browne.

Robert Browne saw the Church of England in a state of moral disrepair and in need of reform from outside. He advocated an early form of Congregationalism, and separation from the Church of England. Browne was only an active Separatist from 1579-1585.

Browne was actively criticized by those who came after him for recanting his principles in order to win his own personal liberty. This did not stop the spread of his writings or of other Brownist congregations.

The writings of Robert Browne were major contributions in the early development of Elizabethan English religious dissent, the beginnings of the English Separatist movement, during the later reign of Elizabeth I. His light may have shown only briefly, but it lit the way for many others to follow with more "radical" points of view. Browne has often been called **the father of Congregationalism**. His writings influenced both the Pilgrims and the Puritans of New England.

___

1. Write 2 Corinthians 6:17 twice.

Chapter 11—The Churches of the Sixteenth Century Part 2

2. What was it about the Church of England that was different from the Protestant churches of Europe? *Origins political instead of religious*

3. What two major movements prepared the foundation of the English Reformation? *Wycliffe rebellion, Spread of Northern independence*

4. In the beginning, was the Reformation movement in England a deeply religious movement? *no*

5. Name Henry VIII's two Protestant advisors. *Thomas Cranmer & Thomas Cromwell*

6. What was the most notable group from the Counter-Reformation and who founded it? *The Jesuits; Ignatius of Loyola*

7. The Puritans were "militant, Bible-based" what? *Calvinists*

8. Where did some of the Puritans migrate? *Holland (Netherlands)*

9. Who was the father of Congregationalism? *Robert Brown*

10. What was "the Star Chamber?" *A British court to secure admission of guilt*

****

11.1.2

The Martyrdom of Joan Boucher and Edward Wightman

Henry VIII's decree of 1538 approved the penalty of death for refusing infant baptism. **Joan of Kent** (Joan Boucher) was condemned in 1551. Of Joan Boucher, Joseph Ivimey wrote:

The most awful instance of persecution in this year was the burning of **JOAN BOUCHER** of Kent. Burnet says, "She denied that Christ was truly incarnate of the virgin, whose flesh being sinful, he could take none of it; but the Word, by consent of the inward man in the virgin, took flesh of her." [In this Joan opposed the Roman Catholic notion that Jesus Christ received some of His flesh from Mary, ed.]

The commissioners took much pains about her, and had many conferences with her; but she was so extravagantly conceited of her own notions that she rejected with scorn all they said whereupon she was adjudged an obstinate heretic, and so left to the secular power.

> Rogers answered, "Burning alive was no cruel death, but easy enough." Foxe answered, "Well, perhaps, it may so happen that you yourself shall have your hands full of this mild burning." And so it came to pass and Rogers was the first man who was burnt in Queen Mary's time (Thomas Crosby, *History of the English Baptists*, Vol 1, P. 61).

To the other charges preferred against this good woman by her enemies, who would endeavour to blacken her as much as possible in order to justify their own conduct. **It is to be added that she was a Baptist; and perhaps this was the sin which was not to be forgiven.** "When the compassionate young king could not be prevailed upon to sign the warrant for her execution, **Cranmer, with his superior learning, was employed to persuade him.** He argued from the practice of the Jewish church in stoning blasphemers, which rather silenced his highness than satisfied him: for when at last he yielded to the importunity of the archbishop, he told him with tears in his eyes, that if he did wrong, since it was in submission to his authority, he should answer it before God. This struck the archbishop with surprise; but yet he at last suffered the sentence to be executed." (See Burnet, *History of Reformation,* Vol. ii. P. 112.)

The extraordinary efforts used to bring Joan Boucher to retract her sentiments, **prove her to have been a person of note, whose opinions carried more weight and respect than it can be supposed the chimeras of a frantic woman**, as she has been sometimes represented, would have done. The account which Mr. Strype gives of her is truly honourable. "She was (he says) a great disperser of Tyndale's new testament, translated by him into English, and printed at Colen, and was a great reader of scripture herself. Which book also she dispersed in the court, and so became known to certain women of quality, and was particularly acquainted with Mrs. Anne Askew. She used for the greater secrecy to tie the books with strings under her apparel, and so pass with them into the court." (Strype's *Eccles. Mem.* vol. ii. p. 214.) By this it appears that she hazarded her life in dangerous times to bring others to the knowledge of the word of God. To be employed in such a work, and to die in such a cause, is the highest character that could be given to any of the disciples of Christ.

There are some remarks upon this circumstance in Fox's Latin book of Martyrs, which are omitted in the English from a regard, as is supposed, to the reputation of the martyrs who suffered in the next reign. But Mr. Pierce has given us the following translation in his answer to Nichols, p. 33. "In King Edward's reign, some were put to death for heresy. One of these was Joan Boucher, or Joan of Kent. Now, says Mr. Fox, when the protestant bishops had resolved to put her to death, a friend of Mr. John Rogers, the divinity-reader in St. Paul's church, came to him, earnestly desiring him to use his interest with the Archbishop, that the poor woman's life might be spared, and other means used to prevent the spreading of her opinion, which might be done in time, saying too, that though while she lived, she infected few with her opinion, yet she might bring many to think well of it, by suffering death for it."

He pleaded therefore that it was better she should be kept in some prison, without an opportunity of propagating her notion among weak people, and so she would do no harm to others, and might live to repent herself. Rogers on the other hand pleaded; she ought to be put to death. Well then saith his friend, if you are resolved to put an end to her life together with her opinion, choose some other kind of death, more agreeable to the gentleness and mercy prescribed in the gospel; there being no need, that such tormenting deaths should be taken up, in imitation of the Papists. Rogers answered, that burning alive was no cruel death but easy enough. His friend then hearing these words, which expressed so little regard to poor creatures suffering, answered him with great vehemence, and striking Roger's hand, which before he held fast, said to him, **Well, perhaps, it may so happen, that you yourselves shall have your hands full of this mild burning**. And so it came to pass; Mr. **Rogers was the first man who was burned in Queen Mary's reign.** I am apt to think (adds Mr. Pierce) that Mr. Roger's friend was no other than Fox himself (Joseph Ivimey, History *of the English Baptists,* Ch. 3).

Chapter 11—The Churches of the Sixteenth Century Part 2

> **John Foxes' Plea to Queen Elizabeth not to burn heretics**
>
> I understand there are some here in England, not English but come hither from Holland, I suppose both men and women, who having been tried according to law, and having publicly declared their repentance, are happily reclaimed. Many others are condemned to exile; a right sentence in my opinion. But I hear there are one or two of these who are appointed to the most severe of punishments, viz. *burning*, except your clemency prevent. Now in this one affair I conceive there are two things to be considered; the one is the wickedness of their errors, the other, the sharpness of their punishment. As to their errors, indeed, no man of sense can deny that they are most absurd, and I wonder that such monstrous opinions could come into the mind of any Christian; but such is the state of human weakness, if we are left never so little awhile destitute of the divine light, whither is it we do not fall? And we have great reason to give God thanks that I hear not of any Englishman that is inclined to this madness.
>
> As to these fanatical sects, therefore, it is certain they are by no means to be countenanced in a commonwealth, but in my opinion ought to be suppressed by proper correction. But to *roast alive* the bodies of poor wretches, that offend rather through blindness of judgment than perverseness of will, in fire and flames, raging with pitch and brimstone, is a hard-hearted thing, and more agreeable to the practice of the Romanists than the custom of the gospellers; yea, is evidently of the same kind, as if it had flowed from the Romish priests, from the first author of such cruelty, Innocent III. Oh, that none had ever brought such a Phalarian bull into the meek church of Christ!
>
> For so it is perhaps a folly in me; but I speak the truth, that I can hardly pass by a slaughter-house where cattle are killing, but my mind shrinks back with a secret sense of their pains. And truly I greatly admire the clemency of God in this, who had such respect to the mean brute creatures formerly prepared for sacrifices, that they must not be committed to the flames before their blood had been poured out at the foot of the altar. Whence we may gather, that in inflicting of punishments, though just, we must not be over rigorous, but temper the sharpness of rigour with clemency. Wherefore, if I may be so bold with the majesty of so great a princess, I humbly beg of your royal highness, for the sake of Christ, who was consecrated to suffer for the lives of many, this favour at my request, which even the divine clemency would engage you to; that if it may be, (and what cannot your authority do in these cases?) these miserable wretches may be spared; at least that a stop may be put to the horror, by changing the punishment into some other kind. There are excommunications, and close imprisonments; there are bonds; there is perpetual banishment, burning of the hand and whipping, or even slavery itself. This one thing I most earnestly beg, that **the flames of Smithfield**, so long ago extinguished by your happy government, may not be again revived. –John Foxe, 1575.

John Foxe was the Church of England historian who wrote the famous *Book of Martyrs*. Foxe was concerned that the laws in England, written to burn heretics, would damage the history of his country. Furthermore, he feared the burning of the so-called heretics would bring shame to Smithfield, a place where martyrs, killed at the hands of the papacy, had been slain.

At the left is a portion of the letter Foxe sent to Elizabeth pleading for leniency in dealing with *heretics.* The letter was preserved in Joseph Ivimey's *History of the English Baptists.* Foxe feared that the burning of heretics would bring the judgment of innocent blood on England. Even with Foxe pleading, Elizabeth did not change the policy.

Edward Wightman

Edward Wightman was the last Baptist martyr burned in England. He was burned at the stake at Litchfield, April 11, 1612. Wightman was accused of every radical heresy under the sun. Thomas Crosby wrote:

> If Wightman really held all the opinions laid to his charge, he must have been an idiot or a madman, and ought to have had the prayers of his persecutors rather than been put to a cruel death. It is now about two hundred years since Wightman, [Benedict writing in 1813] with his enormous load of heresies, was committed to the purifying flames. Almost half of this time the Baptists in England were, for the most part, in an uncertain state; what earthly enjoyments they possessed were held by a precarious tenure, and persecution and distress were their common lot. They had indeed some short intervals of repose, but these were

succeeded by tempestuous seasons, and the cup of affliction was dealt out to them by their enemies in plenteous measure (David Benedict, *A General History of the Baptist Denomination,* Vol. 1, P. 196-7).

1. Write 2 Corinthians 6:17 twice.

2. Henry the VIII's decree of 1538 did what?
   Penalty for fusing infant Baptism / death to anyone
3. What did Joan Boucher say about Christ's flesh?
   It did not come from the virgin mary
4. Who went to convince the King to burn Joan? *Thomas Cranmer*
5. What historian was against the burning of Joan? *John Foxe*
6. Of what was Edward Wightman accused?
   Every heresy under the sun

****

11.2.1

SECTION TWO

Evidences of the Baptists in England before the Seventeenth Century

In the year 1539, the thirteenth of the reign of Henry VIII, the following enactment was published:

> That those who are in any error, as Sacramentarians, Anabaptists, or any others that sell books having such opinions in them, once known, both the books and such persons shall be detected and disclosed immediately to the king's majesty, or one of his privy council, to the intent to have it punished without favor, even with the **extremity of the law**. (See *Foxe's Book of Martyrs,* Vol. ii, P. 440.)

This was soon after the bands which attached Henry to Rome were severed. It was the first dawn of the Protestant Reformation in England. Henry had divorced Catharine, and married Anne Boleyn. The effects of his quarrel with Rome emboldened the Baptists to leave their hiding-places, "and," says, Fox, speaking of the influence of Anne Boleyn over Henry, "we read of no persecution nor any abjuration to have been in the Church of England, save only that the Registers of London make mention of **certain Anabaptists, of whom ten were put to death in sundry places of the realm**, A.D. 1535; other ten repented and were saved." (See *Fox's Book of Martyrs,* Ed. ii, P. 956.)

Baptist presence is revealed at the very first of the Reformation, when Henry first broke with the pope. The following year a convocation sat, and after some matters relating to the king's divorce had been debated, the lower house presented to the upper house a list of religious heresies which prevailed in the realm, specifying those of the Anabaptists. Several complaints about the Baptists were affirmed or condemned. Among its items were:

Chapter 11—The Churches of the Sixteenth Century Part 2

1. Infants must needs be christened, because they are born in original sin, which sin must needs be remitted, and which only can be done in the sacrament of baptism.
2. That children or men once baptized can or ought never to be baptized again.
3. That they ought to repute and take all the Anabaptists, and every man's opinion agreeing with said Anabaptists, for detestable heresies and utterly to be condemned.

Baptism for believers only by immersion was a truth forced underground until a little liberty let it break out of its concealment, "or," as says the persecuting Dr. Featly, who wrote against the Anabaptists in 1645, "if it broke out at any time, by the care of the ecclesiastical and civil magistrates, it was soon put out." Since the Baptist hating Featly wrote that statement in 1645, it meant that the Baptists were very much present in the mid seventeenth century. Ford wrote:

> "They were found," says Bishop Burnett, "in almost every town and village in England." "They were emboldened," says Durham, and their great increase is accounted for by "the partial toleration in religion."

Again the fact stated by Mosheim: **"Baptists lay concealed in almost all the countries of Europe before the rise of Luther and Calvin."** Yes, and they were concealed by the thousands in England, too, and broke out with great power at the first hint of freedom (S. H. Ford, *the Origin of the Baptists*, Ch. 3).

As we have shown, during the reign of Edward VI (1547-1553), laws were passed against the Baptists. To be a Baptist was a grave crime. The young king was merciful to a great degree, but eventually he let great cruelty against the baptized believers be unleashed.

> A large number of historians testified that Baptists were numerous in England throughout the centuries. According to J. T. Christian, baptism by immersion for believers was common all over England and Europe in the mid-1500's. (See J. T. Christian, *A History of the Baptists*, Vol. 1. P. 115-152.) **In 1880, Dr. William H. Whitsitt, then professor of ecclesiastical history at the Southern Baptist Theological seminary in Louisville, Kentucky, contended that from 1509 to 1641 the Anabaptists of England practiced effusion, and not until 1641 did they begin to practice immersion.** Whitsitt ignored a sea of evidence to the contrary.

Even so, the Baptists steadily increased in numbers. They were everywhere it seemed. They were in the court, in town, country and common. Bishop Burnet said, "There were many Anabaptists in many parts of England." **Even in London** they were great in number. On June 25, 1549, Bishop John Hooper wrote to Henry Bullinger, saying, **"The Anabaptists flock to this place (London) and give me much trouble."** In 1550, Ridley, who was Bishop of London sent this letter to all London ministers to find out if:

> Whether any speak against infant baptism. Whether any of the Anabaptists' sect, or other, use notoriously any unlawful or private conventicle (churches), whether they do use doctrine or administration of sacraments, separating themselves from the rest of the parish (J. T. Christian, *A History of the Baptists*, Vol. 1, P. 197).

From the above evidence, it is obvious that there were fully organized Baptist churches in London by the year 1550.

If the letters of the ministers of the Church of England can be believed, then it is also obvious that **the Baptists were active in Kent**. As early as June 26 of 1550, Bishop John

The Collegiate Baptist History Workbook

Hooper, complained that his **"district is troubled with the frenzy of the Anabaptists more than any other part of the kingdom."** And the historian Strype says: **"There were such assemblies in Kent"** (J. T. Christian, *A History of the Baptists*, Vol. 1, P. 197).

Christian wrote:

> The Baptists of Kent had a number of great preachers. Henry Hart began preaching during the reign of Henry VIII. He was strict and holy in life and fervent in his opinions. He and several others were thrown into prison. Humphrey Middleton was included in another group. When Middleton was cast into prison he said to the Archbishop: **"Well, reverend sir, pass what sentence you think fit upon us; but that you may not say that you were forewarned, I testify that your turn will be next."** Like the fulfillment of an Old Testament prophecy, when Middleton was released the Archbishop was thrown into prison.
>
> Another preacher in Kent was John Kemp who "was a great traveler abroad in Kent, instructing and confirming the *gospellers*" (J. T. Christian, *History of the Baptists* Vol.1 P. 197).

STOP AND THINK

1. Write 2 Corinthians 6:17 twice.

2. How severe was the punishment for violating the enactment of 1539?
   Punished to the extremity of the law without favor
3. What first caused the Baptists to come out from concealment in England?
   The reformation
4. Where were Baptists found in England according to Bishop Burnett?
   almost every town/village in England
5. Name at least two cities in which the Baptists of this time period were found: *Kent, London*
6. In what year was it obvious that there were fully organized Baptist churches in London?
   1559/1550

****

11.2.2

Definitions:

effusion: the act of pouring water over a candidate for baptism
sprinkling (affusion): the act of placing water on the head or face for baptism
immersion: scriptural practice of dipping under the water the believer for baptism
catabaptist: one who practices dipping for baptism

Baptism by Immersion in England before the Seventeenth Century

John T. Christian wrote:

> We have already seen that the Baptists before 1641, while numerous, suffered greatly from persecutions. They did not leave much literature, and so we must largely depend upon their enemies for references to them. We have enough proof, however, to show that they practiced dipping.

149

Chapter 11—The Churches of the Sixteenth Century Part 2

Mr. Christian was doing the Christian world, and especially the Baptists, a favor when he brought forth evidences of immersion among the Baptists of the seventeenth century. We baptized believers of today should know our heritage and protect it.

A book, *The Sum of the Holy Scriptures*, was published in 1523 by the Anabaptists in Holland. It was translated and widely circulated in England. According to Thomas Armitage, the book stated:

> So we are dipped under as a sign that we are, as it were, dead and buried, as Paul writes, Rom. 6 and Col. 2. The life of man is a battle upon the earth, and in baptism we promise to strive like men. The pledge is given when we are plunged under the water. It is the same to God whether you are eighty years old when you are baptized, or twenty; for God does not consider how old you are, but with what purpose you receive baptism. He does not mind whether you are Jew or heathen, man or woman, nobleman or citizen, bishop or layman, but only he who with perfect faith and confidence comes to God, and struggles for eternal life, attains it as God has promised in the Gospel (Thomas Armitage, *History of the Baptists*, Vol. 1, P. 409).

> **Answering William Whitsitt's 1641 Theory**
> Baptist historians William Cathcart and Thomas Armitage answered Whitsitt's error indirectly in their writings. In 1896, John Taylor Christian answered Whitsitt directly with his doctrinal masterpiece, *Did They Dip?* Modern Baptist historians such as Leon MacBeth, Walter Shurden, William McGoldrick, etc., quote Whitsitt as though he were the sole authority on this question. In fact, Baptist historians in convention circles simply accept the English Descent Theory and do not believe Baptists existed before 1641.

The English Church historian Fuller, declares the Anabaptists to be *dippers*. J. T. Christian quoted Fuller:

> A match being now made up, by the Lord Cromwell's contrivance, betwixt King Henry and Lady Anne of Cleves. Dutchmen flocked faster than formerly into England. Many of them had active souls so that, whilst their hands were busied about their manufactures, their heads were also beating about points of divinity. Hereof they had many rude notions, too ignorant to manage themselves and too proud to crave the direction of others. Their minds had a bye stream of activity more than what sufficed to drive on their vocation; and this waste of their souls they employed in needless speculations, and soon after began to broach their strange opinions, being branded with the general name of Anabaptists. These Anabaptists, for the main, are but "Donatists new **dipped**" and this year their name first appears in our English Chronicles; for I read that four Anabaptists, three men and one woman, all Dutch, bare faggots at St. Paul's Cross, Nov. 24th, and three days after, a man and a woman of their sect were burned in Smithfield (J. T. Christian, *A History of the Baptists*, Vol. 1, P. 195).

> The practice of immersion was universal in the reign of Henry VIII. It was the form of baptism of all parties and there is no known testimony to the contrary. The Church of England practiced immersion. The Catholics practiced immersion. The Baptists practiced immersion (J. T. Christian, *History of the Baptists*, Vol. 1, P. 196).

It was at this time that God raised up Robert Cooke, a tremendous man of law who argued for the Baptist cause for over 40 years. Cooke caused a great stir as J. T. Christian relates how the state church fought Cooke: "In 1551 William Turner, 'Doctor of Physick,' devised A Preservative or triacle, agaynst the poyson of Pelagius, lately renued, & Styrred up agayn, by the furious secte of the Anabaptistes."

Even John Knox thought Cooke worthy enough to write against him. (See J. T. Christian, *A History of the Baptists*, Vol. 1, P. 201.)

The Collegiate Baptist History Workbook

There is so much evidence for immersion it is impossible to relate all. Here are some of the facts as recorded by J. T. Christian, concerning the royal family of England and their baptisms during the seventeenth century:

> The Synod of Cashel, A. D. 1172, was held under Henry II:
> It was ordained that children should be brought to the church and baptized in clear water, being thrice **dipped** therein, in the name of the Father, and of the Son, and of the Holy Ghost.
> We have an account of the baptism of Arthur, the oldest son of Henry VII. He married Catherine of Aragon, who after his death became the wife of Henry VIII.
> Leland also gives a description at great length of the baptism of Margaret, the sister of Arthur, 1490, and of Queen Elizabeth, 1533. The royalty were all immersed.

Christian again, quoting the English historian Fuller:

> Anabaptists not only deny believer's children baptism, as the Pelagians and Donatists did of old, but affirm that **dipping the whole body under water** is so necessary that without it none are truly baptized (as has been said) (J. T. Christian, *The History of the Baptists*, Vol. 1, P. 195).

J. T. Christian again, and note the hatred of Featley:

> Daniel Featley, D.D., a fierce opponent of the Baptists, born in 1582, also declares that the Baptists of the reign of Henry VIII practiced dipping. He says: "**Let the punishment bear upon it the print of the sin, for as these sectaries drew one another into their errors, so also into the gulfe; and as they drown men spiritually by rebaptizing, and so profaning the holy sacrament, as also they were drowned corporally**" (J. T. Christian, *History of the Baptists*, Vol. 1, P. 196).

Perhaps the most compelling argument for the practice of immersion by the Baptists of seventeenth century England comes from the pen of the Protestant historian John Foxe:

> There are some Anabaptists at this time in England who came from Germany. Of these there were two sorts; **the first only objected to the baptizing of children and to the manner of it by sprinkling instead of dipping.** The other held many opinions anciently condemned as heresies; they had raised a war in Germany, and had set up a new king in Munster; **but all these were called Anabaptists, from their opposition to infant baptism,** though it was one of the mildest opinions they held (John Foxe, *Book of Martyrs*, Alden ed., P. 338).

1. Write 2 Corinthians 6:17 twice.

2. What is effusion?

3. How does sprinkling differ from immersion?

4. What was Whitsitt's contention?

5. Who answered Whitsitt and how?

Chapter 11—The Churches of the Sixteenth Century Part 2

6. How was the Royal family baptized? Immersion
7. What is a "catabaptist?" Practices dipping (scorn)
8. What did Featly say was a fit punishment for Baptists? drowned to death
9. Who is at least partly responsible for sprinkling replacing immersion for baptism according to Sir David Brewster? John Calvin
10. What is the amazing conclusion of the Westminster Assembly of 1643 about baptism? It was debated and sprinkling became the main form of baptism

Chapter Twelve
The Churches of the Seventeenth Century

Section One: The Authorized Version, The Independents, Puritans, Dissenters and Pilgrims
Section Two: Roger Williams and John Clarke

SECTION ONE

Time Line Seventeenth Century:
1603. King James VI of Scotland becomes King James I of all England
1609. Jamestown Settlement in Virginia
1610. Anglican worship enforced in England
1611. Completion of the Authorized Version
1612. Edward Wightman burned in Lichfield, England for preaching Baptist principles
1620. *Humble Supplication* presented to Parliament
1620. Pilgrims arrive in Massachusetts Bay
1625. Charles I becomes King
1628. Charles I dissolves parliament, pressures Puritans to desist
1629. Massachusetts Bay colony begins under John Endicott
1633. Laud becomes Archbishop of Canterbury
1637. First Baptist Church in America, under Dr. John Clarke, worships in New Hampshire
1644. London Confession (Particular Baptist) published
1644. Richard Baxter publishes his "Plain Scripture Proof" tirade against believer's baptism
1644. Roger Williams publishes *The Bloudy Tenet of Persecution*
1649. Civil War in England, Charles I dethroned and executed. Long parliament under the Presbyterians appointed Oliver Cromwell, Lord Protector
1649. Under the Long parliament, death penalty for denying infant baptism is reinstated.
1651. The Beating of Obadiah Holmes in Boston
1655. The Massacre of the Waldensians
1660. Charles II restored to the throne.
1661. An address of toleration presented to Charles II by Thomas Grantham
1662. Act of Uniformity was passed (the old prayer book of Elizabeth reinstated) 2,000 preachers forced from their churches and homes
1663. Conventicle act; John Bunyan jailed
1665. The Plague **100,000 die in London**
1666. Drought and the London fire, 13,000 homes burnt, 89 churches burnt
1689. Act of Toleration under William of Orange

The Authorized Version of the Bible

The line of English translations leading to the King James Version of the Bible:

William Tyndale: 1483-1536. Tyndale translated from the Old Latin. Tyndale said, "I defy the Pope, and all his laws; and if God spare my life, ere many years, I will cause a boy that driveth the plough to know more of the Scripture than you do!"—Tyndale to a Roman prelate.

Tyndale was skilled in seven languages, Hebrew, Greek, Latin, Italian, Spanish, English and French. His edition of the Bible was printed in 1525. He was strangled and burned at Vilvorde, Germany in 1536. Before his execution he cried, "Lord, open the eyes of the King of England!"

Miles Coverdale: Tyndale's proofreader printed his edition in 1535 in Cologne. Coverdale used the *received text* of the *Itala Biblia* and non-Roman Catholic

Chapter 12—The Churches of the Seventeenth Century

translations. The *received text* was used from that time on for English translations.

Matthews Bible: Translated by John Rogers in 1536.

Great Bible: Translated in 1538.

Geneva Bible: An English edition which was printed in 1560. It was a product of Beza, Knox, Coverdale and Whitingham. It was printed in Geneva, France due to the reign of Bloody Mary in England.

Bishop's Bible: This was translated in 1568.

King James: The King James was translated in 1611. Forty-seven world renowned scholars worked for seven years on the Authorized Version. This Bible brought missions and revival to the world.

Scripture to Memorize

Hebrews 12:3 For consider him that endured such contradiction of sinners against himself, lest ye be wearied and faint in your minds.

The Independents, Puritans, Dissenters and Pilgrims

There is a tremendous amount of history packed into the seventeenth century. Voyages to the New World and the birthing of new colonies filled Europe with wonder and excitement. The migration to the western world eventually produced the greatest republic in the history of mankind. The rise of the American republic is paralleled by the rise of the American Baptists. One movement could not have existed without the other. To discover this truth we start with the Independents of the Church of England.

The Scrooby Congregation

The Separatist (Independent) wing of the Church of England gave birth to two brave churches, the Scrooby congregation and the Gainsborough congregation. Both churches migrated to Amsterdam, Holland in search of liberty. For the Scrooby flock, under the pastoral care of John Robinson and Richard Clifton, Amsterdam was a bit too much liberty. They chose to migrate to Leyden, Holland. The Gainsborough congregation had as their pastor, John Smythe, and his assistant Thomas Hellwys. In a short time, the Mennonite (Baptist) element of Amsterdam had a doctrinal effect on Smythe and Hellwys. Some historians believe Smythe performed baptism upon himself and then upon the rest of his congregation. Amidst great confusion, and in the wake of Smythe's death, the Gainsborough church split, and Thomas Hellwys retraced his tracks to England with his flock. This church supposedly became the first *General* Baptist church in England, officially organized in 1611. However, as we have shown, evidence proves that Baptists were in England much earlier.

The Scrooby congregation stayed together in Leyden and determined to go to yet another country to worship God in peace. This they did in 1620. Over one hundred of them sailed upon a small vessel across the raging Atlantic. We know them as the Pilgrims and their vessel was the *Mayflower*.

The Pilgrims

The Collegiate Baptist History Workbook

The journey of the Pilgrims was a search for religious liberty. The Scrooby congregation had sued for a patent in the New World and for liberty of conscience. The patent was secured from the English government but there was no written agreement as to their separation from the Church of England. So, even without the guarantees of total liberty they came to North America believing the distance would allow them to worship without the liturgy and false forms of the Anglican Church.

The Pilgrims were not Baptist people, but they were closely related. The Pilgrims were not as **the Puritans, who opposed the liturgy, ceremonies and parts of the constitution and discipline of the Church of England**. Nor were they of the same mind as **the Presbyterians** who **opposed the ceremonies, mainly**. They were independents— *Separatists* who wanted a clean break, "seeking to lay aside the liturgy and all ceremonies together" (John Callender, *Historical Discourse on the Civil and Religious Affairs of Rhode Island*, P. 8).

The Pilgrims were aided by God's providence. The providential hand of God in helping these original Americans is a stunning study in the supernatural.

Their intentions were to bring a contingent of Pilgrims, a crew of hired *adventurers,* a military leader (Myles Standish) and an extra ship, the *Speedwell*. But the *Speedwell* was full of holes and even a last ditch effort to patch her ended in failure. The cargo was loaded onto the *Mayflower*, and after a weeping farewell, they sailed for New England.

With roughly half of the crew rough merchantmen, the Pilgrims nearly drove their worldly crew insane with their fervent prayers and psalm singing. One such crewman had enough of it and took to calling the floating churchgoers *pukes*. All criticism of the Pilgrims was stopped when that shipman was knocked overboard by a strong wind and never found.

In 66 days, the *Mayflower* finally reached land. On November 9, 1620 she came along Cape Cod. Some have speculated that the *Mayflower* missed her landing place on purpose, but as time would soon tell the purposes were of God. As the crew and passengers cautiously took days to strike out and carve out shelter, they were amazed at the absence of natives even though there were obvious evidences of a previous settlement. The land had been cleared and the area had plenty of fresh water springs. And there were stashes of corn and grain. It was not until they met their Indian friends and benefactors, Samoset, Squanto and Massasoit, that they learned of the mysterious disease that had wiped out the warlike tribe that inhabited the bay before their arrival.

> It was in those waters that the Pilgrims met their first terror. Before the Mayflower landed at the famous Plymouth Rock, she was anchored in the bay while her genteel ladies waded out into the water to wash their husband's clothes. Incredibly, some caught their death of cold and contracted severe flu. In the terrible winter that engulfed them—they perished.

When the Scrooby congregation landed they were without their original spiritual leader. John Robinson had elected to stay in Leyden, Holland with the remainder of his flock. It was William Brewster who made the journey with them. They did not make it to the Hudson, but landed providentially several hundred miles to the north in a beautiful bay inside of Cape Cod.

The land herself was the Pilgrims worst enemy in that first winter separated from mother England by the cold green waters of the Atlantic Ocean. Of the one hundred and

Chapter 12—The Churches of the Seventeenth Century

one souls that journeyed to the New World, over half of them perished in the first twelve months.

With the help of benevolent natives, the Pilgrims survived and then thrived. Elder Brewster lived to pastor his flock for over 24 years. God began to prosper them, and by 1629 their number increased to over three hundred. With the news of the Pilgrim success, the Puritans of Old England took heart and began immigration to the New World. From 1628 to 1643 21,200 persons came to New England. What was their religious affiliation? Isaac Backus (the first American Baptist historian) reports, "very few had separated from the Church of England."

The Mayflower Compact

All Americans should be aware that in the infancy of our struggling country, the Pilgrims of Plymouth produced **our first independent document of self-rule**: *the Mayflower Compact*.

The document is inseparable from the conduct and character of the pioneers who penned its words. It was drawn inside the bowels of the *Mayflower*, and it was **the first document of separation from mother England.**

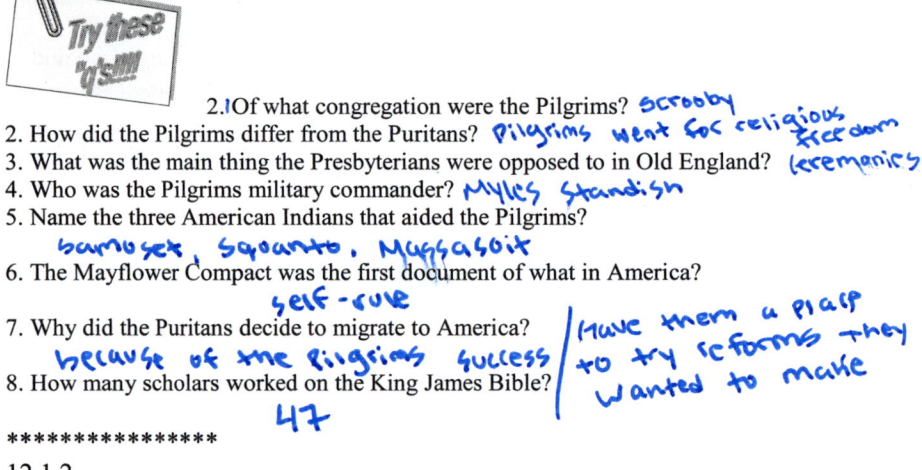

1. Write Hebrews 12:3 two times.
2. Of what congregation were the Pilgrims? *Scrooby*
2. How did the Pilgrims differ from the Puritans? *Pilgrims went for religious freedom*
3. What was the main thing the Presbyterians were opposed to in Old England? *ceremonies*
4. Who was the Pilgrims military commander? *Myles Standish*
5. Name the three American Indians that aided the Pilgrims? *Samoset, Squanto, Massasoit*
6. The Mayflower Compact was the first document of what in America? *self-rule*
7. Why did the Puritans decide to migrate to America? *because of the Pilgrims success / Gave them a place to try reforms they wanted to make*
8. How many scholars worked on the King James Bible? *47*

****
12.1.2

The Puritans in America

The English were interested in the areas north of the Pilgrims, there were definite concerns about what the French were going to do there. In God's Providence, the King of England assigned a despot priest named William Laud to be the Archbishop of Canterbury, a position of rule over the Church of England. Laud burned Baptists, (including Edward Wightman) and other dissenters, and hated the Puritans and tried to silence them. All of this encouraged the flight to the New World.

The Collegiate Baptist History Workbook

In 1629, after eight years of Pilgrim isolation, Charles I granted the Massachusetts charter for a Puritan exodus to *New Israel.* John Endicott (1589-1655) arrived with colonists in September 1628, serving as the colony's first governor until 1630. The Massachusetts Bay Company (March, 1629) began with a royal charter. Their first settlement in Boston was established in 1630.

> **William Laud**
>
> William Laud (1573 1645) Archbishop of Canterbury, born at Reading, Berkshire, England. Studied at Oxford. In 1601, he was ordained and in 1603 he became a chaplain. Advancement was rapid, and by 1611 he was elected the head of the St John's College. In 1621, he was appointed bishop of St. David's. He increased in royal promotions and favor. With the ascension of Charles 1, in 1625, real power in the Church of England began. He believed in the divine right of kings, and the divine right of bishops, and exercised authority accordingly. In 1626, he became Bishop of Bath and Wells, and in 1628, he became the Bishop of London. In 1629 he was made chancellor of the University of Oxford where he pursued a program of scholarly reform, and founded a school of Arabic which is still in existence.
>
> In 1633, he was made Archbishop of Canterbury and began work as head of the church [of England] with great zeal and determination. In his first year there he attempted to force ritualism on the Scottish Presbyterian Church. This led to riot in the churches, and a flare of rebellion in the entire land of Scotland. When the king endeavored to squelch the rebellion, trouble broke out at home, and the Civil War of 1642 to 1649 followed. Laud's severe program against the Puritans incurred their bitter hostility; his dealings with the Queen, who was a Roman Catholic, stirred her to enmity. In 1640, he was impeached for treason. He was confined and sent to the Tower in 1641. He was tried, and in 1643, with great firmness, he met his death on the scaffold of the Tower. He was narrow, cruel, and an enemy of the Baptists.—David L. Cummins.

In Puritan Massachusetts, each community had its own church, which was **an individual unit run by the members of each congregation.** The church and the community were inseparable. The community elected their own minister. This was congregational church-state government. Ministers could not hold public office, but great pressure was exerted in advising public officials. A court of Deputies was elected each year in Boston as judges over the "New Israel."

In the beginning, **the New England Congregational church** set very high standards for its members. They accepted only those who publicly professed their faith, and showed evidences of salvation. To become a candidate for membership, one had to undergo examination in front of the congregation and describe their **conversion experience**.

The Puritans insisted on **literacy** so everyone could read the Bible. Parents were responsible for seeing that their children were not ignorant of the Scriptures. Ministers were to stir the heart and faith of their congregation with moving sermons that could be understood by everyone. **Harvard College** was founded in 1636 to educate ministers of the Gospel.

John Cotton, the famous Puritan Reformer from Boston in England, came to New England in 1630 and became the ruling elder in the congregational church at Boston, Massachusetts. Also arriving was Thomas Hooker, the future founder of Connecticut.

Four ships arrived in March 1630 with the newly elected governor **John Winthrop**. Seven more followed within one month. Winthrop viewed the Massachusetts colony as a sacred experiment, a **city upon a hill**, which would serve as a lighthouse to humanity. Winthrop envisioned a society in agreement with God, which would be a model for the rest of mankind to observe. Instead, Massachusetts exemplified tyranny. A tyranny our Baptist forefathers resisted. Winthrop was governor for nineteen years.

The population settled along the Massachusetts coast north of Plymouth. Within one decade 20,000 settlers immigrated to New England.

Chapter 12—The Churches of the Seventeenth Century

As the Pilgrims of Plymouth and the Puritans of Massachusetts ran on in years they began to blend into a *standing order*, although the Plymouth Pilgrims never really embraced the tyranny of her brother Puritans to the north.

The Pilgrims and the Puritans were destined to run into **the crucible of baptismal legitimacy**. As Joseph Hall, Anglican bishop said to John Robinson, Pilgrim pastor: "Either you must go forward to Anabaptism, or come back to us. If we be a True Church you must return, if we be not you must re-baptize. If our baptism be good then is our Constitution good." (See Hall's *Common Apologie*, s.xi.) In one hundred years his prediction was fulfilled.

American school children are no longer taught the true story of the Puritans of New England. A real understanding of our Republic must begin with an understanding of these pioneering Englishmen who came seeking a better country. The author of this text hates to bring bad light upon the Puritans especially in the current economy of hatred and bigotry toward Christians of all sects in twenty-first century America. Although none could question their character and dependence upon God, the Puritans have a horrific record concerning the *baptized believers*. The Puritans came to America to escape the brutality of the notorious Church of England henchman, Laud. With freedom theirs, the Reformed children of Rome were faced with the same question that dogged Luther and Calvin: Where does the authority of "the Church" begin and end? Would the New World have a feudal government and religious establishment, or civil government and religious liberty? Sadly, our Puritan forefathers chose the former for New England. John Callender alluded that these first Americans were incapable of "mutual forbearance" (John Callender, *Historical Discourse on the Civil and Religious Affairs of Rhode Island*, P. 15). Their religious intolerance would last into the nineteenth century.

> **America's Four Key Documents**
> There were four documents that blazed the trail for liberty and the establishment of the American republic. The first was drawn together inside the *Mayflower*, **the Mayflower Compact**. It was the first document of separation from mother England. The second was **the Providence Compact**, penned in Providence, Rhode Island and was the first document of government order giving power only from the consent of the governed. The third document was **the Portsmouth Compact**. Rarely given the credit it deserves, the compact at Portsmouth was uniquely powerful because of its guarantee of religious liberty. It has been copied in principle in each ensuing generation. The fourth document was **the Rhode Island Constitution**. The constitution was written by Dr. John Clarke, pastor of the first Baptist church in America. Many believe it was the basis of the U.S. Constitution.

---

1. Write Hebrews 12:3 two times.

2. Why were the English interested in the area north of the Pilgrims?
   Concerned about the French
3. What is Congregational church government?
   ruled largely by a congregation
4. What did the Congregational church require of its members?
   describing their conversion stories after baptism

5. What was John Cotton's position in the Congregational church at Boston, Massachusetts?
   The ruling elder
6. What did Bishop Laud try to force into the Scottish Presbyterian Church?
   ritualism
7. What were the Pilgrims and Puritans destined to face?
   The crucible baptismal legitimacy
8. What were America's four key documents?
   The Mayflower Compact, The Providence Compact, The Portsmouth Compact, The Rhode Island Compact

SECTION TWO

Definitions:

Congregationalism: a church governed by the members of each congregation.
Oath of the Freeman: oath signed by new citizens of Massachusetts swearing allegiance to the New England government and the Congregational church
The "Law of Patents:" So called **divine right of Christian Kings** to confiscate lands from the heathen without payment to them
Enforcement of the First Table of the Law: the obligation of the civil government to enforce religious laws of faith and practice upon its citizens. */ separation of 10 commandments/*
Seeker: a religious person seeking the correct way outside of religious establishment
Anabaptist: a name of scorn given to those who baptized only upon a profession of faith in Christ
Antinomian: literally means "without law," was a derisive nickname given to those that believed you could have assurance of salvation based solely on belief in the Bible promises. *(Dr. John Clark)*
Experimental Religion: emerging evangelical belief in the early seventeenth century that you can experience a new birth by believing in Christ, giving you assurance of salvation. */ salvation experience*
Disfranchised: removing your ability to buy or sell at the common markets.
Disarmed: taking the weapons away from those citizens esteemed *dangerous*
Received Text: that group of manuscripts which were accepted by Bible believers and generally rejected by the Roman Catholic Institution

The First Baptists in America and Roger Williams

After the Puritans settled Massachusetts in 1630, a young preacher named Roger Williams came to Boston to become the teaching elder in the Congregational church.

All biographers are certain that Roger Williams was born and lived in London, though the dates are uncertain. His birth was probably around 1599. He attended St. Sepulcher's church and won a scholarship to Cambridge. He studied languages, theology, and the classics and became quite adept at stenography and short hand.

His office skills were profound at an early age and came to the attention of Sir Edward Coke, the famous juror of England who prosecuted Sir Walter Raleigh and later the members of the infamous Gunpowder Plot. Williams became the equivalent of an office manager for Coke and recorded procedures for him in the myriad of court dates

Chapter 12—The Churches of the Seventeenth Century

and duties of England's most famous lawyer. This brought him into contact with the elite band of dissidents whose collective voice was beginning to be heard from on high.

In the 1620's Mr. Williams' association with the Separatist leaders of England built definite principles into his young mind. His Separatist views were nurtured by the independent thinking of Coke and other men opposed to King Charles I. Contrary to modern historical rewrite; his views were not a New England evolution of thought. They were definitely Old England. It is evident that this group of non-conformists wanted nothing less than the right to worship as a separate church, independent of the compromise and unregenerate state of the Church of England.

Upon leaving Cambridge, Mr. Williams was assigned the duty of personal chaplain to Sir William Masham and his Lady Joan. Both were Puritan sympathizers leaning toward Separatism. Mr. Williams fell in love with the niece of Lady Joan, but this was not to be. He instead courted Mary Barnard, a servant for the Mashams and married her in December of 1629.

> The Oath of a Freeman:
> I, A.B. being by God's providence an inhabitant and freeman in this Commonweal, do freely acknowledge myself to be subject to the government thereof, and therefore do here swear by the great and dreadful name of the ever-living God, that I will be true and faithful to the same, and will accordingly yield assistance and support hereunto with my person and estate as in equity I am bound, and will also truly endeavor to maintain and preserve all the liberties and privileges thereof; submitting myself to the wholesome laws and orders made and established by the same. And further, that I will not plot nor practice any evil against it, nor consent to any that shall so do; but will truly discover and reveal the same to lawful authority now here established, for the speedy preventing thereof. Moreover I do solemnly bind myself in the sight of God, that when I shall be called to give my voice touching any such matters of this state wherein freemen are to deal, I will give my vote and suffrage as I shall judge in mine own conscience may best conduce and tend to the public weal of the body, without respect of persons or favour of any man; so help me God in the Lord Jesus Christ.

Williams became acquainted with the arguments of the Puritans and Separatists while serving as chaplain. He even became friends with Thomas Hooker. Williams and Hooker went by carriage together to meet with another young preacher destined for fame in the New World, John Cotton. From Cotton's church in England's Old Boston, the three traveled together to attend the famous meeting for the forming of the Massachusetts Bay Company in Sempringham. What happened on the journey is an open window of understanding early American history.

During their ride to and from Sempringham, the three men of God carried on a lively discussion about theology and church reform, making the trip a memorable one. Williams wrote: "Possibly, Master Cotton may call to mind that the discusser, riding with himself and one other person of precious memory, Master Hooker, to and from Sempringham, presented his arguments from Scripture why he durst not join with them in their use of Common Prayer (Roger Williams, *The Bloody Tenet Yet More Bloody*, N.C.P., Vol. IV, P. 65).

Massachusetts was a colony designed to be a "Holy Commonwealth," it distanced itself from the Church of England and set up its own official church: the New England Congregational Church. It was a violation of the law to be anything but Congregational. In 1635, the Boston Court of Deputies passed a law requiring all citizens to take the "Oath of the Freeman." The *Oath* said that a man must swear allegiance to the commonwealth government and be a member in good standing of the Congregational, or *standing order*, church.

Roger Williams believed the *Oath* was scripturally wrong and preached against it. He resigned the teaching duties of the Boston Congregational Church and began preaching at Salem, just northwest of Boston.

One great burden that Roger Williams had was the salvation of the Native American Indians of New England, and he began to witness to them. He learned their language, wrote a book on learning the dialect, and began to publicly protest the so-called "**Law of Patents.**" *The Law of Patents*, a policy began by the popes in Rome, authorized "Christian" Kings to claim land inhabited by conquest or discovery. To Roger Williams this was nothing but robbery and he lost the pulpit in Salem for opposing the Law of Patents.

Roger Williams also opposed the "Enforcement of **the First Table of the Law**," which gave national government the right to impose religious beliefs upon citizens. Williams rightly defended the emerging idea of religious liberty and liberty of conscience, something all Americans take for granted. For his defense of these rights, he was banished from Massachusetts and ordered out of England.

The Providence Compact

Williams did not wait to be deported. He fled into the American wilderness with his family. After three days, he came to a crossroads named Rehoboth in the extreme west of Plymouth jurisdiction. He found some solace among Pilgrim sympathizers, token evidences of their Separatist feelings. But Governor Winslow of Plymouth suggested that the he travel west, beyond the river Seekonk, into Rhode Island. The territory had been called the *sewer of New England* by the Massachusetts Bay leadership.

The Seekonk River was a river outlet that flowed into the Narragansett Bay and separated the Plymouth colony from the western wilderness. This was Narragansett Indian land and Williams knew he had to make contact with the Sachems and negotiate a land deal. So in the cold of November, 1636, Williams crossed his *Jordan* and sought out his new friends. He did not have to search long for them, for as his canoe reached the western bank of the Seekonk a voice cried out in an Indian accent, "Whattcheer?!" It was the voice of a Narragansett familiar with the English greeting of charity. Williams testified:

> I testify and declare in the holy presence of God, that when at my first coming into these parts I obtained the lands of Secunk of Osamaquin, (Massasoit) the then chief Sachem on that side. The Governor of Plymouth, Mr. Winslow, wrote to me, in the name of their government, their claim of Secunk to be in their jurisdiction, as also their advice to remove but over the river unto this side, where now by God's merciful providence we are, and then I should be out of their claim, and be as free as themselves, and loving neighbors together (Isaac Backus, *Church History of New England*, Vol. 1. P. 57).

Most heavy upon the mind of these banished believers was whether the land could be purchased. When it was agreed that it could be purchased it from the natives, Williams and his wife, two little children and eleven of his followers migrated to the land north of the Narragansett Bay on the banks of the Seekonk River. After fourteen weeks on the run as a fugitive, Williams founded a colony. He called it ***Providence***.

Chapter 12—The Churches of the Seventeenth Century

Two years after the stunning success of their founder, in August of 1638, the people of Providence Plantation approved the first public document establishing government without interference in religious matters. The Providence Compact was the first of a series of American political documents advocating government by the consent of the governed and *liberty of conscience*. It was visionary for its time.

Providence Compact

We whose names are underwritten, being desirous to inhabit in the town of Providence, do promise to submit ourselves in active or passive obedience to all such orders or agreements as shall be made for public good of the body in an orderly way, by the major consent of the present inhabitants, matter of families, incorporated together into a township, and such others whom they shall admit unto the same, *only in civil things*.

STOP AND THINK

1. Write Hebrews 12:3 two times.
   [handwritten: Roger Williams: founded the colony of Providence and established religious liberty / ward that]
2. When was Roger Williams born? *[handwritten: 1599]*
3. Was Williams a Puritan or a Separatist? *[handwritten: Separatist]*
4. True or False: Williams became a separatist after he came to America. *[handwritten: False]*
5. Williams was banished for opposing three things. What were they?
   [handwritten: oath of a freeman, enforcement of the first table, law of patents]
6. How did Williams acquire the land for his new colony?
   [handwritten: purchased the land]
7. The Providence Compact was the first government document that advocated "government by the
   [handwritten: people / consent of the governed]
8. What was the *Received Text*?
   [handwritten: rejected by roman catholics / majority text]

****

12.2.2

Dr. John Clarke

At this time, there were **four** great settlements in New England: **Plymouth, 1620; Massachusetts Bay, 1630; Hartford, 1635, and Providence, 1636**. A very important but little known American was about to participate in the fifth.

Born in Suffolk, England, in 1609 and educated in London, John Clarke became a practicing physician. He arrived in Boston in November 1637. Like Roger Williams before him, there was something about reaching the New World, that made all tyranny out of place. The Boston Court of Deputies made *anabaptism* a crime, and the government of Massachusetts was now a church government through and through, even making the rejection of certain Calvinist doctrines a crime. Isaac Backus wrote:

The Collegiate Baptist History Workbook

> But what followed among them [at Boston in 1638] may be a warning to all after ages, against confounding church and state together in their government. For disputes and divisions about grace and works, between their chief rulers and ministers, came on in Boston, and spread through all the country to a great degree (Issac Backus, *A Church History of New England*, P. 40).

The Boston Court banished a preacher named Wheelwright for his opinions about how a person could know he was saved. Many in Boston believed you could have assurance of salvation based on the scriptures alone after experiencing the convicting power of the Holy Spirit. This became known as ***experimental religion*** or ***being born again.*** Incredibly the Boston Court deemed this illegal to believe or preach. (See John Callendar, *Historical Discourse on the Civil and Religious Affairs of Rhode Island*, P. 25.) After refusing to stop preaching these sentiments, John Wheelwright was **disfranchised, disarmed and banished.**

The most obnoxious turn of events occurred as house meetings held across the area were condemned. The best way for the Boston Court to stigmatize these home Bible studies was to find a fiend among them. They found the fiend in Anne Hutchinson.

There is no evidence to suggest that Mrs. Hutchinson was unique to the controversy other than the fact that she was

> The "Ann Hutchinson Thing" is a result of feminist re-writers who desire to give this sweet lady more credit than she is due. The historians on the side of the Boston synod such as Cotton Mather and Neal in his *History of the Puritans* distort the place of Mrs. Hutchinson in this dispute to make it appear that she was the ringleader in a seditious movement. Modern historians use this distortion (without consulting the Baptist accounts) to build a case that this poor woman's rights as an individual were violated. Eyewitness accounts indicate neither assessment is true.

bright, attractive and articulate. She was conducting ladies meetings in her home with her husband's approval. The meetings were held primarily in support of John Cotton, the Hutchinson's hero and mentor. It came to pass that Ann Hutchinson was also banished. The banished people of Boston were called *Opinionists*.

In the midst of this controversy, Dr. John Clarke arrived in Boston. He sensed the danger of possible conflict as Mr. Wheelwright and the other disfranchised citizen were extremely popular. When the Boston Court ordered 76 men *disarmed*, Clarke sprang into action.

Perhaps his skills as a physician had quickly won the *Opinionists*' respect, or, perhaps they had known him for years in Old England. We do not know from the record. But whatever the reason, John Clarke assumed the reigns of leadership of the banished, disarmed and disfranchised brethren and became the Moses of Aquetneck Island.

Dr. Clarke suggested that they move for the sake of peace. Before blood was shed, he led a group of 18 families to New Hampshire in the winter of 1637-38. The cold of the New Hampshire winter influenced them to move again and by sailing vessel they were on a journey they hoped would lead them to Delaware. They never made it to Delaware. On their journey around Cape Cod, they sailed into the Narragansett Bay to lodge with an understanding and kind Roger Williams. It was during that time of repose and reflection

Chapter 12—The Churches of the Seventeenth Century

that Mr. Williams convinced the band of believers to look at the beautiful garden of the Island of Aquetneck. It was the spring of 1638.

After traveling there, the banished believers from Boston received assurance from Plymouth that the island was out of both Pilgrim and Puritan jurisdiction. That being settled, through the communicative skills of Roger Williams, they purchased Aquetneck from the Indian sachems, Caunannicus and Miantinomi, and promptly renamed their paradise *the Isle of Rhodes* or Rhode Island. There on the north neck of the Island, approximately 75 miles southwest from Boston, was the signing of the first governmental document protecting religious *opinion*, **the Portsmouth Compact**.

The chief architect of this concise and powerful piece of political history was Dr. John Clarke, beloved physician and banished believer from Boston:

The document, written on the Isle of Rhodes and signed on March 7, 1638, was the singular point in the conception *of the land of liberty*. It was the first document in history that **severed both political AND religious ties with mother England**. An idea was being incubated that would give birth to something called the Constitution and the Bill of Rights.

Portsmouth Compact

We whose names are underwritten, do here solemnly, in the presence of Jehovah, incorporate ourselves into a body politic, and as He shall help, will submit our persons, lives and estates, unto our Lord Jesus Christ, the King of kings, and Lord of lords, and to all those perfect and most absolute laws of his, given us in His holy word of truth, to be guided and judged thereby.

signed by:

William Coddington, John Clarke, William Hutchinson, John Coggshall, William Aspinwall, Thomas Savage, William Dyre, William Freeborne, Philip Sherman, John Walker, Richard Carder, William Baulstone, Edward Hutchinson, Edward Hutchinson Junior, Samuel Wilbore, John Sanford, John Porter, Henry Bull.

---

1. Write Hebrews 12:3 two times.

2. What were the four settlements in America at the time of Dr. John Clark's arrival?

3. About what were the people of Boston disputing?

4. Define antinomian, disfranchised, disarmed and experimental religion.

5. What was the "Anne Hutchinson Thing?"

6. What did the Portsmouth Compact do concerning England?

****

12.2.3

The First Baptist Church in America?

After the signing of the Providence compact, the men of Providence moved to form a church. Since they had been excommunicated, they believed that a new church ought to be formed on Baptist principles. Mr. Holliman baptized Roger Williams and Mr. Williams baptized the other candidates for membership. As Isaac Backus expressed it, "now we are come to an event that had made much noise in the world": the baptism of Roger Williams and the church in Providence. According to Governor Winthrop, this baptism took place in March, 1639 with Ezekiel Holliman baptizing Roger Williams who in turn baptized Holliman and *some ten more*.

However, in just a few months Mr. Williams rejected his own baptism and became a *Seeker,* not knowing whom God meant to lead his churches. The church at Providence sometime after that reorganized with Thomas Olney as pastor. (See Isaac Backus, *A Church History of New England*, P. 45-48.)

But Williams' church was not the first.

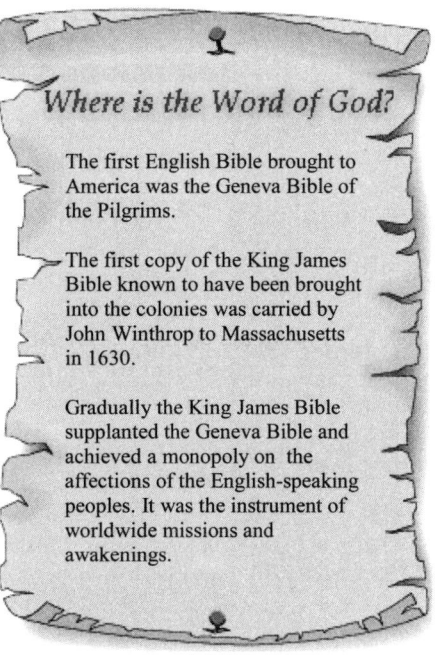

Where is the Word of God?

The first English Bible brought to America was the Geneva Bible of the Pilgrims.

The first copy of the King James Bible known to have been brought into the colonies was carried by John Winthrop to Massachusetts in 1630.

Gradually the King James Bible supplanted the Geneva Bible and achieved a monopoly on the affections of the English-speaking peoples. It was the instrument of worldwide missions and awakenings.

Dr. John Clarke

The First Baptist Church in America*

Not long after the company of believers signed the compact at Portsmouth, some of them migrated to the south end of the island and founded the city of Newport. John Winthrop mentioned a church on Aquetneck as early as 1639. However, this group of believers was worshipping in the wilderness of New Hampshire in the winter of 1637.

John Clarke is perhaps the most underrated man in American history. He organized the first Baptist church, held the first revival meeting on American soil and wrote the third and fourth most important documents in American history: **the Portsmouth Compact** and **the Rhode Island Constitution**. At various times of his life, he was called upon to state his beliefs. He left behind a statement of faith that leaves no doubt about his belief in the Bible, the blood atonement, man's sinful and

---

* Please read Appendix A.

Chapter 12—The Churches of the Seventeenth Century

impotent condition, and the work of grace in the hearts of those receiving Christ as Saviour. His theology was scripturally sound with a fervent zeal for souls. His theology was what might be termed mild Particular Baptist (of which we will shortly learn).

STOP AND THINK

1. Write Hebrews 12:3 two times.

2. Who baptized Roger Williams? *Ezekiel Holliman*
3. What was the name of Williams' settlement? *Newport*
4. What happened to Roger Williams concerning his leadership as a preacher? *rejected his baptism and became a seeker*
5. What was the first Baptist church in America? *Newport — John Clark*
6. Who brought the first King James Bible to America? *John Winthrop*
7. When did the first Baptist church in America begin to worship together? *1637*
8. What were John Clark's basic beliefs? *Blood atonement, man's sinful and impotent condition, work of grace in the hearts of those recieving Christ as his savior*

Chapter Thirteen
The Churches of the Seventeenth Century part II

Section One: Baptist Struggle in England. London Confession. The Waldensian Massacre.

Section Two: Baptist Struggle in America. Obadiah Holmes. The Baptist Church at Boston.

SECTION ONE

Scripture to Memorize

Isaiah 53:1 Who hath believed our report? and to whom is the arm of the LORD revealed?

The Struggle of the Baptists in England

In 1612, after the public burning of Edward Wightman, the Baptists of England began to petition the King and the House of Lords for *liberty of conscience*. Edward Bean Underhill preserves their petitions in the compilation, *Tracts on the Liberty of Conscience*. J. T. Christian quoting a portion of a 1614 petition:

> ...when we fall into the hands of the bishops we can have no benefit by the said oath, for they say it belongeth only to Popish Recusants and not to others; but kept have we been by them in lingering imprisonments, divided from wives, children, servants and callings, not for any other cause but only for conscience toward God, to the utter undoing of us, our wives and children (J. T. Christian, History of the Baptists, P. 217-8).

None of the petitions were granted.

We cannot emphasize the profound effect these documents had on American history. Perhaps **the most influential tract was written in 1620 by an anonymous sufferer of the Newgate Prison**. The petition, or tract, was written in *milk*, only readable by burning the parchment with candles (Roger Williams, *The Complete Writings of Roger Williams, Vol. 3, The Bloudy Tenet of Persecution*, P. 61). It was called the *Humble Supplication* and it directly influenced the life and writings of John Locke, John Milton and Roger Williams. Williams, using the scriptural arguments from the *Humble Supplication*, wrote the *Bloudy Tenet of Persecution* and the *Bloudy Tenet* influenced the founding fathers of Virginia, especially Thomas Jefferson.

But, let us return to the troubles of Old England. According to Doctor Featley and others, the Baptists were growing; and it was terrifying to the Church of England, or the Presbyterians, whichever were in power at any given time. Doctor Featley, the foe of the Baptists said:

> But of late this sect has rebaptized hundreds of men and women together, in the twilight, in rivulets and some arms of the river Thames (Daniel Featly, *The Dippers Dipt, Infant Bap.*, Vol. ii, P. 316).

The government in England continued to change hands with no real progress for Baptist people. J. M. Cramp wrote:

Chapter 13—The Churches of the Seventeenth Century Part II

Charles I. succeeded his father, James I., in 1625. In religion, he was a Romish Protestant. Politically, he believed in the one-man system of government, regarding the people as ciphers, and lost his life by pertinaciously laboring to put his belief in practice. Morally, he was made up of negations. He wanted principle, sincerity, and steadfastness. The Church of England used to call him a "martyr," but the annual service in commemoration of his death is now discontinued. (See J. M. Cramp, *History of the Baptists*.)

In 1811, Joseph Ivimey wrote:

There was a congregation of protestant dissenters of the Independent persuasion in London, gathered in the year 1616, of which Mr. **Henry Jacob** was the first pastor; and after him succeeded Mr. **John Lathorp**, who was their minister in 1633. In this society several persons, finding that the congregation kept not to its first principles of separation, and being also convinced that baptism was not to be administered to infants, but to such as professed faith in Christ, desired that they might be dismissed from the communion, and allowed to form a distinct congregation in such order as was most agreeable to their own sentiments.

The church, considering that they were now grown very numerous, and no more than could in those times of persecution conveniently meet together, and believing also that those persons acted from a principle of conscience, and not from obstinacy, agreed to allow them the liberty they desired, and that they should be constituted a distinct church; which was performed Sep. 12, 1633. And as they believed that baptism was not rightly administered to infants, so they looked upon the baptism they had received at that age as invalid, whereupon most or all of them received a new baptism. Their minister was a Mr. **John Spilsbury**. What number they were is uncertain, because in the mentioning of about twenty men and women, it is added with divers others.

In the year 1638, Mr. **William Kiffin**, Mr. **Thomas Wilson**, and others, being of the same judgment, were upon their request dismissed to the said Mr. Spilsbury's congregation. In the year 1639, another congregation of Baptists was formed, whose place of meeting was in Crutched-friars; the chief promoters of which were Mr. Green, Mr. Paul Hobson, and Captain Spencer.

The account of **Mr. Spilsbury's** church is said in the margin to have been written from the records of that church; but from any thing that appears there is nothing to justify the conclusion of Crosby, [Thomas Crosby, English Baptist Historian] that this was the first Baptist church; as the account relates simply to the origin of that particular church, to state which it is probable was **Mr. Kiffin's** design, rather than to relate the origin of the Baptist churches in general, and which he must certainly have known were in existence previously to that period.

It has not been uncommon for the enemies of the Baptists to reproach them with the manner in which this practice was restored. In a work published at the close of the seventeenth century by Mr. John Wall, entitled *Baptism Anatomized*, the writer says, "Their baptism is not from heaven, but will-worship, and so to be abhorred by all Christians; for they received their baptism from one Mr. Smyth who baptized himself; one who was cast out of a church, and endeavoured to deprive the church of Christ of the use of the Bible." (See Joseph Ivimey, *History of the English Baptists*, Ch. 5).

> In 1648 came the "**Peace of Westphalia**." Among other things which resulted from that peace pact was the triple agreement between the great denominations Catholic, Lutheran and Presbyterian, no longer to persecute one another.
>
> However, all other Christians, especially the Anabaptists, were to continue to receive from them the same former harsh treatment: persistent persecution.

The Collegiate Baptist History Workbook

Mr. Ivimey's remarks remind us, there was **controversy** concerning when the Baptists of England actually began and when they baptized by immersion. However, **we believe we have shown baptism by immersion for believers only has existed since the time of the first missionaries to the present day**, using the writings of the enemies of the Baptists. The principles of the baptized churches, which baptized only believers, can be traced without breaking any time line.

Even so, when speaking of **English Baptist** *written* history, we can generally trace two groups: the **General Baptists** and the **Particular Baptists**.

Definitions:

General Baptists: held to the belief in *general* atonement, that is, the belief that salvation is *available* to all men. General Baptists are sometimes called ***Arminian*** after the English theologian Jacob Arminius who believed in the free-will of man to accept Christ. This is opposed to the Calvinist belief of *Irresistible Grace*. Severe Arminianism believes you can lose your salvation.

Particular Baptists: held to the belief in *particular* atonement, that is, the belief that salvation is only *available* to the elect of God. Sometimes called *Calvinistic* after the French theologian John Calvin. The *Particulars* did more writing and gained influence in England through their books. The extreme end of Particular theology is Hyper-Calvinism, which can result in faded zeal for soul winning, failing to give invitations to the lost to receive Christ, or a fatalistic view of the Christian life.

1. Write Isaiah 53:1 twice.

2. What happened to the petition of 1612? *not granted / don't know*
3. Which tract or petition was the most influential? Whom did it influence?
   The humble supplication (1620); John Locke, John Milton, Roger Williams
4. What was happening among the Baptists in and around 1645 according to Dr. Featley?
   they were growing
5. What is a Particular Baptist?
   Particular atonement / only to the chosen
6. What is a General Baptist?
   Salvation is available to all

****

13.1.2

Definitions:

five-mile rule: English rule which forbade church members or ministers from venturing more than five miles to attend church or minister the Gospel.
conventicle act: forbade any unauthorized church services not approved by the government

169

Chapter 13—The Churches of the Seventeenth Century Part II

Leaders among the General Baptists of England

John Smythe
Smythe earned a master's degree from Cambridge in 1593. He wrote *Character of the Beast* in 1609. Smythe wrote his confession in 1611, and migrated to Holland with Hellwys. He eventually split with Hellwys. Smythe died around 1612.

Thomas Hellwys and John Murtin
Hellwys and Murtin returned to England in 1611, and began the first "General" Baptist church in England. (This is debatable.)

Thomas Grantham
This preacher delivered the petition of grievances and declaration of faith to Charles II in 1667. Grantham pastored in Norwich and suffered many imprisonments and persecutions. He died in 1671.

> 1626: There were 5 *General* Baptist churches in England
> 1644: There were 47 General Baptist churches in England
> 1768: There were 69 General Baptist churches according to Morgan Edwards.

****

Leaders among the Particular Baptists of England

Thomas Collier:
Collier pastored the first Particular Baptist church (debatable) in 1630.
> By 1644 - 7 churches

William Kiffen:
Born in 1616 in Wales, Kiffen was saved at an independent church of dissenters. He became a member of the Baptist church where John Spilsbury was the pastor. Soon Kiffen became a pastor and a merchant. His success in business helped support the Baptists in England in the 17th century. He died in 1701.

Hanserd Knollys:
Knollys was a preacher of Church of England, the Peterborough church in 1629. He became a part of the Separatist (Puritan) movement in 1636. He sailed to Boston in 1638, and eventually became a pastor at Dover, New Hampshire. He began to oppose infant baptism. In 1641 he was summoned home to be with his ailing father. Knollys refused to baptize his infant child. In 1645, he began to pastor a Baptist Church in London. Knollys was forbidden to preach under the Presbyterian rule and was imprisoned at age 84 for 6 months. He died at age 93.

John Spilsbury:
Spilsbury was pastor of the first Particular Baptist Church, in Broad-street, Wapping, London. His signature is affixed to the Confession of Faith published in 1646, and other public documents, the last being the *Humble Apology of some Commonly Called Anabaptists*, presented to Charles II in 1660. He joined William Kiffen in a letter to the Baptists in Dublin, persuading them to submit quietly to the Protectorate, he afterwards along with several others sent a letter to Oliver Cromwell, protesting against his assumption of the kingly title. His writings became influential and his converts had an effect in America.

Samuel Oates:
Oats was a popular English Baptist preacher who in 1646 was accused of murdering Anne Martin by baptizing her and causing her subsequent death. He was cleared of all charges, but was dragged from his house and drowned.

The Collegiate Baptist History Workbook

John Bunyan, William Cathcart's account of his life:

John Bunyan, was born at Elstow, England, about a mile from Bedford, in 1628. His father was a man of more intelligence than those who generally followed his calling, and he had taught John to read and write. When the little boy was ten years of age he first became conscious that he was very sinful. He speedily shook these fears.

He was "drawn out" in 1645, with others, at the siege of Leicester to perform sentinel's duty before the city, when another member of his company expressed a desire to take his place, the request was granted, and that night Bunyan's substitute was shot in the head and, died. This deliverance produced a powerful impression upon Bunyan.

Soon after he left the army he married, and his wife and he were so poor that they had neither a "dish nor a spoon."

His first permanent conviction of sin was produced by a sermon denouncing the violation of the Lord's day by labor, sports, or otherwise. This came home to Bunyan with peculiar force for his greatest enjoyment came from sports on the Lord's day.

A long while after this, Bunyan, in passing through the streets of Bedford, heard, "three or four poor women," sitting at a door, "talking about the new birth, the work of God in their hearts, and the way by which they were convinced of their miserable state by nature. They told how God had visited their souls with his love in Christ Jesus, and with what words and promises they had been refreshed, comforted, and supported against the temptations of the devil; moreover, they reasoned of the suggestions and temptations of Satan in particular." From these women Bunyan learned to loathe sin and to hunger for the Saviour. He sought their company again and again, and he was strengthened to go to Jesus. One day, as he was passing into the fields, he says, "This sentence fell upon my soul, 'Thy righteousness is in heaven.' I also saw that it was not my good frame of heart that made my righteousness better, nor yet my bad frame, that made my righteousness worse, for my righteousness was Jesus Christ himself, the same yesterday, to-day, and forever." Then, as he says, "his chains fell off," and he went home rejoicing.

In 1655, Mr. Bunyan was immersed by John Gifford, of Bedford. The same year he was called to preach the gospel.

Bunyan was arrested Nov. 12, 1660, [**for violating the five-mile rule and the conventicle act**] and he was in jail **more than twelve years**. His imprisonment was peculiarly trying. "The parting with my wife and poor children," says Bunyan, "hath often been to me, in this place (the prison), like pulling the flesh from my bones." And of his blind daughter he adds, "Poor child, what sorrow thou art like to have for thy portion in this world! Thou must be beaten, must beg, suffer hunger, cold, nakedness, and a thousand calamities, though I cannot now endure if the wind should blow upon thee." *The Pilgrim's Progress* was written in Bedford jail.

During Bunyan's lifetime there were 100,000 copies of that book circulated in the British islands, besides which there were several editions in North America. And in the ten years which Bunyan lived, after his wonderful book was first issued, it was translated into French, Flemish, Dutch, Welsh, Gaelic, and Irish. Since Bunyan's death it has been translated into Hebrew for Christian Jews in Jerusalem, and into Spanish, Portuguese, Italian, Danish, German, Armenian, Burmese, Singhalese, Orissa, Hindostanee, Bengalee, Tamil, Maratthi, Canarese, Gujarratti, Malay, Arabic, Samoan, Tahitian, Pihuana, Bechuana, Malagasy, New Zealand, and Latin. This list of translations ends with 1847. Since that time it has been rendered into several additional tongues of our race. Nor will *The Pilgrim's Progress* stop in its travels until it visits every land occupied by human beings, and tells its blessed story in the language of all nations.

Chapter 13—The Churches of the Seventeenth Century Part II

There is a French Roman Catholic version of *The Pilgrim's Progress*, greatly abridged, with the head of the Virgin on the title-page. It leaves out giant Pope and the statement that Peter was afraid of a sorry girl. An English ritualistic clergyman has tried to adapt it to the sacramental jugglery of his system. Of Bunyan's [book] *the Holy War*, Lord Macaulay says, "If *The Pilgrim's Progress* did not exist it would be the best allegory that ever was written" and he proclaims "John Bunyan the most popular religious writer in the English language."

The pardon which secured Bunyan's release from prison was ordered by the Privy Council, presided over by the King, May 17, 1672. After his liberation he became the most popular preacher in England; 3000 persons gathered to hear him in London before breakfast. Men of all ranks and of all grades of intelligence listened to his burning words, and heralded the fame of his eloquence to the King. The learned Dr. John Owen told Charles II that he would relinquish all his learning for the tinker's preaching abilities.

While Bunyan was journeying upon an errand of mercy he was exposed to a heavy rain, which brought on a violent fever, from the effect of which he died in ten days, in London, Aug. 12, 1688. His last hours were full of peace. He was buried in Bunhill Fields Cemetery, where his monument is still seen.

Bunyan's church, now of the Congregational denomination, is still in Bedford. His chair is in the meeting-house, and some other relics of the immortal dreamer. A few years since, the Duke of Bedford erected a handsome monument to Bunyan in Bedford, on which a statue of the great dreamer stands. John Bunyan was one of the few men of our race who possessed genius of the highest order (William Cathcart, *Baptist Encyclopedia*, Vol. 1, P. 159).

The London Confession of Faith

In 1644, in an attempt to stem the tide of criticism and to make plain the beliefs of the Baptist churches in England, the Particular Baptists of London published their Confession of Faith. It appeased the Calvinists of the Church of England and resembled the Westminster Confession of faith being prepared by the Presbyterians. The outstanding part of the confession was its emphasis on grace and the plan of salvation. It emphasized believers' baptism as a prerequisite for church membership. The confession also advocated religious liberty and freedom of conscience. It was written mostly by William Kiffin and contained fifty articles. It helped establish the Baptists of England as "orthodox" in the minds of many enemies.

However, in one generation the abuse of the "particular" outlook of it discouraged inviting sinners to Christ. Although certainly not intended, it gave credence to covenant relationship (infant Baptism, patriarchal salvation, predestination and election) in the local church rather than baptismal relationship.

In 1689, there was a revision of the London Particular Confession of Faith. At that time, there were 107 Particular Baptist Churches in England according to the historian Joseph Ivimey. One hundred years later, 1768, there were 217 Particular Baptist congregations; and by 1798, there were 450.

According to David Benedict, the Particular Baptist Churches in England averaged about 80 members per church.

Other great leaders and writers of the Seventeenth century English Particular Baptists were: Benjamin Cox, John Tombes and Henry Jesse.

Overview of Baptist Confessions by William Cathcart:

1611: A church of English Baptists, residing in Holland, adopted a confession of faith, prepared most probably by Thomas Helwys, their pastor. Has 26 articles, most sound.
1644: London Confession adopted by seven London churches. Fifty-seven articles. Particular atonement. William Kiffen, author. The appendix to this confession of faith was written by Benjamin Cox.
1656: Confession of Faith of Several Churches of Christ in the County of Somerset. Sixteen churches. Authored by Thomas Collier. Particular in makeup.
1660: London Confession of Faith. General Baptist document. Twenty-five articles.
1678: Orthodox Creed. General Baptist confession with fifty articles. Its mode of describing election, providence, free will, and final perseverance is, in the main, scriptural. The extent of the atonement is the only question about which it differed from the opinions of our orthodox brethren of that day.
1689: The London Confession "put forth by the elders and brethren of many congregation of Christians, baptized (immersed) upon profession of their faith, in London and the country."
Thirty-two articles. After dropping its lengthy appendix, and inserting two new articles, it became, in
1742: The Philadelphia Confession of Faith. Adopted by most of the early Baptist Associations in America.
18??: The New Hampshire Confession of Faith. Cathcart admitted, "we very much prefer the Philadelphia Confession.

The Massacre of the Waldensians 1655

Before the focus of God's power left the continent of Europe, the old Vaudois party, weary of the debauchery and satanic ways of the Roman Catholic institution, sought asylum with the Reformers and gained security in their protection. As related in chapter ten, **Geofroi Varaile,** a converted monk to the Reformed faith, came to the Vaudois valley, and with the promise of peace and protection, almost single-handedly converted the primitive believers of the Piedmont to the Reformed ideas of John Calvin.

In 1622, Pope Gregory XV formed the "Society for the Propagation of the Faith." This paved the way for the most barbarous persecution in the history of cruelty. In 1650 the Council of the Propagation began making plans to exterminate all non-believers. In January, the infamous order of Gastaldo ordered the Vaudois out of their valleys. The Waldensians were to convert to Roman Catholicism, or move from the valleys. If they did not move, they would be exterminated.

Death of the daughter of Moyses Long, from Samuel Morland's *Hist. of the Ev. Churches of the Piedmont*

On April 17, 1655 the inhuman toad Marquis de Pianeza brought an Army of 15,000 monsters to the foot of the Piedmont and commenced the slaughter of these innocent men, women, and children. We cannot begin to describe the unmitigated fury these mercenary maggots unleashed upon the poor Waldensians. Wylie, writing of the 1655 atrocity:

> There is no town in Piedmont, under a Vaudois pastor, where some of our brethren have not been put to death. Hugo Chiamps of Finestrelle had his entrails torn from his living body,

Chapter 13—The Churches of the Seventeenth Century Part II

at Turin. Peter Geymarali of Bobbio, in like manner, had his entrails taken out at Lucerna, and a fierce cat thrust in their place to torture him further; Maria Romano was buried alive at Rocco-patia; Magdalen Foulano underwent the same fate at San Giovanni; Susan Michelini was bound hand and foot, and left to perish of cold and hunger at Saracena. Bartholomew Fache, gashed with sabres, had the wounds filled up with quicklime, and perished thus in agony at Fenile; Daniel Michelini had his tongue torn out at Bobbio for having praised God. James Baridari perished covered with sulphurous matches, which had been forced into his flesh under the nails, between the fingers, in the nostrils, in the lips, and over all his body, and then lighted. Daniel Revelli had his mouth filled with gunpowder, which, being lighted, blew his head to pieces. Maria Monnen, taken at Liousa, had the flesh cut from her cheek and chin bone, so that her jaw was left bare, and she was thus left to perish. Paul Garnier was slowly sliced to pieces at Rora. Thomas Margueti was mutilated in an indescribable manner at Miraboco, and Susan Jaquin cut in bits at La Torre. Sara Rostagnol was slit open from the legs to the bosom, and so left to perish on the road between Eyral and Lucerna. Anne Charbonnier was impaled and carried thus on a pike, as a standard, from San Giovanni to La Torre. Daniel Rambaud, at Paesano, had his nails torn off, then his fingers chopped off, then his feet and his hands, then his arms and his legs, with each successive refusal on his part to abjure the Gospel. Thus the roll of martyrs runs on, and with each new sufferer comes a new, a more excruciating and more horrible mode of torture and death (J. A. Wylie, *The History Of The Waldenses*, P. 69).

What was left of the Waldensians fled to a safer country where they eventually recovered. In 1689 the Vaudois returned to their valleys under the military leadership of Henry Arnaud.

---

1. Write Isaiah 53:1 twice.

2. Why was John Bunyan imprisoned?
   For breaking the 5 mile rule and Conventical act

3. Why did the Baptists of London feel a confession was needed? *(Statement of belief)*
   Clarify baptist belief and to help stop criticism

4. What courageous thing did Thomas Grantham do?
   delivered petition of grievances and declaration of faith (1661)

5. What did the London Confession resemble? *westminister confession*

6. What was the best part of the London Confession?
   emphasis on grace and salvation

****

13.2.1

SECTION TWO

The Struggle of the Baptists in America

After the banishment of Roger Williams and John Clark to the newfound haven of Rhode Island, the Baptists of America were still finding it hard to live according to the dictates of their conscience. Massachusetts and Connecticut were off limits, Virginia and

The Collegiate Baptist History Workbook

Georgia had established the Church of England, and as the number of Baptists arriving in New England increased, the harder it became to stay hidden. The urge to preach the Gospel was second nature to these persecuted believers.

Obadiah Holmes

Obadiah Holmes migrated to Massachusetts Bay in 1638. He was born in Reddish, near Manchester England around 1607. At the tender age of 23 he experienced a "spiritual awakening" (Edwin S. Gaustad, *Baptist Piety*, P. 8-9). England was a confusion of religious faces in Holmes' young lifetime. As a boy working on his father's farm, England was a mild Puritan under James I. As a teen, the crown returned to rigid Anglicanism under Charles I. In 1628 Charles appointed William Laud as Bishop of London. Laud then became the Archbishop of Canterbury or religious head of the Church of England in 1633. Laud had a vendetta against the Puritans and the Baptists and fought them, banished them, and discredited them all the years of his "ministry."

Holmes married and came to America in 1638 and settled in Salem, Massachusetts. But things did not work out for the Holmes family in Salem. From there Obadiah Holmes moved to Seekonk, Massachusetts.

At this time, **John Cotton** was involved in a battle with Roger Williams over the book, The *Bloudy Tenet of Persecution*. Cotton wrote a book and pamphlet arguing against liberty as proposed by Williams. In the end, Williams won the battle of ideas.

There at Seekonk Obadiah Holmes managed to get into a scrap with the *standing order* pastor, Mr. Samuel Newman. Obadiah Holmes established a "separate" Congregational Church in Seekonk. This courageous act stirred up the entire Congregational church organization against him and earned him the reputation of being "the arrantest rogue and rascal" in that part of burgeoning America. (See Edwin S. Gaustaud, *Baptist Piety*, P. 15.)

> It was from William Witter that the Lynn church jurisdiction had experienced marked protest in the past. Witter had been arrested in 1646 and testified that "infant baptism was *the badge of the whore*."

Dr. Clarke's zeal for the lost was revealed as he **conducted the first revival in American history**. Clarke and a group of soul-winners from the church on Rhode Island saw Seekonk as a mission field. Roger Williams described the 1649 revival for us in a letter to a horrified John Winthrop:

> At Seekonk a great many have lately concurred with Mr. John Clarke and our Providence men about the point of a new Baptism, and the manner by dipping; and Mr. John Clarke hath been there lately (and Mr. Lucar) and hath dipped them. I believe their practice comes nearer the first practice of our great Founder Christ Jesus; than other practices of religion do. (See Bartlett, *Letters of Roger Williams*, VI: 187-88, and the *Massachusetts Colony Records*, III. 173.)

Obadiah Holmes was baptized by Dr. John Clarke, early in 1649, and became a member of the Baptist church at Newport.

Sometime in the summer of 1651, Newport Baptist Church received a request from the aged William Witter, who desired to be visited so that he may hear the word of God and be comforted. Dr. John Clarke and the church received this request, made by a distant

Chapter 13—The Churches of the Seventeenth Century Part II

member of the church. It was complicated because it would require navigation to the mainland and a trip to Lynn in the Massachusetts jurisdiction. Not only was the trip dangerous, expensive, and exhausting, the proposition of traveling anywhere close to Boston could mean imprisonment and/or death for the missionaries. We would be correct in assuming Clarke knew all of the ramifications of such a trip. He knew well the violence of the Boston Court. He knew the visit would cause a crisis with the law. But leaving behind him an example of apostolic leadership, (Acts 5:29: *"Then Peter and the other apostles answered and said, We ought to obey God rather than men."*) Clarke and others were willing to pay the price. All options weighed, it was decided that Mr. Witter's request be honored. In July, 1651, Dr. John Clarke, Obadiah Holmes and a church member, John Crandall journeyed into Massachusetts's territory.

They arrived in Lynn on Saturday evening, and having enjoyed fellowship with William Witter, they prayed, and decided to stay over until the Lord's Day and have service. News in Lynn spread fast and a quick warrant for the arrest of the strangers was delivered to the constable. The officers came and arrested the three missionaries.

Clarke, Holmes and Crandall were escorted first to the Congregational church for the end of service, then to the jail. After weeks of imprisonment, the trio was transferred to the Boston court. Clarke was fined 20 pounds, or be "well whipt," Holmes 30 pounds or be "well whipt," and Crandall five pounds, or be "well whipt."

Clarke wanted a chance to debate and defend the Bible principles of the Baptists. He never got the opportunity to defend his principles in an open dispute, for someone paid his fine and he was released. Crandall was released also, leaving only the "rascal" Holmes in custody.

From July until September, 1651 Obadiah Holmes remained imprisoned. His pastor, John Clarke, had returned to Newport along with John Crandall. Obadiah Holmes was not alone in Massachusetts because loyal John Hazel, a convert from his Seekonk days, came to Boston to stand by his old friend and pastor.

The day of the execution of his sentence came and a larger than usual crowd gathered for the macabre entertainment. He was to receive thirty lashes, ten less than the death penalty of forty. Obadiah Holmes wrote an account of his sufferings, which was sent to the Baptist churches in London. The account was published in a short history entitled *Ille Newes from New England*, written by John Clarke. Here is the account from Obadiah Holmes:

> I desired to speak a few words, but Mr. Nowel answered. "It is not now a time to speak," whereupon I took leave, and said, "Men, brethren, fathers and countrymen, I beseech you to give me leave to speak a few words, and the rather because here are many spectators to see me punished, and I am to seal with my blood, if God give strength, that which I hold and practice in reference to the word of God, and the testimony of Jesus. That which I have to lay in brief is this, although I am disputant, yet seeing I am to seal with my blood what I hold, I am ready to defend by the word, and to dispute that point with any that shall come forth to withstand it."
>
> Mr. Nowel answered, "now was not time to dispute;" then said I, "I desire to give an account of the faith and order which I hold," and this I desired three times; but in comes Mr. Flint, and saith to the executioner, "Fellow, do thine office, for this fellow would but make a long speech to delude the people;" so I being resolved to speak, told the people, that which I am to suffer for is the word of God, and testimony of Jesus Christ. "No," saith Mr. Nowel, "it is for your error, and going about to seduce the people;" to which I replied, "Not for error, for in all the time of my imprisonment, wherein I was left alone, my brethren being gone, which of all your ministers came to convince me of error? And when

upon the Governor's words, a motion was made for a public dispute, and often renewed upon fair terms, and desired by hundreds, what was the reason it was not granted?"

Mr. Nowel told me, it was his fault who went away and would not dispute; but this the writing will clear at large. Still Mr. Flint calls to the man to do his office; so before, and in the time of his pulling off my clothes, I continued speaking, telling them that I had so learned that for all Boston I would not give my body into their hands thus to be bruised upon another account, yet upon this I would not give the hundredth part of a "wampum peague," to free it out of their hands; and that I made as much conscience of unbuttoning one button, as I did of paying the thirty pounds in reference thereunto. I told them moreover, that the Lord having manifested his love towards me, in giving me repentance towards God, and faith in Christ, and so to be baptized in water by a messenger of Jesus, in the name of the Father, Son, and Holy Spirit, wherein I have fellowship with him in his death, burial and resurrection, I am now come to be baptized in afflictions by your hands, that so I may have further fellowship with my Lord, and am not ashamed of his sufferings, for by His stripes am I healed.

Beating of Obadiah Holmes, depiction courtesy of the Baptist History Preservation Society

And as the man began to lay the strokes upon my back, I said to the people, though my flesh should fail, and my spirit should fail, yet God would not fail; so it pleased the Lord to come in, and to fill my heart and tongue as a vessel full; and with an audible voice I break forth, praying the Lord not to lay this sin to their charge, and telling the people that now I found he did not fail me, and therefore now I should trust him forever who failed me not; for in truth, as the strokes fell upon me, I had such a spiritual manifestation of God's presence, as I never had before, and the outward pain was so removed from me, that I could well bear it, yea, and in a manner felt it not, although it was grievous, as the spectators said, the man striking with all his strength, spitting in his hand three times, with a three corded whip, giving me therewith thirty strokes. When he had loosed me from the post, having joyfulness in my heart, and cheerfulness in my countenance, as the spectators observed, I told the magistrates, "**You have struck me as with roses**;" and said moreover, "although the Lord hath made it easy to me, yet I pray God it may not be laid to your charge."

Obadiah Holmes sentence of 30 lashes was the same punishment given to those guilty of adultery, rape and counterfeiting. From all accounts, the beating was an attempt to kill Holmes. From the crowd came protests and exclamations of outrage. In the aftermath, Holmes wrote:

After this many came to me, rejoicing to see the power of the Lord manifested in weak flesh; but sinful flesh takes occasion hereby to bring others into trouble, informs the magistrates hereof, and so two more are apprehended as for contempt of authority, their names are **John Hazel and John Spur**, who came indeed and did shake me by the hand, but did use no words of contempt or reproach unto any. No man can prove that the first spake anything; and for the second, he only said, "Blessed be the Lord;" yet these two, for taking me by the hand, and thus saying, after I had received my punishment, were sentenced to pay forty shillings, or to be whipt. Both were resolved against paying their fine: nevertheless, after one or two days imprisonment, one paid John Spur's fine, and he was released; and after six or seven days

Chapter 13—The Churches of the Seventeenth Century Part II

imprisonment of brother Hazel, even the day when he should have suffered, another paid his, and so he escaped, and the next day went to visit a friend about six miles from Boston.

When I was come to the prison, it blessed God to stir up the heart of an old acquaintance of mine, who with much tenderness, like the good Samaritan, poured oil into my wounds, and plastered my sores; but there was present information given what was done, and inquiry made who was the surgeon, and it was commonly reported he should be sent for: but what was done, I yet know not. Now thus it hath pleased the Father of mercies to dispose of the matter, that my bonds and imprisonment have been no hindrance to the gospel; for before my return, some submitted to the Lord, and were baptized, and divers were put up on the way of inquiry; and now being advised to make my escape by night, because it was reported that there were warrants forth for me, I departed; and the next day after, while I was on my journey, the constable came to search at my house where I lodged; so I escaped their hands, and by the good hand of my heavenly Father brought home again to my near relations, my wife and eight children, the brethren of our town and Providence having taken pains to meet me four miles in the woods, where we rejoiced together in the Lord.

Thus have I given you, as briefly as I can, a true relation of things; wherefore, my brethren, rejoice with me in the Lord, and give all glory to him, for he is worthy, to whom be praised forevermore, to whom I commit you, and put up my earnest prayers for you, that by my late experience, who trusted in God and have not been deceived, you may trust in him perfectly; wherefore, my dearly beloved brethren, trust in the Lord, and you shall not be ashamed nor confounded. So I rest, yours in the bond of Christ—Obadiah Holmes.

John Spur later testified that he was saved at the beating of Obadiah Holmes, saying, "I, John Spur, being present, it did take such an impression in my spirit to trust in God, and to walk according to the light that God had communicated to me, and not to fear what man could do unto me." But **John Hazel** never made it back to Newport. Ten days after leaving Boston, he died of complications stemming from his imprisonment.

STOP AND THINK
1. Write Isaiah 53:1 twice

2. From where was Obadiah Holmes?
3. Who baptized Obadiah Holmes?
4. Why didn't William Witter have a local church pastor visit him?
5. How many lashes did Holmes receive?

6. What was Holmes reaction, and what did he say after the beating?

****

13.2.2

The Story of the Boston Baptists

The first four Baptist churches in America were: The First Baptist Church, Newport, Rhode Island, 1638; the First Baptist Church, Providence, Rhode Island, 1639; Second Baptist Church, Newport, Rhode Island, 1656; and the First Baptist Church, Swansea,

> It is thought that Henry Dunster, the first president of Harvard came under the influence of Obadiah Holmes as a result of his public beating and attempted murder. In any event, Dunster refused to have his infant child "baptized" and was forced to resign his presidency of Harvard as a result. This happened in 1653.

Massachusetts, 1663. A group of brave Americans now proceeded to plant the fifth such church.

Thomas Gould was a member of the first Congregational church in Boston and was one of the many in the colony who were weighing the issues of church membership, regeneration and infant baptism. **Henry Dunster**, after losing his position as President of Harvard, for his opposition to the practice of infant baptism, began communicating with Gould. Both men influenced each other and gained strength and courage. Sometime in that fateful year of 1655, Gould began voicing his doubts about the validity of infant baptism.

Events were put into further motion when Thomas Gould refused to take his daughter to receive her infant baptism at the hands of Zechariah Symmes, the pastor of the church at Charlestown. In December of 1655, he was summoned to a meeting at the church to discuss his delinquency.

Thus began an ordeal such as never has been seen in America. For the next several years, the first Congregational church in Charlestown tried to convince Gould of his errors. Mr. Gould protested as dissenters did, by walking out during infant baptism, or turning his back while a christening was conducted. He was threatened with beatings, spent time in jail, and threatened with excommunication. On May 28, 1665, a very courageous group of believers officially began the Baptist church in Boston. They followed the Lord in believers' baptism and signed a covenant agreement organizing themselves into a church. The members were: Thomas Gould, Thomas Osburne, Edward Drinker, John George, Richard Goodale, William Turner, Robert Lambert, Mary Goodale, and Mary Newell. (See Isaac Backus, *An Abridgement of Church History of New England*, P. 96.)

The dispute over the First Baptist Church, Boston, was a generational ordeal. As the antichrist is credited with "wearing out the saints of God" in Daniel 7:25, the Boston Baptists were subjugated to a relentless attempt of the *standing order* to disrupt their worship. The tactics of our adversary were in full force as Gould and his flock were dragged (sometimes literally) before countless councils and courts. In Boston, a new scornful identification was given to the baptized believers: *antipaedobaptist.*

After serving three different sentences in prison, Thomas Gould and the Boston Baptist Church sent this petition to the Boston Court:

> For our Gathering together and practice we have already given in our Grounds which we Judge were according to Scripture. Secondly Wee humbly consider the Patent Gives us leave for soe doeing, as his Majesty hath explained in his letter to the general Court saying that the principal end and foundation of that Charter was and is the freedom and liberty of conscience. Thirdly, Wee consider the Law of the Colony doth not deny it to us, though with some Provisoes added which soe far as wee failed of Attending unto wee humbly crave Pardon or Submit to the Penalty of the Law therein. (See Suffold Co. Court files, 744a(3), October 24, 1665. Suffolk Col Courthouse, Boston.)

The court reacted by ignoring the plea of the church and began to move in more aggressive ways.

Governor Bellingham became successor to John Winthrop. Holding the office of governor several times from 1644 to the time of his death, he was re-elected governor of

Chapter 13—The Churches of the Seventeenth Century Part II

the Massachusetts colony soon after Winthrop's death. He is well known as a character in the now famous classic novel, *The Scarlet Letter* by Nathaniel Hawthorne. With as much or more zeal as Winthrop, he was determined to rid the colony of "poisoned and paralyzing" opinions. Bellingham had a sister, Anne (Bellingham) Hibbins who was one of the unfortunate women burned as a witch in the Salem Witch Trials. As far back as 1642, Bellingham wrote:

> We have had some experience here of some of their undertakings, who have lately come amongst us, and have made public defiance against magistracie, ministrie, churches, & church covenants, &c. as antichristian; secretly also sowing the seeds of Familisme, and Anabaptistrie, to the infection of some, and danger of others, so we are not willing to joyne with them in any league or confederacie at all, but rather that you would consider & advise with us how we may avoyd them, and keep ours from being infected by them. (See the Collections of Massachusetts Historical Society, Fourth Series, III., P. 386-7.)

So with great pride of purpose Bellingham presided with his "council," or Court of Assistants, **over the great Baptist debate,** which began April 14, 1668.

All of New England was there. John Clark sent Hilcox, Torrey and Hubbard to assist their brethren in the debate, but it became quite clear that none of them were going to be allowed to speak. The *standing order* stuck to a rigid game plan and basically demanded an answer to this:

> Whether it be justifiable by the word of God for these persons and their company to depart from the communion of these churches, and to set up an assembly here in the way of Anabaptism (William McGlothlin, *New England Dissent 1630-1833, Vol. 1*, P. 63).

Ah, but this friends, was an unlearned question and not the real issue. The issue was not "departing from communion." The issue for the Baptist church at Boston was: MAY WE HAVE CHURCH WITHOUT YOUR APPROVAL?

Thomas Gould never wanted to break communion, but the battle over baptism was about to force him. In this debate as recorded by Thomas Danforth and preserved in the

---

The Plight of the Quakers

On October 20, 1659, William Robinson, Marmaduke Stevenson, and Mary Dyre, were condemned to die for returning to Massachusetts after they were banished. Knowing that they would be put to death simply for returning to the colony, the two men were hanged on the 27th of October, 1659. Mary stood at the foot of the hanging tree and watched as her fellow Quakers were executed under John Wilson. There was a delay with fair Mary, because not everybody wanted her dead. She was strikingly beautiful and had suffered extreme persecution and slander at the hands and pens of the Boston Court. Ever since she and her husband William escaped with the Wheelwrights to Rhode Island, Mary was a subject of scorn. She was said to have given birth to a "monster," a "hideous thing" according to the ridiculous account of Cotton Mather. Of course this was construed as judgment upon her for befriending William and Anne Hutchinson, the banished believers who settled on the Island of Rhodes.

So, in delay, Mary was allowed to escape to Rhode Island once again. But her conscience bothered her that she should be given preferential treatment and so she returned to Boston against the better wishes of her husband. Even with a pleading letter of mercy from William Dyer in his hand Governor John Endicott condemned her to death. From the gallows Mary said, "Nay, I cannot save my life; for in obedience to the will of the Lord God I came, and in His will I abide faithful to the death" (Horatio Rogers, *Mary Dyer of Rhode Island*, P. 31).

She was hung June 1, 1660 and buried somewhere on the common. William Leddra, followed her to the hanging tree for dissident beliefs March 14, 1661. One hundred years later Isaac Backus wrote, "And from hence we may see, that the use of force in religious affairs is a bloody practice" (Isaac Backus, *An Abridgement to the Church History of New England*, P. 93).

Massachusetts Historical Society, John Crandall and Benanual Bowers, even though they were not supposed to speak, argued that the Puritan churches were so corrupt as to be null and void. This of course was correct and in forty years the *Separate Baptists* would repeat it loud and often. But at this particular moment of time, some of the other Baptists did not know how to say it. In light of all they had suffered how could they be justly criticized? In any event, the *standing order* was not about to let anybody from Clarke's crowd speak. Even when Thomas Gould set forth unanswerable arguments against infant baptism, the *standing order* evaded the issue and of course, declared themselves the victors.

> **First appearance of the "half-way" covenant:** *The* controversy in New England was the doctrine which allowed unregenerate parents to bring their children to the *standing order* church for infant baptism. Connecticut was the culprit in the propagation of the **half-way covenant**, of which her founder, Thomas Hooker, was opposed. Connecticut promoted it when all common sense said no. Connecticut promoted it when the best of her native sons preached against it. It was a denial of being born again—*experimental religion*.

The most telling exchange in the debate came when Thomas Gould eloquently explained: "Christ dwelleth in no temple but in the heart of the believer." Whereupon Mr. Shepard answered by quoting, "I will dwell in *them*, therefore it is not true, that He dwelleth only in a particular believer"(William McGlothlin, *New England Dissent 1630-1833, Vol. 1*, P. 70). And with that, the armies for *experimental religion* and against *experimental religion* began to line up. We will look at the concept of "experimental religion" in the next chapter. After the debate, Thomas Gould and his faithful helper, William Turner, were returned to prison.

The ministers of Massachusetts passed their judgment against the Baptists of Boston. They were: "an enemy in the habitation of the Lord; an anti-New England in New England. If this assembly be tolerated, where shall we stop?" On May 7, 1668, the General Court of Deputies took the advice of the most reverend fathers and banished Thomas Gould, William Turner and John Farnum, Sr. They were put in prison to await their escort out of Massachusetts. The Boston Court received many letters of protest from the colonies and England against the sentencing of these men.

Meanwhile the Boston Baptist church had a temporary solution for the threat of imprisonment for meeting as a church: they assembled by rowing across a short watercourse and gathering together in a home on Noodles Island in Massachusetts Bay. At times the aged and venerable Obadiah Holmes preached to them.

Apparently out of pity, the Court granted a 3-day release for Gould and Turner and like John Clarke before him, Gould organized a church service as soon as he was released. They were all discovered and in the confusion, while 15 other church members were taken custody Gould and Turner made their escape to Noodles Island.

For five years, Thomas Gould held forth the word of God on Noodles Island, preaching to whomsoever would take the short trip across the watercourse to hear him. Souls were saved and lives were touched on that remote oasis of freedom in Massachusetts Bay.

One night, William Turner made the mistake of rowing back to the mainland. He was immediately arrested. But somehow he made his escape to military immortality by leading a band of Baptist volunteers, defeating the Indian armies of King Phillip, at the battle of what is now known as: *Turners Falls*.

Chapter 13—The Churches of the Seventeenth Century Part II

During this time the grand jury of Boston presented indictments to no less than nine Baptist congregations from 1669-1680. Churches sprang up in Woburn, Concord, Cambridge, Newbury, Malden, Reading and Billerica. Elsewhere, the Seventh day Baptist church sprang from the Newport Church in 1671. It was the third Baptist church birthed from Dr. Clarke's congregation and the sixth church of the *baptized believers* in America.

Then the hand of God began to move for the Boston Baptists. Unexpectedly, Governor Bellingham died in 1673. This brought the more tolerant John Leverette into power.

In the midst of a tremendous struggle for liberty and the souls of men, Thomas Gould died on October 27, 1675. His nation should honour him, but does not know who he is. It must have been a lonely funeral dirge that fall as the exiled saint of Noodles Island was laid to rest in an inconspicuous grave.

The Baptist church of Boston petitioned the court for the right to meet and worship late in 1680 and waited for an answer of mercy from a group of men who were their avowed archenemies. **Almost as an afterthought, the church was granted permission by the court to meet as a CHURCH in February of 1681!!** The sufferings and testimony of **50 years** by noble saints finally paid off. From the portals of glory, Thomas Gould must have been cheering.

1. Write Isaiah 53:1 twice

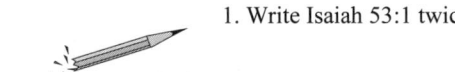

2. Who was the first president of Harvard? What happened when the time came to baptize his child?
   Henry Dunster, he refused

3. Name the first five Baptist churches in America:
   The first baptist church, Newport, Providence
   Second baptist Newport, Swansea

4. Who was the pastor of the Boston Baptists? Who influenced him?
   Thomas Gould

5. To what Island did the Baptist flee? Did their pastor live to see the victory of their church?
   Noodles Island   No!

Chapter Fourteen
The Churches of the Eighteenth Century

Section One: The Decline of Religion in England and America.
Section Two: The Philadelphia Baptist Association of 1707. The Philadelphia Confession of Faith.

SECTION ONE

Scripture to Memorize

Revelation 2:5 Remember therefore from whence thou art fallen, and repent, and do the first works; or else I will come unto thee quickly, and will remove thy candlestick out of his place, except thou repent.

A Time Line for the Eighteenth Century.
1700. The Adoption of the Half-way covenant by the Congregational Church (— allowed children to be baptized regardless of parent membership)
1702. Publishing of Cotton Mather's *Magnalia*
1703. Birth of Jonathan Edwards, Windsor, Connecticut
1704. Birth of John Comer
1706. Birth of Daniel Marshall, Windsor, Connecticut
1706. Birth of Shubal Stearns in Boston, Massachusetts
1707. The Philadelphia Baptist Association, the first Baptist association formed in America.
1708. The first Baptist church in Connecticut formed by Valentine Wightman
1714. Birth of George Whitefield, Gloucester, England
1724. Birth of Isaac Backus, Norwich, Connecticut
1727. Birth of John Gano
1732. Birth of George Washington
1754. Birth of John Leland

The Church bodies that came out of the Reformation

The Greek Church split from the Roman Catholic in 909. The Greek Orthodox did not come out of the Reformation. These did:

1. **The Lutheran Church** split from the Roman Catholic institution in 1530, under the leadership of Martin Luther.
   All of the major Lutheran bodies came from this branch: Missouri Synod, Evangelical Lutheran, and German Reformed.
2. **The Church of England** (Anglican or Episcopalian) split from the Roman Catholic in 1531, under the leadership of King Henry VIII.
   From the Church of England came **the Congregational** church in America (1630) and **the Methodists** of England and America
3. **The Presbyterian Church**, based on John Calvin's theology, split from the Roman Catholic institution in 1541.
   From the Presbyterians came **the Cumberland Presbyterian, the Disciples of Christ** (1820's) and various twentieth century branches of the Presbyterian denomination.

Some would argue that Baptist churches came out of the Reformation, (some would say the 1640's out of English Separatism) but as we have learned, Baptist churches existed from the time of the resurrection until the present day.

Chapter 14—The Churches of the Eighteenth Century

The Decline of Religion in America

Solomon Stoddard, the venerable old man, a sage among the ministers of the *standing order*, had opinions that carried a lot of power. His opinion concerning the **half-way covenant** elevated that false doctrine to common doctrine in the early days of the eighteenth century. No one could explain Stoddard's affection for this destructive doctrine, yet as Mr. Stoddard pressed on with this, New England spiraled into an apathetic and lifeless spirituality, which resulted in the judgment of God. The solution for this error led to the bringing together of the American nation. Surprisingly, the leadership for the solution to the **half-way covenant** was provided from Stoddard's own descendents. The argument for *experimental religion*, first voiced in Boston by John Clarke, then by Thomas Gould, was about to be tested. Emerging from New England came a voice for revival.

Within the bounds of Providence, God gave Solomon Stoddard a lovely daughter named Sarah. Sarah married the preacher, Timothy Edwards and they had a son named Jonathan. In a few short years, Jonathan Edwards would stand in the pulpit of his grandfather Stoddard's church in Northampton and begin a journey to correct the wrongs of the **half-way covenant** and see revival come to America.

Though Edwards was not a Baptist, his influence on the baptized believers was deep and lasting. The English Baptist historian, Thomas Crosby mentions him with great respect; the first American Baptist historian Isaac Backus, credits him with opening the fires of the Great Awakening; and Alvah Hovey, who gave us the biography of Backus, said Edwards' influence and belief in *experimental religion* gained a great foothold for the Baptist people.

Jonathan Edwards was born in Windsor Connecticut in 1703, the only son of Timothy and Sarah Edwards. His father was a preacher, a believer in *experimental religion*, and a witness of great revivals. Edward's mother, Sarah was of a sharp pedigree, and her father was the famous Solomon Stoddard.

Edwards was educated at Yale, and it was in those days deep in study that Edwards came to realize the mistakes of his grandfather. For years he was suspicious of the **half-way covenant**, but since that doctrine had become synonymous with his beloved grandfather we may imagine his dilemma in exposing it as error. Nothing but love and respect towards Stoddard was in his heart and his honorable constitution would make it difficult to become critical of his mother's father. Still, the belief system had to be corrected, because in Edwards' words, since 1704, the sacrament of baptism "was viewed as a converting ordinance" (Sereno E. Dwight, *Memoirs of Jonathan Edwards*, P. xxviii). We will detail more of Edwards' life in chapter fifteen.

The dulling effect on *experimental religion* by the **half-way covenant** was brutal. Churches began to die. Between 1718 and 1727, Mr. Stoddard's church as well as all of New England experienced in Edwards' own words, "a far more degenerate time among his people, particularly among the young, than ever before" (Sereno E. Dwight, *Memoirs of Jonathan Edwards*, P. xxviii).

Definitions:

the half-way covenant: the doctrine which allowed unregenerate parents to bring their children to the *standing order* church for infant baptism.
Christi Magnalia Americana: the history of New England written by Cotton Mather in which the Baptists are slandered.

1. Write Revelation 2:5 twice.

2. Write the definition for "half-way covenant:"
   doctrine that allowed unsaved parents to bring children into church to be baptized
3. What was *Christi Magnalia Americana*?
   Cotton Mather
4. Since 1704, how was baptism viewed in the *standing order* churches?
   As a saving ordinance
5. Where did Jonathan Edwards attend college? *Yale*
6. Concerning his mother, why was opposing the Saybrook platform a problem for Edwards?
   His mother was the daughter of Solomon Stoddard
7. Name the three main church bodies that came out of the Reformation.
   Lutheran = German   *Scotland - Presbyterian*
   England = Church of England   *John Calvin*

****

14.1.2

Definitions:

Regular Baptists: these were the "Particular" Baptists of America in the Seventeenth and Eighteenth century, holding to the doctrine of Particular redemption
Six Principle Baptists: these were the "General" Baptists of America in the Seventeenth and Eighteenth century holding to the doctrine of General atonement. They held to the six principles of Hebrew 6:1-2 - repentance, faith, baptism, laying-on-of-hands, the resurrection of the dead and eternal life. Of these, the laying-on-of-hands was the only one really distinctive to them, because it was mandatory to membership and an ordinance of the church. They also opposed hymns or music in the church services.

What caused the Decline of Religion in England and America?

In England, the government had changed hands so many times that the act of toleration had been a pessimistic solution. No one knew for sure how long the toleration would last, but the suffering of dissidents grew less and less frequent. The Church of England had been practicing a form of the **half-way covenant** before the American colonies had ever put it into practice. Now with a slight bit of freedom the non-conforming Baptists settled into a happy mediocrity. This caused a decline in the religion of the heart. There was growth, but along with the slight growth in the Church of England

Chapter 14—The Churches of the Eighteenth Century

and the Presbyterians there was entirely too much formalism and not enough heart-felt conviction.

What is the Ground of Thy *Controversie?*
Salem Witch Trials

A sad chapter in American history occurred in 1692. There was confusion about witchcraft.

A certain blood fever was demonstrated in the confusion over witchcraft in Salem, Massachusetts. There is not room to narrate the odd proceedings, but suffice it to say, that the Baptists of New England had no part in the destruction of those 20 people who in a matter of four months were executed. Some of those that died were in actuality, Baptist.

In the wake of the deaths of the so-called witches, Michael Wigglesworth's solemn words written to Increase Mather are important to note:

> I fear (among our many other provocations) that God hath a Controversy with us about what was done in the time of the Witchcraft. I fear that **innocent blood hath been shed**; and that many have had their hands defiled therewith. I believe our Godly Judges did act Conscientiously, according to what they did apprehend then to be sufficient Proof: But since that, have not the Devil's impostures appeared? And that most of the Complainers and Accusers were acted by him in giving their testimonies. Be it then that it . . . was done ignorantly. Paul, a Pharisee, persecuted the church of God, shed the blood of God's saints, and yet obtained mercy, because he did it in ignorance; but how doth he bewail it, and shame himself for it before God and men afterwards (Bernard Rosenthal, *Salem Story, Reading the Witch Trials of 1692*, P. 183).

> **Valentine Wightman**; who was a direct descendent of Edward Wightman, the last *baptized believer* burned in England; founded the first Baptist church in Connecticut in Groton in June 1708. It was a "Six Principle Baptist Church."
>
> He was born in North Kingston, Rhode Island in 1681. On February 10, 1702, he married Susannah Holmes, the granddaughter of Obadiah Holmes and the great-granddaughter of Roger Williams.
>
> He continued his ministry at Groton for more than forty years, and died June 9, 1747, aged sixty-six years. His son, Timothy Wightman, who filled the pulpit for a period of more than forty years, succeeded him as pastor.
>
> Timothy's son, John Gano Wightman, pastored the church for another forty years. The Wightmans pastored in Groton for over 125 years!

In New England in 1702, there were five histories telling the story of the Puritans. There was Mitchel, Johnson, Hutchinson, Morton, and the most popular of all: *Magnalia Christi Americana*, written by Cotton Mather.

In England, Daniel Neal finished his *History of the Puritans* in 1732. It was well received in England and became the standard non-Catholic history text of the eighteenth century. According to Baptist historian Thomas Crosby, Dr. Neal had promised his book would give a fair account of the English Baptists. Large amounts of materials were sent to him documenting the troubles and persecution of the English Baptists. However, when his history was published the obvious distain for the Baptists came through without a veil. Neal basically ignored the evidence and material set before him. Thomas Crosby rescued those documents from Neal and wrote the *History of the English Baptists*, which was published in 1740.

As Cotton Mathers' *Magnalia* became the standard Christian history of America, Neals' became the standard in England. Re-write had early proponents.

It became clear that the Baptists needed a history of their own. The battle for an accurate American Baptist history began with the birth of **John Comer** on August 1, 1704.

Comer was born in Boston and attended Yale College. From August to November 1721, while a student at Yale, John Comer was in travail of soul over his salvation, even moving to Cambridge for fear of the small pox epidemic. Providentially, the family with whom he lived contracted the disease. Those circumstances led to his conversion to Christ.

Soon, Bro. Comer came under conviction about baptism by reading *Treatise on Baptism* by the English Baptist preacher, Joseph Stennet.

The *real crucible of New England* was increasingly being debated: **if an infant is baptized and converted in older years, what scriptural term describes the unregenerate person in the intervening years?** Indeed, the debate about baptism would drive a new generation of Americans into **independence** from all *standing order*, and toward a deeper dependency on God.

> ### The Five Mile Rule
> As was done in England, a *Five-Mile Rule* was established in New England. An exemption was made in 1728 for Baptists and Quakers for relief from ministerial taxes IF they lived less than five miles from their place of worship. Now came the necessity of territorial policing. Backus likened this to the pharaoh allowing the Israelites to worship—but not to worship *too* far away. In 1729, 28 *baptized believers* went to jail in Bristol, Massachusetts for refusing to pay the Congregational ministerial rates (taxes).

The passages that brought John Comer to conviction about baptism by immersion for believers only were Acts 8, Matthew 3, and Romans 6.

> **John Comer** diligently researched the hardships of the pioneer Baptists in New England. God did not allow Mr. Comer to finish. He died May 23, 1734 from consumption. His work fell into the hands of his good friend John Callender, who became the pastor of John Clarke's church at Newport.
>
> Sadly only a few of Comer's writings ever reached the Baptist historians Morgan Edwards, Isaac Backus, and David Benedict. His materials and remains were vandalized and many documents stolen. Only his diary remained intact. (William Wilmarth records this sad commentary in his notes in Comer's diary.)

John Comer began the most important work of his life. As Mather's *Magnalia* was reprinted, and quoted against the Baptists, Comer began to work to preserve the true record of his heritage. On pages 92 and 93 of his diary, he wrote of his desire to communicate with Henry Loveall to gain information on the churches in "the Jerseys." He began gathering information in October of 1729. He wrote to Thomas Symonds, a pastor in South Carolina, for information. He wrote to Paul Palmer in North Carolina, and to Nicolas Eyres in New York. In March of 1731 he traveled south to New Jersey and Pennsylvania. Comer recorded two Seventh-day Baptist churches in New England making the number of churches of the baptized believers in that part of the country 18 total. No one knew the number elsewhere, a problem he tried desperately to remedy.

Chapter 14—The Churches of the Eighteenth Century

In 1732, Comer reported, "According to my best knowledge that there were 26 Baptist churches in America under their several divisions and about 2,110 communicants, reckoning from North Carolina to Boston."

What is the ground of thy Controversy?

Mr. Comer pointed to the following disasters as proof that God was displeased with the "progress" of New England: The great Boston fire of 1711. In 1721, a small pox epidemic in Boston, with over 1,000 people killed in one year. **The death of Increase Mather occurred in 1723**. Comer said, "This year (1727) proved trouble-some to the state of this Colony, which was in a distressing condition. There never was so many supporters of the State taken away in one year as in this remarkable year. It looks like a sad token of God's displeasure" (John Comer, *Diary*, P. 47). 1728 started as badly: "January 17, 1728, This night Mary Dye went and drowned herself as the Jewry [jury] gave it; but most concluded she was murthered by her husband. **Cotton Mather died on February 13, 1728**. Deborah Brinman, was killed by lightning at Narraganset on May 31st 1728. A hild drowned at Connanicut on August 23rd 1728. April 7, 1728 five more citizens drowned in a sailing incident. On May 31, 1728, Deborah Grinman was killed by lightning." In addition, a terrible appearance of the aurora borealis frightened the population of New England in October 1728.

John Comer reported an example of an unregenerate church preacher named Joseph O'Hara. An Episcopalian, Mr. O'Hara was ousted, literally, from his pulpit November 3, 1728 by "an extraordinary gust of wind" which blew both he and a large window out into the street. O'Hara was later jailed for theft.

Other evidences of God's judgment from Comer's diary: Dec 8, 1728 a woman was found dead in Dyre's swamp. Four more drowned off Hog Island on Dec 21, 1728. **Solomon Stoddard died on February 11, 1729**. A man drowned on the Seventeenth of March, 1729.

John Comer recorded in his diary: "A number of Baptists, Churchmen, and Quakers, in all 30 persons, belonging to the township of Rehoboth (Mass.) were committed to Bristol jail, by reason of their refusing to pay the ministers' rate. The measles brought into town and spread. Same day. March 3, 1729" (John Comer, *Diary*, P. 62).

Comer wrote, "**the voice of sudden death** warns us, **be ye also ready**." He reported five more dead with their funerals in one day in October of 1729. October 22, 1729, small pox *again* reported in Boston. It was brought to Massachusetts on an Irish vessel, from which 19 fell victim and were cast into the sea. **On October 29, 1729, the Great Earthquake hit.** Both secular and religious historians tell of the magnitude of it. There has not been an earthquake of such magnitude in New England since. Isaac Backus wrote: "at ten in the evening, came on the greatest earthquake that had then been known in this country, and great numbers were awakened thereby."

On November 5, 1729 the light came back. Mr. Comer identifies it on Jan 4, 1730 when he says he saw the "aurora borealis, in the north." Finally concerning the Northern Lights, Mr. Comer on October 22, 1730 records, "This evening between six and seven of the clock came on **the most terrifying awful and amazing Northern light as ever was beheld in New England as I can learn**. There was at the bottom of the horizon a very great brightness and over it an amazing red bow extending from North to East like a dreadful fire and many fiery spears, and the East was wonderfully lighted and some part of the appearance continued many hours, and people were extremely terrified. Words can't express the awfulness of it. **What God is about to do is only known to Himself.**"

After seeing strange lights in the sky four times in three years, reporting numerous drownings and suicides, unjust jailings and hangings, a measles outbreak, the small pox epidemics in Boston, July heat, August lightning, a September hurricane, the October earthquake, John Comer wrote:

> February 15, 1730. The interest of Christ in the Baptist churches looks very dark at this time; the harvest is great, but the labourers are few. Oh that the Lord of the harvest would furnish and send forth into his harvest! I mourn over the churches. Lord show us, **what is the ground of thy controversie**? (John Comer, *Diary*, P. 101)

STOP AND THINK

1. Write Revelation 2:5 twice.

2. Define *Regular Baptist*:
   regular = particular

3. Define *Six Principle Baptist*: → *became General Baptists*

4. What was the main reason for the decline of religion in America?
   Doctrine of the halfway covenant

5. What did Wigglesworth think of the death of the witches of Salem?
   worried that innocent blood had been shed.

6. Who was the first man to record history for the Baptist people in America? *John Comer*

7. What happened to Comer's papers?
   They were vandalized, mostly destroyed (diary survived)

8. Name at least three disasters that Comer pointed to as judgments of God. Which one is the most unusual in your opinion?
   Northern lights 3 times

9. What was the condition of the Baptist churches according to Comer in 1730?
   very dark

****
14.2.1

SECTION TWO

The Philadelphia Association

Historians try with every given opportunity to trace American Baptist roots to Roger Williams and the First Baptist Church of Providence. The truth is that the First Church of Providence under Williams birthed no children. She passed her baptism down to no one. Baptism in America has its roots in three basic streams: English, Welsh and German

Chapter 14—The Churches of the Eighteenth Century

ancestry. American mother churches are too numerous to pinpoint one great grandmother. However, the Baptists of America do have a place where they settled what they believed and set off to aggressively win souls and birth churches. That place was Philadelphia.

Elias Keach arrived in Pennsylvania in 1686. He was the son of the celebrated Benjamin Keach of England, one of the most prominent Baptists of his day. Elias was only 19 when he stepped into the new world and fancied himself quite a preacher.

He lobbied for an opportunity to preach to a gathering at **Pennepek**. Using his pedigree and promoting himself as a "young London divine," Elias dressed in black garb and clerical collar, drummed up a crowd and began to speak. He was barely into his discourse when the power of God fell upon the meeting. The first person to fall under conviction was Keach himself. He paused in his delivery and weeping, left the meeting and went to **Cold Spring, Bucks County, Pennsylvania** on the Delaware River to speak to a seasoned Baptist preacher named Thomas Dungan.

> The father of the noted **Dr. Benjamin Rush**, a signer of the Declaration of Independence, was a member of this Baptist Church at Cold Spring. William Penn, it is supposed, caught his liberal [political] views from Algernon Sidney, also from Cold Spring Baptist Church. Penn had suffered much for Christ's sake, and had adopted quite broad views of religious liberty; for at the very inception of legislation in Pennsylvania, the Assembly had passed **the "Great Law,"** the first section of which provides that in that jurisdiction no person shall "At any time be compelled to frequent or maintain any religious worship, place or ministry whatever, contrary to his or her mind, but shall freely and fully enjoy his or her Christian liberty in that respect, without any interruption or reflection; and, if any person shall abuse or deride any other for his or her different persuasion and practice, in matter of religion, such shall be looked upon as a disturber of the peace, and be punished accordingly (Thomas Armitage, *History of the Baptists, Vol. 2*, P. 706).

Dungan, had come from Rhode Island to Cold Spring in 1684, and gathered a Baptist church there. Dungan came from Ireland to Newport because of the persecution of the Baptists under Charles II. The church, as Armitage puts it, "lived at a dying rate" and passed out of existence in 1702. But before it "died," it brought forth life in Elias Keach, whom Thomas Dungan brought to Christ and baptized.

At Pennepeck, a work began among the Baptists west of the Connecticut River. The end result of the work became the great work of the Philadelphia Association, the first Baptist association in America.

As Cold Spring paved the way for the revival at Pennepek and Elias Keach, Pennepek was the place in Pennsylvania from which the first churches of the first association of Baptists in America were birthed. Armitage informs us on how **Pennepeck church** was formed:

From Wales:

> By the good providence of God, there came certain persons out of Radnorshire, in Wales, over into…Pennsylvania, and settled in the township of Dublin, in the County of Philadelphia, namely, John Eaton, George Eaton and Jane, his wife, Samuel Jones and Sarah Eaton, who had all been baptized upon confession of faith, and received into the communion of the Church of Christ meeting in the parishes of Llandewi and Nantmel, in Radnorshire.

From Ireland:

> John Baker, who had been baptized, and was a member of a congregation of baptized believers in Kilkenny.

From England:

In the year 1687 there came one Samuel Vans out of England, and settled near the aforesaid township and went under the denomination of a Baptist, and was so taken to be. These, with Sarah Eaton, and Rev. Elias Keach, formed the Church.

From Converts from Pennsylvania:

Ashton and his wife, with Fisher and Watts, had been baptized by Keach at Pennepek, November, 1687 (Thomas Armitage, *History of the Baptists, Vol. 2*, P. 707).

In January of 1688, the Baptist church at **Pennepek** was organized. This was the second Baptist church in Pennsylvania and a mother of many churches.

Keach became a powerful evangelist, pastoring the Pennepek church and preaching the Gospel all around the Philadelphia area. He preached the Gospel in Trenton, Philadelphia, Middletown, Cohansey, Salem, and many other places. He baptized his converts into the fellowship of the Church at Pennepek, so that all the Baptists of New Jersey and Pennsylvania were connected with that body except the little band at Cold Spring.

After a time the branch churches or chapels of **Pennepek** under Elias Keach began to meet twice a year for public preaching and exhortation. "Morgan Edwards tells us that twice a year, May and October, they held 'General Meetings' for preaching and the Lord's Supper, at Salem in the spring and at Dublin or Burlington in the autumn, for the accommodation of distant members and the spread of the Gospel, until separate churches were formed in several places" (Thomas Armitage, *History of the Baptists, Vol. 2*, P. 708).

Elias Keach returned to London in 1689 where he began a work for God, baptizing 130 in a nine month span. He died in 1701 being only 34 years of age. His influence in America was felt in the power and integrity of the work he left behind, manifesting itself in the Philadelphia Association. Armitage further comments:

The **Pennepek** Church, after some contentions, built its first meeting-house in 1707, on ground presented by Rev. Samuel Jones, who became one of its early pastors; for many years it was the center of denominational operations west of the Connecticut River, and **from its labors sprang the Philadelphia Association, in 1707**. It was natural that the several Baptist companies formed in different communities by this church should soon take steps for the purpose of becoming independent churches in their several localities. This was first done in New Jersey, then in Middletown in 1688, Piscataqua in 1689, and Cohansey in 1690 (Thomas Armitage, *History of the Baptists, Vol. 2*, P. 708-9).

In 1707, the Philadelphia Association was formed of the five following churches: **Pennepeck (now Lower Dublin northwest of Philadelphia), Middletown (Pennsylvania), Piscataqua (New Jersey), Cohansey (New Jersey), and Welsh Tract (Delaware)**.

Here is Thomas Armitage on the Baptist Church at Cohansey:

Chapter 14—The Churches of the Eighteenth Century

Another Church was established at **COHANSEY**. The records of this Church for the first hundred years of its existence were burned, but, according to Asplund's Register, the Church was organized in 1691. **Keach** had baptized three persons there in 1688, and the Church was served for many years by Thomas Killingsworth, who was also a judge on the bench. He was an ordained minister from Norfolk, England, of much literary ability, eminent for his gravity and sound judgment, and so was deemed fit to serve as Judge of the County Court of Salem. About 1687 a company had come from **John Myles's Church, at Swansea**, near Providence, which for twenty-three years kept themselves as a separate Church, on the questions of laying on of hands, singing of psalms and predestination, until, with Timothy Brooks, their pastor they united with their brethren at Cohansey. It was meet that before this remarkable century closed the nucleus of Baptist principles should be formed in the great Quaker city of Philadelphia, and this was done in 1696. **John Fanner and his wife, from Knolly's Church in London, landed there in that year, and were joined in 1697 by John Todd and Rebecca Woosencroft, from the Church at Leamington, England**. A little congregation was held in Philadelphia by the preaching of Keach and Killingsworth and slowly increased. The meetings were held irregularly in a store-house on what was known as the "Barbadoes Lot," at the corner of what are now called Second and Chestnut Streets, and formed a sort of out-station to Pennepek. In 1697 John Watts baptized four persons, who, with five others, amongst them John Hohne, formed a Church on the second Sabbath in December, 1698. They continued to meet in the store-house till 1707, when they were compelled to leave under protest, and then they worshiped, according to Edwards, at a place "near the draw-bridge, known by the name of Anthony Morris's New House." They were not entirely independent of Pennepek till 1723 (Thomas Armitage, *History of the Baptists, Vol. 2*, P. 711).

> **A most interesting Church was organized in 1689 at Piscataqua** (in New Jersey) This settlement **was named after a settlement in New Hampshire (now Dover), which at that time was in the Province of Maine**. We have seen that Hanserd Knollys preached there in 1638-41, and had his controversy with Larkham respecting receiving all into the Church (Congregational), and the baptizing of any infants offered. Although Knollys was not a Baptist at that time, **his discussions on these subjects proved to be the seed which yielded fruit after many years**. In 1648, ten years after he began his ministry at Dover, under date of October 18th, the authorities of the day were informed that the profession of *Anabaptistry* there had excited much trouble.
>
> When Knollys left, in 1641, a number of those who sympathized with his Baptist tendencies left with him, and when he returned to London they settled on Long Island, and remained there until that territory fell under the power of English Episcopacy, when they removed to the vicinity of New Brunswick, N. J. There they formed the settlement of Piscataqua (afterward Piscataway, near Stelton) and organized a Baptist Church, which has exerted a powerful influence down to this time. The township confined about 80 families, embodying a population of about 400 persons.
>
> From the earliest information this settlement was popularly known as the **"Anabaptist Town,"** and from 1675 downward the names of members of the Baptist Church are found amongst the law-makers and other public officials, both in the town and the colony, showing that they were prominent and influential citizens (Thomas Armitage, *History of the Baptists, Vol. 2*, P. 710-11).

Thomas Armitage described the beginnings of the **Baptist church at Welsh Tract**:

The new century, however, opened with the emigration of sixteen Baptists, from the counties of Pembroke and Carmarthen, Wales, under the leadership of Rev. **Thomas Griffith**, whose coming introduced a new era in Pennsylvania and the region round about. They had organized themselves into what Morgan Edwards calls "a Church emigrant and sailant" at Milford, June, 1701, and landed in Philadelphia in September following. They repaired immediately to the vicinity of Pennepek and settled there for a time. In 1703 the greater part of

The Collegiate Baptist History Workbook

them purchased lands containing about 30,000 acres from **William Penn**, in Newcastle County, Delaware. This they named the **Welsh Tract** and removed thither. There they prospered greatly from year to year, adding to their numbers both by emigration and conversion. For about seventy years their ministers were Welshmen, some of them of eminence, and **six Churches in Pennsylvania and Delaware trace their lineage to this church**. As early as 1736 it dismissed forty-eight members **to emigrate to South Carolina**, where they made a settlement on the **Peedee River, and organized the Welsh Neck Church there**, which during the next century became the center **from which thirty-eight Baptist churches sprang**, in the immediate vicinity (Thomas Armitage, *History of the Baptists, Vol. 2*, P. 712).

Thomas Armitage noted the importance of the Welsh Baptist churches:

> Humanly speaking, we can distinctly trace the causes of our denominational growth from the beginning of the century to the opening of the Revolutionary War. In the Churches west of the Connecticut there was an active missionary spirit. At first the New England Baptists partook somewhat of the conservatism of their Congregational brethren, **but in the Churches planted chiefly by the Welsh in New Jersey and Pennsylvania, South Carolina and Virginia**, the missionary spirit was vigorous and aggressive. As from a central fortress they sent out their little bands; here a missionary and there a handful of colonists, who penetrated farther into the wilderness, and extended the frontiers of the denomination (Thomas Armitage, *History of the Baptists, Vol. 2*, P. 713).

---

1. Write Revelation 2:5 twice.

2. What was the unusual thing about Elias Keach's salvation? *He almost converted himself*
3. Who baptized Elias Keach? *Thomas Dungen*
4. What was the first Baptist church west of the Connecticut River? *Pennepeck*
5. What preacher from Wales led the congregation which started the Welsh Tract church? *Thomas Griffith*
6. How many churches were birthed from the Welsh Tract church in Delaware? *six*
7. How many churches were birthed from the Welsh Neck church in South Carolina? *38*
8. What five churches constituted the Philadelphia Association? *Pennepeck, Cohansey, Piscataway, Welsh tract, Middletown*

****

14.2.2

Definitions:

open communion: the practice of allowing those who were baptized in non-Baptist churches to participate in the Lord's supper in Baptist churches.

Chapter 14—The Churches of the Eighteenth Century

close communion: the practice of allowing only baptized believers to participate in the Lord's Supper in Baptist churches.

The Philadelphia Association 1707
The First Baptist Association in America

As the Baptist historian William Cathcart said, "Formed on the twenty seventh day of the seventh month on the seventh day of the week," the Philadelphia Association began its work. The purpose of this first Baptist Association was declared on numerous occasions: **It was established for communication and unity of doctrine**. The early Baptist associations had no intention to control or manipulate the churches. All churches were independent and the thought of a hierarchy among them was contemptible.

The Philadelphia Association grew to contain fifty-three churches in its membership by 1791. In 1742 the association adopted the Philadelphia Confession of Faith, a confession of faith nearly identical to the London Baptist Confession of Faith of 1689. Benjamin Franklin printed the confession in 1743 for the general public. This brought about a good sense of unity among the Baptists, who for so many years had to struggle just to survive. Now there was hope that there would be some settling of doctrine and practice. Those that adhered to the confession became known as **"Regular"** Baptists. Nearly all of the pioneer Baptist associations of America eventually adopted the Philadelphia Confession of Faith.

The main difference between the London confession of 1689 and the Philadelphia confession of 1742 had to do with the Lord's Supper, or Communion. The London Confession has an admission in its appendix that some Baptist churches practiced **"open communion,"** that is receiving persons who were baptized as infants at the Lord's Supper. The Philadelphia Confession has no such admission and is definitely a **"close communion"** confession, taking a stand that only baptized believers are allowed to participate in the Lord's Supper in Baptist churches.

1. Write Revelation 2:5 twice.

2. Define open communion.

3. Define close communion.

4. What was the first association of Baptists in America? When was it formed?
   Philadelphia association 1707

5. What was the purpose of the first Baptist associations that were formed in America?
   For communication and unity of doctrine
   → Starting churches and doing missions

Chapter Fifteen
The Churches of the Eighteenth Century Part II

Section One: The Great Awakening in America and England. Jonathan Edwards. George Whitefield.
Section Two: The New Lights, Separates, and Isaac Backus.

SECTION ONE

We have seen how the state of religion in America greatly declined in the early eighteenth century and the judgment of God fell upon the colonies. We have seen how God raised up Jonathan Edwards in Northampton, Massachusetts, a preacher of the *"standing order"* who believed in experimental religion. His preaching was different from the dead orthodoxy of the established churches of New England. As we have seen, the **half-way covenant** was having a chilling effect. All young Americans should take heed to the events leading up to what has since been called "the Great Awakening."

Definitions:

Old Lights: those established churches that did not embrace the Great Awakening.
New Lights: churches that embraced the Great Awakening and believed in revival.
dead orthodoxy: believing the right doctrines, but having no vital power, or lack of belief in the new birth.

Scripture to Memorize

> 2 Chronicles 7:14 *If my people, which are called by my name, shall humble themselves, and pray, and seek my face, and turn from their wicked ways; then will I hear from heaven, and will forgive their sin, and will heal their land.*

The Beginning of the Great Awakening

The Great Awakening commenced in 1734. The early defining moments of this tremendous event were recorded in **Jonathan Edwards'** *Narrative of Surprising Conversions*. The roots of the Great Awakening were in Edwards and his church, the Congregational Church of Northampton, Massachusetts.

According to Jonathan Edwards the awakening started among a specific group in his church: "There began a better attitude and a disposition to yield to advice **in the young**" (Sereno E. Dwight, *Memoirs of Jonathan Edwards*, P. xxii).

Mr. Edwards had been concerned about the lax attitude toward Sunday services. Not absences, but inattention. He preached on it one Sunday and the next evening a large number of adult church members came to his home wanting to do something about their complacent attitudes. He challenged his people to warn their families, but to the surprise of Mr. Edwards and the adults of the church, **the young people** were already discussing their mediocrity and repenting of their complacency. God began to move in their midst. This began a stirring across Massachusetts and New England.

A small revival stir occurred from there to the little village of Pascommuck. This then spread across Massachusetts and New England. Jonathan Edwards preached his epic

Chapter 15—The Churches of the Eighteenth Century Part II

sermon, *Sinners in the Hands of an Angry God* in the parish church of Enfield, Connecticut on July 8, 1741. The Great Awakening was under way.

Baptists owe much to Edwards for his stand on experimental religion and his support of George Whitefield, whom we shall presently meet. Edwards put an emphasis on the personal drawing and convicting power of the Holy Spirit and convinced just about every American of their most important need: "Ye must be born again."

The Effect of Jonathan Edwards

Jonathan Edwards practiced physical exercise, slept very little, and ate very little. Thirteen hour days of study were NORMAL for him. He used investigation and argument in his works and prospered under long constrained applications of study. He lived by a great schedule and self watch, and he was a man of self-denial. A great principle found in Edward's life: *The force of habitual duties creates a change of habit*. He said, "When at any time I have a sense of any divine thing, then I seek to turn it in my thoughts to a practical improvement."

> Jonathan Edwards said, "When at any time I have a sense of any divine thing, then I seek to turn it in my thoughts to a practical improvement."

Edwards devoted large amounts of his time to study. He desired to be a theologian, but God made of him an unusual combination of theologian and revivalist.

Physically, he was frail and he knew it. He worked on his health, and paid close attention to his diet, even to the point of noting what foods affected his body and mind. But most obviously he WALKED WITH GOD. He kept a rigorous office schedule and made himself easily available to those in distress of soul, where they were treated with "all desirable tenderness, kindness and familiarity" (Sereno E. Dwight, *Memoirs of Jonathan Edwards*, P. xxxix).

In 1750, Edwards was voted out of his church by the "parish committee" by one vote.

In early 1758, he became the President of Princeton College in New Jersey. On March 22, 1758, he died of a small pox inoculation.

We cannot make revival happen but we can pray, work, and apply our talents, and so not hinder its approaching fragrance. Jonathan Edwards certainly left a testimony of how to prepare for its coming.

> **Sarah Pierrepont Edwards**
>
> Edwards' wife (married July 28, 1727) was the beautiful Sarah Pierrepont, the daughter of James Pierrepont the *standing order* preacher of the New Haven Congregational church. Pierrepont was author of the *Saybrook Platform*, and a supporter of the **half-way covenant**. Complications set in when Edwards came to reject and then publicly oppose Saybrook and the "half-way."
>
> "Sarah was born January 9, 1710. She was a young lady of uncommon beauty. The native powers of her mind were of a superior order. In her manners she was gentle and courteous, amiable in her behaviour, and the law of kindness appeared to govern all her conversation and conduct. She was also a rare example of early piety; having exhibited the life and power of religion, and that in a remarkable manner, when only five years of age" (Sereno E. Dwight, *Memoirs of Jonathan Edwards*, P. xxxix).

The Collegiate Baptist History Workbook

1. Write the definitions above one time:

2. Write the memory verse for this chapter twice:

3. Which group of Christians from the Great Awakening would Baptists most identify with, the new lights or the old lights?
   new lights
4. What church saw the beginning of the Great Awakening?
   Congregational Church at Northampton, MA
5. What group of people in the church began to seek the Lord earnestly leading to the beginning of the great awakening?
   The young people
6. Name the most outstanding trait in the life of Edwards? *he walked with God*
7. For what purpose did Edwards work in his office 13 hours each day?
   1. to study 2. he made himself available to counsel others

****

15.1.2

The Great Awakening and George Whitefield

At the same time the American colonies were experiencing the first flames of the Great Awakening, God was raising up a group of men in England to bring revival to a needy empire and a waiting world.

These men were preparing for the Gospel ministry at Oxford University. They called themselves "the Holy Club." They were earnest and fervent with their walk with God and their desire to be used. John and Charles Wesley were the founders of this "Holy Club" and they consecrated themselves to God in an unusual fashion. We must remember that there was no college or university for a Baptist Christian to attend. Baptists were still outlawed in most places. But these Anglican preachers in the "Holy Club" would one day live to be a blessing to the *baptized believers*, even though they did not intend to be.

→ Anglican

George Whitefield

One of the young preachers in the "Holy Club" was George Whitefield, a converted theatre enthusiast who now

Chapter 15—The Churches of the Eighteenth Century Part II

dedicated his tremendous talents for communication to the Gospel ministry. Whitefield had a great passion to know God and be used of him. He began preaching at age 19 just after graduating from Oxford and soon became a hated and beloved man.

Whitefield immediately began to declare *ye must be born again*. He drove several people "mad" during his first sermon. He was soon driven from the Anglican churches by the pastors, because he preached experimental religion and at times exposed them as unsaved men posing as ministers of Christ.

His preaching startled England. His style and pathos were unique. His delivery was **loud** and gripping. It was his intense relationship with God and passion for souls that came through to his hearers. It is abundantly evident that the mighty power of God fell upon him, and his listeners were convicted, converted and helped. According to Benjamin Franklin, Whitefield's sermons could be heard clearly from a mile away! (See Arnold Dallimore, *George Whitefield, The Life and Times of the Great Evangelist*, Vol. 1, P. 439.)

After a short but important ministry of two months in the town of Dummer, England, Whitefield took responsibility of an orphan house, which had been established near Savannah, Georgia by John and Charles Wesley. He sailed for America in the latter part of 1737 and continued there about a year. The needs of this orphan house, often occupied him. Some question to this day the wisdom of Whitefield's involvement in it, but it is the opinion of the author that God used that ministry and Whitefield's loyal obligation (partly his loyalty to the Wesleys) to keep him in America for large portions of time.

> **From Whitefield's Influence**
> **Robert Robinson, *Ecclesiastical Researches* and *the History of Baptism***
> Robert Robinson was converted under the ministry of George Whitefield in London, England in December of 1755. He began to preach among the Methodists. He concluded that infant baptism was of none effect and was immersed at Ellingham sometime around 1758. He became the pastor of the Baptist church at Cambridge in 1761. William Cathcart wrote, "His success in Cambridge was marvelous. The meeting-house, which had been first a barn, afterwards a stable…became too strait for the audiences which assembled there. In 1774 he had a congregation of 600 or 700 persons. His popularity occasioned numerous preaching engagements, yet by his methodical habits and incredible industry he found time for extensive reading, and few years passed without some publications from his pen. He was occupied for several years with a history of the Baptists, undertaken at the suggestion of the Rev. Dr. Gifford and other prominent members of the denomination" (William Cathcart, *Baptist Encyclopedia,* Vol. 2, P. 998).
> Robinson's *Ecclesiastical Researches* and *the History of Baptism* were published after his death, which occurred suddenly in June of 1790. He was 55 years of age.
> Sadly, we must say that Robert Robinson conformed to the tide of Unitarianism, imported from apostates from New England. His brilliant mind was corrupted by evil influences. Nevertheless, his historical works, written when in his right mind, contain some of the most compelling evidences of the Baptist witness throughout the ages.

Whitefield returned from Georgia to England in 1738. His voyage across the Atlantic took **nearly a year** due to what we believe was a direct attempt on his life by satanic forces. When he arrived in England he found himself in a storm of controversy. The majority of the clergy of the Church of England were now in opposition to his ways, means and doctrine. The greatest criticism was his insistence on regeneration, or the new birth. The number of pulpits in which he had access rapidly diminished. Churches and ministers were filled with indignation at a man who declared fully the atonement of Christ and the work of the Holy Ghost. Mr. Whitefield began to preach in the open fields.

Mr. Whitefield established a list of convictions that he believed would establish his relationship with God and benefit his quest for holiness and sincerity. He would judge himself each day by asking: Have I,

1. Been fervent in private prayer?
2. Used stated hours of prayer?
3. Used short communicative prayers every hour?
4. After or before every deliberate conversation or action, considered how it might tend to God's glory?
5. After any pleasure, immediately given thanks?
6. Planned business for the day?
7. Been simple and recollected in everything?
8. Been zealous in undertaking and active in doing what good I could?
9. Been meek, cheerful, affable in everything I said or did?
10. Been proud, vain, unchaste, or enviable of others?
11. Recollected in eating and drinking? Thankful? Temperate in sleep?
12. Taken time for giving thanks according to Law's (William Law) rules?
13. Been diligent in studies?
14. Thought or spoken unkindly of anyone?
15. Confessed all sins?

According to Mr. Whitefield, the main problem in the established churches was the lack of regenerate or saved men in the pulpits. On his second tour of America in 1739, he preached throughout the colonies and extensively in New England and influenced the burgeoning revival to become an awakening—the Great Awakening. Jonathan Edwards came out publicly for Whitefield even when the vast majority of the *standing order* church ministers were against him.

On that second tour, Whitefield landed in Lewistown, Delaware with the express purpose of going to Philadelphia. In nine days the town was turned upside down and the wrath of the clergy came wildly upon him. He set out on horseback to New York where he met an anxious Gilbert Tennent, whose Presbyterians had split over the Awakening into "New Sides" and "Old Sides." The "New Sides" were in favor of the revival, and Mr. Tennent emerged as the leader of the "New Sides."

Mr. Whitefield immediately went to obtain permission from Mr. Vessey, the commissary of the Church of England in New York, but Vessey had already sent a scathing rebuke and refused Whitefield to grace the Anglican church of New York. So, Whitefield took to the fields. Here is a partial account of that first field meeting, related by a critic of the meeting:

> When Mr. Whitefield came to the place before designed, which was a little eminence of the side of a hill, he stood still and beckoned with his hand, and dispos'd the multitude upon the descent, before and on either side of him. He then prayed most excellently. The assembly soon appeared to be divided into two companies. The one were collected round the minister, and were very serious and attentive. The other had placed themselves in the skirts of the assembly, and spent most of their time in giggling, scoffing, talking and laughing. Towards the last prayer the whole assembly appeared more united, and all became hush'd and still; a solemn awe and reverence appeared in the faces of most, and a mighty energy attended the Word. I heard and felt something astonishing, but I confess, I was not at the time, fully rid of my scruples (Arnold Dallimore, *George Whitefield, The Life and Times of the Great Evangelist*, Vol. 1, P. 435).

Chapter 15—The Churches of the Eighteenth Century Part II

After his arrival in New York, he was invited to the Wall Street Presbyterian Church. He then returned to Philadelphia where he caught the attention of Benjamin Franklin. Franklin remarked on the marvelous change in the people of Philadelphia after Whitefield had preached:

> It was wonderful to see the change soon made in the manners of our inhabitants, From being thoughtless or indifferent about religion, it seems as if all the world were growing religious, so that **one could not walk thro' the town in an evening without hearing psalms sung in different families of every street** (Arnold Dallimore, *George Whitefield, The Life and Times of the Great Evangelist*, Vol. 1, P. 439).

In late November 1739, Mr. Whitefield preached his last sermon of that tour in Philadelphia to a crowd of 10,000 solemn hearers. They knew he was to leave their city and wept for their great sorrow in parting with him. Whitefield set out to see the rest of America on horseback in the direction of Georgia and the orphanage. Over two hundred horsemen followed him along the road south. During the first one hundred miles he stopped often to preach. His journal recorded the results:

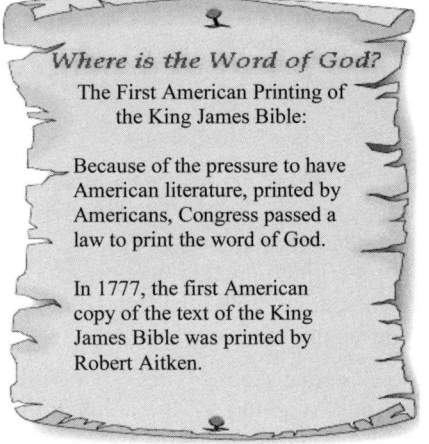

Where is the Word of God?
The First American Printing of the King James Bible:

Because of the pressure to have American literature, printed by Americans, Congress passed a law to print the word of God.

In 1777, the first American copy of the text of the King James Bible was printed by Robert Aitken.

Chester, Thursday, Nov. 29. I preached to about five thousand people from a balcony. It being court-day, the Justices sent word that they would defer their meeting till mine was over.

Wilmington, Friday, Nov. 30. Preached at noon and again at three in the afternoon. Received several fresh invitations to preach at various places, but was obliged to refuse them all. Oh, that I had a hundred tongues and lives, they should all be employed for my dear Lord Jesus.

Newcastle, Saturday, Dec. 1. Preached to about two thousand from a balcony, but did not speak with so much freedom and power as usual, God being pleased to humble my soul by inward visitations and bodily indisposition. Lay on the bed after sermon, which much refreshed me.

Whiteclay Creek, Sunday, Dec 2. The weather was rainy, but upwards of ten thousand people were assembled. It surprised me to see such a number of horses. There were several hundreds of them. I preached from a tent erected for me by Mr. William Tennent…I continued my discourse for an hour and a half, after which we went into a log-house near by, took a morsel of bread and warmed ourselves. I preached a second time from the same place. My body was weak (Arnold Dallimore, *George Whitefield, The Life and Times of the Great Evangelist*, Vol. 1, P. 441).

Of the Whiteclay Creek meeting, Benjamin Franklin reported over 3,000 horsemen alone as part of the throng gathered to hear him.

Whitefield preached to huge crowds, crossed the Atlantic on six different occasions, and saw thousands saved. The large number of converts began to search the scriptures for the will of God. Many of his converts saw *believer's baptism* as being the scriptural way.

Many of his converts became Baptist. So many in fact, that he said, "All my chickens have turned to ducks!"

Mr. Whitefield died of complications from asthma on September 30, 1770. He is buried under the pulpit of the Old South Church in Newburyport, Massachusetts.

We stated that the change in the Presbyterian Church was a split with those on the side of the revival known as "New Sides." Those opposed to the revival were known as the "Old Sides." Now a new group arose from the New Light Congregationalists: *the Separates*.

STOP AND THINK

1. Write *2 Chronicles 7:14* twice.

2. What was the name of the group of young preachers at Oxford that John and Charles Wesley started? *Holy Club*

3. What was the difference between the "Old Lights" and the "New Lights?" *New lights believed in the necessity of salvation*

4. The Congregationalists divided into the "Old Lights "and the "New Lights." Into what two groups did the Presbyterians divide? *old sides and new sides*

5. Name two ways in which Whitefield would "judge himself."

6. What famous American patriot documented the strength of Whitefield's voice? *Benjamin Franklin*

7. What English Baptist historian who studied the history of Baptism, was converted under the ministry of Whitefield? *Robert Robinson*

8. What new group arose from the "New Light" Congregationalists? *Seperates*

****

15.2.1

SECTION TWO

Isaac Backus and the Rise of the Separates in America

The preaching of Whitefield left thousands of converts hungry to receive the word of God. The result of the preaching was the beginning of *separate* Congregational and Presbyterian churches, all seeking truth from the scriptures. Most Congregationalists were simply not satisfied with the *standing order* churches and broke away to become "Separates." To give you an idea of how many Congregational churches became *Separate*, here is a list of a fraction of them as recorded by Isaac Backus:

Congregationalists become *Separate* Congregational:

> John Hovey, Mansfield, October 1745; Solomon Paine was ordained at Canterbury, September 10, 1745; Thomas Stevens at Plainfield, September 11, 1745; Thomas Dennison at Norwich Farms, October 29, 1745; Jedidiah Hide at Norwich Town, October 30, 1745; Matthew Smith at Stonington, December 10, 1745; John Fuller at Lyme, December 25, 1745; Joseph Snow at Providence, February 12, 1747;

Chapter 15—The Churches of the Eighteenth Century Part II

Samuel Wadsworth at Killingly, June 3, 1747; Paul Park at Preston, July 15, 1747; Elihu Marsh, at Windham, October 7, 1747; Ebenezer Frothingham at Weathersfield, October 28, 1747; Nathanael Shepard in Attleborough, January 20, 1748; Isaac Backus at Bridgewater, April 13, 1748; John Paine at Rehoboth, August 3, 1748; William Carpenter at Norton, September 7, 1748; John Blunt at Sturbridge, September 28, 1748; Ebenezer Mack at Lyme, January 12, 1749; Joshua Nickerson at Harwich, February 23, 1749; Samuel Hide at Bridgewater, May 11, 1749; John Palmer at Windham, May 17, 1749; Samuel Hovey at Mendon, May 31, 1749; Samuel Drown at Coventry, October 11, 1749; Stephen Babcock at Westerly, April 4, 1750; Joseph Hastings at Suffield, April 17, 1750; Nathanael Ewer at Barnstable, May 10, 1750; Joshua Morse at New-London, May 17, 1750; Jonathan Hide at Brookline, January 17, 1751; Ezekiel Cole at Sutton, January 31, 1751; Ebenezer Wadsworth at Grafton, March 20, 1751; Shubael Stearns at Tolland, March 20, 1751; Nathanael Draper at Cambridge, April 24, 1751; Peter Werden at Warwick, May 17, 1751.

Immediately the Separate bodies began to suffer. They were looked upon with the same contempt as the Baptists. Just one instance of the contempt in Connecticut concerned Congregational minister Philemon Robbins. Robbins was pressured to say that he broke the law of God because he went to a Baptist meeting house to preach the Gospel. In 1747, he was deposed from preaching the gospel. Robbins wrote a narrative of his experiences (Isaac Backus, *Abridgement of the History of the Churches of New England*, P. 184).

The preachers studied infant baptism and whether baptism should be given before salvation. Since salvation was a definite "birth," and one would need to be a conscious, thinking person to receive salvation, then the command for baptism would be something impossible for an infant to obey.

Isaac Backus was one such Congregationalist preacher who thought along those lines. He realized that baptism by immersion for believers only was the correct baptism. **Isaac Backus was placed providentially by the hand of God**

> ### Isaac Backus (part 1) by William Cathcart
>
> **Isaac Backus** was born at Norwich, Conn., Jan. 9, 1724, of parents who were actively identified with the "pure" Congregationalism as opposed to the Saybrook platform, and his early religious training influenced greatly his future life. He was converted in 1741 during the Great New England Awakening, but did not join himself to the church until ten months later, and then with much hesitation, owing to the laxity of church discipline and its low state of religious feeling.
>
> From this church—the First Congregational of Norwich — he and others soon separated themselves, and began to hold meetings on the Sabbath for mutual edification. Feeling himself called by God to the work of his ministry, he shortly after began to exhort and preach, although there were at that time penal enactments against public preaching by any except settled pastors, unless with their consent and at their express desire. He was, however, unmolested, and addressed himself earnestly to the work of a pastor and evangelist, his first pastorate being that of a Separate church at Middleborough, to which he was ordained in 1748. In the following year he married Susannah Mason, of Rehoboth, with whom he lived fifty-one years, and of whom he wrote near the close of his life that he considered her the greatest earthly blessing God had given him."
>
> "The subject of baptism was agitating the church of which Mr. Backus took charge, and it was only after a long and bitter struggle with himself that two years later he was enabled to put aside all doubts and perplexities on the subject and come out unreservedly for baptism through a profession of faith. His stand on this subject and his baptism by Elder Pierce, of Rhode Island, soon led to his exclusion from the church, although he did not consider himself a Baptist, nor did he desire to connect himself with that denomination. He continued his labors as an evangelist until 1756, when, with six baptized believers, a Baptist church was formed in Middleborough, and Mr. Backus was ordained its pastor. In 1765 he was elected a trustee of Brown University, which position he held for thirty-four years (William Cathcart, *Baptist Encyclopedia*, Vol. 1, P. 52).

in New England for the religious and political struggle that would bring liberty to all Americans. Backus had to settle the tremendous baptism question.

Isaac Backus was saved after hearing Eliazer Wheelock, first president of Dartmouth College. Backus realized there was something wrong with his Congregational church at Norwich, Connecticut, because the pastor, Benjamin Lord was not in favor of the Great Awakening. In fact, Backus waited several months before presenting himself for church membership.

Meanwhile, all over the country, Separate Congregational churches were springing up. The *standing order* scrambled to enforce a 1742 law in Connecticut forbidding churches from "settling ministers" who were not Yale, Harvard, or foreign educated (Alvah Hovey, *Life and Times of Isaac Backus*, P. 59). This was done to try to counter the large number of unordained "exhorters" who were engaged in preaching the Gospel all over New England.

Isaac Backus was called of God to preach the Gospel in September of 1746. He gave a testimony of this call in his 1753 published sermon, *Discourse on the Nature and Necessity of an Internal Call to Preach the Everlasting Gospel*. If the call to preach is an *internal call*, Backus argued, then it must be in the life of a regenerate person. If it is an *internal call*, then a corrupted church form cannot produce it.

This was not to say that Isaac Backus rejected the local church, he wrote: "A converted person, has an internal right to all the privileges of the Christian church, yet has no external right to them, till he is openly received as a member; so a person who is called to preach has no right to act in duties peculiar to an officer of the church, till he is publicly set apart therein. Praying, exhorting, and preaching, though duties to be performed in the church, are not so confined to it, that they may not rightly be performed where there is no church at all. **But only those who have a visible standing in the church** can administer *special* ordinances or act in cases of discipline, for these are things peculiar to a visible church" (Alvah Hovey, *Life and Times of Isaac Backus*, P. 64).

Obviously, this was a source of consternation to Backus, for he could not agree with the forms of the Congregational church. Backus did not have a visible church to administer special ordinances in the beginning of his ministry, but he decided he could pray, exhort and preach. So Backus defied the 1742 law against lowly preachers. For five years he preached as an itinerant evangelist until the year 1748 when he gathered a "Separate" (independent Congregational) church in Middleborough, Massachusetts. Then the most nagging question needed an answer. It was about infant baptism. After a lengthy study, Isaac Backus came to this essential question in the debate about infant baptism:

*Where, and in what relation to the church of God do those stand who have been baptized and yet are **not** believers?* (Alvah Hovey, *Life and Times of Isaac Backus*, P. 87).

He came to the conclusion that baptism must be for believers only.

---

1. Write *2 Chronicles 7:14* twice.

Chapter 15—The Churches of the Eighteenth Century Part II

2. Name three Congregational preachers who became "Separate."

3. For what reason was Philemon Robbins rebuked?
   He went to a baptist church to preach

4. According to Cathcart, why did Backus hesitate to join his own church?
   laxity of church discipline, a low state in religious feeling

5. Where did Backus pastor his "Separate" church? *Middleborough MA*

6. What sermon did Backus publish that gave testimony of his call?
   Discourse on the nature and necessity of an internal call
   what was to preach the everlasting gospel

7. Quote ~~exactly~~ the essential question Backus came to ~~concerning infant baptism~~.
   Baptism

****

15.2.2

Backus records the suffering of the Baptists

Isaac Backus received the papers of John Comer and began to write the first true history of the Baptists of America. What he discovered astonished him and he was the first to record the sufferings of Roger Williams, John Clarke, Thomas Gould, (who founded the first Baptist church of Boston) and Obadiah Holmes.

It was from the pen of Isaac Backus that we have much of our early American Baptist heritage recorded. In addition, his journals, essays and diaries record the struggles he encountered with men such as John Adams, in securing liberty for the Baptists of Massachusetts, thereby securing liberty for all Americans.

> *Pivotal Points to Ponder*
>
> The Great Awakening led to a progression in religious thought in America, especially in New England.
> 1. There was a *standing order*
> 2. It became corrupt
> 3. God sent an awakening.
> 4. The churches were too corrupt to handle the fire and converts.
> 5. A *Separate* standing order was attempted.
> 6. The *Separates* developed a zeal for the Bible.
> 7. The Separates sought believer's baptism.

Many who now came out in a separation from the *standing order* churches, descended from the Plymouth fathers. Plymouth colony (the Pilgrims) was milder than the Puritans of Massachusetts for Plymouth believed the ministers of Christ were to be supported only by influence, and not by laws enforced by the sword. That principle, borrowed from **the anonymous Baptist from Newgate prison** and **Roger Williams**, was now bearing fruit.

Elisha Paine visited Canterbury, Massachusetts and was imprisoned in Windham for illegal preaching. In November of 1752 he wrote: "I cannot but marvel to see how soon the children will forget the sword that drove their fathers into this land, and take hold of it as a jewel, and kill their grand-children therewith. O that men could see how far this is from Christ's rule!" Paine spent only a gracious five days in prison, but he was not able to return to Long Island to finish the home he had attempted to build. It was a long winter for his family. Elisha Paine died in 1775, at age 84.

The people of the Separate (Congregational) church at Norwich were fined to support Benjamin Lord and his church and when they refused, forty persons, both men and women, were imprisoned in a single year. Isaac Backus was informed of a tax levied against him in support of the *standing order* minister of Middleborough. He refused to pay it. On February 6, 1749 an officer, who commenced to take him to jail, seized him. Upon that tragic scene a friend came who stopped the imprisonment and paid Mr. Backus' tax.

But this scene would repeat itself many times. The church of Canterbury, for 15 years had its people imprisoned, property stolen, and church harassed simply because they did not want to support a minister they did not choose. (See Isaac Backus, *Abridgement of the History of the Churches of New England*, P. 177.) "To these were added the imprisonment of Mr. Frothingham five months, Mr. John Paine eleven months, and Mr. Palmer four months all at Hartford, for preaching without the consent of parish ministers. And three gentlemen, only for being members and deacons in these separate churches, were, at different times, expelled out of their legislature, namely, Captain Obadiah Johnson, of Canterbury, Captain Thomas Stevens, of Plainfield, and Captain Nathan Jewet, of Lyme" (Isaac Backus, *Abridgement of the History of the Churches of New England*, P. 175-185). All this occurred in Connecticut.

> Isaac Backus received this letter from an imprisoned "Separate," jailed for refusing to pay the ministerial tax:
>
> I have heard something of the trials among you of late, and I was grieved till I had strength to give up the case to God, and leave my burthen there. And now I would tell you something of our trial. Samuel lay in prison twenty days. October 15, the collector came to our house, and took me away to prison about nine o'clock, in a dark rainy night. Brother Hill and Sabin were brought there next night. We lay in prison thirteen days, and then were set at liberty, by what means I know not. Whilst I was there, a great many people came to see me; and some said one thing and some another.
>
> O the innumerable snares and temptations that beset me, more than I ever thought of before! But, O the condescension of Heaven! Though I was bound when I was cast into this furnace, yet was I loosed, and found Jesus in the midst of the furnace with me. O, then I could give up my name, estate, family, life and breath, freely to God. Now the prison looked like a palace to me. I could bless God for all the laughs and scoffs made at me. O the love that flowed out to all mankind! Then I could forgive, as I would desire to be forgiven, and love my neighbour as myself. Deacon Griswold was put in prison the 8th of October, and yesterday old brother Grover. [They] are in pursuit of others; all which calls for humiliation. This church hath appointed the 13th of November to be spent in prayer and fasting on that account. Do remember my love to you and your wife, and the dear children of God with you, begging your prayers for us in such a day of trial. We are all in tolerable health, expecting to see you.
>
> These from your loving **mother, Elizabeth Backus.**

Massachusetts also continued her tyranny at this juncture. Peter Thacker, minister, passed away in 1744 having seen his church, the Congregational Church at Middleborough grow during the Great Awakening to over 340 communicants. The parish committee (which was the county legislature under the Saybrook platform), worked against the congregation in calling another pastor. (Oh, the intrigue when the church is

Chapter 15—The Churches of the Eighteenth Century Part II

mixed in with the state.) The parish committee called another man and sent him to the church. Middleborough church refused to hear him and withdrew to examine the man of their choice. But the parish in a general election rejected the wishes of the church. Then, the church called for a council of five other churches to settle the matter and they ordained the church's choice of pastor. But the parish committee went ahead and ordained the man of their choosing, occupied the meetinghouse and taxed the people for support of a preacher they did not choose. Yes, it was TAXATION WITHOUT REPRESENTATION.

On January 16, 1756, after years of study and struggle, Isaac Backus founded the Baptist church at Middleborough, Massachusetts. It was a congregation of "Separate" Baptists. **In his spiritual journey leading to the founding of the Baptist Church in Middleborough, Isaac Backus represented a microcosm of the America mind, with baptism being the single most important intellectual debate before the Revolution.** Backus was sharp, independent, pious, and spiritual. He wanted what was real in religion and government. He rejected the establishment or status quo and struck out on his own seeking the truth and finding kindred spirits. He rejoiced in new found truth, stood for it, and then suffered and paid a price for it. His courage ultimately led him to triumph in it. He is the quintessential citizen of *Baptist Nation*. —> perfect

The New Lights were left in a vacuum as their Baptist breakaway brethren rode off into the sunset and ended up saving the country. The number of Separate Congregationalists who became "Separate" Baptist was astounding. Many of the Separates passed through *the real crucible of New England* and became Baptist. Here is a partial list of the Separate Congregational preachers who became Baptist from 1745 to 1760:

Matthew Smith of Stonington, Elihu Marsh, of Windham, Isaac Backus of Bridgewater, William Carpenter of Norton, John Blunt of Sturbridge, Ebenezer Mack of Lyme, Samuel Hovey of Mendon, Samuel Drown of Coventry, Stephen Babcock of Westerly, Joseph Hastings of Suffield, Joshua Morse of New-London, **Shubal Stearns of Tolland**, Nathanael Draper of Cambridge, and Peter Werden of Warwick.

---

1. Write *2 Chronicles 7:14* twice.

2. What papers did Isaac Backus receive? The papers of John Comer
3. Give the last 4 steps in the progression of religious thought in America after the Great Awakening. 1. The Churches were too corrupt to handle the fire and converts
   2. A seperate standing order was attempted
   3. The seperates developed a zeal for the bible
   4. The seperates sought believers baptism.
4. From whom were many of the "Separates" descended? Plymouth fathers (Pilgrims)
5. When did Backus found his "Separate" church? 1748
6. When did Backus found his "Separate Baptist" church? 1756

7. Based on the letter recorded in this section, why would Isaac Backus become such a champion for religious liberty?

Because it was personal

Chapter Sixteen
The Churches of the Eighteenth Century Part III

Section One: Shubal Stearns and the Separate Baptist Revival in America.
Section Two: Baptists in the Revolution. John Gano. John Leland. The Forging of the American System of Government from Baptist principles.

SECTION ONE

Scripture to Memorize

Ephesians 6:20 *For which I am an ambassador in bonds: that therein I may speak boldly, as I ought to speak.*

Definitions:

Regular Baptists: Particular Baptists in America, holding to particular atonement.
General Baptists (America): Same as their mother churches in England, holding to the doctrine of general atonement.
Separate Baptists: Baptists who came out of the Great Awakening and led in the great revival of the South. Held a milder *Particular* view of the atonement. Many considered themselves neither *Particular* nor *General* in their view of the atonement, neither *Calvinist* nor *Arminian*.

The state of the Baptists in America in 1700:
1. Still required to register in some states, the Baptists were still outlawed in other states.
2. Small number of churches in open existence.
3. General Baptists were scattered (holding to a general atonement).
4. Particular Baptists were gathered in Pennsylvania and New Jersey (holding to a limited atonement-Particular). These Particular Baptists formed the first American Baptist Association in Philadelphia in 1707, uniting under the *Philadelphia Baptist Confession*. Baptists holding to this confession became known as **Regular Baptists**.

The Separate Congregationalists become Regular Baptists

As we have stated, many of the converts from the Great Awakening separated from the Congregational Church. Many of these Separates became Baptist. The Separate Congregationalists, who were New Lights; when coming to Baptist principles, became *Regular Baptists*. The term *Separate Baptist* came to be used **in the South** in the wake of the revival under **Shubal Stearns**. Most Baptists who came out of the Congregational church, such as Isaac Backus, remained in the North and simply became part of the "Regular" Baptists under the leadership of the Philadelphia Baptist Association.

The Charleston Association, the Second Baptist Association in America

Remember the plight of the Boston Baptist Church? One of the members at Boston, William Screven, led a group of persecuted Baptists to Kittery, Maine to begin a work for God. However, persecution was greater in Maine than Boston, and Screven and his

Chapter 16—The Churches of the Eighteenth Century Part III

church soon set sail for Charleston, South Carolina. They established the Charleston Baptist Church, the first Baptist church in the South.

That group of Baptists grew and birthed other churches as well, and in 1751 established the Charleston Association, the second such Baptist association in America. Charleston Association adopted the *Philadelphia Confession of Faith*, which of course meant it was a **Regular** Baptist association.

The Regular Baptists in Early Virginia

We must date the origin of the Regular Baptists in Virginia about the year 1750, but it was not until ten years after, that they began to flourish and prevail to any considerable extent. In 1762, **David Thomas**, who had often visited the State in his evangelical excursions, removed to the county of Fauquier, and became the pastor of the Broadrun church, which was gathered soon after he removed to the place.

Outrageous mobs and individuals frequently assaulted and disturbed him. Once he was pulled down as he was preaching, and dragged out of doors in a barbarous manner. At another time a malevolent fellow attempted to shoot him, but a by-stander wrenched the gun from him, and thereby prevented the execution of his wicked purpose. "The slanders and reviling," says Mr. Edwards, "which he met with, are innumerable; and if we may judge of a man's prevalency against the devil, by the rage of the devil's children, Thomas prevailed like a prince." But the gospel flourished and prevailed; and Broadrun church, of which he was pastor, in the course of six or eight years from its establishment, branched out, and became the mother of five or six others (David Benedict, *History of the Baptists*, Vol. 2, Pp. 26, 30-1).

Shubal Stearns and the Separate Baptists—America's *Greatest* Revival

The "Separate Baptists" who migrated to the South, did not become Regular Baptists. In fact, they became a part of one of the most unusual awakenings in the history of the New Testament churches.

One Congregational preacher converted under Whitefield came to understand Baptist convictions and was baptized by Wait Palmer in Tolland, Connecticut. His name was **Shubal Stearns**. Stearns is not well known in American history, but he should be. Shubal Stearns migrated to the South and began the greatest revival in the history of the United States. Today, we think of the South as "the Bible Belt" when in reality, it should be known as "the Separate Baptist Belt." While the Separate Baptists of the North were organizing as Regular Baptists, the Separate Baptists in the South, so different and so influential, kept their own identity and were for many years called *the Separate Baptists*. Their beliefs were identical to the Regular Baptists, but were more "general" in their belief about the atonement. However they were not General Baptists, either. William Cathcart on Stearns:

> Historians believe that the preaching of Stearns and the Separate Baptists closely resembled George Whitefield's. The "Southern style" as it is sometimes falsely called, was actually the result of copying the earnest, urgent preaching of Stearns and those that followed him.

Shubal Stearns, was born in Boston, Mass., Jan. 28, 1706. He was the son of Shubael Stearns and Rebecca Larriford. About 1745, Mr. Stearns joined **the New Lights**, as the converted Congregational communities that originated from the ministry of George Whitefield in New England were designated. Called of God to proclaim the unsearchable riches of Christ, he speedily became a minister among the pious New Lights, and exercised his gifts among them until 1751. At this time, like many of his brethren, **he was constrained by reading the scriptures to accept believer's immersion as the baptism of the New Testament**; and after this conviction, as the Saviour alone was his master, he came out boldly as a Baptist. He was immersed on a profession of his faith, in Tolland, Conn., by Rev. Wait Palmer, in 1751, and on May 20th of that year he was ordained to the Baptist ministry by Mr. Palmer and Rev. Joshua Morse.

Mr. Stearns received an impression, as he thought from God, that there was a great work for him to do outside of New England, and he obeyed what was undoubtedly a divine call, and started in 1754 for his expected field of labor. He stopped for a time at Opeckon Creek, Va, but anticipating greater success in his ministry than he enjoyed in that place, he removed, with his relatives, to Sandy Creek, N.C. There, he constituted a Baptist church of sixteen persons. Daniel Marshall and Joseph Breed were appointed to assist the pastor in his ministerial duties.

In the region around Sandy Creek the people knew nothing of the Christian religion except what they had learned from Episcopal clergymen, who in that section, at that time, were unconverted men, and their irreligious darkness was dense. The instructions of Mr. Stearns and the godly lives of the church members were an astonishing revelation to their neighbors. A mighty outpouring of the Holy Spirit fell upon the truth proclaimed by the pastor and the preachers of the Sandy Creek church, and as a result, throngs of converts surrounded the gospel banner, and **mission communities were organized far and near**. The parent body in a few years had **606 members, and in seventeen years from its origin it had branches southward as far as Georgia, eastward to the sea and the Chesapeake Bay, and northward to the waters of the Potomac. It had become the mother, grand-mother and great-grandmother of forty-two churches, from which 125 ministers were sent out**.

[Shubal Stearns] of Sandy Creek church was of small stature, had a very expressive and penetrating eye, and a voice singularly harmonious; his enemies, it is said, were sometimes captivated by his musical **voice**. Many things are related of the enchanting sound of his **voice**, and the glance of his eyes, which had a meaning in every movement.

[Tidance Lane said], "He managed his voice in such a way as to make soft impressions upon the heart and bring tears from the eyes, and anon to shake the very nerves and throw the physical system into tumults and perturbations. **All the separate Baptists copied after him in tones of voice** and actions of body. When the fame of the preaching of Mr. Stearns reached the Yadkin, where I lived," says Mr. Tidance Lane, "I had a curiosity to go and hear him. Upon my arrival I saw a venerable old man sitting under a peach-tree with a book in his hand and the people gathering around him. He fixed his eyes upon me immediately, which made me feel in such a manner as I never had felt before. I turned to quit the place, but could not proceed far; I walked about, sometimes catching his eyes as I walked. My uneasiness increased and became intolerable. I went up to him thinking that a salutation and shaking hands would relieve me, but it happened otherwise. I began to think that he had an evil eye, and ought to be shunned, but shunning him I could no more effect than a bird can shun the rattlesnake when it fixes its eyes upon it. When he began to preach my perturbations increased, so that nature could no longer support them, and I sank to the ground." Mr. Lane afterwards became a very useful Baptist minister.

And in after-years the power that God gave Shubal Stearns and his Sandy Creek church in its early years swept over Virginia, North Carolina, Georgia and South Carolina with resistless force, and brought immense throngs to Christ, and established multitudes of Baptist churches. There are today probably **thousands of churches** that arose from the efforts of Shubal Stearns and the church of Sandy Creek (William Cathcart, *Baptist Encyclopedia*, Vol. 2, P. 1098-9).

Chapter 16—The Churches of the Eighteenth Century Part III

1. Write Ephesians 6:20 twice.

2. What was the "Separate Baptist" view of the atonement?
   mild particular atonement
3. True or False: Baptists enjoyed great freedom by 1700. False
4. Baptists holding to the Philadelphia Baptist Confession of Faith became known as what?
   regular
5. Who started the Baptist church at Charleston, South Carolina? William Scheven
6. What was the second Baptist association formed in America, and when was it founded?
   Charleston association
7. What man did God use to begin the greatest revival in the history of the United States? Shubal Stearns
8. Describe the growth of Sandy Creek church in the period of its first few years.
   they went from small to big in a couple of years
9. Describe the preaching of Shubal Stearns.
   enchanting, loud, musical

****
16.1.2

Sandy Creek Association—The Third Baptist Association in America

William Cathcart concerning Sandy Creek Baptist Association:

> Mr. Stearns traveled extensively in his own region, preaching Jesus, organizing churches, and giving counsel to the new communities which were formed. And his labors in every department were blessed. Through him, **in 1758**, three years after the Sandy Creek church was formed, **the Sandy Creek Association** was organized. For twelve years, all the separate Baptist churches in Virginia and the Carolinas were members of this body. All who were able, traveled from its remote extremities to attend its annual meetings, which were conducted with great harmony, and afforded such edification as induced them to undertake with cheerfulness long and laborious journeys. By means of these meetings the gospel was carried into many new places where the fame of the Baptists had previously spread. As great multitudes attended from different places, chiefly through curiosity, many of them were charmed with the piety and zeal of this extraordinary people, and petitioned the association to send preachers into their neighborhoods. In these associational meetings Shubal Stearns exerted an enormous influence. Other men among the separate Baptists were conspicuous for their ability and usefulness, but in the entire body in the several states Mr. Stearns wielded a founder's

> Elder James Read, in speaking of the first meeting of the Sandy Creek Baptist Association said, "The great power of God was among us, the preaching everyday seemed to be attended with God's blessing. We carried on our association with sweet decorum and fellowship to the end. Then we took leave of one another with many solemn charges from our reverend old father, Shubal Stearns, to stand fast until the end."

authority. This association conducted its annual meetings without a moderator for several years after it was formed, which shows the extraordinary modesty of Mr. Stearns; its harmony, when we remember that its members and ministers were nearly all new converts without experience, proclaims the great power possessed by Mr. Stearns in its deliberations (William Cathcart, *Baptist Encyclopedia*, Vol. 2, P. 1099).

The man who recorded the history of the Separate Baptist revival was **Robert Baylor Semple**, a preacher trained in law who was saved in a Separate Baptist church in Virginia. His book, *The Rise and Progress of the Baptists of Virginia*, though primarily about the Virginia Baptists, gives the best history of the Separate Baptists and their beginnings. Semple gives us some detail on the salvation of the early converts and preachers who were called from the revival. Because of the corrupt condition of the Episcopalian Church in North Carolina and Virginia at the time of Stearns' ministry, Robert Semple wrote: "The hearts of the people being touched by a heavenly flame could no longer relish the dry parish service conducted for the most part as they thought, by a set of graceless mercenaries" (Robert Semple, *The Rise and Progress of the Baptists of Virginia*, P. 1).

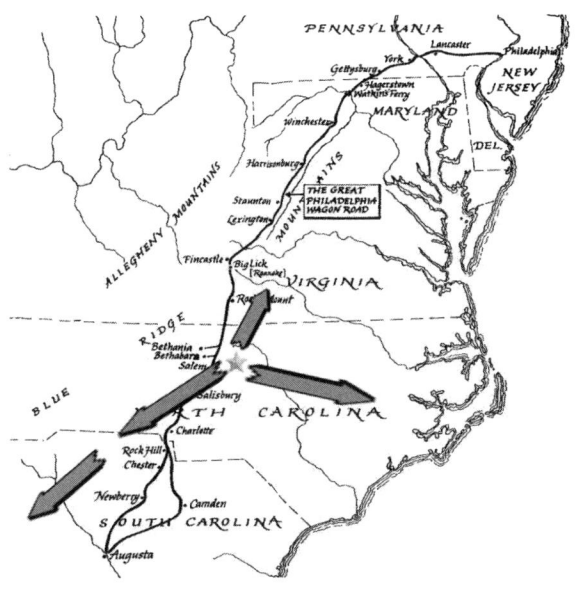

Shubal Stearns had 17 men who answered to the call to preach in the first three years of his ministry at Sandy Creek. Here are their names and their initial field of labour:

To **North Carolina**: William Murphy, Joseph Murphy, Ezekiel Hunter, Charles Markland, James McDaniel and Elnathan Davis. To **South Carolina**: Philip Mulkey Joseph Rees and Joseph Murphy. To **Virginia**: William Murphy, Samuel Harris, Dutton Lane, John Waller, Jeremy Walker, James Reed, John Newton and Elijah Craig.

It was from this group of men that 42 churches were formed and 125 men surrendered to the gospel ministry by the year 1770.

Robert Semple describes the work of Stearns and his preachers and also introduces the ministry of the remarkable **Daniel Marshall**. Marshall birthed churches in North Carolina, South Carolina and especially Georgia where he is considered the father of the Baptists in that state. All of this was accomplished *after* he was 50 years of age.

Semple wrote this concerning Marshall and the advance of the Gospel into Virginia:

> Into the parts of Virginia, adjacent to the residence of this religious colony, the gospel had been quickly carried by Mr. Marshall. He had baptized several in some of his first visits. Among them was **Dutton Lane**, who shortly after his baptism, began to preach, a revival succeeded, and Mr. Marshall at one time baptized 42 persons. In August 1760, a church was

Chapter 16—The Churches of the Eighteenth Century Part III

constituted under the pastoral care of the Rev. Dutton Lane. This was the first Separate Baptist Church in Virginia, and, in some sense, the mother of all the rest (Robert Semple, *The Rise and Progress of the Baptists of Virginia*, P. 3).

David Benedict, in speaking of Daniel Marshall, said:

> **Daniel Marshall**, though not possessed of great talents, was indefatigable in his labours. He sallied out into the adjacent neighbourhoods, and planted the Redeemer's standard in many of the strong holds of Satan. At Abbot's-creek, about thirty miles from Sandy-creek, the gospel prospered so largely, that they petitioned the mother church for a constitution, and for the ordination of Mr. Marshall as their pastor. The church was constituted; Mr. Marshall accepted the call, and went to live among them.

From North Carolina, Daniel Marshall served in South Carolina. When in his *60's* he went to Georgia where his greatest work was accomplished.

From Daniel Marshall's influence in Virginia, **Dutton Lane most influenced Virginia by being the instrument God used to bring Col. Samuel Harris to Christ.** Harris was a man of great respect and influence in Old Virginia. He attended a meeting led by Dutton Lane where Joseph and William Murphy were preaching. He hid behind a pole in the building but the power of God was so strong that he cried out at the conclusion of the meeting and was saved. He was baptized by Daniel Marshall in 1758 and began the ministry of an evangelist throughout Virginia, preaching to enormous crowds and baptizing hundreds into the Separate Baptist churches. Harriss was the best-known man in Virginia, and some said it was doubtful if Patrick Henry himself could control a vast assemblage with a power superior to that of Samuel Harriss. His ministry was attended by conversions in very large numbers; churches sprang up on the line of his missionary travels. He was correctly considered the *Apostle of Virginia*.

> **Regular Baptist prejudice against the Separate Baptists**
>
> [Daniel Marshall's] ordination, however, was a matter of some difficulty. It required, upon their principles, a plurality of elders to constitute a presbytery. Mr. Stearns was the only ordained minister among them. In this dilemma, they were informed, that there were some Regular Baptist preachers living on Pedee river, (S.C.) To one of these, Mr. Stearns applied, and requested him to assist him in **the ordination of Mr. Marshall. This request he sternly refused**, declaring that he held **no fellowship with Stearn's party**; that he believed them to be a disorderly sect; suffering women to pray in public, and permitting every ignorant man to preach that chose; and that **they encouraged noise** and confusion in their meetings (David Benedict, *History of the Baptists*, Vol 2., P. 39).
>
> There was ill will from the Regular Baptists toward the Separate Baptists. The division between them would last for about 20 years.

The Power of God upon the Separate Baptists

Great illustrations of the power of God in salvation came from the meetings of the "Separate Baptists." Here is one of those illustrations:

> Elnathan Davis had heard that one John Steward was to be baptized by Mr. Stearns on a particular day, and, as Steward was a large man, and Stearns of small stature, he concluded that there would be some diversion, if not drowning. Therefore he gathered about eight or ten of his companions in wickedness, and went to the spot. When Mr. Stearns began to preach, Elnathan drew near to hear him, while his companions kept at a distance. He was no sooner among the crowd than he perceived that some of the people began to tremble as if in a fit of the ague. He felt and examined, to see if it was not pretense. Meanwhile one man leaned on his shoulder, weeping bitterly. Elnathan, perceiving that he had wet his new white coat,

pushed him off, and ran to his companions, who were sitting on a log away from the congregation, to one of whom he said, "There is a trembling and crying spirit among them, but whether it be the spirit of God or the devil, I don't know. If it be the devil, the devil go with them, for I will never more venture myself among them!" He stood awhile in that resolution, but the enchantment of Mr. Stearns voice drew him to the crowd once more. He had not been long there before the trembling seized him also. He attempted to withdraw, but his strength failing, and his understanding being confounded, he, with many others, sank to the ground. When he came to himself he found nothing in him but dread and anxiety, bordering on horror. He continued in this situation some days, and then found relief by faith in Christ. Mr. Davis afterwards became a successful minister of Jesus (William Cathcart, *Baptist Encyclopedia*, Vol. 2, P. 1100).

> **America's First Camp Meeting**
>
> The participants turned the associational meeting into an encampment. Thus in 1758, the era of the "camp-meeting" in America began at Sandy Creek, under Shubal Stearns.
>
> In most Baptist institutions of higher learning, credit for the origin of the camp meeting is given to the Presbyterians or the Methodists, who supposedly were the driving force of the great revival of Kentucky 1799-1805. Supposedly, the camp meeting was a by-product of the ministry of the Presbyterian James McGready. The large meetings held at Red River and Cane Ridge, Kentucky are cited as the first camp-meetings.
>
> But even Presbyterian and Methodist historians such as Charles Johnson recognize the fact that the camp meeting had its beginning 50 years earlier in the foothills of the Appalachians in central west North Carolina at Sandy Creek

In 1758 seven congregations organized themselves into the Sandy Creek Baptist Association: Sandy Creek, Abbot's Creek, Grassy Creek, Deep River, Little River, New River and Southwest. This new association eventually included churches in Virginia and South Carolina.

STOP AND THINK

1. Write Ephesians 6:20 twice.

2. When was Sandy Creek Baptist Association organized and what were the first six churches in the association?
1758, Abbot's Creek, Grassy Creek, Deep River, Little River, New River and Southwest

3. What Virginia law student wrote much about the Separate Baptist Revival? Robert Baylor Semple

4. In what three states did Daniel Marshall birth churches and in which state was he the most influential?
North Carolina, South Carolina, Georgia

5. Dutton Lane was saved as a result of Daniel Marshall's ministry. What prominent Virginia military man was saved in the Murphy's revival led by Dutton Lane?
Col. Samuel Harris

Chapter 16—The Churches of the Eighteenth Century Part III

6. How did the "Regular Baptists" feel about the "Separate Baptists" in the beginning years? *They were unruly and noisy*

7. What attracted Elnathan Davis to go and see Shubal Stearns? *The baptism of John Steward*

****

16.1.3

The Separate Baptists In The South Expand From The Ministry Of Sandy Creek

The churches listed below are first generation starts from Sandy Creek:

These churches were started in **NORTH CAROLINA**
1- Sandy Creek: 1755, Shubal Stearns
2- Abbot's Creek: 1756, Daniel Marshall
3- Grassy Creek : 1756, James Reed
4- Deep River: 1757 Joseph Murphy, Phillip Mulkey
5- New River: 1758, Ezekiel Hunter
6- Little River: 1759, Joseph Murphy
8-Black River: 1760, John Newton
10- Trent: 1761, James McDaniel
11- Southwest: 1762, Charles Markland
12-Haw River: 1764, Elnathan Davis
Lockwood's Folly: 1772 Nathaniel Powell, James Turner, Ezekial Hunter
Shallow Fords: 1768, Joseph Murphy

> Little River grew to 500 members in 3 years.
> Little River had four branch churches in ten years:
> Little River 2, Rocky River, Jones Creek, Mountain Creek.

> Haw River from 1765 to 1772 grew to five branches in 7 years: Deep River 2, Rocky River 2, Tick Creek, Collins mount, Caraway Creek.

These churches were started in **SOUTH CAROLINA**
9-Fairforest: 1760, Philip Mulkey
Congaree: 1766, Joseph Rees
Stephens Creek: 1766, Daniel Marshall

These churches were started in **VIRGINIA**
7- Dan River: 1759, Dutton Lane
Upper Spottsylvania Church: 1767, Lewis Craig
Staughton River: 1768, William Murphy
Lower Spottsylvania: 1769, John Waller, Jeremiah Walker
Fall Creek: 1769, Samuel Harris
Goochland: 1771, William Webber

```
*the numbers in front of the names of the churches indicate the order in
which they were established.
```

The Breakup of the Sandy Creek Baptist Association

Morgan Edwards, a Baptist historian, reported that in 1771, fifteen-hundred families left the Sandy Creek area of North Carolina. **Fifteen-hundred families** left the area. Sandy Creek Association split into three associations and the Sandy Creek church went from over 600 in attendance to just a handful. What happened?

The Regulators and the Battle of Alamance in North Carolina

216

The Collegiate Baptist History Workbook

One of the first rebellions of the colonists against their established governments came in 1769 in North Carolina. It was the War of the Regulators. The Regulators were patriots who believed the British government of North Carolina was abusing its citizens through fees and duties. The **Battle of Alamance,** May 16, 1771, is considered by some to be **the first battle of the American Revolution.** The colonial *Regulators* fought bravely but lost. Their leader Benjamin Merrill (a member of the Baptist church at Jersey settlement) was captured, hung and *quartered.* What did that have to do with the Sandy Creek Baptist Church and Association?

Evidence shows that Baptist people were the majority of the population in the areas disputed by the Regulators. In fact, many Regulators were Baptist. According to the account given by Morgan Edwards, in 1769, the Sandy Creek Baptist Association had before it a resolution **opposed** to the Regulators. It was Shubal Stearns first and only controversy at the Association. The Association waited for three days praying and fasting. They decided to divide the association into three parts. Some believe that most of the preachers simply did not want to oppose their beloved leader and did not wish to embarrass him. Some believe the Regulators themselves put pressure on the Association to split. Looking back and seeing the final results, we note that the pain inflicted by the enemy of souls was turned on its head by the power of God. Like Joseph of old, an attempt to do harm turned out to do good and the verse *"all things work together for good"* (Romans 8:28) is *still* in the Bible. The division resulted in even greater works in the following twenty years.

Shubal Stearns died Nov. 20 1771, just six months after the defeat at the Battle of Alamance. His remains are buried by the Sandy Creek church. Sandy Creek became an association containing just the original three churches: Sandy Creek, Abbott's Creek and Deep River. The three new associations were now set up. The churches in **North Carolina** kept the name **Sandy Creek**, the churches in **South Carolina** took the name **Congaree**, and the churches in **Virginia** adopted the name **Rapid-ann.** (Rapid-ann soon changed its name to the **General Association of Separate Baptists**.) The families of the Sandy Creek Association moved on in disappointment over the defeat of the Regulators and the loss of their spiritual leader. However, as the spiritual children of Stearns **scattered over the mountains into Tennessee, Kentucky and Georgia**, they spread the Gospel and birthed churches at a rate much like their departed leader.

1. Write Ephesians 6:20 twice.

2. What was the apparent emphasis of the churches of the Sandy Creek Baptist Association? *Soulwinning & churchplanting*

3. How many families moved out of the Sandy Creek area after the War of the Regulators? *1,500*

4. Who was the leader of the Regulators and what happened to him? *Benjamin Merill was hung and quartered*

5. What was Shubal Stearns attitude toward the Regulators? *He was opposed*

217

Chapter 16—The Churches of the Eighteenth Century Part III

6. What were the two other associations started when Sandy Creek Association divided?

The trial of Lewis and Joseph Craig and Aaron Bledsoe.
"For preaching the Gospel of the Son of God in the colony of Virginia."

PATRICK HENRY, who, on hearing of this prosecution, had rode some fifty or sixty miles from his residence in Hanover county, to volunteer his services in their defense. He listened to the further reading of the indictment with marked attention, the first sentence of which that had caught his ear was, "For preaching the Gospel of the Son of God." When it was finished, and the prosecuting attorney had submitted a few remarks, Henry arose, reached out his hand and received the paper, and addressed the Court:

May it please your worships: There are periods in the history of man, when corruption and depravity have so long debased the human character, that man sinks under the weight of the oppressor's hand, and becomes his servile, his abject slave; he licks the hand that smites him; he bows in passive obedience to the mandates of the despot, and in this state of servility he receives his fetters of perpetual bondage. But, may it please your worships, such a day has passed away! From that period, when our fathers left the land of their nativity for settlement in these American wilds, for LIBERTY, for civil and religious liberty, for liberty of conscience, to worship their Creator according to their conceptions of Heaven's revealed will; from the moment they placed foot on the American continent, and in the deeply imbedded forests sought an asylum from persecution and tyranny, from that moment despotism was crushed; her fetters of darkness were broken, and Heaven decreed that man should be free-free to worship God according to the Bible. Were it not for this, in vain have been the efforts and sacrifices of the colonists; in vain were all their sufferings and bloodshed to subjugate this new world, if we, their offspring, must still be oppressed and persecuted.

But, may it please your worships, permit me to inquire once more, for what are these men about to tried? This paper says, "For preaching the Gospel of the Son of God." Great God! For preaching the Gospel of the Savior to Adam's fallen race. And in tones of thunder, he exclaimed: "WHAT LAW HAVE THEY VIOLATED?" while the third time, in a slow, dignified manner, he lifted his eyes to heaven, and waved the indictment around his head.

The face of the prosecuting attorney was pallid and ghastly, and he appeared unconscious that his whole frame was agitated with alarm; while the judge, in a tremulous voice, put an end to the scene, now becoming excessively painful, by the authoritative declaration, *"Sheriff, discharge those men."*
(See the author's book, *America in Crimson Red* for documentation of this disputed account.)

---

7. Why did the 1500 families leave the Sandy Creek area?

8. What good thing happened after the split of Sandy Creek Baptist Association?

****

16.2.1

SECTION TWO

Definitions:

Tory: colonists loyal to the British crown during the Revolutionary war
patriot: colonists loyal to the cause of independence for the American colonies

Imprisoned Preachers in Old Virginia

Virginia proved to be the battleground in which religious liberty would be first won and then spread to the rest of the colonies. We have already stated that several states had established religions much like the nations of Europe. In **Massachusetts** and **Connecticut** the state religion (*standing order*) was the Congregational Church. In **Georgia** and **Virginia** the established religion was the Episcopal (Anglican) Church of England.

Some political leaders in Virginia such as Thomas Jefferson, James Madison and especially Patrick Henry saw the **establishment** of religion as a threat to the liberty of all. These men had Baptist pastor friends whom they respected. They were concerned for the freedom of these men to preach the gospel freely and worship according to the dictates of their conscience. We do not know the true spiritual condition of Jefferson and Henry, but their admiration for the Baptists of Virginia was obvious.

After the break up of Sandy Creek Association, the Baptists of Virginia had a tremendous revival mostly influenced by Samuel Harriss. Other preachers having a hand in this great revival were Lewis Craig, John Waller, James Ireland, John Weatherford, and John Leland. We will examine Leland after a few pages, but first the other four.

Lewis Craig

Lewis Craig was a distinguished Baptist preacher of Virginia and Kentucky, was born in Orange Co., Va., about the year 1737. He was first awakened by the preaching of **Samuel Harriss**, about the year 1765. A great pressure of guilt induced him to follow the preacher from one meeting to another, and after the sermon he would rise in tears and assert that he was a justly condemned sinner, and unless he was born again he could not be saved. His ministry thus began before he had hope of conversion, and after conversion he continued preaching a considerable time before being baptized; many were led to Christ under his labors. Soon after his conversion and before his baptism (there being no ordained ministers near to baptize him) he was indicted for "preaching the gospel contrary to law." The celebrated John Waller was one of the jurors in the case. The pious and prudent deportment of Mr. Craig during the trial was blessed to the conviction and conversion of Mr. Waller. (John Waller—see below.)

The exact period of Mr. Craig's baptism is not known. He continued preaching with great zeal until the 4th of June, 1768, when being engaged in public worship, **he and John Waller and James Childs were seized by the sheriff and brought before three magistrates in the meeting-house** yard, who held them to bail in the sum of 1000 pounds to appear before court the next day. They were required by the court to give security not to preach in the county within twelve months. This they refused to do, and were committed to jail. As they passed through the streets of Fredericksburg, from the court house to the jail, they sang the hymn beginning, "*Broad is the road that leads to death.*"

During his confinement **Mr. Craig preached through the prison bars to large crowds**. He remained in jail a month and was then released. He immediately hastened to Williamsburg, and soon secured the liberation of his companions. Their imprisonment seemed only to inflame their zeal, and they went everywhere preaching the Word. Mr. Craig was ordained and became pastor of Upper Spotsylvania church in November 1770. But this did not prevent his preaching in the surrounding counties. **In 1771 he was again arrested and imprisoned for three months in Caroline County**. He continued preaching with great zeal and success until 1781, when he and a majority of his church moved to Kentucky (William Cathcart, *Baptist Encyclopedia*, Vol. 1, P. 285).

John Waller

Born December 23rd, 1741, in Spotsylvania, county, he acquired for himself the infamous appellation of *Swearing Jack* Waller, by which he was distinguished from others of the same name. He was one of the grand jury who presented Louis Craig for preaching. Mr. Craig addressed [the grand jury]: "I thank you, gentlemen of the grand jury, for the honour you have done me. While I was wicked and injurious, you took not notice of me; but since I have altered my course of life, and endeavored to reform my neighbors, you concern yourselves much about me. I forgive my persecuting enemies, and shall take joyfully the spoiling of my goods." When Mr. Waller heard him speak in that manner, and observed the meekness of his spirit, he was convinced that Craig was possessed of something that he had never seen in the man before. He thought within himself, that he should be happy if he could be of the same religion with Mr. Craig.

Chapter 16—The Churches of the Eighteenth Century Part III

[Later, Waller related upon attending a preaching meeting], "I had long felt the greatest abhorrence of myself, and began almost to despair of the mercy of God. On a sudden, a man exclaimed that he had found grace, and began to praise God. Leaving the meeting, I hastened to a neighboring wood, and dropped on my knees before God, to beg for mercy. In an instant I felt my heart melt, and a sweet application of the Redeemer's love to my poor soul."

By the time Messrs. Harris and Read came on their second tour into this region, Mr. Waller was there baptized by Mr. Read, some time in the year 1770. He conferred not with flesh and blood; but began to preach, that men ought everywhere to repent. That arch enemy of souls, succeeded in raising up a powerful opposition.

He was ordained June 20th, 1770. **He baptized William Webber**, who afterwards became a distinguished preacher among the Virginia Baptists, being the first he did baptize. October, 1770, he traveled down as far as Middlesex, where his ministry was attended with great success, and where he also met with violent opposition. Wherever he went, he was attended by a divine power, turning many to righteousness. His name sounded far and wide. The Baptists and their adherents looked upon him as set for the defense of their cause, and with much confidence rallied round him as their leader.

[After a controversy over Particular and General atonement] Mr. Waller proclaimed himself an independent Baptist preacher. The only thing in which he was deficient, was, that he could not be happy while separated from his brethren. He yearned after the people of God, from whom he had with-drawn. He was again fully reinstated in connexion with his brethren, in 1787; when a full union between Separates, Regulars, and Independents, was accomplished.

A very great revival commenced under Mr. Waller's ministry, in 1787. In this revival he was greatly engaged; and baptized from first to last many hundreds, and his church in a short time increased to about 1500 members. November 8th, 1793, moved his family to Abbeville district, in the State of South Carolina. This removal was said to [come] from a strong desire to live near a beloved daughter, who had married Rev. Abraham Marshall, of Georgia. He remained faithful in the cause, until his death, July 4th, 1802 (David Benedict, *A General History of the Baptist Denomination*, Vol. 1, P. 393-399).

James Ireland

Rev. James Ireland was born in Edinburgh, Scotland, in 1748. He was brought up in the Presbyterian Church of his fathers. His education and talents were respectable. He came to America after reaching manhood, with pleasing manners, and without Christ in his heart. He was something of a poet, and in revising one of his religious pieces he was deeply convicted of guilt, from which faith in a suffering Saviour delivered him. He became eminent as a preacher soon after his baptism [he was the first person baptized by **Samuel Harriss**]; his learning and the tenderness of his manner produced a powerful impression upon his hearers, and the Spirit's blessing upon the truth he proclaimed made him a great enemy of Satan's empire. He formed several Baptist churches during his ministry, which extended over forty years, and his influence in favor of truth was very great.

This led the Episcopal clergy of Virginia to stir up social and legal persecutions against him. **He was thrust into jail in Culpeper** for preaching without the authority of law; abuse was heaped upon him on his way to prison; within its walls **an attempt was made to blow him up with gunpowder**, and on its failure an effort was put forth to suffocate him by burning brimstone at the door and window of his jail. It was also planned to poison him. [One of his children died as a result of the poisoning.]

His persecutions permanently injured his health; two accidents completed the work began by State church tyranny, and Mr. Ireland entered his rest May 5, 1806 (William Cathcart, *Baptist Encyclopedia*, Vol. 1, P. 585).

John Weatherford

John Weatherford had been imprisoned in the Chesterfield County jail of the colony of Virginia for five months in the year 1773. Like his brethren, Weatherford preached through the grates of the prison. The opponents of Weatherford and his Baptist friends would stand by the window and slash his hands with knives causing the blood to run down the walls of the prison.

After being held in close prison for some time, Weatherford was allowed the privilege of the prison bounds. Sometime later an order for his release was secured. The jailer refused to free Weatherford until the jail fees (room and board) were paid, which amounted to a considerable sum because of the length of his imprisonment. Not long afterward, this fee was paid by someone whose name was concealed, and Weatherford was released. More than twenty years later, **Patrick Henry** moved to Charlotte County and became a neighbor to John Weatherford, who was pastoring a nearby Baptist church. It was not until this time in discussing their early experiences in the fight for liberty, that Pastor Weatherford learned for the first time that **Patrick Henry had paid his fine** and brought about his release. Of course Weatherford never lost his love and admiration for Patrick Henry.

During his last illness, he would often try to win the lost from his bedside. Each day towards the end of his life, he requested "Amazing Grace" to be sung. John Weatherford went to his eternal reward on January 23, 1833. He was more than ninety years of age (Lewis Peyton Little, *Imprisoned Preachers and Religious Liberty in Virginia*, P. 358).

Forty-four Baptist preachers were jailed in Virginia before the Revolutionary War. Their sufferings were on the minds of Henry, Jefferson and Madison.

Isaac Backus Fights for Liberty in Massachusetts

Isaac Backus

In Massachusetts, Isaac Backus was in a political fight with none other than John Adams himself. Mr. Adams had taken the liberty to put Baptists in a bad light after the meeting of the Continental Congress of 1774. Isaac Backus had petitioned the Massachusetts delegation at the Congress, asking for religious liberty. He had brilliantly debated the points of liberty with Adams at Independence Hall. Adams, upon returning to Massachusetts wrote published articles accusing the Baptists of division of the patriot cause. Backus answered in the Boston papers that Baptists were indeed patriots and simply wanted the liberty to practice Christianity according to "tender conscience."

William Cathcart on the twilight years of Isaac Backus:

Under the direction of the Association, which met that year at Warren, [the fourth Baptist Association in America] Mr. Backus drew up a letter to all the Baptist societies asking for a general meeting of their delegates for devising the best means for attaining their religious freedom. **In 1777 he read an address before the Warren Association** "To the People of New England" on the subject of religious freedom, and the same year **his first volume of the "History of New England"** was issued. In the following year he read before the Warren Association another paper on religious liberty, which was published at their unanimous request. In 1779, he published in the *Independent Chronicle* of Boston, a reply to the statement made at the drafting of the proposed new State constitution, that the Baptists had never been persecuted, and they had sent their agent to Philadelphia in 1774 with a false memorial of their grievances in order to prevent the union of the colonies. **This false assertion** was made in

Chapter 16—The Churches of the Eighteenth Century Part III

order to obtain votes necessary to carry an article in the Massachusetts Constitution which gave to civil rulers powers in religious matters. In 1780 the Baptist Convention published an appeal to the people **against this article**, which led to a newspaper controversy, in which the Baptists were defended by Mr. Backus. A protest was then issued by the Association, but the General Court nevertheless adopted the objectionable article, and the Warren Association through their agent again addressed the Baptists of the State. Under the new constitution the Baptists, "**if they gave in certificates to the ruling sect that they belonged to a Baptist society, and desired their money to go to the minister thereof, he (the minister) could sue the money out of the hands of those who took it.**" Mr. Backus met the Committee of Grievances in 1785 [of the Baptists] to consult with them in relation to their course of action under such ruling. **They concluded to accept the compromise despite the earnest objections of Mr. Backus**. Had they been willing to resist, even to the loss of their property, the giving in of certificates, and had they demanded the entire separation of church and state, the desired end would no doubt have been attained many years before it was. [Note: **It was not until 1833** that Massachusetts finally disestablished Congregationalism and made the state free.]

In 1789, Mr. Backus visited Virginia and North Carolina, at the request of the brethren, for the purpose of strengthening and building up their churches. He spent six months in this work, and was the means of accomplishing much good. The distance he traveled while there—some 3000 miles—and the number of sermons preached—126, show the marvelous energy of the man, and the immense amount of work he must have accomplished during his ministerial life.

Mr. Backus continued in the active duties of a pastor and evangelist until within a short time of his death, which occurred Nov. 20, 1806. In appearance he was tall and commanding, and in later years inclined towards portliness. He possessed an iron constitution, and was capable of great physical endurance.

The historical works of Mr. Backus are of great value on account of the deep research he made in the collection of his material, and his impartiality in presenting the facts. The Baptists owe much to him for the discovery and preservation of many interesting and important events concerning their history during colonial times (William Cathcart, *Baptist Encyclopedia*, Vol. 1, P. 53-4).

The Baptist Chaplains in Washington's Army and the Immersion of George Washington

When war broke out between the colonists and Britain the Baptists of America stood nearly unanimous. The most outstanding Baptist patriots were David Jones and John Gano.

David Jones was born in Newcastle Delaware in 1736 and became a part of the Welsh Tract Baptist Church in Delaware. He was one of the students of Isaac Eaton at Hopewell Academy in New Jersey. One of the early proponents of independence, Jones was appointed chaplain in Col. St. Clair's regiment and was at the battle of Ticonderoga. He served under Horatio Gates and Anthony Wayne. He had his horse shot from under him at the Battle of Brandywine, and continuing to shoot at the enemy, he flung his pistol at advancing troops when his ammunition would not fire. He miraculously escaped injury to serve at Valley Forge and to the end of the war at Yorktown. He was greatly trusted by Washington.

John Gano was chosen to be Washington's personal chaplain of the portion of the Continental Army under his direct command. At the close of the war, Washington asked

Gano to baptize him by immersion. (See the *Evidences of General Washington's Baptism* by L.C. Barnes in the archives of the American Baptist Historical Society, Rochester, N.Y.)

Although this event in history is doubted by some and even made fun of by modern historians, the evidence shows that it is a fact of history. General Washington was an Episcopalian. His pastor at Williamsburg, Virginia was a Loyalist (Tory) in sympathy with the British crown. It is no wonder that George Washington would sit outside the window of the Baptist church in New York City and listen to the preaching of Gano.

Cathcart, writing about John Gano:

Portrait of Gano Baptizing Washington. Commissioned by the Gano family. The portrait is hanging in the lobby at the John Gano Memorial Chapel in Liberty, Missouri.

Mr. Gano was deeply interested in the Revolutionary struggle, and when fighting began he entered the army as chaplain to Gen. Clinton's New York brigade, and performed services which rendered him dear to the officers and men with whom he was associated. Nor did he ever shun the scene of danger, though his duties were entirely peaceful. Headley, in his *Chaplains and Clergy of the Revolution*, says, "In the fierce conflict on Chatterton's Hill, Mr. Gano was continually under fire, and his cool and quiet courage in thus fearlessly exposing himself was afterwards commented on in the most glowing terms by the officers who stood near him." In speaking of his conduct on that occasion, he said, "My station in time of action I knew to be among the surgeons, but in this battle I somehow got in the front of the regiment, yet I durst not quit my place for fear of dampening the spirits of the soldiers, or of bringing on myself an imputation of cowardice." Headley states that when he "saw more than half the army flying from the sound of cannon, others abandoning their pieces without maintaining a conflict with the whole British army, filled with chivalrous and patriotic sympathy for the valiant men that refused to run, he could not resist the strong desire to share their perils, and he eagerly pushed forward to the front." Any wonder that Washington should say of chaplains like Mr. Gano, (and there were other Baptists of his spirit) that "Baptist chaplains were the most prominent and useful in the army?" (See William Cathcart, *Baptist Encyclopedia*, Vol. 1, P. 434.)

When the war was over, General Washington had John Gano give the final prayer of thanksgiving.

1. Write Ephesians 6:20 twice.

Chapter 16—The Churches of the Eighteenth Century Part III

2. What was a Tory?
   A British loyalist
3. Were the Baptists generally Loyalist (Tory) or Patriot? *Patriot*
4. Name at least two Baptist preachers imprisoned in Virginia before or during the Revolution.
   John Wetherford, Lewis Craig
5. Who was responsible for Lewis Craig's salvation? What was John Waller's nickname?
   Colonel Samuel Harris "Swearing Jack"
6. What terrible thing happened to John Weatherford while he was in prison?
   His arms were slashed while he was preaching from jail
7. What terrible thing happened to James Ireland's family?
   They were poisoned
8. Why do you think Washington wanted John Gano to be his personal chaplain during the war?
   For his patriotism and desire
9. What ordinance of God did Washington desire at the hand of John Gano?
   Immersion

****

16.2.2

Significance of the Baptists and How They Affected American History

After the division of Sandy Creek Association, the Baptists of Virginia and Georgia met the same persecution as the Baptists of Massachusetts. Yet even following this division, the churches continued to grow and multiply. In Virginia especially, a stunning revival took place. In 1771 the Virginian churches had 1,355 members. By 1773, they had increased their enrollment to 3,195 members.

They steadily increased and immediately after the Revolutionary War, another astounding revival took place in Virginia. Because of the great revival, they became **the largest religious body in the state**. One great leader among them was **John Leland**, who was a personal friend to Thomas Jefferson and James Madison. It is a known fact that Jefferson envisioned a republic styled after the order of a Baptist church and that he greatly admired the Baptists' zeal and courage.

Jefferson, the Baptists and a Brief History of Liberty

Door at Newgate Prison

Referring to the Declaration of Independence, Thomas Jefferson said he "turned neither to book nor pamphlet." He also wrote, that the principles of the document were not original to him, but were instead, "intended to be an expression of the American mind." Historians falsely give credit to the English philosopher, John Locke for helping Jefferson develop his "American mind." However, **forty-five years before Locke** put his ideas on paper, Roger Williams, basing his "American mind" on the writings of the anonymous Baptist from Newgate prison, wrote:

First, whereas they say, that **the Civill order may erect and establish what forme of civill Government may seeme in wisedome most meet**, I acknowledge the proposition to be most true, **both in itself**, and also considered with the end of it, that a civill Government is an Ordinance of God, to conserve the civill peace of people, so farre as concernes their Bodies and Goods, as formerly hath beene said.

> But from the Grant I infer, (as before hath been touched) that the Soveraigne, originall, and foundation of civill power lies in the people, (whom they must needs meane by the civill power distinct from the Government set up.) And if so, **that a People may erect and establish what forme of Government seemes to them most meete** for their civill condition: **It is evident** that such Governments as are by them erected and established, **have no more power, nor for no longer time, then the civill power or people consenting** and agreeing shall betrust them with. This is cleere not only in Reason, but in the experience of all common-weales, where the people are not deprived of their naturall freedome by the power of Tyrants (Roger Williams, The Complete Writings of Roger Williams, Vol. 3, The Bloudy Tenet of Persecution, P. 249-250).

Let an astute mind now compare the Baptist prisoner of Newgate/Williams with the **first principles of the American republic**, immortalized in the Declaration of Independence. Jefferson wrote:

> We hold these truths to be **self-evident**, that all men are created equal, that they are endowed by their Creator with certain unalienable Rights, that among these are Life, Liberty and the pursuit of Happiness.--That to secure these rights, Governments are instituted among Men, **deriving their just powers from the consent of the governed**, --That whenever any Form of Government becomes destructive of these ends, **it is the Right of the People to alter or to abolish it, and to institute new Government**, laying its foundation on such principles and organizing its powers **in such form, as to them shall seem most likely to effect their Safety and Happiness**—Thomas Jefferson, Declaration of Independence.

When comparing Jefferson with anonymous/Williams, it is clear that Jefferson had in his mind the principles of the Baptists when he wrote the **founding** document of the American nation.

Thomas Armitage wrote:

> There was a small Baptist Church which held its monthly meetings for business at a short distance from Mr. Jefferson's house, eight or ten years before the American Revolution. Mr. Jefferson attended these meetings for several months in succession. The pastor on one occasion asked him how he was pleased with their Church government. Mr. Jefferson replied, that it struck him with great force and had interested him much, that he considered it the only form of true democracy then existing in the world, and had concluded that it would be the best plan of government for the American colonies. This was **several years before the Declaration of Independence** (Thomas Armitage, History of the Baptists, Vol. 2, P. 734).

Madison and Leland

John Leland told Madison that the Virginians would not approve of the Constitution without a guarantee of religious liberty. William P. Grady wrote:

> Leland was nominated to be the Orange county delegate to the Virginia convention for ratification. [of the U.S. Constitution] Knowing that Reverend Leland's concerns were not so much with what the Constitution said but rather with what it specifically did not say, Madison embarked upon an historic private conference with the influential Baptist. When Madison assured the man of God that he would lobby for a favorable amendment as a forthcoming member of the Virginia House of Representatives, his would-be rival not only pledged his

Chapter 16—The Churches of the Eighteenth Century Part III

personal support but graciously stepped aside, allowing the more persuasive and articulate Madison to attend the convention in his place (William P. Grady, *What Hath God Wrought?*, P. 167).

Virginia ratified the Constitution July 28, 1788. Within a year Madison went to congress and helped draw up the Bill of Rights, fulfilling the promise made to Leland. Cathcart, on Leland:

> Leland was born in Grafton, Mass., May 14, 1754. Within a month after his conversion, in June, 1774, he made his first attempt at public speaking. Having connected himself with the church in Culpeper Co., Va., he was ordained by the choice of the church. He preached from place to place, everywhere proclaiming "the unsearchable riches of Christ." Wonderful revivals everywhere followed the labors of Mr. Leland in Virginia. Hundreds came under the power of converting grace, and professed their faith in Christ. The summary of his labours during the fifteen years of his ministry in Virginia is thus recorded, -- 3009 sermons preached, 700 persons baptized, and two large churches formed, one of 300 members, and another of 200.
>
> Having finished the work which he thought his Master had given him to do in Virginia, Mr. Leland returned to his native State, and made his home for the most of the remainder of his life in Cheshire, Mass. Here, and in the region about, the same power and the same success followed his ministry. He reports the whole number of persons whom he had baptized down to 1821 as 1352. "Some of them," he says, "have been men of wealth and rank, and ladies of quality, but the chief part have been in the middle and lower grades of life. Ten or twelve of them have engaged to preach." Missionary tours were made in almost every direction, and multitudes crowded to hear him."
>
> A sensational preacher he was not, nor a mere bundle of eccentricities. The discriminating and thoughtful listened to him with the most interest and attention. He was evidently "a born preacher." The life of a settled pastor would have been irksome to him. He wanted freedom from all restraint, and to do his own work at his own time and in his own way. His warmest sympathies went out to his Baptist brethren in their efforts to secure a complete divorce of the Church from the State. Everywhere he pleaded with all the energy of his soul for civil and religious liberty, and he had the satisfaction of seeing it at last come out of the conflict victorious over all foes. Among the class of ministers whom God raised up during the last century to do the special work which it was given the Baptist denomination to perform, John Leland occupies a conspicuous place. We doubt if his equal will ever be seen again. Mr. Leland Died Jan. 14, 1841" (William Cathcart, *Baptist Encyclopedia*, Vol. 2, P. 683).

---

1. Write Ephesians 6:20 twice

2. What happened to the Baptists of Virginia just before and after the Revolutionary War?

they grew / had great revival

3. According to Leland and the Baptists of Virginia, what was wrong with the Constitution of the United States?

It did not guarantee religious liberty (in the beginning)

The Collegiate Baptist History Workbook

4. True or False: The Virginia Baptists were so insignificant they just held on and prayed for deliverance. _false_

5. How did Leland help Madison?
He withdrew his bid for election

6. In three sentences explain how the Virginia revival and the Baptist people of that state brought about the formation of the Bill of Rights?

𝒫𝓋𝒾𝓉𝑜𝓁 𝒫𝑜𝒾𝓃𝓉𝓈 𝓉𝑜 𝒫𝑜𝓃𝒹𝑒𝓇

The real meaning of the
<u>**Separation of Church and State**</u>
—**A promise made to the Baptists**.

"The Separation of Church and State" is **not found** in the Declaration of Independence or the Constitution of the United States or in the Bill of Rights. **The phrase is found in a letter from Thomas Jefferson written to the Danbury Baptist Association of Virginia**. The reason for the letter is obvious if you know the Baptist history of America. Jefferson assured these *baptized believers* that no church denomination would become established as the national religion. America would **not** be as Europe and establish a national church, persecuting those that did not conform. Roger Williams first used the phrase, "<u>wall of seperation</u>."

Chapter Seventeen
The Churches of the Nineteenth Century

Section One: The Rise of English Baptist Missions and American Baptist Missions.
Section Two: The 100-Year War for Souls in America. Satan's Plan for America.

SECTION ONE

Scripture to Memorize

2 Peter 3:9 The Lord is not slack concerning his promise, as some men count slackness; but is longsuffering to us-ward, not willing that any should perish, but that all should come to repentance.

Definitions:

Hypercalvinism: extreme form of Reformed Calvinist doctrine, which discourages inviting sinners to receive Christ
Arminianism: on the other end of the spectrum from Hypercalvinism, Arminianism diminishes the sovereignty of God and denies the eternal security of the believer.

The Rise of English Baptist Missions and American Baptist Missions

In England, by the year 1800, there were nine Particular Baptist Associations, which included 361 churches and, according to David Benedict, about 36,000 members. No one was sure how many General Baptist churches there were. There were at least three General Baptist Associations and several hundred churches. Growth of Baptist churches in England was dramatically slower than in America, which we will see, and by the beginning of the nineteenth century, growth in England had ground nearly to a standstill. The events in England we are about to relate took place at the end of the eighteenth century. Their effect on the nineteenth century was profound.

The **cause** of slow growth in Baptist churches in England was **theological and practical.** While America owed much of its spiritual heritage to England and Wales, what remained in England and Wales was a shell. Under the extreme form of Calvinism sometimes called "Hypercalvinism," the appeals of aggressive preaching and soul winning were criticized and considered "Arminian." The most notable Particular Baptist writer of the period was London pastor John Gill, whose books are renowned to this day. However, with all due respect, Dr. Gill so extended his views on Particular redemption, that his church, from 1719-1771 dwindled to a handful as Dr. Gill refused to publicly invite sinners to Christ. Of Gill, Thomas Armitage wrote:

And yet, with all his ability, he was so high a supralapsarian, that it is hard to distinguish him from an antinomian. For example, he could not invite sinners to the Savior, while he declared their guilt and condemnation, their need of the new birth; and held that God would convert such as He had elected to be saved, and so man must not interfere with His purposes by inviting men to Christ. Under this preaching his church

Chapter 17—The Churches of the Nineteenth Century

steadily declined, and after half a century's work he left but a mere handful (Thomas Armitage, *History of the Baptists*, Vol. 2, P. 561).

It was Gill's theology that affected English Baptist practice. England needed its own Separate Baptist revival, but none came.

One man that Gill influenced was John Ryland. Ryland had pastored first in Northampton in 1781, and then the famous Broadmead Baptist Church in 1791. He was a leader in the Northamptonshire Baptist Association.

It was at the Northamptonshire Association meetings that **William Carey** and **Andrew Fuller** spoke out on the need to take the Gospel to the people of eastern Asia. At one juncture Mr. Ryland, marked with Hypercalvinism, told Carey, "Sit down young man, when the Lord gets ready to convert the heathen, he will do it without your help or mine!" Thankfully, Ryland later had a change of heart.

The short biographies of William Carey and Andrew Fuller are well worth our reading:

> **William Carey** was born in Purey, Northampton, England, August 17, 1761. In his boyhood he was an extreme Episcopalian, regarding dissenters with sovereign contempt. [However as a young man he was saved, and after a study in the Bible became a Baptist.] Mr. Carey was baptized by Dr. Ryland, Oct. 5, 1783.
>
> He was ordained pastor of the church of Moulton Aug. 1, 1787.
>
> Mr. Carey had probably the greatest facility for acquiring foreign languages ever possessed by any human being, no one ever possessed a larger measure of this extraordinary talent. **In seven years he learned Latin, Greek, Hebrew, French, and Dutch**, and in acquiring these languages he had scarcely had assistance.

William Carey

> In reading the voyages of the celebrated Captain Cook he first had his attention directed to the heathen world, and especially to its doomed condition. The topic soon filled his mind and engrossed his heart. And though the subject was beset by innumerable and apparently insurmountable difficulties, and though the work was novel to him and to every one of his friends, yet he felt impelled by an unseen power to go and preach the gospel to the heathen.
>
> He issued a pamphlet entitled **"An Inquiry into the Obligation of Christians to Use Means for the Conversion of the Heathen."** Mr. Carey became pastor of the church in Leicester in 1789, and there he labored with untiring faithfulness among his flock, and formed plans with unquenchable zeal for the salvation of the heathen. From this church he went to India to give God's Word to its vast population.
>
> At the meeting of his Association, which was held at Nottingham, **May 30, 1792**, he preached on Isaiah liv. 2,3, announcing the two memorable divisions of his disclosure: **"Expect great things from God; attempt great things for God."** The sermon stirred up the hearts of his hearers as they had never been before. At Kettering, the church of Andrew Fuller, **the Baptist Missionary Society** was organized Oct. 2, 1792. The society was formally instituted in the house of the widow of Deacon Beeby Wallis. The little parlor which witnessed the birth of this society was the most honored room in the British Islands, or in any part of Christendom; **in it was formed the first society of modern times for spreading the gospel among the heathen**, the parent of all great Protestant missionary societies in existence.
>
> He sailed June 13, 1793. At Seramore the missionaries set up printing presses and a large boarding school, and in process of the time founded a college. They preached incessantly, and Carey particularly studied the languages of the country with a measure of success never

equaled before or since by any other settler in India. He soon became the most learned man in the country.

Carey was the author of a Mahratta grammar, and of a Sanscrit grammar, extending over more than a thousand quarto pages, a Punjabi grammar, a Telinga grammar, and of a Mahratta dictionary, a Bengali dictionary, a Bhotanta dictionary, and a Sanscrit dictionary, the manuscript of which was burned before it was printed. He was also the author of several other secular works. The versions of the Sacred Scriptures appeared in six of these tongues. The New Testament appeared in 23 languages. Carey and his brethren rendered the Word of God accessible to one-third of the world. And even this is not all: before Carey's death 212,000 copies of the Scriptures were issued from Serampore in 40 different languages, the tongue of 330,000,000 of the human family. Dr. Carey was the greatest toolmaker for missionaries that ever labored for God. His versions are used today by all denominations of Christians throughout India.

The first Hindoo convert baptized by Dr. Carey in India was the celebrated Krishna Pal. Dr. Carey founded churches and mission stations in many parts of India, and planted seed from which he gathered precious harvests, and from which his successors have reaped abundantly.

He died June 9, 1834, in his seventy-third year—the **father of modern missions** (William Cathcart, *Baptist Encyclopedia*, Vol. 1, P. 182-4).

Andrew Fuller, was born in Wicken, Cambridgeshire, England, Feb. 6, 1754. When about fourteen years of age he first became the subject of religious exercises. This question arose in his mind. What is faith?

He was considerably affected at times by reading Bunyan's "**Grace Abounding to the Chief of Sinners**" and his "**Pilgrim's Progress**," and once he was led to weep bitterly in reading Ralph Erskine's "**Gospel Catechism for Young Christians**." At this time Job's words came to him, and soon created ...resolution in him. "Though he slay me yet will I trust him;" and the words of Esther intensified his purpose, "If I perish, I perish," but I must go to Jesus; and driven by his sins, and attracted by the redeeming power of the Lamb, he trusted Christ for the full salvation of his soul, and soon his guilt and fears were removed.

In March 1770, he saw two young persons baptized. He had never witnessed an immersion before, and it made such an impression upon him that he wept like a child, and he went away fully convinced that what he saw was the solemn appointment of the royal Saviour. One month after this baptism he was immersed himself into the membership of the church of Soham.

In the spring of 1775 he was ordained pastor of the church of Soham. In October 1782, he removed to Kettering, in Northhamptonshire, where he spent the rest of his life.

A pamphlet published by Jonathan Edwards on the importance of general union in prayer for the revival of true religion, led to a series of prayer meetings among the ministers of the Northhamptonshire Association for this special purpose. It is with some reason believed that these prayer meetings started that missionary tidal wave that soon rolled over England and America.

At a meeting held in Kettering on **the 2d of October 1792**, **the Baptist Missionary Society** was formed. Mr. Fuller was appointed its first secretary, and while others nobly aided, Andrew Fuller **was** the society till he reached the realms of glory. [Concerning the mission movement Fuller said,] "We had no one to guide us, and while we were thus deliberating, Carey, as it were, said, 'Well, I will go down if you will hold the rope.' But before he went down he, as it seemed to me, took an oath from each of us at the mouth of the pit to this effect, that while we lived we should never let go the rope." And Mr. Fuller held it fast till his hand fell powerless in death.

231

Chapter 17—The Churches of the Nineteenth Century

He traveled all over England very many times, pleading for foreign missions; five times he journeyed through Scotland on the same errand of love; and he visited Ireland once to advocate the cause of the perishing. The noblest cause that stirred up Christian hearts, the cause that brought the Saviour himself from the heavens, found in Andrew Fuller its grandest champion, and to him more than to any other human being was the first foreign missionary society of modern times indebted for its protection in infancy, and the nurturing influences that gave it the strength of a vigorous organization (William Cathcart, *Baptist Encyclopedia*, Vol. 1, P. 420-422).

1. Write 2 Peter 3:9 two times.

2. What was the cause of the slow down in growth of the Baptist churches of England?

3. What is Hypercalvinism?

4. How did Hypercalvinism affect the churches of England during the last part of the eighteenth century?

5. What was John Ryland's reaction to William Carey's burden for missions?

6. What was the title of the sermon Carey preached which led to the formation of the Baptist Missionary Society?

7. What position of importance concerning missions did Andrew Fuller hold until his death?

****

17.1.2

American Missions

At the close of the Eighteenth century there were over 90 Baptist associations in America. This included close to 2000 churches representing nearly 150,000 people.

The first five Baptist churches were: First Baptist Church of Newport, Rhode Island; First Baptist Church of Providence, Rhode Island; Second Baptist Church, Newport, Rhode Island; First Baptist Church of Swansey, Massachusetts; and First Baptist Church of Boston, Massachusetts. The first five Baptist associations in America were: **Philadelphia**, Pennsylvania (1707); **Charleston**, South Carolina (1751); **Sandy Creek**, North Carolina (1755); **Kehukee**, North Carolina (1765); and **Ketocton**, Virginia (1766). The next 100 years would bring an explosion of growth and the "War for Souls."

As you would think of **William Carey and Andrew Fuller in England** in bringing about the revival of missions in that country, you should think of **Adoniram Judson and Luther Rice** bringing the mission emphasis to the forefront in **America**.

Adoniram Judson

The Collegiate Baptist History Workbook

Adoniram Judson, was born in Malden, Mass., Aug. 9, 1788. **When he was 16**, he entered the sophomore class in Brown University, becoming a member of the institution on the 17th of August 1804. He graduated in 1807 with the highest honors of his class. The death of a classmate caused him to question his own salvation and led to his conversion. In 1809, he was admitted into the Andover Theological Institution and became a member of the Third Congregational Church in Plymouth, Mass., of which his father was the pastor. In February 1810, Judson made a decision to follow the Lord in foreign missions. He sought out other young men at the Andover seminary who joined with him in praying for revival and missions at "Missionary Rock."

The young men prepared a paper to be presented to a general association of all the evangelical ministers of Massachusetts, which convened at Bradford in 1810, urging the leaders to attend to the great need of preaching Christ in foreign parts. They asked boldly for an appointment in the East. The result of this action was the formation of **the American Board of Commissioners for Foreign Missions**; and later, the **Baptist General Convention of 1814**.

Soon after his graduation, Judson was sent to England by the **American Board** to confer with the London Missionary Society on the matter of combining the efforts of the **American Board** and the **London Society** in the work of carrying the gospel to the heathen. These boards were both "Congregational" as Adoniram Judson had not yet come to his conviction of baptism. Incredibly, he was kidnapped at sea by pirates but was quickly released and made it to England. The London Missionary Society appointed him and his fellow-students, Newell, Nott, and Hall, as missionaries to India. However, the American Board decided to send them without the help of London.

Judson, with his wife, Ann; and Nott, Newell, Hall, and Rice, sailed February 19, 1812, from Salem, Massachusetts. They reached Calcutta the 17th of the following June. By the time he reached India, Judson had come to see the need for scriptural baptism and was immediately immersed by William Carey, September 6, 1812, in the Baptist chapel in Calcutta. His wife also was baptized. This of course displeased the American Board of Commissioners for Foreign Missions, and they immediately withdrew support from Judson.

This turn of events put **Luther Rice** into a ministry, which had great and lasting effects. It led to the formation of **the Baptist Triennial Convention. This convention was held for the first time on the 18th of May 1814**. This first national Baptist organization in America was founded simply to meet the need of sponsoring and encouraging missionaries at home and around the world.

It became apparent that the Congregational East India Company was opposed to the work of Adoniram Judson and so he moved his mission to Burma and there he made a stand for God. Even after the Burmese king forbade Judson's work, Mr. Judson continued to preach the Gospel and devote himself to the translation of the scriptures and the preparation of religious tracts, to be circulated among the people.

After an extreme amount of government interference, in which Judson was imprisoned, the harshness of travel and constant sickness caused Ann Judson to become violently ill. Mrs. Judson died at Amherst, Burma on October 24, 1826. A two-year-old daughter also died from fever a few months later. Dr. Judson removed to Maulmain

Chapter 17—The Churches of the Nineteenth Century

November 14, 1827, and preached the Gospel with power. He began works in Maulmain, Prome, Rangoon, and other places, becoming especially interested in the conversion of the Karens.

On April 10, 1834, he married Sarah Boardman, who served with him until her death in 1845.

For many years Dr. Judson devoted a part of his time to the translation of the Scriptures into the Burmese language, and the compilation of a Burmese dictionary. He completed the Burmese Bible in 1834, but did not finish the dictionary. He sailed for America in April of 1850 and on April 12, died aboard ship and was buried at sea. Adoniram Judson made a difference that is felt to this day and has encouraged and inspired hundreds and thousands to surrender to preach the Gospel on the mission field.

The Triennial Convention: First National Baptist Convention

As mentioned in the short biography of Adoniram Judson above, the **Triennial Convention**, the first national Baptist organizational meeting, was formed to solve the problem of foreign and home missionary support. This organization served a great purpose and was among the greatest Baptist revival efforts of the nineteenth century. It was formed on **May 18, 1814** at the **First Baptist Church of Philadelphia**. Richard Furman, the pastor of First Baptist Church in Charleston, South Carolina, with his fiery Separate Baptist background, became the first president of the Convention. Its usefulness was short lived.

Luther Rice

Rice was a part of the **"Haystack Revival,"** so named for the famous prayer meeting involving Samuel Mills, Judson, Nott, Newell and Richards. These young men met together to pray under a haystack during a thunderstorm on the campus of Williams College. That one time prayer meeting brought about the birth of foreign missions in America. William Cathcart on Luther Rice:

> **Rice** was born in Northborough, Worcester Co., Mass., March 25, 1783. His parents were members of the Congregational Church, his mother being a woman of remarkable intellectual vigor. He attended the public schools of the neighborhood, and was apt in acquiring knowledge. While still a mere youth, the wonderful self-reliance, for which he was always distinguished, displayed itself; for, **at the age of sixteen**, he entered into a contract to visit the State of Georgia to assist in obtaining timber for ship-building, without consulting his parents, and was absent six months. Soon after this he became greatly concerned about his soul, and suffered the acutest mental agony for many months. At the age of nineteen, in March of 1802, he united with the church at Northborough.
>
> He was from the beginning a most consistent and active Christian worker, he infused a new and higher type of piety into his own family and the church, and made it a special duty to converse frequently with the impenitent. He was from the start of his Christian career deeply interested in missions and missionary publications. During all this time he was laboring upon his father's farm. His mind was now directed to the Christian ministry, and he resolved to secure a collegiate and theological education. He spent three years at Leicester Academy, and paid his expenses by teaching school during the vacations and giving lessons in singing at night. He made such rapid progress at the academy that he was able to complete his collegiate course in three years, having entered Williams College, Mass., in October of 1807. While in college he became deeply interested in missions, and he infused the same enthusiasm into the

minds of his friends, Mills and Richards. In a letter, written March 18, 1811, he says, "I have deliberately made up my mind to preach the gospel to the heathen." A society of inquiry on the subject of missions was formed through his instrumentality, and about the same time a branch society at Andover Seminary, where Judson and his friends met, caught the new awakening.

[Following Judson's appointment] Rice [also] had set his heart upon going, and he was permitted to do so upon the condition that he would himself raise the money necessary for his outfit and his passage, which he did within a few days. Having been previously licensed, he, with his companions, was ordained at the Tabernacle church, Salem, Mass., Feb. 6, 1812, and sailed from Philadelphia, February 18 in the packet "Harmony," destined for India.

Dr. Judson and wife, who had sailed from Salem, having **changed their minds on the subject of baptism, were baptized by Dr. Carey** soon after their arrival at Calcutta; and Mr. Rice, having also been led, after a thorough investigation, to change his views on the same subject, was also baptized, on Nov. 1, 1812, by Mr. Ward, a few weeks after Mr. and Mrs. Judson.

Owing to the continued and bitter opposition of the English authorities in India, Mr. Rice concluded to sail for the Isle of France, and thence to the United States, to adjust his relations with the Congregational board, to enlist the Baptist churches in the cause of missions, and to recruit his health. He arrived at New York, Sept. 7, 1813; went immediately to Boston, and communicated with the board, who, however, received him with much coldness, and, rather rudely, dissolved his relations with themselves.

Mr. Rice now completely identified himself with the Baptists. At a consultation, in Boston, it was determined to appoint him an agent to visit all parts of the country, and enlist churches and individuals in the cause. He journeyed throughout the entire length of the country, and met with the most encouraging success. Delegates were appointed from all parts of the land to meet for conference, and on the 18th of May 1814, a large number assembled at Philadelphia, Dr. Richard Furman presiding. After several days deliberation **the General Convention of the Baptist Denomination in the United States for Foreign Missions** was formed, that organization which has accomplished so much in heathen lands for the glory of God and the good of men. On his Southern tour Mr. Rice collected about $1300, made arrangements for future contributions, and organized about twenty missionary societies, and throughout the country about seventy societies.

At the meeting of **the Triennial Convention** in Philadelphia, **in 1817**, he reported that he had traveled, during a very short time, 7800 miles, collected nearly $3700, and aroused a warm interest in missions everywhere. These journeys were "through wildernesses and over rivers, across mountains and valleys, in heat and cold, by day and by night, in weariness and painfulness, and fastings and loneliness."

To Mr. Rice, more than to any other man is due the awakened regard in ministerial education. He was deeply interested in the school opened in Philadelphia, under Staughton and Chase, for the instruction of young men for the ministry. Eighteen were in course of preparation there, he urged the founding of a college at Washington, D. C., [Columbian College] and through his efforts forty-six and a half acres were purchased adjacent to the city of Washington, and a building capable of accommodating eighty students was begun. The [Triennial] Convention took the new institution under its supervision, and in the report made to the Convention in **1821**, there was set forth a most gratifying statement of the progress of the college. Mr. Rice was appointed its agent and treasurer. About this time he originated the *Columbian Star,* published at Washington.

Mr. Rice sacrificed his life for the welfare of the institution which be originated, [note: Columbian College eventually passed out of Baptist hands and is now George Washington

Chapter 17—The Churches of the Nineteenth Century

University] and which he loved so well. During a collecting tour through the South he was taken seriously ill, and soon after died at the house of his friend, Dr. Mays, Sept. 25, 1836. He was buried at Pine Pleasant Church, Edgefield District, S. C. Part of his memorial stone reads:

> "A minister of Christ, of the Baptist Denomination.
> He was a native of Northboro, Massachusetts,
> And departed this life in Edgefield District, S. C.
> In the death of this distinguished servant of the Lord, 'is a great man fallen in Israel.'
>
> Perhaps no American has done more
> Than he, for the great Missionary enterprise.
>
> It is thought the first American Foreign Mission, on which he went to India, associated with Judson and others, originated with him.
>
> And if the Burmans have cause of gratitude towards Judson, for a faithful version of God's Word, so they will through generations to come arise up and call Rice blessed;' for it was his eloquent appeals for the Heathen, on his return to America, which raised our Baptist churches to adopt the Burman Mission and sustain Judson in his arduous toils."

(See William Cathcart's *Baptist Encyclopedia*, Vol. 2, P. 978-980.)

1. Write 2 Peter 3:9 two times.

2. What two men are responsible for the early missionary burden in America?

3. What was the Haystack prayer meeting and what did it produce?

4. Other than preaching the Gospel, what were the two things Adoniram Judson was trying to accomplish?

5. What role did Luther Rice play concerning Judson?

6. Basically, why was the Triennial Convention formed?

7. What college did Luther Rice found?

****

17.2.1
SECTION TWO

The 100 year war for Souls in America

With a burst of freedom, the Baptists of America spread across the country like an army. At the turn of the nineteenth century, all Bible believing denominations enjoyed good growth, especially the Methodists and Baptists. A sort of spiritual war took place in which the souls of Americans were being sought. It is a good thing to know that the doctrines of salvation, atonement and eternity were being faithfully preached from most every denominational pulpit. We will see how much of Christianity attempted a union in America, then split apart, then united again for a common cause. Then in our last chapter we will see how the unity unwittingly became a threat to Baptist distinctives.

Across the Alleghenies: The "Travelling" Church

Just before the end of the revolution, the Baptist churches of the Piedmont area of Virginia and the Carolinas saw the need to migrate into the wilderness west of the Blue Ridge and the Allegheny Mountains. The most profound example of this burden for the west can be seen in the pioneer preacher **Lewis Craig**. The following narrative was typical for those pioneering Baptists. For your edification:

Craig, the Separate Baptist, had seen revival in his church in Spotsylvania, Virginia and felt compelled of God to move **his entire church** into the new country of Kentucky. Only Daniel Boone and a handful of others had ever ventured past the Cumberland Gap into the new territory.

Craig knew the dangers, and like Shubal Stearns, knew the importance of establishing churches among the pioneers. This was vital to the future of America.

Sometime in September 1781 Lewis Craig led a group of Baptist pioneers and their acquaintances in a farewell service at Upper Spotsylvania Baptist Church. The area is now known as Craig's Station. The group of over 600 souls made their way across Virginia southwest to the Cumberland Gap and then northwest into Kentucky country, a journey of over 600 miles.

Among them, according to tradition, was Elijah Craig, the bold exhorter of the Blue Run church who had lunched in jail more than once on rye bread and water for conscience sake: Ambrose Dudley who had often labored with him: William E. Waller, pastor of County Line and William Ellis the aged shepherd of the Nottaway flock who had realized what "buffetings" meant long before the Revolution brought its blessed heritage of religious freedom. They had many relatives among the departing throng and all of them but the venerable Ellis soon followed them to the land of Boone (George Ranck, *The Travelling Church*, P. 6).

Along the old Catharpin road toward the west, their route turned into "the mountain road" past the hamlet of Gordonsville and thence to the cluster of houses known as Charlottesville. They found themselves in the midst of the noted Piedmont country and their road extended from Albemarle to the James. By this established route the travelers reached the James River and after they had slowly forded it to the little knot of dwellings on its southern bank, where Lynchburg was to be, they camped.

Next, the old red road through the rolling tobacco lands of Bedford brought them to the village of Liberty where they saw the "everlasting hills" of the Blue Ridge and the Peaks of Otter. This was the beginning of a great succession of mountain barriers forever cutting them off from old Virginia.

Chapter 17—The Churches of the Nineteenth Century

From Buford's Gap on the crest of the winding way they saw the endless mountains and started a journey for old Fort Chriswell. After fording the Roanoke they climbed the rugged ascent of the Alleghany divide. From there they descended down the mountain road and crossed New River. They arrived at Fort Chiswell, which was located about nine miles east of the present Wytheville. There they gave up their wagons for the journey's sake, because the terrain and road could not allow wagons. The close of the third week of September found them safely encamped at the desired point, the "Wolf Hills" now know as Abingdon.

During the "halt at Abingdon" the glorious news came of the British surrender at Yorktown. A group of stranded pioneers also from Virginia had been in Abingdon for nearly a year. Lewis Craig formed them into a church, which was called Providence.

> **From Kentucky across the Ohio Isaac McCoy—the greatest missionary in the history of America.**
>
> For 30 years (1816-1846), Baptist missionary Isaac McCoy preached the Gospel to the Indians of the Ohio, Mississippi, and Missouri Valleys. He birthed churches among the natives in Kentucky, Indiana, Ohio, Illinois, Michigan, Missouri, Kansas, Nebraska and Oklahoma.
>
> Sensing evil men within the government were attempting to commit genocide against the people he loved, McCoy lobbied and succeeded in creating reservations for the Indian tribes of the Great Plains.
>
> McCoy was a tireless worker who was used of God to see a large number of Indian chiefs and tribal members brought to a saving knowledge of Christ.

The Travelling Church was forced to stay in Abingdon for a month and built a group of primitive huts to live in.

Lewis Craig and his group of pioneers had determined before they ever left Virginia that they would strive to migrate to Gilbert's Creek, a tributary of the Dix River in central Kentucky territory. About the first of December, nearly three weeks after leaving Abingdon and the North Fork of the Holston River, the dauntless pioneers crossed the Cumberland Gap. They entered Kentucky, passing intimidating mountain drop offs and an enormous wilderness.

Light was breaking through for them, and they moved on about five miles north of Rockcastle River, where the buffalo path led toward the already famous Boonsborough. They followed this branch of the Wilderness Road to the place now known as Mt. Vernon. Within a short time, the emigrants were marching toward English Station which they reached without any added trouble.

Now they passed the cabins of "The Crab Orchard" and filing northwestwardly through the woods and canebrakes headed for Logan's Fort near the spot where Stanford was afterwards established. The settlers of the area were ready for them. The settlers, some of whom were their own friends and kindred from Virginia, had gathered to meet them and when they appeared in sight of the stockade they were greeted with the firing of rifles and shouts of welcome. Then came a touching scene of hearty hand-shaking, affectionate embraces, eager inquiries, tears of joy and repeated exclamations of delight.

They located on the little tributary of Gilbert's Creek, two miles and a half southeast of the then forest-covered site of the present town of Lancaster and in that part of the original County of Lincoln which now constitutes the County of Garrard.

Spurred on by cold weather and dire necessity, the Baptists quickly made a clearing in the woods at Gilbert's Creek and established Craig's Station on land afterwards owned by John Simpson, and there in that lonely outpost before the close of **the second Sunday in December, 1781**, (See *Ford's Christian Repository, March, 1856.*) they gathered and worshipped around the same old Bible they had used in Spotsylvania. There, the word of God was preached by their pastor, Lewis Craig. So met the first church that ever assembled in central Kentucky

They had traveled 600 miles in 4 months, an average of about 5 miles a day. Cathcart noted this about Lewis Craig:

The next year he [Lewis Craig] gathered Forks of Dix River in the same county. In 1783 he and most of Gilbert's creek church moved to the north side of Kentucky River and organized South Elkhorn church, in Fayette County. Here he remained about nine years, laboring zealously in all the surrounding country. Cathcart wrote:

> A number of churches were founded, **and Elkhorn Association was formed Oct.1 1785**. About 1792 he moved to Bracken Co., Ky. Here he formed several churches, and "became in a manner the father of Bracken Association." About the year 1828, he died suddenly, of which he was forewarned, saying, "I am going to such a house to die," and with solemn joy went on to the place, and with little pain left the world (William Cathcart, *Baptist Encyclopedia*, Vol. 1, P. 285).

William Hickman

One of the most famous of the pioneer Baptist ministers in Kentucky, was born in King and Queen Co., Va., Feb. 4, 1747. He was by early training an Episcopalian, and entertained great contempt for the Baptists. During a sermon by the renowned John Waller, in 1770, he was deeply impressed. After struggling with his sins and his prejudices about three years, he obtained peace in Christ and was baptized by Reuben Ford, in April, 1773. At this time he lived in Cumberland County. There being few preachers in that region, he, with others, established prayer meetings. In February 1776, he started to Kentucky, and arriving at Harrodsburg, he remained several weeks, and during the time, though not licensed, he attempted on one occasion to preach. Upon his return home to Virginia he was soon set apart for the ministry, and spent several years as a preacher in his native State. In 1784 he removed to Fayette Co., Ky., where he preached with great zeal and activity in the surrounding settlements. In 1788 he changed his residence to what is now Franklin County. Here, in the same year, **he formed the Forks of Elkhorn church**, and was chosen the pastor. From this place he made preaching tours among the settlers, often attended by a guard of soldiers to protect him from the Indians. The new churches he formed were watched over and nurtured until they grew strong and the savages were driven from the country. He was greatly blessed in his ministry. A contemporary supposes that in his day he **"baptized more people than any other minister in Kentucky."** He probably formed more churches than even the famous Lewis Craig. He baptized over 500 during one winter. He died suddenly in 1830. His son William was long pastor of South Benson church, and Hickman Co., Ky., was named after his son, Col. Paschal Hickman, who fell in the battle of the river Raisin (William Cathcart, *Baptist Encyclopedia*, Vol. 1, P. 521-2).

STOP AND THINK
1. Write 2 Peter 3:9 two times.

Chapter 17—The Churches of the Nineteenth Century

2. Describe briefly the 100-year war for souls in America:

3. What was Lewis Craig's vision for his church in Spotsylvania?

4. How far did the travelling church travel and how long did it take them?
5. Who was the greatest missionary in American history?
6. What state received the pioneers along the "Wilderness Road?"
7. What Baptist association formed in Kentucky as a result of Craig's efforts?

8. Hickman's ministry was greater than Craig's in what ways?

****
17.2.2

The Great Revival of 1796-1802

When Francis Asbury passed through the Wilderness Road, not long after the Baptists were led by Lewis Craig, he began the inroad of the Methodists through the western frontier. Methodist men such as Asbury, Peter Cartwright and Jessie Walker fought the war for souls with the Baptists along with the few Presbyterians who had come into the rough land. Kentucky was soon filled with wild settlers who established counties such as "Bourbon" and towns like "Dog Walk."

As our Baptist forefathers pioneered Kentucky, a flood of ungodly men came on their heels and more than one historical account talked of the profane way the wilderness was forming. God miraculously sent what most historians believe to be **The Second Great Awakening**, which began in western Kentucky and grew into an avalanche of salvation shaking the Kentucky and Tennessee countries. The revival headed east and flamed all the way to the east coast including all of the original colleges of the colonies in its fire.

The Baptists of Kentucky were profoundly affected. Clear Creek, which was an offshoot from the Forks of Elkhorn church, with its pioneer pastor **John Taylor**, grew to over 600 members in the woods south of Lexington. Taylor's influence fanned what became known as the "Wilderness Revival."

Education

On the heels of the Revolutionary war and the Second Great Awakening, the *baptized believers* now desired education. The first institution for educating Baptist preachers was the **Hopewell Academy** in Hopewell, New Jersey. Its initial instructor was a brilliant and fervent teacher named **Isaac Eaton**. Eaton's influence among the pre-Revolution preachers was tremendous. The Hopewell Academy eventually served as the basis of the forming of Brown College in Providence, Rhode Island.

Time and space does not allow us to tell much detail about the lives of these great servants of God, but briefly:

The Collegiate Baptist History Workbook

James Manning

James Manning, was the founder and first president of Brown University in Providence, Rhode Island. He was born October 22, 1738. About the age of eighteen, he went to Hopewell, N. J., to prepare for college, under the instruction of Isaac Eaton. There was a strong feeling among the Baptists of the great need of an educated ministry, and the Philadelphia Association, which met in 1762, resolved to establish a denominational college in Rhode Island. To Mr. Manning was entrusted the carrying out of this object. A charter was obtained from the General Assembly in 1764, authorizing the birth of the College of Rhode Island, which eventually became Brown.

The Warren Association was formed in Rhode Island in 1776. It began with four churches, but soon extended over New England. Mr. Manning was a part of this association and Warren was a great help to Brown College. In 1771, Manning became pastor of the First Baptist Church of Providence and the beautiful building, still standing, was built during his pastorate.

Jessie Mercer

Jessie Mercer, the son of Silas Mercer, was born in Halifax Co., North Carolina, Dec. 16, 1769. His father removed to Georgia about 1775, and settled in Wilkes County, but fled to North Carolina at the outbreak of the revolution. He did not return until after the war, when Jesse was about fourteen years old. Before he was twenty years of age, Jessie was ordained on the 7th of November 1789, by Silas Mercer and Sanders Walker. He pastored six churches in 50 years and was successful in refuting the anti-mission movement. For several years he was the editor of *the Christian Index* and was the founder of Mercer University.

Richard Furman

Furman was baptized **in his sixteenth year**. His roots were Separate Baptist. He was an active patriot and his early speaking ability and powers to persuade made him a special enemy of Lord Cornwallis. The British general offered a large reward for the capture of Furman.

In 1787 he became pastor of the First Baptist church in Charleston, S.C. which was greatly weakened from the war. For 37 years Furman pastored the church and God granted them revival and strength.

He was unanimously elected the first president of the **Triennial Convention in 1814**. He worked in agreement with Luther Rice for the formation of Columbian College. He exercised what influence he could for the education of preachers in the South. His efforts led to the formation of **Furman University**, in South Carolina: **Mercer**, in Georgia: **Hamilton**, in New York; and eventually the Baptist Theological Seminary. He died in August 1825.

The Revival of 1858, City Revivals, and the Evangelical Alliance

The Baptists, as well as other denominations, became widely successful during the nineteenth century. The denominations that had a love and burden for souls were: 1. The Congregationalists, 2. The Methodists, 3. The Presbyterians, and 4. The Baptists.

Chapter 17—The Churches of the Nineteenth Century

As the cities of America began to grow the Protestant churches began to use "Union" meetings to try to reach the growing populations. In the eastern part of America, the Presbyterian evangelist, **Charles Finney** began seeing great success in the 1830's. Two early citywide evangelists were **Edwin Payson**, a Congregationalist, and **Jacob Knapp**, a Baptist. Although the Baptists did not oppose these "Union" meetings, the majority of Baptists did not participate.

Just before the Civil War, **in 1858,** the **Third Great Awakening** in the history of America occurred. It began as a prayer meeting in New York City, led by a member of the Dutch Reformed Church, Jeremiah Lamphere. In the beginning, just a handful met at lunchtime to pray for America. Within a few weeks as many as 10,000 souls were meeting. It became known as **the Fulton Street Prayer Revival** and it quickly spread to every corner of America. Every church and every denomination benefited. Reports of revivals, awakenings and conviction of sin were given to the American public by way of newspapers each and every day. Many secular historians even refer to the awakening as the "event of the century."

After the Civil War, the Bible-believing denominations formed **the Evangelical Alliance**. Meetings of the "**Alliance**" were held in most major cities. It was good in that a large number of city dwellers were heard the Gospel. It was harmful in that Baptist distinctives took a back seat. Not many Baptists joined the Evangelical Alliance. Thomas Armitage, great pastor and Baptist historian from New York City wrote respectively against the city campaigns, believing the campaigns would eventually erode the importance of believer's baptism. After the war, from 1870 to 1910, the great Evangelical Alliance evangelists were **Dwight L. Moody**, the Congregationalist; **Sam Jones** and **Gipsy Smith**, Methodists; **J. Wilber Chapman** and **Billy Sunday**, Presbyterian. The great Baptist evangelists were: **Abraham Marshall, John Taylor, Jeremiah Vardemann, Alfred Taylor, T. J. Fisher, Jacob Knapp, Jabez Swan, William Penn, J. R. Graves, A. B. Earl,** and **"Cyclone Mac" McClendon.**

> **No Great Baptist Evangelists?**
>
> Often, uniformed preachers and teachers will lament the absence of great Baptist evangelists during the era of the great revivals. The lament is unnecessary, as Baptists did the first works in evangelism (John Clarke 1639, and the Kentucky evangelists 1781-1840). They pioneered the camp-meeting (Sandy Creek 1758); and produced the greatest of America's evangelists: Shubal Stearns, Samuel Harriss, Abraham Marshall, John Taylor, Jeremiah Vardemann, Alfred Taylor, T. J. Fisher, Jacob Knapp, Jabez Swan, William Penn, J. R. Graves, A. B. Earl, and Cyclone Mac McClendon.

Satan's Devices

The Devil lost a lot of ground in America between 1776 and 1840, but he began to make up for lost time with a 5-prong attack using the following devices:

Satan's Plan for America

Anti-Mission Movement

The anti-missions movement began among the Baptists in protest of Luther Rice and his "methods." Some Baptists of the South looked at the missions movement as a non-scriptural "innovation" and a means to gather money. Others were Hypercalvinistic and rejected the aggressive preaching of the Gospel. This outlook led to the "Primitive" Baptist or "Hardshell" movement. This movement killed many churches. Issues involving missions would prove to be a crucial point in the rise of the Independent Baptists of the twentieth century.

Bible Revision Movement

Bible revision was the second part of satan's plan for America. Alexander Campbell, the founder of the Church of Christ called for a revision of the King James Bible as early as 1840. Some well meaning Baptist leaders followed suit. They reasoned that the word "baptize" in the Greek was "immerse" and so the text of the King James should read "immerse." This movement lost momentum during the Civil War and died shortly afterwards as the Westcott and Hort controversy concerning revision began.

Wescott-Hort Revision Movement

The third part of satan's plan for America involved the English revision movement of Wescott and Hort. Instead of just revising a few words, now a movement sprang from the Protestants to revise the Authorized Version. In essence, the revisers wanted to go to a "more reliable" and more ancient text and rewrite the word of God. This plot had its roots in German Rationalism and came to the American educational system by way of the German apostates Immanual Kant (1724-1804), Johann Griesbach (1745-1812), Carl Lachmann (1793-1851), and Friedrich Tischendorf (1815-1874). There is no evidence that any of these men ever won a soul to Christ, or led a revival campaign, yet they influenced Protestant and Baptist colleges in America. They were the founders of modern *Textual Criticism* and the *Modernist* attack on the Bible.

In 1856 a group of five Church of England clergymen petitioned the English government for authorization of a "revision" of the King James Bible. For several years they lobbied for parliamentary resolution and wrote portions of a revision. In 1870, the Anglican Church approved a revision and a committee was approved to begin work.

A text of the Hebrew and Greek was needed in which the English could be revised, corrected, and changed. Instead of using the existing received text, known as the *Textus Receptus*, along with other sources available to the King James translators, the revisers of 1870 chose a text from the Alexandrian-Jerome line. (See chapter four.) It had been compiled from two Anglican scholars; Brooke Wescott, and Arthur Hort. They used the flawed scholarship of Origen, Eusebius and Pamphilus, along with two supposedly more ancient and "accurate" texts: **the Sinaiticus** and **the Vaticanus**. Changing the word of God had a devastating effect and **the modernist movement** was benefited.

The Rise of the Modern Cults

Campellism (Church of Christ)

This group of Baptist people, blinded by the false doctrine of "baptismal regeneration" gave rise to the **"Church of Christ"** and **"Disciples of Christ."** They originated from the great revival of 1800 and had roots in the Baptist churches of Kentucky. They came under the influence of English apostate Alexander Campbell who desired a union with Protestant groups. Campbell believed that the Gospel was preached in four parts: 1. Hearing 2.

Chapter 17—The Churches of the Nineteenth Century

Believing 3. Being baptized 4. Following on to obey. Campellism clearly teaches salvation by works.

Watchtower Society (Jehovah's Witness)

Started as a rejection of the Presbyterian Church, the "Russellites" are **the disciples of denial** as they deny the deity of Christ, the resurrection, the Second Coming of Christ, and the existence of Heaven and Hell. Their founder is Charles Russell, who became a Seventh Day Adventist, but disagreed with them and started the Watchtower Society in 1879. Modern "witnesses" forget Russell as he was found guilty of fraud when he lied under oath about his ability to read Greek. At Russell's death in 1916, Joseph Rutherford took his place. Rutherford was a lawyer and a judge and used his organizational powers to found "Kingdom Halls" all over America. He wrote many books and pamphlets, and started the J. W. way of writing all articles anonymously. The J. W.'s predicted Christ would return in 1914. When He did not come, they covered the lie and said He came back in spirit form and is in the atmosphere now.

Latter-Day Saints (Mormons)

Many believe John Smith of upstate New York began the "Latter-Day Saints" as a joke. Smith said that in 1823 the angel Moroni gave him the secret gold plates which contained God's new record, which he was allowed to translate into Elizabethan English to give us the book of Mormon. The plates have disappeared but the Mormons remain. Their first "church" was in Fayette, New York. They teach "baptism for the dead" that is, you can have yourself baptized on behalf of loved ones who have gone before, which explains their infatuation with genealogy records. (They have the largest archive of genealogical records in the world.) Mormonism is a works salvation, which teaches you may attain Godhood status. The earth was created and populated by "Adam-God" and Jesus was his off spring. Jesus is just one god of many gods. The Mormons believe that Joseph Smith reinstated the church.

The Modernist Attack

As German textual criticism invaded the seminaries and colleges across America, the result was a flood of unbelief called "*modernism.*" Corrupt textbooks polluted the theological seminaries of most Protestant and Baptist colleges and professors, who believed themselves enlightened by great thinkers and scientists, encouraged unbelief. Evolution was advancing upon the minds of intellectuals and unbelief found its way into the pulpits of America. A battle for the Bible was about to be waged.

The Split of the Baptists in the North and South

An entire book could be written to tell the story of the split of the Baptists. The Baptists were fairly unified in their effort to birth churches, win the lost and send missionaries. But the support of missionaries who were pro-slavery could not be tolerated by the Baptists of the North. Simply put, the civil war over slavery among the Baptists erupted 15 years before the firing on Fort Sumter. In 1845 at a convention in Augusta,

Georgia, the "Southern Baptist Convention" was formed. It was formed because the churches of the North would not support pro-slavery missionaries of the South. In addition, the southern churches did not like the direction of the associations of the North. The South viewed the North as being too controlling of the churches. The Triennial Convention was dead. The Northern Baptist Convention, (now known as the American Baptist Convention) was formed in 1907.

 1. Write 2 Peter 3:9 two times.

2. Where did the "Second Great Awakening" begin?

3. What was the first educational institution for Baptists and where was it located?

4. What did James Manning accomplish?

5. What did Jessie Mercer successfully refute?

6. Who was the first President of the Triennial Convention?

7. What four denominations had a love and burden for souls during the nineteenth century?

8. What exactly was The Third Great Awakening in America?

9. Name two great citywide Evangelists:

10. Describe briefly "the Evangelical Alliance:"

11. What was Thomas Armitage' warning about citywide revival campaigns?

12. Name the five prongs of Satan's Devices in the nineteenth century:

13. Why did the Baptists split North and South?

Chapter Eighteen
The Churches of the Twentieth Century

Section One: Evangelical Alliance gives way to Modernism
Section Two: Fundamentalism and the fight for
Baptist Principles (First Principles)

Ecumenicalism, Fundamentalism and Baptist Principles

SECTION ONE

Scripture to Memorize

> Jude 1:3 Beloved, when I gave all diligence to write unto you of the common salvation, it was needful for me to write unto you, and exhort you that ye should earnestly contend for the faith which was once delivered unto the saints.

Definitions:

modernism: the modernizing of Biblical doctrine or standards, removing some or all supernatural truth
fundamentalism: the militant defense of fundamental beliefs found in the word of God.
ecumenicalism: the attempt of modernists to unite all of Christendom without requiring fundamental belief.
new evangelicalism: the unscriptural attempt to duplicate the Evangelical Alliance which existed before the rise of modernism
post-modernism: the attempt made by modern (or new) evangelicals to convince Christianity that the era of modernism is over. It is **not over**, the affects of the poison of modernism are with us to this day.

The fundamentalist battle and the history of the Baptists in the twentieth century could fill a volume of several hundred pages. Space constrains, but we will introduce you to some of the main characters that with brave voices fought for the cause of biblical standards and pure doctrine in the twentieth century.

We have stated that the Bible believing Protestants of the nineteenth century, mostly without the consent or help of the Baptists, formed an Evangelical Alliance to help their efforts to preach the Gospel during the era of the great citywide revival campaigns.

The Civil War caused the Evangelical Alliance to break up for a time. The Methodists, Presbyterians, and Baptists split north and south. By the time the Methodists, Presbyterians and Baptist came back together their schools and colleges had embraced *modernism*.

The Congregationalists

The Congregationalists did not split before the war, but after the death of D.L. Moody in 1899, they went into a doctrinal free fall. They eventually united with the German Reformed Church and parts of the "Christian Church," formerly of Kentucky fame, and became **the United Church of Christ**. This merger occurred in 1957.

Chapter 18—The Churches of the Twentieth Century

The Methodists
The Methodists split several times to form the Nazarenes, and the Wesleyans and all manner of Pentecostal groups including the Assemblies of God. The Methodists of the North and South reunited to form the United Methodists.

The Presbyterians
The Presbyterians north and south reunited as the United Presbyterian Church.

The Baptists never reunited. However the separate conventions north and south became entangled with **modernist** errors and the battles over doctrine waged well into the twentieth century.

In the twentieth century, **fundamentalism** was the reaction of Bible believers to the Protestant retreat from the Bible. The retreat was **unbelief. Liberalism is unbelief.** Unbelief produces nothing. Fundamentalism is the opposite, fundamentalism is belief, and the militant defense of the same.

The days of the old Evangelical Alliance are forever over. The good that the Evangelical Alliance did was great. However, a large portion of what is called Protestantism lost what it had when it embraced *modernism*. **Today, you cannot duplicate the Evangelical Alliance without compromising the standards of the word of God.** This fact **fundamental Baptists** realized. New Evangelicalism has been trying to reproduce the **Evangelical Alliance** since the mid-twentieth century.

---

1. Write Jude 1:3 two times:

2. Write out the 5 definitions above once each:

3. The Bible warns us not to infiltrate, but to _____ .

4. What does unbelief produce?

5. Why is the day of the Evangelical Alliance over?

6. What three church organizations became the United Church of Christ?

****

18.1.2

The Emergence of Fundamentalism

There was no official birth of **Fundamentalism**. Fundamentalism, if it's meaning *is* **belief**, has always been in Christianity. It is a sad fact of history that Fundamentalism ever had to become a "movement." Fundamentalism is simply **stating and defending** what is surely believed. What we recognize as the Fundamentalist movement was an attempt to rescue the old Evangelical Alliance from apostasy.

In America, Fundamentalism began when the established pastors of the major denominations realized their colleges were being operated by **the German Rationalist movement**. In addition, unbelieving professors were training their preachers. Publications began to sound the warning of the dangers of Bible rejection. *The Watchword* (Baptist), *the Truth* (Presbyterian) and others made the *modernist* movement well known to all Americans.

A conference was held from October 30 to November 1, 1878, at the Church of the Holy Trinity (Episcopal) in New York City, where Stephen H. Tyng Jr. was the minister. Another conference was held in Farwell Hall in Chicago, November 16-21, 1886. The men leading these conferences were of several denominations. This was the beginning of the **Fundamentalist** movement. The Baptists in the meetings were: George C. Needham, A. J. Gordon, and G. C. Lorimer; the Methodists were: L. W. Munhall, W. E. Blackstone, and Henry Lummis; Presbyterians were Albert Erdman, W. J. Erdman, and James H. Brookes; Congregationalists were: E. P. Goodwin and D. W. Whittle; Episcopalians included Stephen Tyng Jr. and Maurice Baldwin; the Lutherans also were involved with Bishop Joseph A. Seiss and G. N. H. Peters.

Fundamentalism's Creed

One of the first doctrinal creeds defining Fundamentalism came from the Niagara Bible Conference in 1878. The Creed listed fourteen articles:
1. The verbal, plenary inspiration of the Scriptures.
2. The Trinity.
3. The Creation of man, the Fall into sin, and total depravity.
4. The universal transmission of spiritual death from Adam.
5. The necessity of the new birth.
6. Redemption by the blood of Christ.
7. Salvation by faith alone in Christ.
8. The assurance of salvation.
9. The centrality of Jesus Christ in the Scriptures.
10. The constitution of the true church by genuine believers.
11. The personality of the Holy Spirit.
12. The believer's call to a holy life.
13. The immediate passing of the souls of believers to be with Christ at death.
14. The premillennial Second Coming of Christ.

The most famous listing of the Fundamentals, which are commonly cited today, are the so-called **five Fundamentals**, identified by the 1910 General Assembly of the Northern Presbyterian Church: (1) Inerrancy, (2) Virgin Birth, (3) Substitutional Atonement, (4) Bodily Resurrection, and (5) Authenticity of Miracles or the Second coming of Christ.

We should note that there is no mention of **baptism** in any creed of the Fundamentalists.

This diverse group demonstrates the concern of the Fundamentalists to recover the belief of the old Evangelical Alliance. The attempt, in all actuality, failed. The **Evangelical Alliance** evolved into **New Evangelicalism** and the **Ecumenical Movement**. After a generation (by 1950) **Fundamentalism** became largely a Baptist movement.

What Is Surely Believed?

According to some sources, the editor of the Baptist periodical *Watchman-Examiner* coined the term ***Fundamentalist*** in 1920 to describe a conference of Baptists at the Delaware Avenue Baptist Church in Buffalo, New York. They met to discuss the problem of ***modernism*** in the Northern Baptist Convention. This is considered by some

Chapter 18—The Churches of the Twentieth Century

to be the beginning of **Fundamentalism**. There are others that point to a meeting at Swampscott, Massachusetts in 1876 for the beginning of the Fundamentalist movement in America. Still others point to the release of the book, *The Fundamentals* in 1922.

One of the first Baptists to take a stand as a Fundamentalist was Adoniram Judson Gordon. Cathcart wrote these words about him when he was just a young man:

> **A. J. Gordon** was born in New Hampton, N. H., and graduated at Brown University in the class of 1860. He took the full course of theology at the Newton Theological Institution, and graduated in the class of 1863. He was ordained June 29, 1863, and became pastor of the church at Jamaica Plain, near Boston, Mass., where he remained six years, and then removed to Boston, where, since 1869, he has been the pastor of the Clarendon Street church, formerly Rowe Street, being the immediate successor of Rev. Dr. Baron Stow. Dr. Gordon was one of the compilers of the "Service of Song." He is also the author of one or two books of a devotional character, which have been favorably received by the religious public.
>
> Dr. Gordon is a trustee of Brown University, and received from that institution, in 1877, the honorary degree of Doctor of Divinity. Though a comparatively young man, Dr. Gordon exerts a wide influence in Boston, and his name is favorably and deservedly known throughout the denomination in this country (William Cathcart, *Baptist Encyclopedia*, Vol. 1, P. 459-460).

A. J. Gordon best defended the word of God through his publication *Watchword*. It ceased publication with his death in 1897.

1. Write Jude 1:3 two times:

2. How long has fundamentalism been a part of Christianity?
3. What was wrong with the college professors?

4. What was wrong with the colleges?

5. Name two publications that sounded a warning about Bible rejecting:

6. Name two early fundamental Baptist leaders before the turn of the twentieth century:

7. Name three fundamentals from the creed above:

****
18.2.1
SECTION TWO
Fundamentalism and "New Evangelicalism"

In the twentieth century, Fundamentalism was lead by these leaders: the Presbyterian Fundamentalists were led by Oliver Bushnell, Merrill T. MacPherson (excommunicated by the Presbyterian Assembly for standing for the truth), **Ian Paisley** (in Britain), and Carl McIntire. The Methodist Fundamentalists were **Bob Jones, Sr**. and "Fighting Bob" Shuler. The Baptist protest was led by **W. B. Riley** in the North, **J. Frank Norris** in the South, **John Roach Stratton** in the East, and **T. T. Shields** in Canada.

New Evangelicalism

The **doctrinal controversy** that made Fundamentalists re-state the basic beliefs of Christianity was **modernism**. As a result of the public stand against modernism, new colleges standing for the truth arose in that generation 1875—1935. Those Fundamentalist colleges included: Moody Bible Institute, Bible Institute of Los Angeles, Bob Jones College, Wheaton College, Philadelphia College of the Bible and Fuller Theological Seminary.

When the Fundamentalists took their stand, "**New Evangelicalism**" emerged. What is New Evangelicalism and where did it come from?

New Evangelicalism came from those in the "Evangelical Alliance" who chose not to separate from unbelief. It rejected separation from unbelievers and modernism and embraced *infiltration*. It was a rejection of the principles of Bible-believing Fundamentalism. The Bible warns us not to infiltrate, but to separate:

"*wherefore come out from among them and be ye separate*" 2 Cor. 6:17

Separation is stating, believing and living the truth while unbelief retreats. The unbeliever, will always retreat from the believer.

One of the biggest problems hindering revival today is the sad fact that the church is comfortable around the world, and worse, the world is comfortable around the church. Separation has always been the fuel for the New Testament church. From the Novatianists, to the Paulicians; from the Albigenses to the Waldensians; from the Anabaptists, to the Separate Baptists; separation from unbelievers always led to two things: **persecution upon the separatists** and **astonishing power for preaching the Gospel**.

> **Independent Protestants**
> In the early twentieth century, independent congregations began to spring up. On the national scene were churches such as the Chicago Gospel Tabernacle, pastored by Paul Rader; Cicero Bible Church, Cicero, Illinois, pastored by Billy McCarrell; Cadle Tabernacle in Indianapolis, Indiana, pastored by Howard Cadle; and the Church of the Open Door, Philadelphia, Pennsylvania, pastored by Merrill T. MacPherson. These types of independent Protestant churches brought about the emergence of independent fellowships such as the Congregational Methodists, and the Independent Fundamental Churches of America (IFCA).

Belief determines separation. The English Bible in its Authorized Version gave the world its belief system. The word of God produces belief and belief produces emotion, philosophy, principle and action. Unbelief is erosion. Christianity is all about belief.

An evangelical educator, Harold J. Ockenga (1905-1985) coined the term *New Evangelical* in his 1948 presidential convocation speech for Fuller Theological Seminary. Dr. Ockenga said that New Evangelicals were a "new breed." He said that New

Chapter 18—The Churches of the Twentieth Century

Evangelicals should **reject** Fundamentalism for these reasons: Fundamentalist suspicion toward modernists and liberals, and the Fundamentalist stand on separation.

Ockenga wanted co-operation with the unbelieving crowd in evangelistic meetings without considering doctrinal differences. This of course was a violation of "come out from among them and be ye separate" and "touch not the unclean thing" (II Corinthians 6:17).

Liberalism had taken over virtually all of the schools of the mainline denominations, including the Southern Baptist Convention, and the New Evangelicals aimed to "capture denominational leadership" (Ernest Pickering, *The Tragedy of Compromise*, P. 13).

According to Ockenga, there are four major agencies of the New Evangelical movement: **(1) the National Association of Evangelicals, (2) Fuller Theological Seminary, (3) the journal *Christianity Today*, and (4) Billy Graham's ecumenical evangelism**.

New Evangelicalism has changed Christianity forever and its promotion of ecumenicalism (the coming together of all religious bodies in the world) will pave the way for **antichrist**.

The Baptist Fight in the Northern Baptist Convention

William B Riley was the Northern Baptist Convention preacher who fought modernism in the convention for over fifty years. He withdrew from the NBC in the last few months of his life.

Riley was called to pastor the First Baptist Church in Minneapolis, Minnesota, in 1897 and pastored there until his retirement in 1942. In forty-five years the congregation grew from 585 to 3,500 members. In 1902 he founded the Northwestern Bible and Missionary Training School. Eventually the enrollment exceeded 800. He also established a seminary. He was greatly used as an evangelist. Dr. Riley authored 60 books and edited a paper. David Cummins wrote:

> Riley envisioned purging liberalism from the Northern Baptist Convention and rallied forces to assist in the battle. Thus he became a leader in the Fundamentalist/Modernism battles from 1920 through the 1940s. With unbounded energy, Riley participated in the formation of the World Christian Fundamentals Association in 1919 and served as president. He spoke in the formational meeting of the Fundamental Baptist Fellowship in Buffalo in 1920. In 1923 he shared in the constituting of the Baptist Bible Union. Riley wrestled the Minnesota Baptist Convention from the Northern Baptist Convention while serving as president of the state body in 1944-45.
>
> True to his convictions and unable to alter the course of the Northern Convention and failing during his tenure as pastor to lead his congregation out, W.B. Riley personally resigned his membership in the Northern Baptist Convention in May 1947, just seven months before his death on December 5, 1947 (David L. Cummins, *This Day in Baptist History*, P. 117).

The Baptist Fight in the Southern Baptist Convention

J. Frank Norris was a Texas preacher who started the Fundamentalist Baptist Fellowship, which eventually pulled out of the Southern Baptist Convention.

Dr. Norris was the valedictorian of his class at the Southern Baptist Theological Seminary in Louisville, Kentucky in 1899. He began his ministry as editor of "The Baptist Standard" and became a staunch opponent of the liquor industry and horse racing, leading to passage of new laws in Texas. Along with Dr. B. H. Carroll, he helped in the forming of Southwestern Baptist Theological Seminary in Fort Worth, Texas.

He accepted the pastorate of the First Baptist Church of Fort Worth, Texas, in 1909. The church had tremendous success and with the help of Louis Entzminger and later, Beauchamp Vick. First Baptist of Fort Worth became the largest church in the world.

On two occasions Norris' church burned to the ground, and he led the people to rebuild. He led in numerous revivals in Fort Worth and Dallas, using any means possible to win the lost. He also baptized the incomparable "Cyclone Mac" McClendon, the "Billy Sunday of the South."

> **INDEPENDENT BAPTIST MISSION BOARDS**
>
> A partial list of the independent Baptist mission boards include: Baptist World Missions, Russian Fundamental Baptist Missions, Baptist Mid-Missions, Independent Baptist Fellowship, Fundamental Baptist Missions International, World Baptist Fellowship, Macedonia World Baptist Missions, Maranatha Baptist Missions. This list is not complete. These and other boards along with several hundred unaffiliated Baptist missionaries represent nearly 4,000 missionaries, the **largest number of missionaries of any Christian body in the world**.

Dr. Norris became pastor of Temple Baptist Church, Detroit, Michigan, in 1935 and pastored both Temple **and** First Baptist for over 15 years. Both churches had enormous Sunday schools with over 5,000 in attendance at each. His newspapers, *The Fundamentalist* and *The Searchlight* had the largest circulation of any religious newspapers in the Southwest.

His fight with the Southern Baptist Convention was over **modernism**, **evolution** and **communism**. He often organized separate conferences at the same time of the yearly Southern Baptist Convention and drew larger crowds, using the opportunity to expose the errors of the convention.

In 1939, with the help of Dr. Louis Entzminger, he founded the Bible Baptist Seminary. It was located in Fort Worth, Texas. Dr. Norris died in Keystone, Florida, August 20, 1952, and was buried in Fort Worth.

The Emergence of the Independent Baptists

Independent Baptists of the North

A major independent, fundamental, Baptist group started in the north, and in 1932 formed the General Association of Regular Baptists (GARB). **Dr. Bob Ketcham** led this group. The GARB started colleges in Cedarville, Ohio, and Grand Rapids, Michigan, as well as a seminary in Denver, Colorado.

In 1940, **Dr. Myron Cedarholm** formed the Conservative Baptist Association of America (CBA), which withdrew from the Northern Baptist Convention. Dr. Cedarholm founded Maranatha Baptist Bible College in Watertown, Wisconsin.

Independent Baptists of the South

The independents withdrew from the Southern Baptist Convention over these issues.
1. The teaching of evolution in Baptist colleges.
2. The rejection of premillennialism.
3. The lack of evangelism, standards, ecclesiastical separation, and personal separation.
4. The need of *believing* Mission boards

Chapter 18—The Churches of the Twentieth Century

When Dr. Norris left the SBC, he built a school in Fort Worth, Texas, which later relocated in Arlington, Texas. Some of those that followed J. Frank Norris were Dr. Lee Roberson, Dr. Beauchamp Vick, Dr. Bill Dowell, Dr. Al Janney, Dr. Verle Ackerman, Dr. Harold Heninger, Dr. Dallas Billington, Dr. Bruce Cummons, Dr. Gerald Fleming, Dr. John Rawlings and a host of others.

The Fundamental Baptist Fellowship broke up into the World Baptist Fellowship with J. Frank Norris as its leader and the Baptist Bible Fellowship with Dr. G. B. Vick as its leader. From the roots of the Baptist Bible Fellowship, the Baptist Bible College in Springfield, Missouri was founded in 1950. Seven great influences on the independent, fundamental Baptists of the twentieth century were:

    The Baptist Bible Fellowship. J. Frank Norris and Beauchamp Vick
    The General Association of Regular Baptists. Dr. Bob Ketchem.
    The Conservative Baptist movement. Dr. Myron Cedarholm.
    The Southwide Baptist Fellowship. Dr. Harold Sightler, Dr. Lee Roberson.
    The Sword of the Lord influence. Dr. John Rice.
    The Pastor School influence. Dr. Jack Hyles.
    The Christian School movement.

STOP AND THINK

1. Write Jude 1:3 two times:

2. Name the four Baptists who protested against modernism in the early twentieth century.

3. Where did "New Evangelicalism" come from and what did it reject?

4. Ockenga said fundamentalism should be rejected for what reasons?

5. According to Dr. Harold Ockenga, the self-proclaimed founder of "New" Evangelicalism, what are the four major agencies of the New Evangelical movement?

6. Who led the fight against modernism in the northern and the southern Baptist conventions?

7. Name two of the four reasons the independents pulled out of the Southern Baptist Convention?

8. Name three of seven great influences on the independent Baptists of the twentieth century.

> As we have seen, Fundamentalism could be viewed as an attempt to rescue the Evangelical Alliance from apostasy. Even though sincere, the Bible-believing Baptists, who had not given in to modernism and liberalism, were absorbed by "fundamentalism."
>
> As a result and most astounding, Baptists for the most part do not have knowledge of their own history. How is this? The unbelieving educational system was not going to inform them. But moreover, when the fundamentalists began their own schools to train ministers of the Gospel, they were broad based and ecumenical in nature, to cover the spectrum of the movement. Eventually, fundamentalism evolved into a predominantly Baptist constituency. The educational centers for fundamentalism while training mostly Baptist ministers, educated them with the Evangelical Alliance as their heritage. The fruit of this mistake is the near total ignorance of Baptist testimony in the pulpits.
>
> Today, in a new era of birthing colleges exclusively for Baptists, *the problem ought to be corrected.* **Educating an entire generation of Baptist preachers who know nothing about Backus, Stearns, Marshall, Harris, Waller, Leland, Ireland, the Craigs, the Murphys, Taylor, Vardeman, et al., must not be repeated.**

****

18.2.2

Other Baptist groups

The group associating themselves with the Landmark position (see below) separated from the Southern Baptist Convention in 1905 and formed the American Baptist Association. Other Baptist groups include the Baptist General Conference (Swedish Baptists) and the North American Baptist Conference (coming from the old German Baptists).

There are more than 50 Baptist groups in the United States.

The Fight for Baptist Heritage

The effect of the Evangelical Alliance on the Baptists, predicted by Thomas Armitage has come to pass. Baptists are now groping for their heritage.

Baptist historian **Henry Clay Vedder** rejected the findings of Cathcart, Armitage, Ford, and Benedict and claimed the Baptists began their heritage as part of the Separatist movement in England and did not baptize by immersion until 1641. Vedder was following the theory of William Whitsitt, professor and later president of Southern Baptist Seminary. **Vedder** himself was a modernist who embraced the false theory of Whitsitt. Vedder's book was made popular when it was given as a gift to the Southern Baptist Convention attendees of the early 1900's. Vedder is still used widely in **Independent** Baptist circles.

The fight for Baptist heritage actually began in the nineteenth century when the educators of Baptist preachers could not decide on the origin of the Baptists. **James R. Graves** fought nationally for the recognition of Baptist churches back to apostolic times. He and fellow Baptist heritage defender, **James M. Pendleton,** were labeled "Landmarkers" for their stand. But history shows most Baptists of the mid to late nineteenth century agreed with their findings. In fact, the Baptist historians **William Cathcart**, **Thomas Armitage** and **John Christian** found Baptist churches existing to the time of Christ. But after the deaths of these men, Baptist colleges neglected, or worse, rejected their works.

Chapter 18—The Churches of the Twentieth Century

There is a need, an urgent need, to express a Baptist Christian worldview, in opposition to the Pagan worldview, or the catholic Reformed worldview. For too long, Baptist Christian school students have been taught to reject the Pagan worldview in favor of the catholic Reformed. Certainly we reject the Pagan worldview, but we cannot abide the catholic Reformed worldview either. **The indoctrination of the catholic Reformed worldview by the standard Christian school textbook industry has all but destroyed Baptist heritage, and with it the first principles of the American republic.**

1. Write Jude 1:3 two times:

2. Which Bible is the accepted Bible among fundamental Baptists?

3. What was Whittsitt's theory about Baptist origins and baptism?

4. For what did J. R. Graves fight?
5. Name three worldviews.

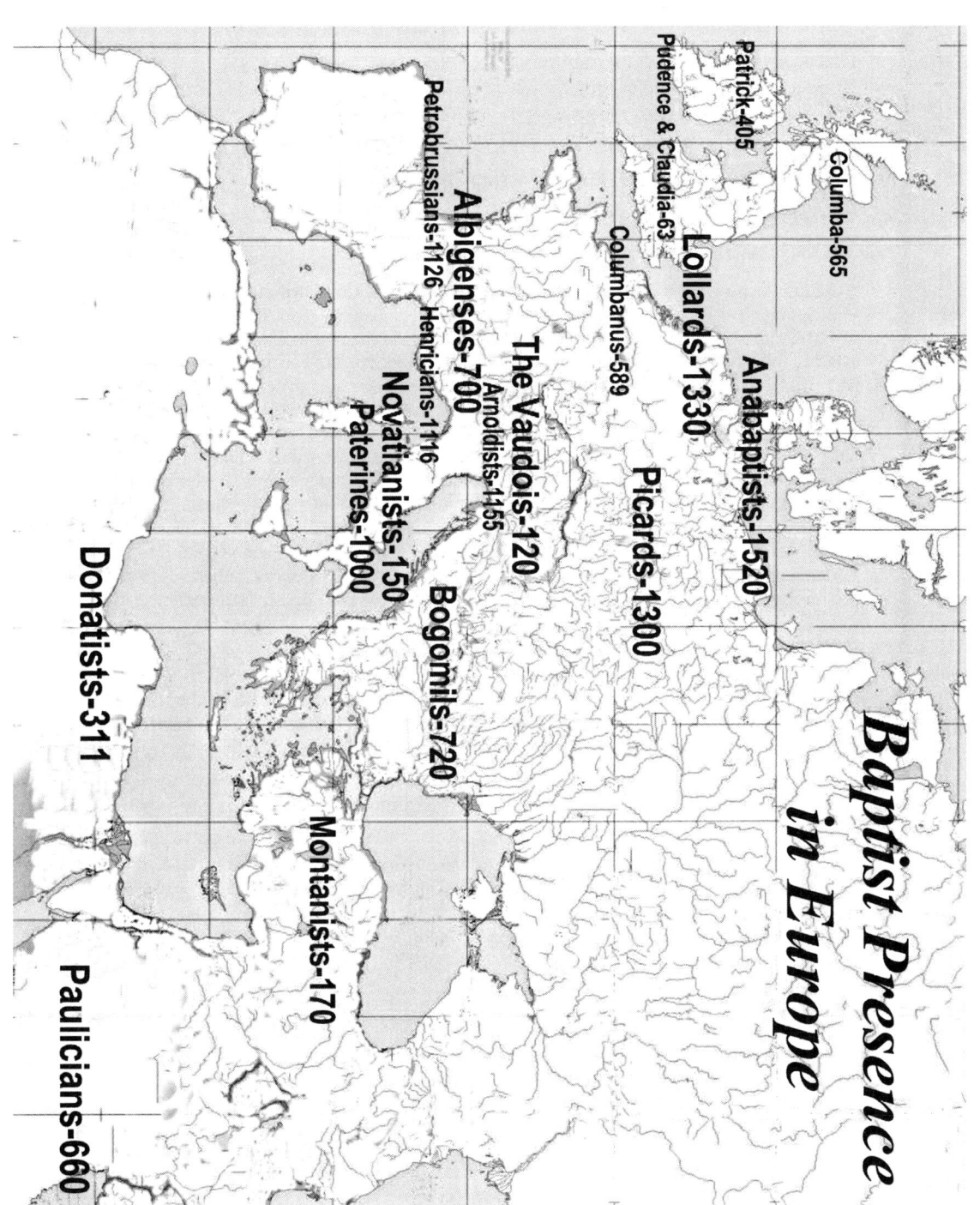

Appendix

Appendix A
Which church was the first Baptist church in America?
From the book, *America in Crimson Red*, by James R. Beller.

The following article appeared in the *Western Watchman* September 22, 1853:

The Oldest Baptist Church in America

A correspondent of the Christian Chronicle, writing from Newport, R.I., says of the First Baptist church in that city: "Though usually bearing the date of 1644, it was really constituted in 1638, and is the oldest Baptist church in America. It stands a monument of the preserving care of God; for it is the only church in all New England that has existed for over two hundred and fifteen years, that has not departed from its original faith; every other church in New England of the same age having gone to Unitarianism. Its founder and first pastor was the distinguished Dr. John Clarke, the original projector of the settlement on the island; the man who, in 1651, with Obadiah Holmes, and John Crandall, was imprisoned in Boston, and condemned to a fine, or to be whipped, for preaching Baptist sentiments in Massachusetts. It was he too, by his own unaided but preserving efforts, who obtained that distinguished character of Rhode Island, the root of our American liberties—securing perfect liberty of conscience to all. Though this church has existed two hundred and fifteen years, it has had but thirteen pastors, including Rev. S. Adlam; its present successful incumbent; and a large proportion of its present members are descended form those who first constituted the church."

Isaac Backus states on page 45 of his *Abridgement to the Church History of New England*, that Roger Williams "formed the first Baptist church in America March 1639." He further states on page 48 that the Newport church under John Clarke began in 1644. In his unabridged *History of New England, with Particular Reference to the Baptists*, Vol. 1, page 123, he says, "about the year 1644."

Backus, justifying the actions of Williams in baptizing without so-called apostolic succession (also known derisively as "se-baptism") quoted Mr. Williams' apology to John Cotton:

> As sacrifices and other acts of worship were omitted by the people of God, while his temple lay in ruins; and that they were restored again by immediate direction from Heaven, so that some such direction was necessary to restore the ordinances of baptism and the supper, since the desolation of the church in mystical Babylon.[1]

According to Isaac Backus, Roger Williams' church in Providence disbanded after he could not defend his own baptism. Backus states: "In March, 1639, he was baptized by one of his brethren, and then he baptized about ten more."[2] Williams then abandoned "such administrations among them."

---

[1] Isaac Backus, *An Abridgement of the Church History of New England* (1804, reprint ed., Harvard: Harvard Library, 1935), P. 45.
[2] *Ibid.*

Thomas Crosby in his *History of the English Baptists*, said "Roger Williams' church came to nothing."[3] Evidence shows that Thomas Olney picked up the pieces and re-gathered the church at Providence. This occurred in July 1639.

About the year 1653, the First Baptist Church of Providence experienced a church split over the controversy of "laying on of hands." Thomas Olney remained the pastor of the "six-principled" First Baptist Church while Wickenden, Dexter and Browne began the "five–principled" new First Baptist Church of Providence. Thomas Olney pastored the old church until his death about 1682.

The old Olney church disbanded according to Callender's discourse on page 61, and the Wickenden, Dexter and Browne congregation lived on as the First Baptist Church of Providence. This is the church that David Benedict testified became a prolific mother of many Baptist communities.

John Comer's papers, the most ancient record of the Baptists in America, may have indicated that the Newport church was the first in America. Unfortunately, as James Willmarth wrote, "the two manuscript volumes [of his diary] of the Rhode Island Historical Society are but a small portion of his writings, for through the centuries lay vandal hands upon manuscripts and unbound memoranda."[4]

It is evident that Callender, and then Isaac Backus, had Comer's papers when they wrote. Backus' *Abridgement* indicates this on page 156. But we do not know how much material remained.

Barrows' notes in Comer's diary, page 35:

> The organization of the First Church [Newport] was effected probably early in 1638, the year of the settlement of the colony. Mr. Clarke began his ministry as soon as the colonists arrived. John Winthrop, the governor of Massachusetts, assures us of this fact in a written statement made that very year; in 1638 he affirmed that Mr. Clarke was "preacher to those of the Island."

The most obvious argument for the Newport church as the first Baptist church in America has to do with the banishment of the *Opinionists* in the winter of 1637-38. This made them **a church in the wilderness**. We cannot believe that such devout people would not have formed themselves into a church in 1637. They certainly would have not waited until "about 1644," which is the date that Isaac Backus assumes. I admit it is difficult to disagree with the findings of Isaac Backus, who I admire with unfeigned respect. But surrounded by the excitements of persecution and the imposing testimony of the men of Providence and Brown University, Backus may have regarded their opinions as correct. Or, Backus simply recorded the plain fact that the Newport *version* of the 1637 wilderness church was finally and officially organized in about 1644.

John Callender became the sixth pastor of the First Baptist church in Newport, beginning his ministry in 1730. He made this footnote in his *Historical Discourse*:

---

[3] Thomas Crosby, *History of the English Baptists, Vol. 1* (London: sp, 1734), P. 17.
[4] James W. Willmarth, Supplementary notes, *John Comer's Diary* (Providence: Published by the Rhode Island Historical Society, Edited by C. Edwin Barrows, D. D., 1893), P. 125.

Appendix

> Since this was transcribed for the Press, I find some Reasons to suspect, that Mr. Williams did not form a Church of the Anabaptists, and that he never join'd with the Baptist Church there. Only, that he allowed them to be nearest the Scripture Rule, and true primitive Practice, as to the Mode and Subject of Baptism. But that he himself waited for new Apostles, etc. The most ancient inhabitants now alive, some of them above eighty Years old, who personally knew Mr. Williams, and were well acquainted with many of the original Settlers, never heard that Mr. Williams formed the Baptist Church there, but always understood that Mr. Browne, Mr. Wickenden, Mr. Dexter, Mr. Olney, Mr. Tillingast, etc, were the first Founders of that Church."[5]

If Callender is correct, then the first Baptist church in Providence began in 1639. Callender also wrote:

> The people who came to Rhode-Island, who were Puritans of the highest Form, had desired and depended on the Assistance of Mr. Wheelwright, a famous Congregational Minister aforementioned. But he chose to go to Long-Island, where he continued some Years. In the mean Time Mr. John Clark, who was a Man of Letters, carried on a publick Worship **at the first coming**."[6]

Which means they had church services in 1638. I believe they were simply carrying on what they had begun in the New Hampshire wilderness a few months earlier.

Callender, having already confirmed the 1638 ministry of John Clarke on the Island, makes this statement, "It is *said*, that in 1644, Mr. John Clark, and some others, formed a Church on the Scheme and Principle of the Baptists." The meaning is clear, that the church had already commenced in 1638, and the official forming may have been 1644. He continues by saying, "It is *certain* that in 1648 there were fifteen Members in full Communion." The meaning here is also clear, that the first official record of any kind does not appear until 1648.[7]

Dr. S. Adlam became the pastor of the First Baptist Church of Newport, Rhode Island in 1850. He soon discovered that the Warren Association, of which the Newport church belonged, had recently examined the confusion concerning the first Baptist church in Rhode Island and the first Baptist church in America. The Warren Association concluded that the Newport church had formed first. This caused Adlam to set forth his arguments that John Clarke and the church at Newport formed the first Baptist church. At the conclusion of his booklet, *The First Church in Providence, not the Oldest Baptist Church in America*, the clerk of the Newport church, Asa Hildreth, wrote the following:

> The matter of the formation of the First Baptist Church was brought before the Warren Association at its meeting in 1847, and at the annual meeting of the association in 1848 the following votes were passed by that body:
>
> First—That the date of 1638, inserted under the name of the First Baptist Church in Newport, contained in the tabular estimate in the minutes of last year, be stricken out and the date (1644) be inserted, as in the minutes of the years preceding.

---

[5] John Callender, *Historical Discourse on the Civil and Religious Affairs of Rhode Island* (Boston: Kneeland and Green, 1734), P. 56.

[6] John Callender, *Historical Discourse on the Civil and Religious Affairs of Rhode Island* (Boston: Kneeland and Green, 1734), P. 62.

[7] Callender, *Discourse*, P. 62.

Second—That a committee, consisting of T. C. Jameson, J. P. Tustin, and Levi Hale, be appointed to inquire into the evidence as to the date of the First Baptist Church in Newport, with instructions to report at the next session of the association.

This committee reported in 1849, that they are of the opinion that this church was formed certainly before the 1st of May, 1639, and probably on the 7th of March, 1638.

This called out a review of the fore-named report by a committee of the First Baptist Church in Providence, whose report is dated August 22, 1850, which led Rev. S. Adlam, who had just settled over the first Church in Newport, to make a thorough investigation of the matter which resulted in his book upon the First Baptist Church in Providence.

It was expected that this book would call out a reply from some one of the First Church in Providence, as there were several very able members of that church professors in Brown University, but as no reply came, Mr Adlam asked one of their ablest men (I am reliably informed) when his little book was to be answered? He replied: "**It is unanswerable**."[8]

This finding was either ignored or overlooked by the historians Thomas Armitage and William Cathcart. Those historians copied from David Benedict, who copied from Isaac Backus. A host of others have followed suit. The Baptists of America are continually pointed to the First Baptist Church of Providence as the first in America. It is high time to stop.

The truth is, Roger Williams baptized no one legitimately, trained no preachers, and birthed no churches. First Baptist of Providence presently (2005) accepts any mode of baptism from any denomination as legitimate and no longer insists on the new birth as a prerequisite for membership.

---

[8] S. Adlam, D. D., *The First Church in Providence not the Oldest Baptist Chruch in America*, (Texarkana: Baptist Sunday School Committee, 1939).

Appendix

Appendix B
Ten Affirmations Concerning Our Baptist Heritage
by James R. Beller

1. Baptists are ancient, and our ancestry can be traced through the vital principles established and set forth by our Lord Jesus Christ and His disciples in New Testament churches.

2. Baptists are not "Protestants," as our testimony extends much further in history than that of Martin Luther or John Calvin.

3. Baptists are not "Reformed" in theology or practice, for our view of the church could never allow the marriage of church and state.

4. Baptists are not "Calvinists," for the doctrines of grace were believed and preached long before John Calvin preached in Geneva.

5. Baptists are not "Arminian" in theology, for our forefathers preached the Gospel with fervor long before the time of Jacob Arminius, and believed they were enabled by God to persevere.

6. Immersion was in common use among Baptists before 1641. We reject the 1641 theory of William Whitsitt and oppose the conclusions of Henry Veddar about baptism. We view as suspect the modern histories of Robert Baker, Leon McBeth, Walter Shurden, Robert G. Torbet, and James Edward McGoldrick as they submit to the thoroughly disproved theory of William Whitsitt.

7. Baptist heritage is far older than Fundamentalism,* or the era of the city-wide revival campaigns, or the time of the old Evangelical Alliance.

8. Because Baptists have suffered at the hands of Papists and Pedobaptistic Protestants alike, we ought to venerate and remember our historic testimony far above the testimony of our persecuting enemies. That is, we ought to revere the testimony of the Paulicians, Peter de Bruys, Henry of Clugny, Balthasar Hubmaier, Henry D'anvers, John Clarke, Obadiah Holmes, Valentine Wightman, Isaac Backus, Shubal Stearns, Samuel Harris, John Leland, John Taylor, Isaac McCoy, et. al. These names should be more commonly known among Baptists than those of D. L. Moody, Ira Sankey, R. A. Torrey, Sam Jones, Gipsy Smith, John Wilbur Chapman or Billy Sunday.

9. Infant baptism is the badge of antichrist, and flirtation with that badge is akin to treason against God's word.

10. Ignorance of Baptist heritage, which is so infectious in our pulpits and pews today, is dangerous and must be over come with a renewed teaching of our Baptist heritage and heroes of past generations.

*Interdenominational Fundamentalism of the turn of the twentieth century.

Selected Bibliography

Allix, Peter. *Some Remarks upon the Ecclesiastical History of the Albigenses*, Oxford, England: Clarendon Press, 1821.

Armitage, Thomas, D.D., LL. D. *A History of the Baptists*, New York, NY: Bryan, Taylor & Co., 1887.

Asher, Louis Franklin, Ph.D. *John Clarke (1609-1676), Pioneer in American Medicine & Liberty*, Pittsburgh, PA: Dozrance Publishing Co., 1999.

Backus, Isaac. *History of New England, with Particular Reference To the Baptists, 2nd Ed. Vol.1 & 2*, Paris, AR: reprint of 1871 work by the Backus Historical Society, 2000.

_____. *An Abridgement to the Church History of New England*, Boston, MA: reprint of 1804 work by Harvard University, 1935.

_____. Papers and Remains, Providence, RI: n.p. John Hay Library, Brown University, n.d.

Barnes, Lemuel Call. *Was General George Washington Baptized by Chaplain John Gano?*, Pittsburgh, PA: n.p. in the archives of Colgate Historical Library, Rochester, NY., 1891.

Bax, E. Belfort. *Rise and Fall of the Anabaptists*, New York, NY: American Scholar Publications, Inc., 1966.

Belcher, D. D. *The Religious Denominations in the United States*, Philadelphia, PA: John E. Potter, 1856.

Beller, James R. *The Soul of St. Louis*, St. Louis, MO: Prairie Fire Press, 1998.

_____. *Why I Left the Roman Catholic Church*, St. Louis, MO: Prairie Fire Press, 1996.

Bender, Harold S., *The Origin of the Mennonites, and the Mennonites of Europe*,

Benedict, David. *Papers and Remains*, Providence, RI: n.p., Rhode Island Historical Society Manuscript Archive, n.d.

_____. *History of the Donatists*, Pawtucket, RI: Nickerson, Sibley and Company, 1875.

_____. *A General History of the Baptist Denomination, Vol. 1 and 2*, Dayton, OH: 1813 edition, reprinted by Church History Research and Archives, 1985.

Bicknell, Thomas W., A.M. *The Story of Dr. John Clarke*, Providence, RI: by the Author, 1915.

Burgess, W. J. *Baptist Faith and Martyrs' Fires*, Little Rock, AR: Baptist Publications Committee, 1964.

Callender, John. *Historical Discourse on the Civil and Religious Affairs of Rhode Island*, Boston, MA: Kneeland and Green, 1734.

Selected Bibliography

Cammack, Melvin Macye. *John Wyclif and the English Bible*, New York, NY: American Tract Society, 1938.

Carroll, J. M. *The Trail of Blood*, Lexington, KY: Ashland Avenue Baptist Church, 1931.

Cathcart, William, D. D. *The Baptists in the American Revolution*, Philadelphia, PA: published by the author, 1876.
_____. *The Baptist Encyclopedia*, Philadelphia, PA: Louis H. Everts, 1883.

Chapin, Howard M. Librarian of the RIHS, *Our Rhode Island Ancestors*, Providence, RI: Rhode Island Historical Society, nd.

Christian, John T. *Close Communion*, Louisville, KY: Baptist Book Concern, 1892.

Clarke, John. *Ille Newes from Newe England*, Boston, MA: Collections of the Massachusetts Historical Society VII, 4th Series, 1854.

Coalter, Milton J. Jr. *Gilbert Tennent, Son of Thunder*, Westport, CT: Greenwood Press for the Presbyterian Historical Society, 1986.

Comer, John. *The Diary of John Comer*, Providence, RI: Rhode Island Historical Society, edited by C. Edwin Barrows, D. D., 1893.

Cramp, J. M. *Baptist History: From the Foundation of the Christian Church*, Philadelphia, PA: American Baptist Publication Society, 1888.

Crosby, Thomas. *The History of the English Baptists, Vol. I and II*, London, England: 1738.

Crouzel, Henri. *Origen,* New York, NY: Harper and Row, Publishers, Inc. 1989.

Cruse, C. F., Editor. *Ecclesiastical History of Eusebius*, Pamphilus, London, England: Henry G. Bohn, York Street, Covent Garden, 1851.

Dallimore, Arnold A. *George Whitefield, The Life and Times of the Great Evangelist*, London, England: The Banner of Truth Trust, 1970.

Dwight, Sereno E. *Memoirs of Jonathan Edwards, from the Works of Jonathan Edwards*, Edinburgh, Scotland: Banner of Truth Trust, 1834, reprinted 1998.

Easton, Emily. *Roger Williams Prophet and Pioneer*, Freeport, NY: Books for Libraries Press, 1930.

Edwards, Morgan. *Materials for a History of the Baptists in Rhode Island*, Boston, MA: Collections of the Massachusetts Historical Society I, 4th Series, 1854.

Ernst, James. *Roger Williams, New England Firebrand*, New York, NY: The MacMillan Company, 1932.

Eusebius Pamphilus, translated by C. F. Cruse, *Ecclesiastical History*, London, England: Henry Bohn, 1851.

The Collegiate Baptist History Workbook

Ford, S. H., D.D., LL.D. *Ecclesiastical History, Condensed from the Apostles to the Reformation*, St. Louis, MO: *Christian Repository*, 1889.

_____. *The Origin of the Baptists*, St. Louis, MO: *Christian Repository*, 1889. [Online] http://www.reformedreader.org/history/ford/ (22 Oct. 2002).

Foxe, John. *Foxe's Book of Martyrs*, London, England: Morgan & Scott 1929.

Fuller, David Otis. *Which Bible?* Grand Rapids, MI: Grand Rapids International Publications, 1970.

Gaustad, Edwin S. *Baptist Piety*, Grand Rapids, MI: Christian University Press, 1978.

Gillette, A.D., Editor. *Minutes of the Philadelphia Baptist Association, Philadelphia, PA*: American Baptist Publication Society, 1851.

Grady, William P. *Final Authority* Schererville, IN: Grady Publications, 1994.
_____. *What Hath God Wrought?*, Schererville, IN: Grady Publications, 1996.

Hislop, Alexander. *The Two Babylons or The Papal Worship*, Neptune, NJ: Loizeaux Brothers, 1916.

Holmes, Col. J.T. *The American Family of Obadiah Holmes*, Columbus, OH: Published by the Author, 1915.

Horsch, John. *Mennonites in Europe*, Scottdale, PA: Herald Press 1942, revised 1950.

Hovey, Alvah. *The Life and Times of Isaac Backus*, reprinted Harrisonburg, VA: Gano Books, 1991, originally published, 1858.

Ivimey, Joseph, *A History of the English Baptists Including an Investigation of the History of Baptism in England from the earliest period to which it can be traced to the close of the seventeenth century.* To which are prefixed, testimonies of ancient writers in favour of Adult Baptism: extracted from Dr. Gill's piece, entitled, "The Divine Right of Infant Baptism Examined and Disproved." [Online] http://www.reformedreader.org/history/ivimey (2 Nov. 2002).

King, Henry M. *Early Baptists Defended*, A Review, Boston, MA: Howard Gannett, Publisher, for the Rhode Island Historical Society, 1880.
_____, A Summer Visit of Three Rhode Islanders, Providence, RI: Rhode Island Historical Society, 1896.

Leland, Elder John. *The Writings of Elder John Leland, Including Some Events in his Life*, New York, NY: G. W. Wood, 1845.

McCabe, James D. Jr. *Cross and Crown*, Philadelphia, PA Jones Brothers & Co. 1874.

McLoughlin, William G. *New England Dissent 1630-1833, Vol. 1*, Cambridge, MA: Harvard University Press, 1971.

Selected Bibliography

Mosheim, John Lawrence. *Ecclesiastical History, Vol. 1 and 2*, New York, NY: Robert Carter and Brothers, 1861.

Muston, Alexis, Dr. Rev. *The Israel of the Alps*, London, England: Strand, 1852.

Neander, Augustus. *General History of the Christian Religion and Church: Translated from the German by Joseph Torrey*, London: Bell and Daldy, 1869.

Orchard, G. H. *A Concise History Of Foreign Baptists*: taken from the New Testament, the first fathers, early writers, and historians of all ages; chronologically arranged: exhibiting their distinct communities, with their orders in various kingdoms, under several discriminative appellations from the establishment of Christianity to the present age: with correlative information, supporting the early and only practice of believers' immersion: also observations and notes on the abuse of the ordinance, and the rise of minor and infant baptism. With an introductory essay, by J. R. Graves. Nashville, TN: Graves & Co., 1855. [Online] http://name.umdl.umich.edu/AJK2016 (15 Nov. 2004).

Paschal, G.W. *History of North Carolina Baptists Vol. 1 and 2*, Raleigh, NC: Edwards & Broughton Co., 1930.

Paul, S.F. *Story of the Gospel in England*, N. Devon, England: Arthur H. Stockwell, LTD., 1948.

Pickering, Ernest D. *The Tragedy of Compromise*, Greenville, SC: Bob Jones University Press, 1994.

Plaidy, Jean. *The Rise of the Spanish Inquisition*, New York, NY: Citadel Press, 1959.

Ranck, George W. *The Travelling Church*, Louisville, KY: Press of Baptist Book Concern, 1891.

Roberts, Alexander and Donaldson, James. *The Ante-Nicene Fathers, Vol. I*, Grand Rapids, MI: William B. Eerdmans Publishing Company, 1953.

Robinson, William. *Select Works of the Rev. Robert Robinson of Cambridge*, London, England: J. Heaton & Son, 1861.

Rogers, Horatio. *Mary Dyer of Rhode Island, Quaker Martyr*, Providence, RI: Reston and Rounds, 1896.

Rosenthal, Bernard. *Salem Story—Reading the Witch Trials of 1692*, Boston, MA: Cambridge University Press, 1993.

Schaff, Phillip. *History of the Christian Church, Vol. VII and VIII*, Grand Rapids, MI: William B. Eerdmans Publishing Company, 1910, reprinted 1977.

Semple, Robert Baylor. *History of the Baptists In Virginia*, Lafayette, TN: reprint of 1810 work by Church History Research 1976.

Simms, Rev. P. Marion, PhD. *The Bible in America*, New York, NY: Wilson: Erickson Inc., 1936.

Sprague, William B., D.D., ed. *Annals of the American Pulpit, Vol. VI and Vol. VIII*, New York, NY: Robert Carter and Brothers, 1865.

Thompson, E. and Cummins, David L. *This Day in Baptist History*, Greenville, SC: Bob Jones University Press, 1993.

Underhill, Edward Bean, ed. *Tracts on Liberty of Conscience and Persecution, 1614-1661*, London: J. Haddon, 1846.

Van Braght, Thieleman J. *The Bloody Theater or Martyr's Mirror*, Scottsdale, PA: reprint of 1660 work by Mennonite Publishing House, 1950.

Williams, Roger. *The Complete Writings of Roger Williams, Vol. 1-7*, New York, NY: Russell and Russell, INC., 1963.

Wylie, J. A., *History of the Waldenses*, London: Cassell and Company, 1860.

INDEX

Anabaptists 3, 78, 83, 91, 120-123, 147-151,170, 251, 260, 263
Arianism 42, 50, 57, 65-67, 83, 258
Armitage, Thomas 4, 17, 19-21, 23-25, 113, 150
Arnoldists (from Arnold of Brescia) 97-101
associations, their original intent 91, 173, 194, 216
Augustine 12, 14, 19, 54-56, 58, 61-62, 65
Auricular confession 65, 102, 125,
Backus, Isaac 156, 161-162, 165, 179, 184, 188
baptism 3, 5, 7, 9-10, 189, 200-204, 206, 211
baptism by immersion 11, 14, 20, 39, 149, 169, 187
baptism debate in the reformation 136
baptismal regeneration 5, 7, 12, 15, 40-41, 51, 90
Baptist Distinctives 237, 242,
Baptists in England 141, 146, 167, 168, 170
Benedict, David 3, 5
Bogomils 75, 83
Britain 29, 43-44, 45, 58, 222
Brownists 143
Bunyan, John 171, 172, 174
Calvin, John; Calvinism, Calvinists 67, 135, 143, 169, 229
Carey, William 230-233
Carroll, J. M. 3, 4, 62
catechumen 48, 56, 66
Cathari 68, 72, 75, 78, 83, 104
Cathcart, William 3, 43, 172
Cedarholm, Myron 253
Celibacy of Priests 104
Charlemagne 75, 80, 84, 86
Charleston Association 209, 210
Christian, John Taylor 83, 149
Church of England 110, 113, 122, 127, 139, 141
Clarke, Dr. John 162-164, 175, 176, 258
Clement of Alexandria 34, 45, 58,138,
Columba, Columbanus 71
Comer, John 187-189, 204, 259
communion, open and close 194
Congregationalism, Congregational Church 157, 159-160, 222
Constantine 36, 48
Cotton, John 157, 160, 163, 175, 258
Craig, Lewis 219, 237-240
Cramp, J. M. 3
Crosby, Thomas 146, 168, 184, 186
dark ages iv, 41, 51, 52, 61
Davis, Jonathan 44
Donation of Constantine 87
Donatists 47, 51, 52, 150, 151
Dunster, Henry 179
Edwards, Jonathan 184, 195, 196, 231
English Separatism 3, 183
Estep, William 3
Eusebius 18, 20, 28, 29, 36, 58, 61
Evangelical Alliance 241, 242, 247
experimental religion 159, 163, 181, 184, 195
Ford, S. H. 3, 12, 21, 120, 121, 148
Franklin, Benjamin 194, 198, 200
Fuller, Andrew 230-232
Fundamentalism 247-252, 262
Galileo 127
Gano, John 210, 222-224
General Baptists 169, 170, 209, 210
general persecutions 6, 8, 25
German Rationalism 243
Gordon, A. J. 249, 250
Gould, Thomas 179-182, 184, 204
Graham, Billy 252
Graves, James R. 3, 255
Great Awakening 194-197, 199, 203, 205
half-way covenant 183-185, 195
Harriss, Samuel 214, 219, 220
Henricians 89, 92-94, 97
Henry VIII 141, 142, 144, 147, 149, 151
Henry, Patrick 214, 218, 221
Hercynian Forest, *men of the* 123, 125, 205
Holmes, Obadiah 167, 175-178, 181, 204, 258
Holy Catholic and Apostolic Church 26, 50, 64, 67, 87
Hubmaier, Balthasar 131, 262
Huguenots 127, 137, 138, 141
Huss, John 116, 118
Hy, island in Britain 69, 71
Hyles, Jack 254
Hypercalvinism 229, 230
infant baptism 10, 12, 13, 15, 16, 22, 40, 41, 44, 45
Inquisition 55, 102-106
Iona 69, 70
Ireland 71, 72
Ireland, James 219, 220
Irenaeus 13, 19, 26, 38, 44, 138
Itala Biblia 42, 138, 153
Jehovah's Witnesses 52
Jerome 58, 61, 64, 72, 79, 118, 139, 243
Jesuits 142
Joan of Kent 127, 144, 145
John Foxe 146, 151
Jones, Bob 251
Judson, Adoniram 232-234, 236, 250
Justin Martyr 13, 15, 21, 22, 30
Keach, Elias 190, 191, 193
Ketcham, Bob 253
Kiffin, William 168, 170, 172
King James, his person and his Bible 142, 154, 156
Latern Councils 101
Law of Patents 159, 161
Leland, John 209, 219, 224-226
Lollards (Walter Lollard) 109, 110, 112

268

The Collegiate Baptist History Workbook

liberty from Newgate 168
Madison, James 218, 224
Manning, James 241
Marshall, Daniel 211
Martel, Charles 75, 84-86
Mather, Cotton 163, 185-188
McClendon, Cyclone Mac 242, 253
McLoughlin, William 3
Mennonites, 78, 120, 129
Mercer, Jessie 241
Miantinomi 164
Mosheim 4, 5, 9, 10, 15, 40, 53, 78, 90, 109
Muhammad 84, 85, 109
Neander 13, 14, 22, 29, 52, 53, 90
New Lights, Old Lights 195, 197, 201, 206, 209
New Sides, Old Sides 199
New Testament church 1, 2, 10, 16, 251
Nicea 42, 50, 51, 56, 57, 63, 81, 82
Norris, J. Frank 251, 252, 254
Novatian, Novatianists 33, 36, 37, 41, 251
Ockenga, Harold 251, 252
Olchan, *the* 122
Orchard, G. H. 37, 79, 90, 97
Origen 34, 243
papal farce 92, 117
Particular Baptists (Regular Baptists) 169, 170, 172, 209
Paterines 62, 68, 90-93
Paulicians 33, 68, 71, 75, 251, 262
Peace of Westphalia 170
Peshito (or Peshitto, Peshitta) 18, 33, 58, 138
Petrobrussians (Petrobrusians from Peter de Bruys) 89, 94-97
Philadelphia Association 189-191, 193, 194, 241
Pilgrims 142, 153-156, 158
Presbyterian Church 26, 127, 159, 183, 200, 201
prophet 2, 3, 11
Protestantism 3, 105, 120, 136, 141, 142, 248
Providence 35, 43, 109, 155, 156, 161
purgatory 35, 64, 66, 67, 81
Puritans 142-144, 152, 154, 155-160, 175, 186
Ray, D. B. 3
reformers, Reformation 72, 80, 120-124, 127, 129
Rice, John R. 254
Rice, Luther 232-234, 241, 242
Riley, W. B. 251
Roberson, Lee 254
Saint Patrick 45, 68
Salem Witch trials 180, 186
Samoset, Massasoit, Squanto 155, 161
Sandy Creek Association 212
Satan's Plan for America 242, 243
Savonarola 116, 118, 119
Sawtree, William 113
School of Alexandria 42
Scotland 68, 71, 79, 139, 220, 232

Screven, William 209
scribe 2, 3, 58
Second Great Awakening 240
Semple, Robert Baylor 213
Separate Baptists 181, 209-212
Sightler, Harold 254
Simons, Menno 130, 132
Spilsbury, John 168, 170
Stearns, Shubal 183, 206, 209-213, 217, 237, 262
Stoddard, Solomon 184, 188
Stratton, John Roach 251
Templar Knights 92
Tertullian 12-15, 19, 22, 29, 30, 33, 39, 138
Third Great Awakening 242
Thomas, David 210
traditores 36, 37, 40, 47, 51
Trail of Blood 3, 11, 63
Transubstantiation 24, 25, 64, 66, 72, 80, 81, 102, 103, 110
Triennial Convention 233-235, 241
Tyndale, William 122, 153
Van Braght, Thieleman J. 107
Vick, Beauchamp 253, 254
Waldenses (Waldensians, the Vaudois) 80, 81, 89, 93, 119, 133, 135, 153, 173, 174
Waldenses, their absorption by the reformers 136, 137
Wales 44, 63, 170, 190, 192
Waller, John 213, 216, 219
Washington, George 222, 223, 235
Weatherford, John 219, 220, 221, 224
Welsh Tract 191-193, 222
Whitefield, George 197-200, 210
Whitsitt, William 150, 255, 262
Wightman, Valentine 186, 262
Wightman, Edward 144, 146, 156, 167, 186
Williams, Roger 186, 189, 204, 224, 258
Wycliffe, John 112, 116, 117
Zwingli, Ulrich 127, 128

About the Author

James R. Beller is a native of St. Louis, Missouri. He grew up a "South Sider," and attended St. Pius V. Grade School on Utah and Grand Avenue.

While attending Fox High School in Arnold, Missouri, Pastor Beller was born again after reading Gospel tracts that had been given to his mother.

While attending Southeast Missouri State University, the author surrendered to the Gospel ministry and enrolled in Bible college, where met his future wife Vickie.

James has pastored the Arnold Baptist Tabernacle in Jefferson County, Missouri since 1987. The church has grown from a storefront to its present properties, and is currently building an educational addition to house its Christian school.

Arnold Baptist Tabernacle has planted five other churches in the St. Louis area since 1994—the Solid Rock Baptist Church, Rock Hill, Missouri; the South Broadway Baptist Chapel, St. Louis, Missouri; the Victory Independent Baptist Church, St. Louis; the Blessed Hope Baptist Church in Farmington, Missouri; and Grace Independent Baptist Church in House Springs, Missouri. The church has plans to begin other works in Missouri.

Pastor Beller is the author of numerous booklets on doctrine and church planting. He is the author of the popular historical narratives, *The Soul of St. Louis*, and *America in Crimson Red*. He and his wife have four children; Jeremy, Nicole, Zackary and Katherine.